A Girl for All Seasons

CAMILLA MORTON

A Girl
for all Seasons

The Year in High Heels

HODDER &
STOUGHTON

First published in Great Britain in 2007 by Hodder & Stoughton
A division of Hodder Headline

A Hodder & Stoughton Book

1

A CIP catalogue record for this title is available from the British Library

ISBN 978-0-340-92259-0

Typeset in Baskerville MT by Palimpsest Book Production Limited,
Grangemouth, Stirlingshire

Printed and bound by Mackays of Chatham Ltd, Chatham, Kent

Hodder Headline's policy is to use papers that are natural, renewable and recyclable
products and made from wood grown in sustainable forests. The logging and manufacturing
processes are expected to conform to the environmental regulations of the country of origin.

Hodder & Stoughton Ltd
A division of Hodder Headline
338 Euston Road
London NW1 3BH

'There is no friend as loyal as a book'
Ernest Hemingway

For *Fabulous* Steven

1968–2007

Contents

Foreword

I first met Camilla in the mid-1990s. She – literally – ended up in my arms at Antonio Berardi's first show. Fresh out of Saint Martin's, she was a wide-eyed, totally English young lady, who even turned out to be polite and well mannered . . . a rarity in the industry, particularly at collection time. I was instantly charmed.

Over the years, I learnt that this wide-eyed, English young lady was made of sterner stuff than her outward appearance would imply. She is witty beyond belief, a wonder with words, and knows fashion like a medic would know the human body. As she has shown in her first book, *How to Walk in High Heels*, she can even play poker, change a light bulb, and climb out of a car properly.

There is even more to her: she never forgets a birthday, she tells the best stories, and loves to have a laugh. It's always a pleasure to bump into her at parties, or, even better, have tea with her – an event which I always look forward to.

Yet above all, Camilla is true and honest. She has a heart of gold and is always there to offer encouragement, help and support. Her writing has pushed the career of many in the business – since she has continuously championed young talent, as well as that of veterans like John Galliano and myself.

All of which makes her the perfect *Girl for All Seasons*: a ray of sunshine to brighten up a bleak autumn's day, a touch of warmth brought to a cold winter. She is as welcome as a beautiful springtime bunch of flowers, and a refreshing tonic on a hot summer's day.

That, for me, is Camilla.

Manolo Blahník, May 2007

January

'When a man is tired of London, he is tired of life'
Samuel Johnson

Wish You Were Here

POST CARD

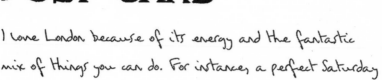
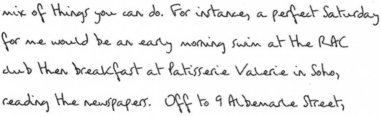

I love London because of its energy and the fantastic mix of things you can do. For instance, a perfect Saturday for me would be an early morning swim at the RAC club then breakfast at Patisserie Valerie in Soho, reading the newspapers. Off to 9 Albemarle Street, Mayfair to spend a hour working in my furniture shop and then onto Portobello Road market, Notting Hill maybe picking up a sandwich at Mr Christian's in Elgin Crescent. I would then spend an hour working in my 'Westbourne House' shop, collect my wife for an early movie at 'The Gate' cinema and finish with supper at The River Café which is my favourite.

Paul Smith

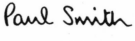

1st January

January was named after Janus – the Roman god of gates and doors, of beginnings and endings. This god was usually depicted with two faces looking in opposite directions (Janus Geminus – twin Janus) and it is his head that was part of the original logo for the House of Fendi. The two faces represented the sun and the moon, and symbolized change and transitions.

Today is the ideal date to put dreams into action. New Year, New Resolutions, New Diary, New You.

If moving from the sofa is difficult, if not impossible, especially after last night's festivities, today's the day to think about areas for improvement. Start with some honest self-analysis. Be sure to upgrade mind, body and soul as well as your wardrobe. No point looking the part in next season's labels if your head is stuck in last year's groove.

Bette Davis admitted, 'I have been uncompromising, peppery, intractable, monomaniacal, tactless, volatile, and at times disagreeable . . . I suppose I'm larger than life.'

And you?

Best foot forward

In English and Scottish folklore first-footing decrees that the first visitor to your house after midnight will determine your year. So this could be where things have been going wrong . . .

A male visitor is said to bring luck (no, you don't say). Getting specific, he should be dark, so why not just add tall and handsome to the wish list and be done with it? Tradition says he will come bearing gifts such as money, bread or coal. Just turning up is a good start.

If he's blond, red-headed or, worst of all, isn't a *he* but a *she* who's first at your front door you're going to have bad luck. Be very cautious who you invite over and use your spy hole before opening the door. You could always refuse to answer. Or tell blond friends to come back tomorrow; they should understand.

How to Pepys

'This morning (we living lately in the garret) I rose, put on my suit with great skirts, having not lately worn any other clothes but them. Went to Mr Gunning's chapel at Exeter House, where he made a very good sermon . . .'

So began Samuel Pepys' Diary, in 1660.

Pepys (23 February 1633–26 May 1703) was an English naval administrator and Member of Parliament who rose to be Chief Secretary to the Admiralty, under King James II. He would have been totally forgotten had it not been for his private diary that he kept religiously for nine years and five months (until his eyesight was too poor to continue). It was published posthumously and his name became linked to history for ever. It's not scandalous but it is the most important primary source of the English Restoration, and includes eyewitness accounts of the Great Plague and the Great Fire of London.

So, as dawn breaks on this first day of January isn't it time you committed to finally committing? Record in a book your deepest thoughts, wild nights and inner feelings, as well as the more bland appointments, like the gas man coming – any time between dawn and dusk.

While the thought that your diary could be read decades, or even centuries, later might seem unlikely, it really depends on you. Aim to make it a page-turner and it could turn into a pension fund.

As Mae West said: 'Keep a diary and one day it will keep you.'

Famous diary keepers to read and be inspired by include:

Real: Ossie Clark, Anne Frank, Kenneth Tynan, Andy Warhol, Virginia Woolf.

Fiction: Bridget Jones, Adrian Mole or, depending on how the week's panning out, Nikolai Vasilievich Gogol's *Diary of a Madman.*

How to blog it

Forget the padlock.

Increasingly diaries are no longer private. Everyone loves to read a diary, from handwritten ones to weblogs for the more technically inclined. If the Internet is anything to go by, diaries are back in fashion – big time. If you feel like giving the world immediate access to your musings, rants or inner turmoil, rather than leaving your diary open on the bus it's time to start a blog. Expose your angst to cyberspace. As author Kingsley Amis said, 'If you can't annoy somebody, there's little point in writing.'

Blogging is an open forum to express your opinions on everything and anything, and a way for everyone, and anyone, to write back. And – be warned – they will.

The best sites to go to for help when setting up your own blog are: *www.blogger.com*; *www.diarist.net*; *www.livejournal.com*. *www.mac.com* have even included an easy to install blog/weblog option within their 'iLife' upgrade packages.

Google have a 'Blogs of Note' section that includes everything from a New York cab driver's rant to a dieter's agony.

Making your opinion heard has never been so easy.

So, first things first . . . what to do?

Follow the steps on your selected programme:

1 Create an account.
2 Name your blog.
3 Choose a template.

www.blogger.com is the most established website, and therefore the most experienced in looking after first-timers. Before clicking on the options decide what you want to use your blog for. What do you want to say, show, discuss or record?

Download a template, follow the instructions and registration steps 1, 2, 3 and let your 'host' site worry about the layout, graphics and HTML. All you need to do is work out the content.

Blog basics

Blogs first appeared in 1999, and by 2005 there were over 20 million blogs and bloggers. Anyone can do it. The blog is like a chain of emails, starting from your most recent, going back to the oldest. It allows you to create an online stream of thoughts.

People can log on or 'post' opinions but essentially it is all about you, by you. You are your own editor, and you decide what stays live. You can post pictures, images and even video or audio, but don't run before you can walk.

Blockbuster blogging

Being a really successful blogger could lead to a new life as a published author. Publishing success stories from blogs are on the up, so much so that there are even publishing houses dedicated to finding budding talent on the web, such as The Friday Project. The notorious call girl 'Belle du Jour' started documenting her life in a blog; it became a bestselling book and has been turned into a screenplay. Proof that computers are no longer only for the geeky. And, because every industry needs to celebrate its stars, there are now the Bloggie Awards, which started in 2000 in America. The 2006 UK winner, *Girl with a One-Track Mind*, got a publishing deal soon after. In the UK 'blooks' (blogs that are online books), are also gaining recognition. So now we can all be Pepys, or at least published authors.

One note of caution, particularly to the shy: you might want to think of a pseudonym before going too far with your online fantasies.

The British Library have recently begun recording the email habits of our time. Any message forwarded to email@emailbritain.co.uk will be included in their archive. Put yourself in the history books.

How to diet and detox

With New Year's resolutions once more comes the annual optimistic trip to join a gym. Time, again, to dust off the tracksuit and trainers, that is if you didn't splash out on a new pair in the sales as part of the 'new you' incentive. January is the gym's busiest joining month, with membership up at least ten per cent on the rest of the year.

Be serious. It will be easy to blend in while getting used to the new regime, and seeing what classes or equipment you can use.

Be brave. Bin any leftover chocolate Father Christmases and mince pies and restock your cupboards. If they were that delicious they wouldn't still be hanging around. Think healthy as well as practical, but also pin a holiday photo nearby so you don't forget the omnipresent threat of a bikini moment.

There are over 4,000 books on dieting and detox available, and, statistics also claim, over 300,000 premature deaths a year in the US due to obesity . . . But how do you sort the fads from the 'feel-goods' and the 'five-minute wonders'? Use your common sense: do something that suits your lifestyle and wallet.

Weigh up the necessity of losing weight and the effect it will have on your health. Before tackling any diet or 'health plan', consult a doctor or nutritionist.

Streamline your food cupboard but don't leave it bare; you also need to make sure your body is getting all the vitamins and minerals it needs. Working in a change of menu is one thing but you should also develop a programme that includes regular exercise and an overall conditioning of your lifestyle to get the best results. This is not something to be entered into lightly.

Above all, don't be a martyr and take all the fun out of food – would you want to hang out with someone who can only eat birdseed and cardboard?

Make informed decisions before you start.

Look at the following websites for advice: *www.simplythebestweightloss.com*; *www.weightlossresources.co.uk*; *www.thedietchannel.com*.

Or read up on the subject. The bestselling diet books include:
  Antony Worrall Thompson's *GL Diet Made Simple*
  Judith Wills' *The Diet Bible: Use to Lose It*
  Nigel Denby's *The 7-Day GL Diet*
  Paul McKenna's *I Can Make You Thin*
  Gillian McKeith's *You Are What You Eat*

Other popular 'dieting' books to dip into this month include:
  The No Diet Diet: Do Something Different by Professor Ben Fletcher, Dr Karen Pine and Dr Danny Penman
  The Money Diet: The Ultimate Guide to Shedding Pounds Off Your Bills and Saving Money On Everything! by Martin Lewis
  Well, credit-card bills need slimming just as much as your thighs . . .

The top diets worth knowing about:

Atkins The high-fat, high-protein, high-profile and low-carbohydrate diet. This means you eat meats, cheese, eggs, poultry, fats and oils. It restricts carbs in foods such as grains, fruits and veggies. Less popular since Dr Atkins died of a heart attack.
Zone Means eating the 'right' foods, which, in this case they say, is 40% carbs, 30% protein and 30% fat.
GI This stands for 'Glycemic Index'. In a nutshell this looks at the effect of carbohydrates on blood glucose levels, ranks them and then compares them gram for gram to other foods. Don't worry about the maths, or what to eat, simply follow their page-by-page 'traffic light' guide, where oat bran is considered bad/red and jellybeans good/green. Go figure.
GL 'Glycemic Load' is an adapted, easier version of the GI way of life. This diet is less restrictive than the GI and takes the carb content and the portion size of your food into account. This says you don't need to cut carbs

completely, so in theory is not totally antisocial. Instead it wants you to eat the right carbs and foods, feel healthier and lose weight.

Weight Watchers This is an old faithful – the low- to moderate-fat diet plan where emphasis is on portion size and calorie control, measured by allocating points to foods. This diet is often supported with diet meetings and public 'weigh-ins' and if it's good enough for the Duchess of York it's worth considering.

Ornish The opposite to the Atkins. Well, we're all different, aren't we? This is a very low-fat diet which allows a complex mix of carbs, a little meat, dairy and next to no fat.

Blood Group Working with the make-up of the four blood types, this prescribes a diet specific to your blood type. It promises you will lose weight and improve your digestion. The theory here is certain foods react negatively with components in certain blood types and are best avoided. First things first: find out what blood type you are and see if the menus appeal.

The Macrobiotic Supposedly Gwyneth Paltrow's choice of diet (and who wouldn't want to look as fabulous as her?) But it's a no-messing, low-fat, high-fibre diet of whole grains, vegetables, sea algae – yuk – and (bird) seeds, prepared in accordance with specific principles. Good grief. It is said to synchronize eating habits with the cycles of nature. Hard core, not for the faint-hearted.

The Popcorn Diet Rumoured to have been tried by Madonna but one that's not generally recommended. They say that as popcorn is high-fibre, low-fat and readily available it's a solution in itself. Well, that seems easy enough, especially if you love going to the cinema, but in reality it should be just one part of a low-fat diet.

The 'best' of the rest

Perricone's Programme Will have you smelling and dreaming of salmon, as that, and melon, is pretty much all you eat. In return it promises to make your skin look younger and 'elasticized'.

Dr Joshi's Detox Loved by celebrities and the very determined; allow time to chop a lot of vegetables, or hire a live-in chef.

The Lemonade Diet Aims to dissolve and eliminate toxins or congestion in any part of the body and generally cleanse your kidneys and the digestive system. It is as bad and as brutal as it sounds, and is a ten- to forty-day form of punishment. Read the horror stories online.

The Shangri-La Diet Dreamed up by a Berkeley professor who worked out that if you take a spoonful of olive oil an hour before each meal it tricks you into thinking you're not hungry, so you eat less, so you lose weight. An alternative to chain-smoking or chewing gum.

Alternatively Beyoncé took a sweet option, using the Maple Syrup Diet to slim down to a sixties-style physique for her role in the 2006 film *Dreamgirls*. The diet consists of maple syrup mixed with water, lemon juice and cayenne pepper, which is taken instead of meals.

'I would never recommend it to anyone unless you are doing a movie and it's necessary and you have proper help,' she said. 'There are ways to lose weight healthily if you want to lose weight, but this was for a film.' She was much happier when her signature curves returned and, regardless of Hollywood stereotyping, who wouldn't want a body like hers?

Question the sanity or necessity of doing the latest fashionable diet as trumpeted by some teenybopper or trophy wife. Do you really want to look like them?

Last, but not least, on the 'Who's Who' of eating hell is the **Cabbage Soup Diet**. Frankly this is the most antisocial of all diets and is a definite *no* for anyone who works in an office environment (you and it stink) unless looking for a new job is high on the list of things to do in January.

The cabbage soup aka new job diet

Ingredients:

   3 large onions
   1 large green pepper
   1 head of celery
   1 half of a dark green cabbage
   1 tin of chopped tomatoes
   1 pack onion soup mix
   3 vegetable stock cubes

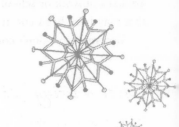

To make:

Cut all vegetables into small pieces, or blend, as you prefer. Place in a saucepan with the other ingredients, cover with water, season and simmer until vegetables are soft. And that's your poison for the week. Day in, day out.

When detoxing this month you could consider what else needs detoxing, such as the taxis home, dreadful dates and cutting down on text messaging.

4th January

Jacob Grimm, father of fairytales, is born, 1785. Read *Sleeping Beauty* in his honour.

How to say your thank-yous

Instead of more TV repeats and/or relatives, early January is the optimum time to sit down and write a few well-chosen words.

'Thank-you' cards should, ideally, be handwritten, and posted no later than a week after the event or gift. Choose either a card or notelet, or why not treat yourself to a nice letter-writing set? Perhaps you got one for Christmas? Whatever you choose, aim to say all your thank-yous before you are back at work or school and are swamped making up for all the corners that may have been cut in the pre-Christmas rush.

Text messages don't count as a proper thank you.

Letter-writing dos and don'ts

Regular correspondence is a good habit to get into. Not only does it show your stunning good manners, but a letter should, in turn, lead to you receiving more than just bills and junk mail through your own letterbox. Letters that are *personally* written to you make opening the post a pleasure rather than a chore.

The tools

For pens this can vary. It is ultimately what you feel comfortable with, from the biro to a bling-bling Montblanc fountain pen. Buy a stationery set, as every workman needs his tools, and yours can be anything from one purchased at the local store to one from the ultimate, Smythsons of Bond Street in London – *www.smythson.com* – or Kate's Paperie in New York – *www.katespaperie.com*. Also log on to *www.mountaincow.com* for quirky and chic stationery ideas, and visit *www.hazlitz.com* to see where the smart set of Chelsea are picking up their thank-you cards. For the ultimate seal and finish you can order your own seal and wax from *www.citycoseals.co.uk*

Punctuation

Good punctuation is essential and you need to keep a strict eye on it or the meaning may be lost altogether. Read *Eats, Shoots and Leaves* by Lynne Truss if in any doubt, or if you feel your punctuation appreciation is lacking.

You must be sure about the difference between colons and semicolons, commas and dashes as well as understand the sensitive nature of an apostrophe. Take Truss's example of the difference between 'Dick's in tray', and 'Dicks in tray'. Well, good heavens, can you see what I mean?

Also make sure you have a current copy of a dictionary close to hand, don't just rely on your computer's 'spell check'. UK English and American English are different. Other essential desk-top books include: *The Oxford Guide to English Usage* and Penguin's *The Complete Plain Words,* as well as books of quotations or elegant fiction to fire your imagination.

Do it the Austen way

Jane Austen's *Pride and Prejudice* was first published on 29 January 1813 and the heroines of this novel, the Bennet sisters, were avid letter writers, as they were nice young ladies of the day.

The book features twenty-one letters, including Darcy's infamous attempt to clear his name with Miss Elizabeth. 'Be not alarmed, Madam, on receiving this letter, by the apprehension of its containing any repetition of those senti-ments, or renewal of those offers, which were last night so disgusting to you,' he begins. Darcy then explains about his feud with Wickham and glosses over the rejected, roundabout proposal he made, and vaguely justifies his behaviour.

In fact, at the time of publication, his letter to Elizabeth was far more scandalous than we now appreciate. As a rule any correspondence between two unmarried, unrelated young people (of marriageable age and material; a nun writing to vicar was *not* classed a scandal) simply did not happen, unless they were soon to be engaged.

'It could not be authorised by anything else,' says Elinor Dashwood solving a similar letter-writing dilemma in *Sense and Sensibility.* No wonder Elizabeth Bennet does not, indeed cannot, reply to his letter. What would people think?

In *Pride and Prejudice* the ghastly Caroline Bingley flirts with Darcy: 'It is a rule with me, that a person who can write a long letter with ease, cannot write ill.' Perhaps. But if you are going to do it; do it properly. Make sure it is well punctuated, has correct spellings and is clearly written; this applies to the handwriting and the contents – and then, yes, anyone will be charmed to receive it.

Your goodness gracious

If you have a coat of arms you should place it on your headed stationery either above a centred address or on the top left-hand side.

It is incredibly naff to pretend to have a coat of arms, so don't. Surprisingly few people who use a coat of arms, or heraldic symbols, today actually have the right to. The rule is you can only use them if you are from the male line of descendents to whom they were originally granted.

If you don't have one, you could create your own headed paper – a fabulous shoe or mischievous angel, drawn by yourself or a friend – and get an order printed.

If you want to look into your entitlement to a coat of arms write to the UK's heraldic societies, who have all the records and lists of who (really) is who. These authorities are:

England, Wales and Northern Ireland:

The College of Arms, Queen Victoria Street, London EC4V 4BT.

Scotland:

The Lyon Office, New Register House, Edinburgh EH1 3YT.

The Republic of Eire:

Chief Herald of Ireland, Genealogical Office, 2 Kildare Street, Dublin 2, Eire.

Envelopes

A bit like knickers and bras, or socks, they must match. Envelopes have to be from the same set as the paper or the card that is being sent. This is especially important for formal correspondence.

When writing the envelope, spare a thought for the postman. Always write the address clearly, and with the full postcode. The post office are very busy and: 'Prince Charming, Peckham, London' may prove problematic to find.

The address on the envelope should contain the proper title of the person you are writing to, such as Miss, Mrs, Lady, Sir, Dr, whatever. It's essential to knock 'Esq.' off the end if addressing a Mr Someone or Sir so-and-so. However, if they have any honours or qualifications you should add these in a formal or professional context.

Stamps

Always put enough on, and be first class rather than second class.

If unsure whether your letter is above the standard weight, take it to a post office and get it weighed. To send a card with postage to pay is unforgivable.

If sending gifts or important documents, absolutely do not cut corners; queue at the post office and send recorded or special delivery. Why waste all the effort you have gone to only for it to be lost in transit? Get proof as well as peace of mind.

For the ultimate finishing touch you can order customized stamps depicting anything from your pet, your shoe – to you! Well, why should the Queen always have all the fun? Email a digital image or send a photograph to Royal Mail and they will do the rest. Go to *www.royalmail.com* for all the info.

International love letters and so on will need special European or worldwide stamps. Your letter won't get to that hunk in Honolulu or the holiday romance in Havana with a first-class stamp, even if it's only a postcard. First class only goes around the UK – from the UK to the UK. Don't unburden your soul only for it never to get to your intended.

A note of caution: *always* check how long it will take and be sure to allow enough time. Forget what the cavalier say about the last date to send Christmas mail; get yours posted by 8 December to be sure.

Muse of the Month

Jane Austen

It is a truth universally acknowledged . . . that if you haven't heard of Jane Austen you must have been living on a different planet. Charlotte Brontë wasn't a fan and Mark Twain snarled 'any library is a good library that does not contain a volume by Jane Austen'. Miaow. Luckily many libraries disagreed as her stories about the trials and tribulations of love and marriage, her caustic wit and social satire have delighted readers for two hundred years and inspired countless adaptations. Not bad for a woman who died a spinster at forty-one and, due to the social restraints of the time, had to publish anonymously.

This month read one of her novels, rent a DVD or write a letter, rather than a text message, in her honour. Remember inspiration can be found close to home.

And thank your lucky stars that, despite the way it sometimes feels, dating can be a lot more romantic now than it used to be. Honestly.

The life and times

Jane Austen was born on 16 December 1775 in Hampshire, England. It was the time of the Napoleonic Wars, the love affair of Emma Hamilton and Horatio Nelson, the art of Constable and the poetry of Byron. The style of Beau Brummell and the sheer decadence of Prince Regent were the talk of the day. Fashions were gentile, restrained rather than refined: hoop skirts, high wigs and heavy make-up were 'out', a more pastoral, classical look was 'in'; think angelic empire-line dresses, bonnets and ribbons, and all things English.

Austen was a rector's daughter, the seventh of eight children born to George and Cassandra Austen who lived in the prosperous parish of Steventon. She briefly attended Mrs Cawley's academy until she caught typhoid. She was then educated at home until her sister Cassandra was sent to the Abbey School in Reading, and Jane insisted she went too. Her father encouraged her reading and writing, and helped fill the gaps in her education with his own extensive library and love of literature. She grew up a devoted reader and loved Byron, Wordsworth and Fanny Burney (whose work was initially published anonymously but due to the success of her first novel *Evelina* her identity was revealed and she became famous overnight). Austen, however, wrote to her sister, 'a woman, especially, if she have the misfortune of knowing anything, should conceal it as well as she can'.

Through her novels, Austen captured the spirit of the times, and her social set. Like the Bennets, Austen and her sister were 'comfortably' middle class, and neither were married as they weren't considered much of a catch because their father couldn't afford great dowries. The rectories, vicarages and country houses of southern England where she'd grown up found their way into her books, as did the experiences of two of her brothers, both young naval officers. Today the towns of Bath, Chawton and Steventon have spawned entire industries to support all the tourists that flock to see where Austen lived and wrote.

She rejected a favourable marriage proposal from a wealthy but 'big and awkward' man named Harris Bigg-Wither as he wasn't 'the one', having earlier enjoyed a 'flirtation' with Irishman Tom Lefroy, but this was called off as his family wanted him to marry a richer girl. (This is the subject of the 2007 film *Becoming Jane*.) 'My tears flow at the melancholy idea,' she confided to her sister. After this knock-back she pledged to confine her affairs of the heart to the page. Her father encouraged this, and indeed never tried to censor her writing, marry her off, or make her fit into the mould of Society. He even wrote to London publisher Thomas Cadell in 1797, hoping to secure publication of her novel *First Impressions*. When her father retired, the family moved to Bath, a fashionable health resort that she despised, until she fell in love again. Sadly fate conspired against her and this potential suitor died soon after they met. It's probable that this heartbreak was the inspiration for *Persuasion* – worth remembering when you're lying on the sofa, eating chocolate and wailing because he didn't call. Can you imagine all this angst without mobiles?

When her father died suddenly in 1805, the Austen women, like the heroines of *Sense and Sensibility*, were left without an income and became reliant on other family members. But, ever defiant, Jane began earning her independence. She wrote to her brother: 'I have written myself into two hundred and fifty pounds which only makes me long for more.' Could she write them out of the debtor's grasp as she did her characters?

Her health deteriorated rapidly as she started work on her last novel, *Sanditon*, in January 1817, and sadly she was never able to complete it. She died on 18 July 1817, of what is now suspected to have been Addison's disease. She was buried at Winchester Cathedral and at last her status as an author was officially unveiled.

The works

Sense and Sensibility (first published 1811)
Originally titled *Elinor and Marianne*. Unlike Mary Ann Evans (aka George Eliot), Jane Austen didn't adopt a pseudonym in a bid to be taken more seriously. Her work was credited simply as 'by a Lady', and that was enough for her. It received favourable reviews, and the first edition earned her a profit of £140. It has been made into four films, including the 1995 version, directed by Ang Lee, starring Kate Winslet and Emma Thompson (who won the Academy Award for Best Adapted Screenplay). Austen has fittingly been referred to as the posthumous *Queen of Genteel Cinema* by the *New York Times*.

Pride and Prejudice (first published 1813)
Without a doubt her most famous work. Originally titled *First Impressions* she referred to it as her 'own darling child'. She sold the rights to the novel for a princely £110 to Mr Egerton of the Military Library, Whitehall. It

has spawned six film versions including the 2005 Academy Award-nominated adaptation, starring Keira Knightley (who got paid rather more than £110), and the Bollywood interpretation *Bride & Prejudice*. It also inspired the love triangle in *Bridget Jones's Diary*.

Mansfield Park (first published 1814)
Fanny Price, the heroine of this story, is renowned for her deep feeling, her 'sensibility', a somewhat intangible trait which (by the end of the eighteenth century) was considered a good thing and became all the rage. This book sold out within six months of being first published. Austen's popularity was growing, and her identity started to be known to a wider circle.

Emma (first published 1816)
By this time Jane Austen's work had come to the attention of the Prince Regent (later George IV), who sent word that he granted permission for her novel to be dedicated to him. She wanted to ignore this as she didn't approve of his lifestyle, but her family pointed out that 'permission' from a Royal wasn't so very different from a command – something to consider when dealing with a difficult boss. Dutifully, she dedicated *Emma* to him – though she couldn't resist a little of her trademark irony: 'This work is, by His Royal Highness's permission, most respectfully dedicated, by his Royal Highness's dutiful and obedient humble servant, the author.' In return he arranged for her to be shown his magnificent London residence, Canton House. This book has been adapted for film five times, including the 1995 teen film *Clueless*, which updated the story and took it to the mall.

Northanger Abbey (first published 1818)
This was the first of her novels to be sold and, according to her sister, was originally to be called *Susan*. Originally sold to a Bath publisher in 1803 for £10, 'the Lady's work' stayed on his bookshelf for many years. It was eventually bought back by her brother for the same sum in 1817, and no way did he reveal she was the 'anonymous' author of four popular novels. Poor publisher didn't know he had sat on a bestseller for years. The novel itself is set in Bath and no doubt reflects her own adventures.

Austen's parody of the popular Gothic novel *The Mysteries of Udolpho* may arguably have ruined Ann Radcliffe's credibilty, although it certainly preserved her for ever in the novel when Austen's heroine is handed a copy to read. Like her other works this novel warns of the danger of confusing life and art and pokes fun at the hypocrisy of her society.

Persuasion (first published 1817)
This was originally published, posthumously, in one volume together with *Northanger Abbey*, and included a 'Biographical Notice of the Author' by her brother Henry, revealing the truth behind the author's life and identity. It is her last completed work and, like *Northanger Abbey*, is set in Bath, where she lived from 1801–5. She had intended to call it *The Elliots*, in reference to the heroine's regret, or indeed the author's own lost love affair. Book yourself a mini-break in Bath – the Jane Austen Festival runs in September. You can take Blue Badge walks round the city and see the sights Austen would have. Go to *www.wessexguides.co.uk*

Austenisms

'I do not want people to be agreeable, as it saves me the trouble of liking them.'

'Where so many hours have been spent in convincing myself that I am right, is there not some reason to fear I may be wrong?'

'There are certainly not so many men of large fortune in the world as there are of pretty woman to deserve them.'

'But when a young lady is to be a heroine, the perverseness of forty surrounding families cannot prevent her. Something must and will happen to throw a hero in her way.'

How to start a book club

You should *never* need an excuse to sit down and read a good book. Make this one of your resolutions and make the time. Weekly gossip magazines don't count. The best way to ensure you read regularly is to join a book club. If you don't fancy a book club full of strangers, even though there might be a brooding bookish type who will gaze at you over the chocolate digestives, why not form your own? Email some like-minded friends and get a gang together.

People's tastes in books are as varied, and as quirky, as their tastes in partners. Try and find between six and eight friends that have reasonably similar (literary) tastes. Remember this is not an enforced school project, but something that will lead to lively conversations and possibly lively arguments. Far better than wasting mindless hours in front of the television or on the telephone, and a fraction of the cost . . .

Once you have established your group, decide what dates to meet on and rotate at each other's houses or meet in a restaurant or a (not too rowdy) pub. You have to be strict that the book is the main topic of discussion. It will certainly be a relief to have a night off from discussing why your flatmate is single/trying a new diet/hates their job. Far more juicy to work out just what Marianne and Elinor Dashwood will do to make ends meet, or why Caroline Bingley is being so spiteful and determined to ruin Jane's happiness, and then there is the problem of Lizzie Bennet – just what on earth should she do about Mr Wickham, or should she go for the uptight Mr Darcy? Yes, it can be rewarding to sink into a really good read.

Take it in turns to choose a book, but make sure you go with something that gets the majority vote – you don't want to lose your members at the starting line. Try and alternate classics with contemporary, heavy with light. Deciding on the book can be as important as the actual reading and dissection . . . sorry, I mean discussion.

Look at Richard and Judy's book club for title ideas, as well as how they organize their book club, by going to *www.richardandjudybookclub.co.uk*. In America there is really only one book club to be in and that is Oprah's – *www.oprah.com*.

Alternatively most newspapers have book clubs, such as the *Mail on Sunday's You* magazine reading group – *www.you.co.uk*. See if any of the Booker Prize contenders catch your eye or if there is a book being made into a film.

Be logical – choose a book list or title ideas from a magazine you read regularly. If you are an avid antique collector you might enjoy novels from the era you are passionate about, while armchair travellers can see the world through the pages and tales of others. If you love biographies you might also like diaries. Above all don't get stuck in a groove or genre. It is often worth reading at least the back covers of the books featured in bestseller lists orin-store highlights. Go to your local library as often as you go to Starbucks, and if you are not a member join immediately – the library, that is – as this is the most essential membership card you can have in your wallet. It could also save you a fortune with this latest venture. That said, if you are going to be making notes on a book you'll need to have a well-thumbed copy of your own.

If you want to know more about the author before committing to their tome go to *www.meettheauthor.com* where contemporary authors explain their books in their own words (sadly it wasn't around at the time of Austen or Dickens). Or indeed log onto *www.amazon.com* or one of the other online bookstores. All the books are available, as well as reader reviews, and they make suggestions for what you might like to read next, based on the books you've already enjoye

The beginning

For your first book club meeting come with a list of, say, five books you have loved and read, and a list of three you are dying to read. This will help establish what you enjoy and what you all have in common. See what everyone else suggests, and if there are groans or anguished looks over a suggested title consider if a) this is the book you want to slog through or b) this is the right mix of members for the group.

You can get an idea of how a book club works in the novel *The Jane Austen Book Club* by Karen Joy Fowler; perhaps this should be set as the initiation research read.

The club in question is founded by Jocelyn in Sacramento Valley, California, a thousand miles away from Austen's original setting but where her novels are discussed by a pot-pourri of new characters. The book weaves the modern-day lives of the club members together with Austen's books. Each month is dedicated to a different Austen work, and each month another character reveals a chink in their armour. It's the perfect mix of how to set up a book club, what the meetings will be like and what to discuss, with a topical sprinkling of Austen.

But don't fret, there doesn't need to be as much 'self-discovery' or revelation in your group as there is in Fowler's, nor does the club have to be limited to one author. The only unbreakable rules are that meetings have to be regular and anyone attending has to have read the book.

When deciding on a book for your club you could always start with diaries, such as *Bridget Jones's Diary* or 'blooks', like *Belle de Jour*, the diary of a London call girl. However noble it is to propose Samuel Pepys' diary, you will find your members falling at the first hurdle. Break in gently to the RRR (Regular Reading Regime).

Why not suggest you start the year with a book that is set in London? Or find out if there's a novel set in your home town. Pick a theme for each month and suggest setting titles around this. Ideally you choose a book that all the group will be reading for the first time.

Once the title has been agreed on set a deadline – say a month – when you will all come back and dissect it, just as you would a date, a bad day in the office, or indeed one of your favourite soaps.

The evening itself

As well as the book there is the social element of bringing like-minded literary bods together. If you are hosting the discussion evening why not take elements from the book and 'theme' it? For *The Jane Austen Book Club*, for instance, what elements of 'Ye Olde Austen England' could you bring to the evening? Would Earl Grey in the bone china tea service with delicate cucumber sandwiches suit the novel, or would a sofa in Starbucks in acknowledgement of the American element be more appropriate? It's up to you how you give the book the setting it deserves. But be original and bring the book to life. Make the hosting as much of a challenge as the discussion; that way people will definitely be more inclined to turn up and try and outshine you when it's their turn.

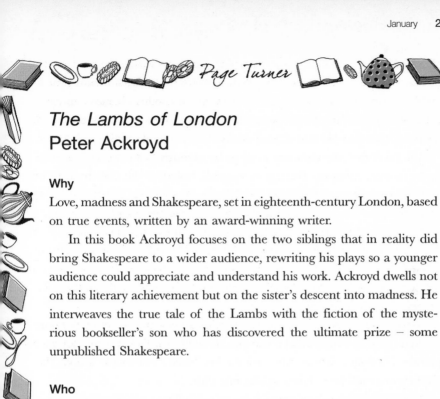

Page Turner

The Lambs of London
Peter Ackroyd

Why

Love, madness and Shakespeare, set in eighteenth-century London, based on true events, written by an award-winning writer.

In this book Ackroyd focuses on the two siblings that in reality did bring Shakespeare to a wider audience, rewriting his plays so a younger audience could appreciate and understand his work. Ackroyd dwells not on this literary achievement but on the sister's descent into madness. He interweaves the true tale of the Lambs with the fiction of the mysterious bookseller's son who has discovered the ultimate prize – some unpublished Shakespeare.

Who

Peter Ackroyd (born 5 October 1949) grew up in a council flat in Acton, West London, and went on to win scholarships to Cambridge and Yale. He's written several prize-winning books including the historical novels *The Clerkenwell Tales*, *Hawksmoor* and the brilliant Booker short-listed *Chatterton*, yet hates award ceremonies and fuss. The day he finished his epic non-fiction bestseller *London* he suffered a heart attack and was in a coma for a week. Yet despite a passion for writing biographies and researching the lives of others he has little interest in talking about his own. In 2004 he told the *Guardian*: 'I don't find myself interesting as a person and the details I find boring, quite frankly. You could sum it up in a few words or sentences really: came from nothing. Self-educated. Luck. Energy. Curiosity. Ambition. That's it.'

The plot

Everyone knows Shakespeare's work, and though he might not have been on your syllabus since school he should still be on your shelf. Those who studied him should have come across Lamb's *Tales from Shakespeare*, the work of siblings Charles and Mary Lamb, first published in 1807. They wrote short, colloquial summaries of twenty of Shakespeare's greatest plays, Charles handling the tragedies, Mary the comedies, which were then gathered together in a miniature pocket book.

Ackroyd's novel follows the events that inspired the creation of their book, and blends fact and fiction to weave an intriguing story.

Children of a lawyer's clerk, life is comfortable for the Lamb family, but Mary Lamb is largely confined to the house, forbidden a career – as were all respectable ladies of the time – and has no husband (reasons for which are later revealed). She lives in London with her ageing father, his new wife and her youngest brother. Her only solace is reading and she escapes the claustrophobia of her life through books, especially Shakespeare. The only person who shows her any real interest is her brother, Charles, an aspiring essayist and poet, who on occasion stages mini performances of the Bard's work in the house with her. Charles Lamb, however, is a bit of a drinker and a gambler and early in the novel is brought home worse for wear by a William Ireland.

Lamb, as a gentleman, looks down on Ireland, the antiquarian bookseller's son. His sister, however, befriends him and starts to visit his shop. An innocent courtship begins. It is not long before Ireland confides in Mary that a mysterious patron has entrusted him with some of Shakespeare's original manuscripts, including an unpublished work. He reads her extracts from this newly discovered play and Mary gets totally caught up in the romance and excitement of his find. Ireland becomes the toast of London, everyone is clamouring to see this treasure, but the literary world is divided over the work's authenticity . . .

Although Ireland is entirely of Ackroyd's invention, the Lambs were real, and Ackroyd uses the dramatic details of their life to shape his book. The actual Mary Lamb suffered a breakdown from the strain of looking after her family and, in 1796, in a sudden fit of insanity killed her mother with a carving knife. In 1799, when his father died, Charles gave up his fiancé in order to care for his troubled elder sister rather than see her committed, and she became his constant and only companion. Ackroyd might play down her mental state, but the distress and intrigue surrounding William Ireland contributed to her distress and provided a motivation for the siblings to transcribe their tales of Shakespeare. Read it and see whether you believe Ireland's tale or the Lamb's Tales.

Hosting

Do you know any Elizabethan-looking ale houses, or a pub by the Globe Theatre or other authentic Shakespearean settings? The Lambs lived in Little Queen Street, Holborn, and the pub Charles Lamb frequented is still serving today at 16 Elia Street, London, N1 (the street was renamed Elia after the pseudonym he often wrote under). Why not go and discuss Ackroyd's work there? Or hold the meeting in your favourite local book-shop in homage to Ireland's shop? Would rock cakes and a light tea make suitable refreshments? Or will you decide to serve a strong ale in line with the times? Just be careful if you do, as your members may need a little nap afterwards, so don't stray too far from home.

Alternative London books include:

Fingersmith by Sarah Waters
Brick Lane by Monica Ali
The Buddha of Suburbia by Hanif Kureishi
White Teeth by Zadie Smith
The Lonely Londoners by Sam Selvon.
Or for modern musings on London, go to *www.smokelondon.co.uk* for words and images inspired by the city – or submit your own thoughts on the number 38 bus.

5th January

Twelfth Night – This is the twelfth day after Christmas and the cultural way to commemorate the night would be to re-read William Shakespeare's *Twelfth Night*, also known as *What You Will*. It was commissioned and first performed as part of the Twelfth Night celebrations at the Middle Temple Hall in 1602.

On this night at the Theatre Royal, Drury Lane, London, Baddeley Cake is served to all the players. This is done in memory of Richard Baddeley, a pastry cook turned comic actor, who bequeathed the theatre a sum of money to spend on wine and Twelfth-Night cake, or 'Baddeley Cake', as it became known when he died in 1794. Thespians, being a superstitious bunch, have kept this tradition up, pausing only during the war but reviving it again in 1947. If the mood takes them, on this night they will also dress up in eighteenth-century garb and really get into cake-eating character.

Two of the most quotable lines in Shakespeare come from this play and are worth having as mottos, or at the very least throwing in at key opportunities.

'Be not afraid of greatness: some are born great, some achieve greatness and some have greatness thrust upon them . . .' Malvolio reads in his letter from Olivia – Act II, Scene V

'Love sought is good, but giv'n unsought is better . . .' Olivia says as she tries in vain to woo Cesario/Viola – Act III, Scene I

If you haven't got time to read *Twelfth Night*, your memory is a little rusty, or your *Lamb's Tales from Shakespeare* isn't around, here are the highlights:

Opening with the immortal lines '*If music be the food of love, play on*', this is a comedy, though bittersweet. It is a quest for love, and concealed identity forms the basis for all the confusion.

Set in the Italian sea port of Illyria, twins Viola and Sebastian are separated when their boat is shipwrecked. Viola is washed ashore and, thinking her brother is dead, disguises herself as a boy so she can survive and get a job working for Orsino, the Duke of Illyria.

Orsino is pining for the love of his neighbour, the Countess Olivia, and sends his new page and confidante Cesario (Viola) to help him woo her. Problem is Olivia falls for Cesario (Viola) *not* Orsino – while Viola falls in love with Orsino. Doh.

As if any further complication is needed it's at this point that Sebastian turns up, rescued by sea captain Antonio, who lends the boy some money to help him on his way. Meanwhile over in Olivia's household there is chaos as her uncle, Sir Toby Belch, is causing trouble, first matchmaking for his own financial gain and then teaming up with the maid Maria for another scam. They forge a love letter from 'Olivia' and send it to her steward, a pompous man named Malvolio. Malvolio falls for it hook, line and sinker and believes that his mistress Olivia is giving him the eye. It backfires horribly and Malvolio is left in yellow stockings and cross-gartering looking so ridiculous that Olivia, as well as the audience, have to forgive him his past arrogance when they see what the cruel joke has done to him.

Anyway, getting back to the main story . . . leave it alone for five minutes and it has become even more complex. Olivia meets Sebastian and, thinking he is Cesario (Viola), literally marches him up the aisle. What a great place, thinks Sebastian and doesn't put up any struggle as he too has fallen for this feisty lady, even if she does seem a little forward.

Once a matter of some stolen gold, mistaken identity and marriage is sorted out Olivia gets her man – (thankfully) a real one: Sebastian. Orsino also gets the girl. By this point he has given up with Olivia and realizes he is in love with Cesario, but is even happier when the *he* turns out to be a *she*. (Even though the original cast would have been all male, gay love affairs weren't very PC in Tudor times.) Orsino can marry Viola, and the twins are reunited. Some Twelfth Night.

6th January

The feast of the Epiphany – Religious reasons aside, Epiphany needs to be circled in your diary as decorations, trees, Santas and so on absolutely *must* come down by today. Any later and you will get a year of bad luck, and no tinsel is worth this risk.

The Western church calendar was adopted in the fourth century and until then Epiphany was observed on different dates. Today the notable exceptions that remain are in some Greek, Russian and Serbian Orthodox Churches who celebrate Epiphany as *Theophany* on 19 January and celebrate Orthodox Christmas on 7 January.

The Christian feast of Epiphany marks the last of the twelve days of Christmas and commemorates the Adoration of the Magi.

This is when the Three Kings – Caspar, Melchior and Balthasar – who had been following the star finally arrived in Bethlehem and presented Jesus with their gifts of gold, frankincense and myrrh.

Also on this date, Joan of Arc was born in 1412.

In 1540, Henry VIII (28 June 1491–28 January 1547) wed Anne of Cleves.

You can keep track of the great monarch's many marriages with the rhyme:

Divorced, Beheaded, Died;
Divorced, Beheaded, Survived.

And the wives were:

Catherine of Aragon, Anne Boleyn, Jane Seymour,
Anne of Cleves, Catherine Howard and Catherine Parr.

Despite ruling England during one of its most golden eras, what people remember Henry VIII most for are his six marriages, and causing England to split with the Pope and Rome. Anne, wife number four, was 'lucky' in some respects, as she survived with a mere divorce (his second). The reason for this divorce was because Henry found her 'dull, unattractive and never consummated the union'. Don't mince your words, Your Majesty. Henry had seen such a flattering – and misleading – picture of Anne that he had proposed, still grief-stricken following the death of possibly his most beloved wife, Jane Seymour (well, she did produce the only male heir). He was furious with the portrait painter, Hans Holbein, the younger, who had done the Tudor equivalent of air brushing. The reality of Anne of Cleves did not rock his boat – so his second divorce followed swiftly.

Plough Monday

Ye Olde England says the first Monday after the twelve days of Christmas is Plough Monday. Back in the day ploughmen would decorate their ploughs, blacken their faces and wear white shirts. The tradition blessed the plough and the harvest it would reap and sow.

9th January

British Prime Minister William Pitt the Younger introduced income tax in 1788. This is a timely reminder. Is your tax return under control? In the UK if you are self-employed you have until the end of the month to file your tax return.

10th January – Eid al-Adha

The Feast of Sacrifice is the most important festival in the Muslim calendar. Beginning today, it is a three-day festival to mark the end of the *Hajj* or the holy pilgrimage to Mecca, one of the five pillars of Islam. (The five pillars of Islam represent the most important acts of being a Muslim, which, in brief, are: the profession of faith in Allah, prayer, paying of alms, fasting and the pilgrimage to Mecca. A Muslim should make at least one pilgrimage in their lifetime.)

The date commemorates Abraham's willingness to obey God by sacrificing his son. The Koran says he was about to sacrifice his son when a voice from heaven stopped him and allowed him to slay a ram instead. The feast re-enacts Abraham's obedience through the sacrificing of a cow or ram. The family will eat a third of the meal, and then donate the rest to the poor.

11th January

Novelist Thomas Hardy died in 1928. (See April Book Club, page 160.)

Also on this date, in 1935, American aviator Amelia Earhart flew across the Pacific. 'I fly better than I wash dishes,' she said and went on to become the first person to fly solo the 2,408-mile distance between Honolulu and Oakland, California, which was also the first flight on which a civilian aircraft carried a two-way radio. Sadly, on her last flight, in 1937, her plane vanished, presumed crashed, and she and her co-pilot have never been found.

14th January

Lohri – this Hindu festival takes place to celebrate the end of the winter season, and is mainly observed in the north of India, where bonfires are lit. It is also known as *Makar Sankrant*, the day for alms-giving and putting right disagreements and quarrels.

Pongal – this three-day festival in southern India blesses the rice harvest. Rice boiled in milk is offered to the sun god, Surya.

15th January

Queen Elizabeth I was crowned in 1559. (Read about her in April's Muse of the Month, page 135.)

The British Museum opened at Montagu House, Bloomsbury, London in 1759.

Martin Luther King Day

In America, the third Monday in January is a national holiday to remember all the late civil rights leader Martin Luther King (15 January 1929 – 4 April 1968) achieved and campaigned for – the date was chosen to fall as near to his birthday as possible.

A devout Christian, his peaceful demonstrations against racism followed the example set by Gandhi. In eleven years he travelled over six million miles, gave over 2,500 public addresses, wrote five books and caught the attention of the entire world with his civil rights movement.

On 28 August 1963, in Washington DC, in front of 250,000 people, King made his famous 'I Have a Dream' speech.

> 'I have a dream that one day this nation will rise up and live out the true meaning of its creed: "We hold these truths to be self-evident: that all men are created equal."'

He was awarded at least twenty honorary degrees and named Man of the Year by *Time* magazine in 1963. He was arrested over twenty times, assaulted at least four times but didn't let this stop him. At thirty-five he was the youngest man to have received the Nobel Peace Prize, and typically gave the prize money of $54,123 to the civil rights movement.

On 4 April 1968, he was assassinated on the balcony of his motel room in Memphis, Tennessee, where he had come to lead a protest march in sympathy with striking garbage workers.

He was thirty-nine years old.

22nd January

Mughal Emperor Shah Jahan died in 1666.

One of the greatest and most glamorous rulers of India, the fifth Mughal Emperor was also a true romantic, and built the world's most famous shrine to love.

When his beloved wife died, just after giving birth to child number fourteen, he was so grief-stricken it is said that his hair and beard went white overnight. As a shrine to her memory he decided to build the most beautiful palace ever seen. After twenty-two years and a fleet of 10,000 elephants commandered to transport the masonry, a new Wonder of the World was unveiled: the Taj Mahal. On the banks of the River Yamuna, the temple is an hour and a half (on an express train) from New Delhi. It has 10–25,000 visitors everyday and has become India's top tourist attraction.

Designed by Iranian architect Ustad Isa, its name means 'Crown Palace'. Legend says that to ensure nothing as beautiful could ever be produced again by his craftsmen, Shah Jahan made one final request when it was completed – for the thumbs of all 20,000 workers and artisans to be chopped off.

The mausoleum has been described as a 'teardrop on the cheek of time' as well as the 'Symbol of Eternal Love'.

In 1992 Princess Diana was famously photographed here, alone. Prince Charles had promised, in 1980, to return with the woman he loved. Headlines blazed all over the world and the photo of her in her brightly coloured suit, sitting in front of the palace, of her 'Temple of Loneliness', is an unforgettable image. If your budget doesn't stretch to you making the journey, read about the love story that inspired it in the un-putdownable *Beneath a Marble Sky: a novel* by John Shors.

25th January

Burns Night – Scotland's most famous poet, Robert Burns (1759–1796) was born on this date and his memory and work are still celebrated today.

Burns was a prolific poet, whose work included: 'O my luve's like a red, red rose, that's newly sprung in June.'

But you already know his most well-known work, the lyrics to 'Auld Lange Syne'. This means 'For Long Ago'. (For the song sheet see New Year's Eve, December, page 498.)

On Burns Night the Scots celebrate by throwing parties, lighting bonfires and downing toddies to keep his memory alive (and to keep warm).

How to make a hot toddy

A hot toddy is an alcoholic concoction made to 'take the chill off things'. Whether you are sick or shivering, the warm elixir of alcohol and sugar is an intoxicating brew, ideal to loosen things up, and has less of an aftertaste than punch.

Ingredients vary from recipe to recipe, but essentially you need to make a mug of hot herbal tea, add a shot of whisky, one to two teaspoons of honey, a slice of lemon, and drink it as hot as you can, sipping slowly. Breathing in the steam helps soothe the sinuses and throat. Be sure to drink it *hot*, as cold toddy (and alcohol cools fast) is revolting.

Ingredients:
   2 measures Scotch whisky
   3 measures boiling water
   $1/2$ measure lemon juice
   1 teaspoon honey (or brown sugar)
   3 drops angostura bitters
   1 slice lemon, studded with cloves
   ground nutmeg

To make:
Put the sugar, bitters, lemon juice, and clove-studded lemon in your mug. Add the Scotch and pour in the boiling water. Stir to dissolve the sugar and sprinkle with ground nutmeg.

25th January

St Dwynwen's Day – she is the Welsh patron saint of lovers and this was an auspicious date for Henry VIII to have married wife number two, Anne Boleyn, in 1533.

27th January

Wolfgang Amadeus Mozart was born in 1756.

Whether you listen to classical music or not, everyone should know this name. Mozart was the most famous child prodigy, composer and performer in musical history and his work is still played, performed and recorded today.

He began touring Europe when he was six, and published his first work, four piano sonatas, before his tenth birthday. He was only thirty when his famed opera *Le Nozze di Figaro* (*The Marriage of Figaro*) debuted, but, despite his genius, he couldn't secure a musical post or fixed patron, while his decadent rock-star-like lifestyle plunged him into debt, and illness.

He died on 5 December 1791 and was buried in an unmarked grave aged only thirty-five.

In his life he composed over 600 works, including 21 for stage and opera, 15 masses, 41 symphonies, 25 piano concertos, 12 violin concertos, 27 concert arias, 17 piano sonatas and 26 string quartets.

Download some of his greatest hits or celebrate the night in style and watch the 1984 Oscar-winning film *Amadeus*, by Peter Shaffer. Such was the success of the film, sales of Mozart's music increased by thirty per cent that year alone. What Mozart do you have on your iPod?

Because Mozart was such a prolific composer catalogues were created to make sure *nothing* got lost and all his archives were preserved. The definitive one for Mozart is the Köchel catalogue, first published in 1862, and it is edited to ensure the chronological preservation of all of his masterpieces.

But why the K?

All his work is listed K1 – K626 in deference to the man who did all the hard work: Ludwig Alois Ferdinand Ritter von Köchel (1800–77). He was a writer, composer, botanist and publisher, and above all a music fanatic. He painstakingly went through, corrected and completed the catalogue of all of Mozart's works and thanks to his hard work his name and Mozart's will last for eternity.

Essential Mozart tunes to listen to/download include:

Church music
Mass in C minor K427
Requiem in D minor K626 (his last uncompleted work)

Operas
Le Nozze di Figaro K492 (The Marriage of Figaro)
Don Giovanni K527
Die Zauberflöte K620 (The Magic Flute)

Symphonies
Symphony No. 40 in G minor K550
Symphony No. 41 in C K551

Serenades and divertimenti
Eine Kleine Nachtmusik K525

Concertos
Piano Concerto in C No. 21 K467

Piano music
Sonata in A K331

Even if you don't recognize the pieces by title, you will when you hear them.

Die Zauberflöte (Der Hölle Rache) is the most downloaded piece of classical music on iTunes, and it's hard to believe how old it is when you listen to it.

As January ends in the western world, in the East celebrations are only just beginning.

The Chinese New Year

The Chinese New Year dates back to 2600 BC, when the cycle of the zodiac was introduced by Emperor Huang Ti, centuries before our calendar was even a consideration.

Similar to the western calendar, it is based on cycles of the moon, and because of this the beginning of the year can fall any time between late January and the middle of February. The date the Chinese New Year falls on is calculated by the date of the second new moon after the winter solstice. Check it out online.

The Chinese New Year rotates around a twelve-year cycle, each year represented by a different animal. According to legend Lord Buddha summoned all the animals in the world to come and say goodbye to him before he departed from the earth, and only twelve turned up. He rewarded those that came by naming a year after them, in the order in which they had loyally arrived.

The Chinese believe that the animal year in which you are born gives an indication of your personality. They have a saying: 'This is the animal that hides in your heart.' See which animal you are, and which you are dating.

Rat: 1912, 1924, 1936, 1948, 1960, 1972, 1984, 1996, 2008
Noted for their charm, and attraction to the opposite sex. They work hard to achieve their goals, acquire possessions and are likely to be perfectionists. Rats are ambitious and love a good gossip, but are easily angered.

Most compatible with Dragon, Monkey and Ox.

Ox: 1913, 1925, 1937, 1949, 1961, 1973, 1985, 1997, 2009

Quiet and eloquent, patient and kind they will inspire confidence. On the downside oxen are often eccentric and opinionated and stubborn – aren't we all? They hate opposition and failure, and are a mass of extremes and contradictions.

Best with Snake, Rooster and Rat.

Tiger: 1914, 1926, 1938, 1950, 1962, 1974, 1986, 1998, 2010

Sensitive, deep-thinking and capable of great sympathy, but likely to be very short-tempered. Some may conflict with their elders or authority while others have respect for them. Can be suspicious but on the whole are courageous and powerful.

Most compatible with Horse, Dragon and Dog.

Rabbit: 1915, 1927, 1939, 1951, 1963, 1975, 1987, 1999, 2011

People born in this year are ambitious, talented, articulate yet reserved. They are virtuous and have excellent taste and are admired and trusted. They are fond of gossip, but are generally kind and seldom loose their temper. Said to be financially blessed, conscientious and never one to back out of a commitment.

Most compatible with Sheep, Pig, Dog.

Dragon: 1916, 1928, 1940, 1964, 1976, 1988, 2000, 2012

Healthy, energetic, excitable on the positive side; stubborn and short-tempered on the negative. They are brave, honest and sensitive. Dragons inspire confidence and trust and are the most eccentric of any in the eastern zodiac.

Compatible with Rat, Snake, Monkey and Rooster.

Snake: 1917, 1929, 1941, 1953, 1965, 1977, 1989, 2001, 2013

Those born in these years are deep thinkers, wise and never have to worry about money. But on the flip side they are often vain, selfish and can be a bit stingy, even though they have great sympathy for others, and do try and help those less fortunate. Determined, snakes hate to fail and although they appear calm on the surface, they are also intense and passionate. They might have marital problems as they are often fickle.

Best with Ox and Rooster.

Horse: 1918, 1930, 1942, 1954, 1966, 1978, 1990, 2002, 2014

Horses are popular, cheerful, skilful with money and perceptive, as well as having the tendency to be chatterboxes. Wise and talented, good with their hands and real flirts, they are impatient and hot-blooded about everything except their daily work. These are party people, who usually ignore good advice.

Best with Tiger, Dog and Sheep.

Sheep/Ram: 1919, 1931, 1943, 1955, 1967, 1979, 1991, 2003, 2015

Elegant and accomplished, they often go into the art world. At first they seem to be better off than any other sign but they are shy, pessimistic and often puzzled about life. Passionate about what they believe in but too timid to be great orators of their thoughts, they are wise, gentle and compassionate.

They are compatible with Rabbit, Pig and Horse.

Monkey: 1920, 1932, 1944, 1956, 1968, 1980, 1992, 2004, 2016

These are the erratic strong-willed geniuses of the cycle. Clever and skilful, inventive and original they can solve most problems and will succeed in most fields. Monkeys have a thirst for knowledge and an excellent memory.

Most compatible with Dragon and Rat.

Rooster: 1921, 1933, 1945, 1957, 1969, 1981, 1993, 2005, 2017

They are capable and talented and like to be busy, devoted beyond the call of duty, and are devastated if they should fail – where would we be without all those early morning cock-a-doodle wake-up calls? Despite giving the impression of being adventurous they have a timid loner side. Roosters are thinkers, perhaps eccentric, but always interesting and brave.

Best with Ox, Snake and Dragon.

Dog: 1922, 1934, 1946, 1958, 1970, 1982, 1994, 2006, 2018

People born in these years possess the best traits of human nature – they have a deep sense of loyalty, they are honest and inspire confidence, and know how to keep secrets. But dogs are not perfect as they can be selfish and annoyingly stubborn. They care not for wealth yet are always in credit. They have a sharp tongue and make great leaders.

Compatible with Horse, Tiger and Rabbit.

Boar/Pig: 1923, 1935, 1947, 1959, 1971, 1983, 1995, 2007, 2019

You are chivalrous and gallant if you are born in these years. Whatever the pig takes on they will do with all their might. Those that they make friends with they will be loyal to for life. They have a great thirst for knowledge, hate arguments and like to be well informed.

Compatible with Rabbit and Sheep.

Chinese New Year celebrations can usually last up to fifteen days, and as with most big events preparations begin way in advance. There is the New Year spring clean to sweep away any traces of bad luck, and, if taking proceedings to heart, doors and window-frames are given a fresh coat of paint, very often in cheery red. Doors and windows are decorated with paper garlands and verses asking for happiness, prosperity and long life.

Eating is an especially significant part of the celebration. Seafood brings different blessings, for example prawns are said to promote liveliness and happiness, dried oysters bring all things good, and raw fish salad, prosperity and good luck.

On the day Chinese New Year is celebrated there is an ancient custom called *Hong Bao*, meaning 'red packet', when married couples give children, and unmarried couples, a gift of money in a little red envelope. Families are meant to go from door to door with New Year greetings and the motto 'let bygones be bygones'.

Chinese New Year superstitions

Death, dying and ghost stories are taboo, and all debts have to be settled, which is all fine and good.

There are a few odd grooming details that are important traditions during the festivities. It is up to you how authentic you want your celebrations to be.

Shoes and pants are considered to be inauspicious purchases. 'Shoe' comes from the Cantonese word 'rough', and 'pants' from the Cantonese word 'bitter'. I feel reluctant to discourage shopping for shoes, but in this case, holding back should at least be considered.

Haircuts are also bad news, as is floor sweeping. Washing your hair is said to wash away luck – so how Cinderella is meant to look her best is a puzzle.

Wear red, which is considered a lucky, happy colour. Another good thing is that candy eating is encouraged for a sweet year.

31st January

The formal deadline for sending back a tax return is today. If it arrives at the Inland Revenue after this deadline you'll be charged an automatic penalty . . . and that's not a good way to start the year. Think of all your resolve.

Foot Note

The court

The court shoe (or 'pump', depending on which side of the pond you are reading this) has been the staple of all stylish wardrobes throughout the ages. The pump came about in 1555 and was taken from 'poumpe', the name given to the slipper worn by footmen. The shoe had to be gripped into place by the heel and toe muscles but before long this elegant sole had slipped its way from the livery men to razzle-dazzling in court. It's a low-cut shoe that has been cutting a dash, slipping on and off, with or without buckles, bows and laces, *comme vous voulez* since the pavane was the dance in fashion (ohhh, way back). From the sixteenth century it has gently waltzed back and forth, its heel rising and falling as style dictated, complementing rather than overpowering trends. On the heel to hem length pulley system, generally speaking, as skirts shrank heels would lower, and vice versa. How very ladylike.

The court shoe is typically black though now it is no longer taboo to have it in other colours – indeed, in the fifties it was positively encouraged to dye them the same shade as your handbag. In the 1880s that simply would never do; it was considered very unbecoming for a lady to draw attention to herself in public, and when Queen Victoria went into mourning so did her court and courtiers' shoes. In the jazz era flappers learned to Charleston and courts got straps, to keep up with the moves.

Leading the way in the ultimate court shoe are names including Roger Vivier, Manolo Blahník, and Raymond Massaro's 1957 two-toned pump for Chanel. The essential classic for any stylish woman, it has gone from court livery to First Lady (think Jackie Kennedy), as the ultimate first footwear.

February

'O Romeo, Romeo! wherefore art thou Romeo?'
William Shakespeare

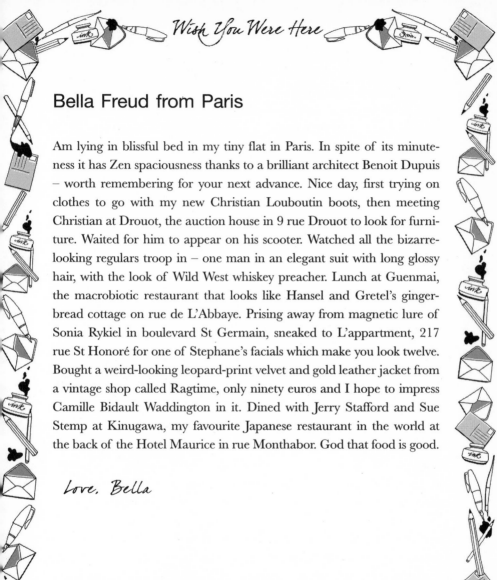

Wish You Were Here

Bella Freud from Paris

Am lying in blissful bed in my tiny flat in Paris. In spite of its minuteness it has Zen spaciousness thanks to a brilliant architect Benoit Dupuis – worth remembering for your next advance. Nice day, first trying on clothes to go with my new Christian Louboutin boots, then meeting Christian at Drouot, the auction house in 9 rue Drouot to look for furniture. Waited for him to appear on his scooter. Watched all the bizarre-looking regulars troop in – one man in an elegant suit with long glossy hair, with the look of Wild West whiskey preacher. Lunch at Guenmai, the macrobiotic restaurant that looks like Hansel and Gretel's gingerbread cottage on rue de L'Abbaye. Prising away from magnetic lure of Sonia Rykiel in boulevard St Germain, sneaked to L'appartment, 217 rue St Honoré for one of Stephane's facials which make you look twelve. Bought a weird-looking leopard-print velvet and gold leather jacket from a vintage shop called Ragtime, only ninety euros and I hope to impress Camille Bidault Waddington in it. Dined with Jerry Stafford and Sue Stemp at Kinugawa, my favourite Japanese restaurant in the world at the back of the Hotel Maurice in rue Monthabor. God that food is good.

Love, Bella

1st February

In 1896 Puccini's Paris-inspired opera *La Bohème* made its debut performance at the Teatro Reggio, Turin, Italy.

However, unlike his previous opera, *Manon Lescaut*, Puccini's fourth opera
was not an instant hit. The Italian newspaper *La Stampa* wrote 'it leaves little
impression in the mind . . . [and] will leave no great trace upon the history
of theatre'. Wrong. Be your own judge and critic. Listen or, better still, find
a performance and go and see *La Bohème* live, and see page 395 for how to
become an opera lover.

Giacomo Puccini (1856–1924) was born in Lucca, Italy, to a family of musicians. His own career began in his teens playing the organ at his local church.
His performance skills, his ingenuity – and Catholic guilt – were tested when
he sold off the church's organ pipes, one by one, to fund his tobacco habit.

La Bohème was inspired by the French poet Henri Murger. The libretto
(musical text) by Luigi Illica and Giuseppe Giacosa took the romantic tale
of *Scènes de la vie de Bohème*, originally magazine sketches that Murger extended
into a popular play, and with the addition of Puccini's music made it
immortal.

The story gives a taste of eighteenth-century bohemian Paris. The
central characters are the philosopher Colline, the painter Marcel, the
musician Schaunard, and the struggling poet Rudolphe (a glimpse of
Murger himself). The gang frequented the Café Momus, where they were
known as the 'four musketeers'. The plot centres around this bohemian
community of artists, particularly the blossoming romance between the
poet Rudolphe (who was to become Rodolfo in Puccini's opera), and the
grisette Mimi, a young, bottom-rung, destitute girl, who in this case does
embroidery. There is also a secondary relationship between his room-mate
Marcello and Musetta, but the main focus rests on the impossible situation of cupid's central characters.

From love follows conflict, confusion, tragedy and inevitably death, all the highs and lows you need to help the music soar. Murger himself was dead within a decade of writing his great triumph – he died on 28 January 1861 aged only thirty-nine. He would never know the high notes his words would hit.

La Bohème remains one of the greatest love stories set to music. Listen to the duet at the end of Act One, '*O Soave Fanciulla*' ('Oh Gentle Maiden') as Rodolfo and Mimi tell each other their stories and love quickly blossoms when she comes to borrow a light for a candle.

Moulin Rouge, the stage musical *Rent*, or Baz Luhrmann's theatrical version of *La Bohème* are all modern adaptations of Puccini's masterpiece.

How to party like a pagan

There are eight major festivals in the pagan cycle – four with Celtic origins, four from points of the solar calendar.

The cycle of pagan festivals is as follows:

Celtic	**Solar**
Imbolc 1–2 February	*Spring Equinox* 20–21 March
Beltane April 30–1 May	*Midsummer* 21–22 June
Lughnasadh 1–2 August	*Autumn Equinox* 20–21 September
Samhain October 31–1 November	*Yule/Winter Solstice* 20–21 December

Note: Due to the seasonal differences across the hemispheres, solar festivals need to be swapped, depending what side of the equator you are on. The above are for the northern hemisphere.

The Celtic Imbolc Festival was celebrated between the 1–2 February at the start of the pagan 'Wheel of the Year' to ensure a good harvest. Rituals included lighting fires, making candles, planting spring flowers as well as reading pagan poetry and performing storytelling. The Imbolc Festival celebrated the increasing power of the sun and the harvest it would provide. Get in touch with your earthy, astrological side.

Stonehenge

When talking about the pagans probably the most famous pile of rocks that springs to mind is the one eight miles out of Salisbury, and to this day it remains a focal point for pagan worship that dates back to over 3–5,000 years ago. It is a gigantic man-made solar calendar that has kept time for centuries. Learn to tell the time by it – no batteries are required, and it is waterproof.

2nd February

This is the date on which the year's supply of a church's candles is blessed. Candlemas's official title is 'The Feast of the Purification of the Virgin'. From the mid-fifth century candles were lit on this day by Christians to symbolize that Jesus Christ was the light and truth of the world.

Today is also Groundhog Day. No, really. In America on this date, legend has it that if a groundhog sees his shadow he'll return to his hole and winter will last another six weeks. Watch Bill Murray in the 1993 film *Groundhog Day* and see what happens when one day repeats itself again and again.

3rd February

The composer of *A Midsummer Night's Dream* and the 'Wedding March', Felix Mendelssohn, was born in Hamburg in 1809. Download one of his master-pieces today – or practise your bridal aisle-gliding in the supermarket; it is after all the right month to find love.

How to learn a language

If the New Year's resolutions are still holding up then it is time to add another skill to your repertoire: a new language. It's only six months until the height of the summer holiday season, in other words, the bikini body-bearing month, so as well as starting the stomach crunches, now's the time to decide where you are going – and what language you'll be needing to learn.

Make sure you can say something new for 'World Hello Day'. 21 November is a day entirely dedicated to greeting people in every language. For more information go to go to *www.worldhelloday.org.*

On the language site *www.everythingESL*.net you can get a head start as here they encourage their students to learn how to say 'hello' in ten new languages such as:

Konichiwa (koh-nee-chee-WAH) is hello in Japanese.
Jambo (JAM-bo) is hello in Swahili.
Hola (OH-la) is hello in Spanish.
Ni hao (nee-ha-OW) is hello in Chinese.
Bonjour (bohn-ZHOOR) is hello in French.
Ciao (chow) is hello in Italian.
Annyong ha shimnikka (An-YOH-HASHim-ni-kah) is hello in Korean.
Czesc (Chesht) is hello is Polish.
Zdravstvuite (ZzDRAST-vet-yah) is hello in Russian.
Al Salaam a' alaykum (ahl sah-LAHM-ah-ah-LAY-koom) is hello in Arabic.

But as well as 'Hello', for which Lionel Richie will always be remembered, there is one other expression that comprises the most important words you will ever learn to say (other than 'don't shoot, we're innocent').

What language do you want to say the magic phrase in? It's not three little words in every country.

Language	I Love You
Danish	*Jeg elsker dig*
Dutch	*Ik hou van jou*
Esperanto	*Mi amas vin*
French	*Je t'aime*
German	*Ich liebe Dich*
Indonesian	*Saya cinta kamu*
Italian	*Ti amo*
Japanese	*Aishite imasu*
Latin	*Te amo*
Mandarin Chinese	*Wo ai ni*
Polish	*Kocham cie*
Romanian	*Te iu besc*
Russian	*Ya vas liubliu*
Spanish	*Te amo*
Swedish	*Jag älskar dig*
Turkish	*Seni seviyorum*

Decide on a language that will be handy for work, wining, dining or shopping. Get the flavour and character of the country you wish to chatter in before tackling the language. This can be done either with a visit, meeting someone from this destination or with a trip to the library or Blockbuster. Rent a DVD, read a book, fictions as well as travel guides, find a willing local and try and communicate in their language rather than your own. Go for dinner to a restaurant specializing in that country's cuisine, or indeed sample a bottle of their wine. It doesn't matter what language you choose, immerse yourself in all aspects. Find out what makes your chosen country tick or swell with pride.

Note: Sweet'n'Sour, like Chicken Tikka or Vindaloo are anglicized adaptations of classic dishes that won't exist in authentic kitchens.

The western creations we know and love came about when the men-folk left their homelands and travelled from East to West, to seek their fortunes. Due to the language barrier and lack of jobs they had to create work. They found they could make a living by imitating their wives' cooking, and so many 'authentic' restaurants from other worlds popped up.

Only problem was, as with men the world over, they had little experience in the kitchen, they would ad lib and serve their own versions (clearly
hoping that 'her indoors' never found out), adding a dash of colouring and
sweetener to get dishes to look and taste how they remembered. The food
we have grown to love wasn't exactly what the women had been slaving
away over a hot stove in the kitchen creating and true connoisseurs are highly
offended by the plastic pizzas and Day-Glo curries that are served up and
delivered twenty-four/seven across the globe.

Know the real from the fake. Don't act like a tourist and ask for one of these
dishes, be more of an honorary local or adventurer and taste the real cuisine
as much as you sample and respect the real culture and treasures of the
well-trodden tourist paths. Be aware of stereotyping and international idiosyn-
crasies and get out and see, taste and try the *real* wonders of the world.

France is very proud of its fine cuisine and cooking; in fact the French supe-
riority in this area is enough to scare off any fast-food junkie quicker than
you can say 'take-away'. But if you think the dishes on the menu look
daunting, take a look at the language, literature and verb conjugations as
well as the Cordon Bleu creations. Make February the month to start understanding what our nearest neighbour is on about on and off the menu, as
well as its claim to own the 'language of love'.

Other language options

Spanish could be sampled with flamenco lessons, castanets, picking up a
matador at the bull-fighting arena or by ordering a paella and sangria. Think
Penélope Cruz, and watch *Volver* to see if it's the language for you.

Italian will mean you need to start making your own pizza and pasta dishes,
and working your way up to rolling your own spaghetti, like a real Italian
mama. Failing that, follow their football teams or fashion designers. Italian
can also be practised with trips to the opera, art galleries or by learning the
sultry style of Sophia Loren as well as following Audrey Hepburn's adventures in the cinema coming-of-age classic *Roman Holiday*.

Mandarin Chinese might be the language spoken by most in the world, followed by Spanish then English, but it's as tricky as chopsticks for a foreigner to master the languages of the East. Oriental languages, as well as some languages of Eastern Europe, use a different alphabet, so you have all kinds of extra challenges here. Make sure it's true love (and not just a taste for a dish best served with rice) before tackling.

A slight note of caution: if learning Italian/German/French through opera-appreciation classes, bear in mind that some of the phrases you memorize could have fallen out of common usage. They might seem dated if tried out in a local bar. However, 'Voi che sapete che cosa è amor?' ('What is this feeling [of love] that makes me so sad?) sounds as beautiful today as it did when it was sung in *The Marriage of Figaro*, which opened in Vienna on 1 May, 1786.

As this is the month for love, let's assume you're going to learn French.

Don't worry if your French teacher terrified you. Moi aussi. It doesn't matter how far you got, whether you have any memory of verb conjugations or how you like your *café*; the second time around, when it's your own choice, it's always much more fun – and much more rewarding.

Decide how you want to tackle the *étude de français*. You could enrol in French classes and learn how to whisper French sweet nothings and socialize with like-minded souls. How chic! There are also countless books, online courses, CDs and lessons to help with conversation and getting the hang of the grammar.

Go to *www.alliancefrancaise.org.uk* and see if they have lessons at times or venues that suit you so you have no excuses to *ne pas comprendre*. Alternatively look at the language courses on offer at *www.berlitzpublishing.com* who effectively publish the bibles of all phrase books.

Paris is the city for lovers and the fashion capital of the world. Think Amélie, Brigitte Bardot and Vanessa Paradis.

How about wetting your appetite by learning some chic sweet nothings.

un cadeau	a present
les fleurs	flowers
les bonbons	sweets
les vêtements	clothes
le parfum	perfume
un amant	lover (male)
une amante	lover (add 'e' to make it feminine)
un copain	boyfriend
une copine	girlfriend
Je t'aime aussi	I love you too
Je t'adore	I adore you
Veux-tu m'épouser?	Will you marry me?

Zee accent

The French do have a bit of a reputation for being sticklers for saying things with zee right accent. *Oh, mon dieu.* But try not to stress too much about this; you are giving it a go and that is worth a few points in itself. Struggle on – like riding a bike, suddenly it'll click. You won't be fluent, but you will get from A to B.

Listen to French CDs, radio or watch films so you can hear the pronunciation and intonations of professionals at speed. However handy phrase books and CDs are, you have to hear it full pelt. But don't totally despair or indeed underestimate the power of body language – eye rolling, pointing and sighing. These will get the point across beautifully should you get stranded (ignore them if they say *non* – they are playing hard to get). The French are great eye rollers and sighers themselves, so they will empathize.

Phrase books usually offer phonetic spellings or suggestions next to the words or phrases. These are OK for your initial crash course and emergency situations but really you should aspire to an authentic Bardot purr, and know how to proceed after the initial 'hello.' *s'il vous plaît*, meaning literally 'if you please' (manners are internationally adored), is pronounced 'see vous play'. Obviously you must *never* admit to reading phonetics, as this is far too touristy and would be like confessing that the fabulous meal you just served was from the microwave.

Bread basket results

Take this challenge seriously. Go to France and visit a *boulangerie* (bakers). This is the perfect place to sample French passion as well as their *pain* (bread). Failing that you must have an 'authentic' café near home. From the baguette to the croissant, even doing the continental for breakfast, will all help put you more in zee mood.

A brief history of the croissant

The most famous French *pâtisserie* has to be the croissant, but like so many things, has got here by default.

On 12 September 1683, Vienna managed to foil a threat of Turkish conquest. The Viennese had been under siege, while the Turks tried everything to tunnel, dig and wiggle their way in and capture the city.

The Turks were actually doing very well until a baker, one Peter Wender, had to go into his basement. Whilst down there he heard a noise and, realizing it was the tunnelling Turks, he tipped off the Viennese. In came the army.

Vienna was saved. Hooray.

To commemorate his part in the victory Wender decided to bake a pastry twisted in the shape of a crescent, which just happened to be the symbol of the [defeated] Ottoman Empire. How true this is is hard to tell – but it's a good tale. Also around the same time a new roll, christened a *Kipfel* (German for crescent), was created.

In 1770 Marie Antoinette took the delicacy with her to France when she married Louis XIV. They took the pastry to their hearts and made it their own. The same can't be said for her, as they chopped off her head.

Language Literate

Rather than opting for the dreary and dry faceless phrase books, stop sweating through *Le Figaro* or *Molière*, and get rid of that panicked look. There are many more chic and fun ways to learn the lingo. Why not subscribe to French *Vogue*, *Numéro* or *l'Officiel* instead?

Magazine captions in the glossies provide good reading as not only will they increase your vocabulary, they will help you acclimatize to French style.

Familiarize yourself with phrases and captions essential for your new look:

Les gants	Gloves
Le manteau	Coat
Les chaussures	Shoes
Le rouge à lèvres	Lipstick
Les lunettes de soleil	Sunglasses
Le sac à main	Handbag
Christian Dior	Christian Dior (note: a stylish label is universal)

If you really want to stretch your vocabulary look at the articles. Start with *Paris Match*, the French glossy gossip bible, their equivalent of *Hello!* They will have lots of pictures that will help the starry interview and 'insight' unfold. Chances are, if up on your celebrity fodder and current love affairs you will be able to guess what word means what when you see the who's who in paparazzi gossip and *scandale*.

When you feel you have mastered this, or indeed if this is going far too slowly for you, you can start looking online at questions and answers on translation sites. Type in phrases you want to learn, click on translate, and see what it says.

Go to *www.babelfish.altavista.com/tr*

Par exemple:

How much for two baguettes?
C'est combien pour deux baguettes?

Where's Chanel?
C'est où Chanel?

Can I have a glass of champagne?
Un verre de champagne; s'il vous plaît.

I'd like a room with a view, please.
Je voudrais une chambre avec vue, s'il vous plaît.

Do you have these Manolos in my size?
Avez-vous ces Manolos dans ma pointure?

When does your sale start?
Quand est-ce que les soldes commencent?

Taxi!
Taxi!

And so on.

Compile a list of key phrases you want to memorize and print off transla-
tions. Another method, still more entertaining than going back to the school
books, is to get a copy of one of your favourite books, or children's stories.
Read the translation *en français*. For example *'Arry Potter, Zee Devil Wears Prada,
'Ow to Walk in 'igh 'Eels*, or why not try *Za Da Vinci Code*? But then again, do
you really want to learn phrases about religious sects, and think how often
you will need to have conversations about wizards . . .

Pick books that will *vous aideront*.

Choose a book that will relate to your specialist subject, or choose a book whose plot you are familiar with and whose tales you can anticipate, and no, this isn't cheating. It is far easier to read and absorb familiar phrases than learning to conjugate *j'aime, tu aimes, il/elle/on aime*. In reality you don't often need to go up to people and rattle off a list of verbs.

Even easier than reading a book is listening to an audio book, which will help you perfect your accent as well as increase your vocab. You can either follow a novel with a copy of the English or fall asleep listening to your story, subliminally absorbing the accent. Train your ear to hear so you can pronounce the words correctly, or at least try to intone them sympathetically. Even if your vocabulary is basic, if you try, and your accent is good, half the battle is won.

French conversation classes, with no cheating or help *en anglais*, are good; a romantic French rendezvous even better. Get on the Eurostar and go for a day trip or a weekend and *parlez seulement français*. This may mean going alone if you are serious about cracking the code and going bilingual. Guaranteed there will be a cantankerous taxi driver or waiter who is picky enough to criticize your phrasing and, although you'll hate them at the time and will possibly want to cry, it will help in the long run, so persevere with this perverse form of torture.

If you are not up to trying your new talent out in public yet, have a French night in. Curl up with your baguette, brie and Bordeaux – or a favourite typical French dish – *coq au vin, croque monsieur, comme vous voulez*.

There are twenty-two wine regions in France with over a million traditional, regional, gourmet and gastro dishes to get through. So you will need an elasticized waistband with this course until you crack *French Women Don't Get Fat* by Mireille Guiliano. Take a look at some books about people relocating to France, such as *Almost French: Love and a New Life in Paris* by Sarah Turnbull, see how she survived and try to avoid it turning into your own *Year in the Merde*.

French and food

Julie and Julia by Julie Powell is the blog-turned-bestseller that didn't involve a move to France, but involved learning the French way of life in the kitchen. It is basically the cooking diary, thoughts and frustrations of an American government drone/secretary by day and amateur chef by night. Powell recorded and logged all her experiences as she cooked her way through all 524 recipes from the book *Mastering the Art of French Cooking,* a first edition by Louisette Bertholle, Simone Beck and Julia Child (the US answer to Delia). She is the woman who brought pasta and the taste of Europe to the US and essentially taught America to cook.

Julie and Julia is not only an inspiring tale and bestseller, it is now becoming a film; or check out her blog at *www.juliepowell.blogspot.com*

Powell could be your mentor when taking on a different language, as well as motivate you in getting creative in the kitchen. This 'blogbuster' is also a timely reminder that your blog/MySpace homepage should be up and running by now.

Another person who used cooking as her method for learning French was Audrey Hepburn (see page 192), when she played the chauffeur's daughter in *Sabrina.* In the film she was shipped off to Paris to learn Cordon Bleu cooking in the hope she would lose her appetite for David Larrabee. She ended up with Linus Larrabee (Humphrey Bogart) the older brother despite never being able to master how to poach an egg.

Why not learn French cooking for yourself? Do it either 'en Français', following a French cook book, find some on *www.booksforcooks.com,* or take a course somewhere like L'atelier des Chefs: *www.atelierdeschefs.com.* Alternatively, log onto *www.lefooding.com* and read where dedicated diners go in Paris.

French on film

Settle down to a French movie.

These are *definitely* better watched at home, as starting to learn a new language may cause a somewhat delayed reaction in the translation filter of the punch lines and jokes and you might irritate or confuse the other viewers with an ill-timed chuckle. Opt for French-speaking films with English subtitles, rather than English films dubbed with French voiceover as the lip-sync will be all over the place and end up making you feel so dizzy you'll be unable to focus on the film let alone the language learning quest.

Start with classics like *La Belle et la Bête,* or *Jean de Florette, Manon des Sources, Jules et Jim, Cyrano de Bergerac* or *Amélie.*

Who is Cyrano de Bergerac?

This is one of the most popular French films and is based on a real person – the French soldier Hector Savinien Cyrano de Bergerac (1619–55).

He was originally made famous when playwright Edmond Rostand published the tale in 1897. It was the basis for the 1987 version *Roxanne* starring Steve Martin and Daryl Hannah before being restored to its full original glory and coming to the big screen in 1990 with Gerard Depardieu as the lead. It was one of the biggest ever box-office smashes for a French-speaking film, as well as being a real weepy, therefore it's an essential part of your DVD collection.

Cyrano is in love with his distant cousin the beautiful Magdeleine Robin, known as Roxane. He is a nobleman, the best swordsman in the King's Guards, a brilliant poet and would be a totally eligible catch but for his oversized nose. He prefers to play the fool rather than risk potential rejection from sweeping his heart's desire, or any maid, off their feet.

Typically Roxane doesn't realize how he feels. She comes to Cyrano to ask his advice on love, as a young cadet in his company has caught her eye (argh, don't you just hate it when that happens?). Enter the dashing young

Baron Christian de Neuvillette. As a rival suitor he looks like Cyrano's worst nightmare. When they are sent off to the front line Roxane asks Cyrano to protect him, and to get him to write to her (as this was the only proper way to flirt in those days). Do you now see what you are missing out on without a letter-writing set?

So Christian might have the looks, but he totally lacks the skills to articulate letters of love. Going beyond the call of duty Cyrano steps in, as what he may lack in looks he more than makes up for in his prose. The combination of Cyrano's words and Christian's looks is intoxicating and has Roxane swooning. In a scene very similar to the Romeo and Juliet balcony scene Cyrano feeds Christian his lines, which are so successful Christian is rewarded with a kiss. How far would you go for true love?

The pair are married – that's Christian and Roxane – but almost immediately Christian, along with Cyrano, is sent off to war. 'Christian' writes daily to his new wife, and she admits how deeply she loves him now more and more for his words and his soul than his looks. Doh. Conveniently at this point he is fatally wounded and dies. Cyrano lives. Perfect, thinks the romantic – not so, as Cyrano is too loyal, too faithful, and never betrays the truth. What a waste.

Fourteen years later Roxane is still living as a widow in a nunnery where Cyrano visits her each week, devoted yet still concealing the truth. One week he is attacked on his way to see Roxane. Let her down? Never. He staggers on.

On this day she asks him to read out Christian's final letter. They had often spoke of it, but only today does he read it to her. It is dark, he is dying, and as the light fades he carries on – as he already knows the soliloquy by heart:

Mon coeur ne vous quitta jamais une seconde et je suis et serai jusque dans l'autre monde celui qui vous aima sans mesure . . .

My heart never left you for a second and I am and will be until in the other world that which loved you without measurement . . .

Pass the tissues.

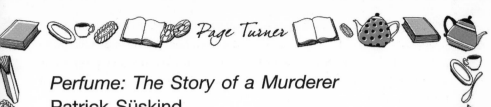

Page Turner

Perfume: The Story of a Murderer
Patrick Süskind

Why

Travel back to eighteenth-century Paris and follow a tale of scent and obsession, with sensual and sinister twists as one man pursues the perfect scent. If you have ever wanted to taste, smell and travel through the streets of Paris's past then Süskind's spooky descriptions are for you. From the opening page the book is crammed full of adjectives to describe every sensory sensation as the gruesome story of Jean Bapiste Grenouille unfolds.

Who

Patrick Süskind was born on 26 March 1949 in Munich, Germany. He read History at Munich University and spent a year in Aix-en-Provence, France, where he gathered the material that would inspire his bestselling novel. His first play *Double Bass* was published to great acclaim in 1980, but it was *Perfume*, translated into English in 1985 by John E. Wood, that really put him on the map. This fictional masterpiece has sold over a million copies worldwide. In 2006 it was turned into a film starring Dustin Hoffman and Alan Rickman, with Ben Whishaw as Grenouille. Süskind himself has retreated from public life and refuses to give interviews. But this doesn't stop people reading and discussing his work. Kurt Cobain said it was his favourite novel, and wrote that 'Scentless Apprentice', from Nirvana's album *In Utero*, was inspired by it.

The plot

Grenouille is abandoned at birth, dumped amongst rotting fish guts and is a strange, unearthly loner from the start. Though his circumstances are tragic, and beyond his control, Grenouille does little to endear himself

to others. He is an unpopular orphan, but not through aggression or manner; what makes him an oddity is that he has no odour, and without it he is invisible to those around him. Despite this odd handicap his own sense of smell is acute and he makes his nose his secret weapon and his hold over the world around him.

Orphan Grenouille is taken on as an apprentice to tanner Maître Grimal to learn a trade. When he delivers a goatskin to famed perfumer Baldini, he cajoles the gentleman into taking him on, sealing the deal when he blends a perfume that Baldini had been trying in vain to copy and dangling the solution as bait: the recipe in exchange for an apprenticeship. For the first time Grenouille finds he has a skill and talent at which he excels and not only feels he can fit in but also feels empowered.

With this strange Grenouille as his hidden protégé, Baldini becomes the greatest perfumer in Paris. Business is booming and his patrons are hypnotized by his new blends. He is unstoppable, unbeatable, rich beyond his wildest dreams yet terrified by this creature who now controls his destiny. He needn't have worried as despite his virtuoso talent, Grenouille doesn't seek fame or fortune. Soon he has learnt all he can and begins his quest in earnest for the ultimate scent. Grenouille leaves all the formulae with Baldini but no sooner has his protégé left than Baldini meets an unhappy end.

Grenouille is now free to wander the countryside searching for a way to blend ingredients to create his own scent. He is tormented and tortured as to how to get the perfect essence when he at last smells what he has spent his life searching for: the sweetest essence of all – that of a young virgin on the cusp of womanhood. He just needs to find a way to bottle it. Ruthlessly he gathers the ingredients he needs to make his scent, but will he succeed?

Perhaps it is not the cosiest of bedtime reads, but it's certainly unforgettable and something sure to spark debate.

Hosting

Ideally this book should be discussed in a dimly lit, red velvet bordello accompanied by perfumed teas, or you could combine the discussion with a wine-tasting session, allowing you to admire the merits of different bouquets, as well as nod to another great French passion. What essence of the book do you want to explore? Customized scents are all the rage; you could arrange for someone (with less deadly intent) to come and create a scent for the group. If the weather is playing fair you could meet in a scented garden, or perhaps this is the perfect excuse to try the newest patisserie, Ladurée in Knightsbridge or the Champs Elysées, or why not hop on the Eurostar for hot chocolate at Angelinas?

Alternative essences of Paris include:

A Year in the Merde by Stephen Clarke
A Tale of Two Cities by Charles Dickens
The Girl at the Lion D'Or by Sebastian Faulks
Bonjour Tristesse by Françoise Sagan
The Many Lives and Secret Sorrows of Josephine B. by Sandra Gulland
Farewell, My Queen by Chantal Thomas
Les Misérables by Victor Hugo

6th February

Poet and playwright Christopher Marlowe was born, 1564.

Marlowe was considered the leading rival to his contemporary fellow actor and playwright Shakespeare. Both were very popular writers and players for Lord Strange's acting company but Marlowe's life, and literature, met with an untimely end. On 30 May 1593 Marlowe and his friend Ingram Frizer got into a quarrel over who was to pay the pub bill, and things got nasty. In a drunken rage Marlowe grabbed a dagger from Frizer's sheath and struck him twice over the head. Frizer then wrestled the dagger off him and, in self-defence, caught Marlowe and accidentally stabbed·him just above his right eye.

Marlowe was only twenty-nine years old when he died. His legacy of work includes *The Tragical History of Doctor Faustus* and *Edward II* as well as the poem:

'Come live with me, and be my love;
And we will all the pleasures prove
That valleys, groves, hills and fields,
Woods or steepy mountain yields.'

'The Passionate Shepherd to His Love' c.1589

7th February

Another literary great, Charles Dickens, was born in 1812.

As a young boy his father was imprisoned for debt and Dickens was sent to work at Warren's Blacking Factory, which haunted as well as inspired him for the rest of his life.

Dickens rose from taking shorthand reports at Doctors' Commons court to becoming Victorian England's most famed novelist. His first story was published in 1833 under the pseudonym 'Boz' and developed into *The Pickwick Papers*. His work captured the hardships of the Victorian and industrial era in Britain.

Dickens went on to write *Great Expectations, Oliver Twist, Hard Times* and *A Tale of Two Cities*.

Also on this date, in 1478, Thomas More, the English statesman, novelist and martyr was born. More's novel *Utopia* (1515), literally meaning 'No Place', described his perfect land. This was a far cry from the situation that he found himself in as devoted Catholic and Chancellor of England during the reign of Henry VIII. He refused to recognize the king's second marriage, and had to choose between Catholicism or the king. He made what his king considered the wrong choice – and was beheaded.

Thomas More was eventually canonized in 1935. He was immortalized in the play *A Man for All Seasons* by Robert Bolt, which was made into a film that scooped six Oscars in 1967.

8th February

Queen Elizabeth I, after years of constant anxiety about plots to seize her crown, reluctantly signed a death warrant for her cousin, Mary Queen of Scots, who was beheaded on this day in 1587.

Mary arrived for her own execution in a long dark cape and perfectly coiffeured hair. When she untied her cape she revealed a defiant blood-red velvet gown the colour of martyrdom. Mary was always a keen follower of fashion. She had shocked many by getting married, when she was sixteen, in black (a French tradition but frowned on by those at home), and it was to this faux pas that all her bad luck was attributed.

It took three blows to chop off her head, perhaps too much information, but when the axe man grabbed her hair to show that the job was complete, all he pulled up was her red wig. Her actual shorn grey hair, and head, stayed in the basket – she was doing things her way, even at the end.

10th February

In 1840, in this the 'month of love', Queen Victoria married her beloved Prince Albert.

Queen Victoria (24 March 1819–22 January 1901) reigned over England for an impressive sixty-three years. She was twenty-one years old when they married, and was totally besotted with Albert – it was she that made the proposal. It was this great monarch who is supposed to have said 'we are not amused' and who created an era of high morals and strict discipline. 'The important thing is not what they think of me, but what I think of them,' she said.

The love match lasted until Albert died in 1861. Grief-stricken, she built the Albert Memorial and the Royal Albert Hall in London as monuments to her late husband. After 1861 she never came out of black mourning dress and for the next forty years she insisted his clothes were laid out each day in his suite.

Aside from making Queen Victoria happy we have many things to thank Prince Albert for, particularly for bringing the Christmas tree tradition to England in 1840. He presented one to his wife, and she so loved the German custom that the whole of England was soon decorating trees, and sweeping up needles as they fell.

To achieve a partnership as successful as that of V&A (Victoria and Albert) you have to look for love. As queen she would have had the pick of the bunch but you have even more choice available. Do a bit of research and find your own Prince Charming.

How to write a personal column

Hopefully one of your New Year's resolutions was to stop dating the dippy, commitment-phobic and unavailable, as well as the undesirable types. The only unrequited love to be tolerated is the love of shoes – and even these should be broken in. There is usually a post-Christmas/pre-Valentine's surge with dating services, personals and onlines. By now it's cutting it fine for this Valentine's but if you're single, there's no time like the present to go in search of cupid's arrow. Get proactive in the search for Mr Right as it's always nice to have someone make you breakfast in bed and put the bins out.

If you don't want to physically go out and see where he's hiding why not look online or place an ad to find him in the personals? If you do decide to go into print, or see if anyone has put a message in the paper that goes straight to your heart, learn the meaning behind the acronyms. Enough of the mixed signals.

Decoding and defrosting

A personal – or personal ad – is one way to find a partner; that is, of course, if you haven't the time to let fate take its course or have been too busy dodging destiny and its attempts to hook you up with Mr Wow. To save space, as much as the applicants' blushes, the ads are printed in code. And guess what, it's even more complex than mobile phone jargon. It's like the cryptic crossword clues with potentially much higher stakes.

Use this guide to help summarize yourself, as well as decode who is worth getting to know.

A: Asian
B: Bisexual
B: Black
F: Female
G: Gay
J: Jewish/Japanese
L: Latino
M: Male/Man
W: White
W: Woman
BBW: Big Beautiful Woman
BDSM: Bondage and Discipline, Domination and Submission, Sado-
    masochism
BF: Black Female/Boy Friend
Bi: Bisexual
BiF: Bisexual Female
BiM: Bisexual Male
CD: Cross-Dresser
DTE: Down-to-Earth
GF: Gay Female (Lesbian)/Girl Friend
GSOH: Good Sense of Humour
GWC: Gay White Couple

GWF: Gay White Female
GWM: Gay White Male
Het: Heterosexual
HWP: Height Weight Proportional (indicates an 'ideal' body weight)
IRL: In Real Life (face to face meeting)
ISO: In Search of
LTR: Long Term Relationship (not letter)
M4M: Man Seeking Man
M4MW: Man Seeking Man and Woman
M4W: Man Seeking Woman
MOTOS: Member of the Opposite Sex
MOTSS: Member of the Same Sex
NS: Non-Smoking
NSA: No Strings Attached
SAE: Stamped Addressed Envelope
SWF: Single White Female
SWM: Single White Male
Str8: Straight (not bisexual or gay)
TLC: Tender Loving Care
W/E: Well Endowed (larger than average male ego)
W4M: Woman Seeking Man
W4MW: Woman Seeking Man and Woman
W4W: Woman Seeking Woman
WLTM: Would Like to Meet

Online and in the mood

Popular sites include *www.datingdirect.com* or *www.match.com*, which had over 60,000 new hopefuls sign up in January 2006 looking for love. If you are worried about clicking on with a love rat/nut case why not log onto *www.mysinglefriend.com*, where hopeful Romeos' and Juliets' profiles are written by a friend. The fact that they have at least one friend is a good start.

Online dating sites can be a good way to meet people and they are a good distraction for a slow day in the office, or an evening in with a face pack on . . . providing you don't have a webcam.

Browse a few dating websites before sending your profile; not only will it give you an idea of the type of people that use the site, it will also help you get the right pitch.

As much as you want to sell yourself, tell the truth. Without pouring out your heart give an accurate, albeit edited, account of your personality, hobbies, likes and dislikes, as well as what you are looking for in a person. You may as well be honest and upfront as you never need meet any of these people. If you don't want long-distance, single-parents, redheads, people who wear glasses or collect snails, that's fine; it's OK to say so (and this way the rebuff isn't to their face).

Reveal as much or as little as you want, but caution: never reveal your personal email address or full name as initially it is best to keep a distance. Use the site to screen things and keep it safe in the browsing-for-boys stage.

Don't fall in love with a photo – appearances can be deceptive. An air-brushed cover shot of them might not be the reality. That said, statistics show that online profiles with a photograph tend to attract ten times the attention. Not putting one up would be the equivalent of going out under an invisible cloak – it's your choice depending on how Harry Potter you feel.

Finally, before clicking send, re-read your profile out loud, or get a friend to. Would either of *you* date you? Try to be witty, and skip any clichéd chat-up lines that make you sound clingy, desperate and way too available.

A brief history of the kiss

ROMEO [TO JULIET]: If I profane with my unworthiest hand
This holy shrine, the gentle sin is this:
My lips, two blushing pilgrims, ready stand
To smooth that rough touch with a tender kiss.

JULIET: Good pilgrim, you do wrong your hand too much,
Which mannerly devotion shows in this;

For saints have hands that pilgrims' hands do touch,
And palm to palm is holy palmers' kiss.

ROMEO: Have not saints lips, and holy palmers too?

JULIET: Ay, pilgrim, lips that they must use in prayer.

ROMEO: O, then, dear saint, let lips do what hands do;
They pray, grant thou, lest faith turn to despair.

Romeo and Juliet, Act 1, Scene 5,
William Shakespeare

This is one of the best bits in all of Shakespeare's plays and really should be committed to memory. Written in 1595, the story of the star-cross'd lovers is set in Verona, Italy. The tragedy has been retold in opera, ballet and on film, including Franco Zeffirelli's beautiful 1968 version and Baz Luhrmann's fast-paced contemporary take. Rather than rewatch these, rent the 1936 Oscar-winning version, directed by Irving Thalberg and starring his wife, Norma Shearer, as Juliet, or order it for an original Valentine's Day gift.

Kissing gets a namecheck right back in the New Testament, where greeting with a kiss was the norm, but don't believe Romeo was really thinking about saints . . .

Kissing has always been very popular. Romans kissed each other on the lips, or eyelids, to show respect. An emperor would deem a person's rank by where they could kiss him, from the feet up. At wedding ceremonies today it is so popular it has become the unofficial finale.

> 'I have found many men who didn't know how to kiss. I've always found time to teach them.' Mae West

The longest recorded kiss lasted 130 hours and 2 minutes, which seems plain antisocial, while the most useful thing to kiss, other than the person you love, is the Blarney Stone in Ireland. It is said to give those who dare dangle backwards off an ancient castle wall the gifts of eloquence and persuasive flattery (that'll be the secret of the luck of the Irish), but then again if you leant off the edge of a battlement you too would expect something pretty great in return.

If you want to see a few cultural kisses look no further than the tongue-locked lovers in Rodin's sculpture *The Kiss* or the entwined pair in Klimt's painting of the same name.

Five of the top on-screen kisses can be found in:

Gone With the Wind
Casablanca
Breakfast at Tiffany's
Lady and the Tramp
From Here to Eternity

But you should also not forget *Sleeping Beauty* and the kiss that broke the spell of a hundred years' sleep, and was the cue for many other Happily Ever Afters.

Sealed with a X

As well as the physical action of a kiss there is also the written sign-off. In 'ye olden days' documents were signed with an X as a symbol to endorse their authenticity. That was in the days when not many people could read – and even fewer could write – but everyone was able to recognize this sign.

As more people started to pick up pen and paper to express themselves letters could be ended with a signature, but the cross was kept as a sign of the sender's integrity. This evolved from business to pleasure, from honour to love, and some added more and more XXXXXXs the greater their love.

In America they like to send hugs as well as kisses – so the letters X and

O are used. Those who like to confuse things argue that the X represents the crossed arms of a hug and the O the puckered lips, ready for a kiss, while some say the reverse – either way it's a sign of affection that isn't standard practice in Europe, nor is it to be confused with a game of noughts and crosses.

12th February

The New Look was unveiled in Paris, 1947.

Fashion designer Christian Dior debuted his post-war collection and brought the entire city to a standstill. Full skirts flounced out, and rationing books had to be ripped up as tiny waists and yards of fabric heralded the return of femininity.

Carmel Snow, then Editor-in-Chief of *Harper's Bazaar* US, famously exclaimed it was 'a New Look'.

The unveiling took place at 30, avenue Montaigne, Paris. At 10 a.m. women in minks and smartly dressed gentlemen waited in the street for the couture house to open its salon doors. Marie-Thérèse (the Linda Evangelista of her day in Supermodel stakes) walked into the salon. She opened the show in a full skirt and hush descended. American *Vogue* fashion editor Bettina Ballard said it was 'magic'.

Coco Chanel was less effusive; she said the show drove her out of retirement. 'Christian Dior doesn't dress women, he upholsters them,' she spat. The revolution had begun and, as Mr Dior said, 'Couture wants to return to its true function – enhancing feminine beauty.'

Since Dior opened its doors it has had illustrious designers at the helm.

Dior designer timeline:
   Christian Dior 1947–57
   Yves Saint Laurent 1957–60
   Marc Bohan 1960–89
   Gianfranco Ferré 1989–96
   John Galliano 1996–

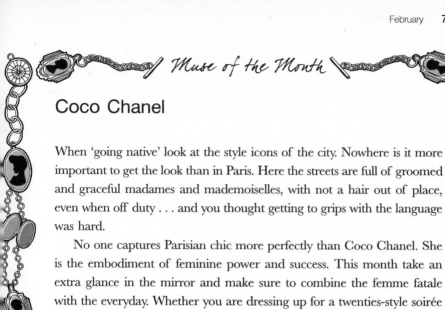

Coco Chanel

When 'going native' look at the style icons of the city. Nowhere is it more important to get the look than in Paris. Here the streets are full of groomed and graceful madames and mademoiselles, with not a hair out of place, even when off duty . . . and you thought getting to grips with the language was hard.

No one captures Parisian chic more perfectly than Coco Chanel. She is the embodiment of feminine power and success. This month take an extra glance in the mirror and make sure to combine the femme fatale with the everyday. Whether you are dressing up for a twenties-style soirée or dressing down for bed, do it in Chanel style. Paint your nails a sinful shade, wear a string of pearls or a camellia, the signature flower, or lounge in luxurious tailored pastel tweeds. Chanel's clothes are simple yet chic. 'Luxury must be comfortable, otherwise it is not luxury,' she said. Chanel claimed the three essential ingredients for looking good were order, poise and good taste, proving it's not just what you wear, but how you wear it. When you're feeling under pressure to conform think of Coco and have confidence in your ability to do things your own way.

Even if you claim not to be a slave to fashion, with or without realizing it, your wardrobe will already have the Chanel touch. Jersey knits, bathing suits, sportswear, ski accessories and the androgynous look all stem from her. It was Chanel and her gamine figure that got women out of corsets and led the craze for the bob haircut. She created the look for a new breed of women who wanted to be man's equal, not his doll.

Chanel created enormous business well beyond those of her era and generation and designed opportunities in clothes through her understanding of how to make women feel empowered and independent. 'With a black pullover and ten rows of pearls she revolutionized fashion,' said rival designer Christian Dior. She became the

first fashion powerhouse, and the first designer to really understand branding and to create her own signature in scent, as well as in style.

Her life and times

Gabrielle Bonheur Chanel was born on 19 August 1883, in Saumur, France, although she always insisted she was born in 1893 in Auvergne.

An illegitimate child, her mother died before her twelfth birthday and she grew up in an orphanage, along with her four siblings. She was educated at a convent, where the black habits worn by the nuns would later inspire her.

She tried her hand as a dancer, a horse rider, an actress and a singer in her endless quest to make her fortune. It was during a spell as a cabaret singer at the Café La Rotonde, where her party piece was performing 'Ko Ko Ri Ko' (the French for cock-a-doodle-do) and 'Qui qu'a vu Coco' that audiences would cry 'Coco' when demanding an encore. The nickname stuck. The career, thankfully for our wardrobes, did not.

Along with an astute business sense Chanel benefited from a string of devoted sugar daddies who helped kick-start her career. She would later boast: 'I was able to start a high-fashion shop because two gentlemen were outbidding each other over my hot little body.' One of the men in question was the English aristocrat Arthur 'Boy' Capel, a shipping and coal magnate said to be the love of her life. He gave her the entrée into society she craved, bankrolled her, loved her but just couldn't marry her – it was a question of class and tradition and ultimately led to a life-time of independence for Chanel. In 1910 he helped her open her first boutique, on rue Cambon, which initially specialized in millinery for clients who were friends from the stage as well as society. In 1919 'Boy' died in a car accident. She was devastated and, though she had numerous glamorous affairs, she never completely gave her heart away again.

As well as ambition she developed a penchant for successful, wealthy men. She collaborated with Picasso, who rejected her as a lover, and the

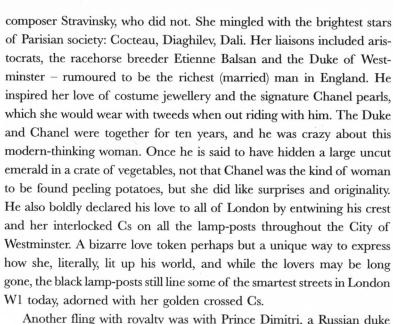

composer Stravinsky, who did not. She mingled with the brightest stars of Parisian society: Cocteau, Diaghilev, Dali. Her liaisons included aristocrats, the racehorse breeder Etienne Balsan and the Duke of Westminster – rumoured to be the richest (married) man in England. He inspired her love of costume jewellery and the signature Chanel pearls, which she would wear with tweeds when out riding with him. The Duke and Chanel were together for ten years, and he was crazy about this modern-thinking woman. Once he is said to have hidden a large uncut emerald in a crate of vegetables, not that Chanel was the kind of woman to be found peeling potatoes, but she did like surprises and originality. He also boldly declared his love to all of London by entwining his crest and her interlocked Cs on all the lamp-posts throughout the City of Westminster. A bizarre love token perhaps but a unique way to express how she, literally, lit up his world, and while the lovers may be long gone, the black lamp-posts still line some of the smartest streets in London W1 today, adorned with her golden crossed Cs.

Another fling with royalty was with Prince Dimitri, a Russian duke involved in the launch of her perfumes. The infamous No. 5, created with Ernest Beaux in 1921, mixed 128 scents together. Chanel was the first person to incorporate floral notes, particularly jasmine, in her perfume. It was named No. 5, with characteristic simplicity, as it was the fifth vial she sniffed. Marilyn Monroe famously quipped that she wore only two drops of Chanel No. 5 in bed. You may need more than this to keep you warm in the winter months.

The signature Chanel cardigan jacket was introduced in 1925, and with her first tweed outfit in 1928 the Chanel attitude was born. Her designs were the perfect armour for the ambitious woman of the twenties. In 1931 she negotiated herself a million-dollar contract with United Artists to dress their Hollywood stars, including Gloria Swanson in *Tonight or Never*, but this was short-lived as her inspirational heart lay in her couture house in Paris.

By 1939 she'd made enough money to retire so closed the fashion house she'd created. She took up residence at the Ritz Hotel. During the war she had an affair with a Nazi intelligence officer and spy, Baron

Hans Gunther von Dincklage, a toy boy ten years her junior. Turned out not to be the best choice of lover in the PR stakes as this led to her being arrested and interrogated by the French police, but she managed to sidestep any major retribution thanks to a friendship with Winston Churchill. She is said to have remarked that 'at my age, when a man wants to sleep with you, you don't ask to see his passport'.

After the Second World War ended she left France and moved to the more neutral Switzerland. But in 1947, aged sixty-four, she returned and re-opened Chanel, claiming it was her duty in the face of Mr Dior and his New Look (see 12 February.) He embodied the very antithesis of all her style principles. Secretly she was delighted to be back in business, especially if she could blame someone else for the inconvenience. She presented her comeback collection in 1954, and there it was – she put the perfect little black dress on the catwalk. It was immediately declared a must-have for well-dressed woman and the 'Chanel look' swept across both sides of the Atlantic.

Coco Chanel worked right up until her death, and died quietly in her bed at the Ritz Hotel, Paris on 10 January 1971. She was still doing fittings for her next collection.

Today her spirit is kept alive and ever young by Karl Lagerfeld who has been Creative Director since 1983. She would probably have hated this – given she thought little of her male rivals – but Lagerfeld has reinvigorated the Chanel brand, and kept it at the forefront of fashion. As well as the fashion, the perfumes and make-up now play a huge part in the empire's business. Following the success of Uma Thurman in *Pulp Fiction* wearing Vamp/Rouge Noir nail varnish, Lagerfeld enlisted the help of children to create a new nail polish in 1997. He asked for pictures of their favourite things and promised to use them as inspiration. From one boy's picture of a starry night sky, Ciel de Nuit was born – a navy lacquer with flecks of silver glitter.

In 2004 Lagerfeld also dared to revamp Chanel's most famous scent, No. 5. The commercial starred Nicole Kidman as the new face of No. 5 and was directed by Baz '*Moulin Rouge*' Luhrmann. It lasted 180 seconds and cost an estimated £18 million. It's big business being beautiful.

Chanelisms

'The most courageous act is still to think for yourself. Aloud.'

'Elegance does not consist in putting on a new dress.'

'Don't spend time beating on a wall, hoping to transform it into a door.'

'Fashion is not simply a matter of clothes. Fashion is in the air, born upon the wind. One intuits it. It is in the sky and on the road.'

'It is the unseen, unforgettable, ultimate accessory of fashion that heralds your arrival and prolongs your departure.'

14th February – Valentine's Day

Today single girls' hearts will sink as the postman will seem to be even later than usual, and couples will be on call to be even more soppy and romantic than usual with their other halves.

The story of St Valentine

In AD 269 St Valentine was martyred. Valentine was a crusader for true love, so it is only fitting that he is the patron saint of lovers.

Roman Emperor Claudius was actively trying to recruit men to join his army. But no one wanted to go to war; they wanted to stay at home with their wives, families and sweethearts. Claudius banned weddings – his 'logic' being that if they could no longer get married they'd sign up and march off to fight for him. As if. He couldn't have been more wrong and there was huge opposition, including that from Valentine, the priest. Our hero started secretly marrying couples. Claudius found out, went ballistic and condemned the romantic priest to be beaten to death.

Legend goes he left a farewell note to the jailer's daughter, who he had not only befriended but had also cured from blindness, signed simply 'From Your Valentine'.

To honour his memory in AD 496 Pope Gelasius set aside this date for romance and ever since then the cards, flowers, chocolates and declarations have been flying faster than cupid's arrow.

How to say it originally

Poetry was made for Valentines, and quoting a Shakespearean sonnet is far more sophisticated than sending images of cupids carrying red satin-shaped hearts.

Can you fail to be moved by Sonnet 18:

Shall I compare thee to a summer's day?
Thou art more lovely and more temperate.

or the hopeless romantic, Lord Byron?

She walks in beauty, like the night
Of cloudless climes and starry skies;
And all that's best of dark and bright
Meet in her aspect and her eyes.

A note of caution, though, when choosing poetry . . . Byron and Shakespeare wrote as men wooing women – you may do better to pick something like Elizabeth Barrett Browning's verse to her husband:

How do I love thee? Let me count the ways . . .

When seeking perfection, romantic letter writers don't come much better than Ludwig van Beethoven in his letter to his 'Immortal Beloved'. 'My angel, my all, my very self – Only a few words today and at that with pencil (with yours)' the written melody begins.

The letters were discovered in March 1827, just after the composer had died. His compelling three-part letter to his mysterious 'Immortal Beloved' was never sent, and to this day no one really knows for certain *who* she is.

How frustrating.

Was it his sister-in-law Johanna or Josephine von Brunswick? Whoever she was, the lady he loved could not be with him. Most biographers claim, trying to crush the intrigue and romance of her concealed identity, that she was Antoine Brentano, a Viennese wife of a Frankfurt businessman, and mother of five. Beethoven met her in Vienna around 1810, and spent considerable time with her, but she was married, so he may have had the affair, but not wishing to leave any incriminating evidence, decided against sending the letters to his secret love.

How different things might have been had he sent them. Read them yourself to see why, or indeed use them as the barometer to judge the standard of any love letters you receive. If you had received these, nothing, surely, would have stood in your way (even though he was said to have a horrible temper). 'Your love makes me at once the happiest and the unhappiest of men,' he lamented.

Other prolific writers, beautifully in touch with their 'feminine side' and great at expressing all the right emotions, include Napoleon Bonaparte, F. Scott Fitzgerald and Dylan Thomas. You may want to casually leave these lying about around this time.

Your letters don't have to be as poetic, but they should come from the heart. Words can be borrowed as long as you credit them, and can stand by the meaning. Once it is in black and white it's hard evidence of how you feel so be careful, as you can't take it back!

How to make truffles

If on St Valentine's Day you are in a double act, as well as producing a card you should lavish affection on that other half – and what better way to show how you feel than by giving him chocolate truffles? If you want to really impress, rather than buying – though Charbonnel et Walker boxes are almost too chic to top – why not make your own? (Slightly in advance, and tested for taste, of course.)

Best place to start would be *www.deliaonline.com*, the chef who is clearly going to have to be named another Patron Saint of Lovers, or at least of Stomachs. Delia Smith is the ultimate, and the easiest to follow, but of course there are *beaucoup de variations*, or maybe your French cooking lessons will have come up trumps.

Here are the basics.

Ingredients:
8oz of double cream
2 tablespoons of unsalted butter
1 teaspoon of syrup
8oz of chopped chocolate (plain) and 6oz for dipping (could use milk or plain)
8oz sifted cocoa powder

To make:
Mix cream, butter and syrup in a saucepan and bring to the boil. Turn off the heat. Gently add your chocolate to the mixture. Don't stir, just let it melt and sink in.

After a soft stir, gently tip the mixture from pan to bowl and place in the fridge for three-quarters of an hour, stirring every fifteen minutes.

Once it starts to thicken, keep a closer eye on it and stir every five minutes. Once the mixture has solidified enough, use a teaspoon and roll mini-balls in the palm of your hand into truffle shapes. Place these on trays (lined with greaseproof paper) and return them to the fridge for a further fifteen minutes.

While they chill out, melt the remaining chocolate in a pan, and allow to cool. Now dip your balls into the melted choco-goo, and roll in a dusting of cocoa powder. This will be very messy, even for Delia.

Place in fridge for a further five-plus minutes to 'set'.

Sample to see how success tastes and then package any that remain in a tissue-lined box and tie – to avoid further temptation – with a bow. After all what greater act of love is there than that of sacrifice?

If this all sounds far too chaotic or time-consuming, go and buy some truffles, cut off all outer packaging and wrap as your own. There is no point being a martyr for a lover, and what they don't know will never hurt them.

How to do Valentine's Day alone

Valentine's Day is the most romantic day in the calendar, bah humbug.

You can always take a sickie or send yourself an *anonymous* bouquet if peer pressure really is making this day too much of a crisis. But don't rise to the bait – there are many benefits to the single life. You can always make the truffles for yourself, and indulge in the occasion by not having to share.

Films which catch the spirit of the night, single or shackled, include:

The Philadelphia Story
Casablanca
To Have and Have Not
Sabrina
Wuthering Heights
Brief Encounter
An Affair to Remember
Sleepless in Seattle

Alternatively, make it an anti-slush night and watch Billy Wilder's *Some Like It Hot,* as amidst all the declarations of love, fluffy messages and sugar-covered candy the action takes place around Al Capone's infamous 1929 St Valentine's Day Massacre. The line-up and the gang massacre in the film parallels the events in crime-rampant Chicago in the Prohibition era – Spats Columbo on film, Al Capone in reality. The film stars Marilyn Monroe, Tony Curtis and Jack Lemmon and ends with the infamous line 'well, nobody's perfect'. Today of all days, ain't that the truth.

Valentine true-love folklore

Go bird-watching

'On Valentine's Day if a woman sees a robin flying overhead she will marry a sailor. If she sees a sparrow she will be happy but marry a poor man. If, however, it is a goldfinch she sees she will marry a millionaire.'

Fact: Goldfinches are usually found in scattered bushes, trees, rough ground or thistles. They also like orchards and parks, and are most common in southern England (the birds, not necessarily the millionaires). There are 230,000 breeding grounds in the UK and at the last count there were 100,000 birds wintering in the UK.

Apple of your eye

Think of four to six names of boys (or girls, as appropriate) whom you could marry. Take an apple and as you twist the stem recite the names you want to research as possibles.

For example: 'John, Paul, George, Ringo' (well, they were all part of the Apple record label).

Whatever name you are on when the stem comes off is the one you will marry.

So now you know the name of your intended the next thing to do is to slice the apple in half. The number of pips you see will be the number of children you have. You may then eat the fruit.

15th February

Astronomer Galileo Galilei was born in Pisa, 1564. See what stars are in the sky tonight or on TV.

25th February

French Impressionist painter Auguste Renoir was born, in 1841. Famous for his studies of Parisian life and ballerinas, let him inspire you to take a sketch book to the bar tonight. (See page 311, for a full art attack.)

Shrove Tuesday

This date varies according to when Easter falls, but is celebrated the day before Ash Wednesday and the start of Lent.

In France this is known as Mardi Gras or Fat Tuesday – this is the date when traditionally all the fats in the kitchen were used up before the fasting began. Fasting is not now commonly observed, but many do like to give something up – such as men, swearing, or chocolate. Today is the last day for excess before the forty days leading up to Easter.

Not everyone observes Lent, but everyone should observe Pancake Day.

The name in England, Shrove Tuesday, derives from people being called to church on this day to confess their sins, and to be 'shriven' – forgiven.

Napoleon loved pancakes, or crêpes as they are known in France, and blamed the failure of his Russian campaign on the fact that he had dropped one the year before. I am sure it was not the real reason for the defeat.

How to toss a pancake

Once you have your batter ready to go, heat the oil/butter and when it's hot pour a small amount of mixture into the pan. The thinner the pancake, the better (and easier to toss).

Let the batter cook and start to take shape, ease it around the edges and give it a little shake to loosen it up before the flip. Hold pan loosely, wrist relaxed. Give it a sharp flick and hope for the best.

If you can't catch don't do this; it will end up either on the ceiling or on the floor.

29th February

Emperor Caesar introduced a new calendar in 45 BC, creating the leap year.

A leap year only happens every four years, like the Olympics, the effect being an extra day is added into the year. February, being the shortest month and being in the right planetary position, is given this honour. It is on this day the tables are turned and a girl can propose to her man.

The reason for that extra day goes right back to the Romans, and Julius Caesar. His calendar – the Julian – helped regulate the long months and years which were playing havoc on the farmers' efforts to organize their crops. His calendar shortened the year to 365.25 days and as there isn't a day that is only six hours long, he created an extra day – 29 February – so that the numbers would add up.

But someone along the line miscalculated – it is thought to have been Emperor Augustus – and so in 1582, to bring things back in sync with the seasons, Pope Gregory XIII created the Gregorian Calendar, which we still use today.

On this magical date Italian composer Gioachino Rossini was born in 1792. He wrote thirty operas – this best-known works include *The Barber of Seville* and *The William Tell Overture*, which went on to become the Lone Ranger's theme tune.

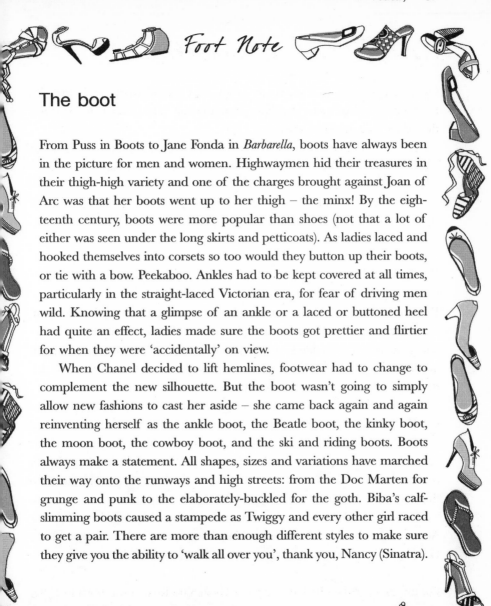

Foot Note

The boot

From Puss in Boots to Jane Fonda in *Barbarella*, boots have always been in the picture for men and women. Highwaymen hid their treasures in their thigh-high variety and one of the charges brought against Joan of Arc was that her boots went up to her thigh – the minx! By the eighteenth century, boots were more popular than shoes (not that a lot of either was seen under the long skirts and petticoats). As ladies laced and hooked themselves into corsets so too would they button up their boots, or tie with a bow. Peekaboo. Ankles had to be kept covered at all times, particularly in the straight-laced Victorian era, for fear of driving men wild. Knowing that a glimpse of an ankle or a laced or buttoned heel had quite an effect, ladies made sure the boots got prettier and flirtier for when they were 'accidentally' on view.

When Chanel decided to lift hemlines, footwear had to change to complement the new silhouette. But the boot wasn't going to simply allow new fashions to cast her aside – she came back again and again reinventing herself as the ankle boot, the Beatle boot, the kinky boot, the moon boot, the cowboy boot, and the ski and riding boots. Boots always make a statement. All shapes, sizes and variations have marched their way onto the runways and high streets: from the Doc Marten for grunge and punk to the elaborately-buckled for the goth. Biba's calf-slimming boots caused a stampede as Twiggy and every other girl raced to get a pair. There are more than enough different styles to make sure they give you the ability to 'walk all over you', thank you, Nancy (Sinatra).

March

'Drama is life with the dull bits cut out.'
Alfred Hitchcock

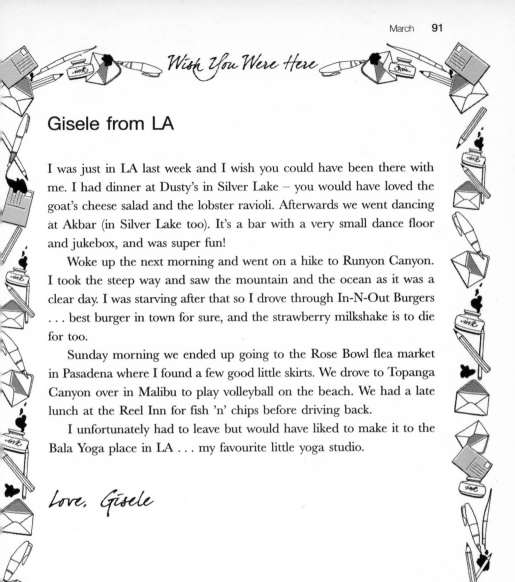

Wish You Were Here

Gisele from LA

I was just in LA last week and I wish you could have been there with me. I had dinner at Dusty's in Silver Lake – you would have loved the goat's cheese salad and the lobster ravioli. Afterwards we went dancing at Akbar (in Silver Lake too). It's a bar with a very small dance floor and jukebox, and was super fun!

Woke up the next morning and went on a hike to Runyon Canyon. I took the steep way and saw the mountain and the ocean as it was a clear day. I was starving after that so I drove through In-N-Out Burgers . . . best burger in town for sure, and the strawberry milkshake is to die for too.

Sunday morning we ended up going to the Rose Bowl flea market in Pasadena where I found a few good little skirts. We drove to Topanga Canyon over in Malibu to play volleyball on the beach. We had a late lunch at the Reel Inn for fish 'n' chips before driving back.

I unfortunately had to leave but would have liked to make it to the Bala Yoga place in LA . . . my favourite little yoga studio.

Love, Gisele

1st March

Today's Saint David's Day, the Patron Saint of Wales. The red dragon (*Y Ddraig Goch*) will fly – albeit only on their national flag – and people will don a leek or a daffodil in their buttonhole to celebrate the occasion.

Famous Welsh names, other than St David, include:

Actors – Anthony Hopkins, Ioan Gruffudd, Jonathan Pryce and Catherine Zeta-Jones.

Designers – clothes and interior designer Laura Ashley and fashion designer Julien Macdonald.

Singers – Shirley Bassey, Charlotte Church, Tom Jones, plus music mogul Ivor Novello.

Welsh writers – Roald Dahl and Dylan Thomas.

On this date in 1810 it is believed that the Polish composer Fryderyk Franciszek Chopin was born to Polish and French parents. He later adopted the French version of his name, which is what we know him by today: Frédéric Chopin.

Chopin was seven when he was recognized as a musical genius, and published two polonaises (traditional Polish folk dances). He toured across Vienna and Poland before finally settling in Paris. Despite all the travel he remained a Pole at heart. 'As an artist, I am still in my cradle, as a Pole, I am already twenty,' the young man remarked as he arrived in Paris.

Chopin wrote a series of twenty-four preludes, mazurkas, nocturnes and waltzes that captured both the essence of Romanticism as well as the traditional folk dances of his homeland and were usually so tricky only someone of his standard could play them.

In 1836 his engagement to first love Maria Wodzinska was forbidden by her mother. His next lover was the married Baroness Dudevant, Amandine-Aurore-Lucile Dupin, who is better known as famed novelist George Sand. This relationship lasted nine years and her work *Lucrezia Floriani* (published in 1847) – a story about a rich actress and sickly prince – is a thinly veiled account of the affair.

Chopin died in 1848, aged thirty-eight, of pulmonary tuberculosis. He was buried in Paris at Père-Lachaise (where Oscar Wilde and Jim Morrison also rest) yet at his request, after his death his heart was cut out and returned to his beloved Poland.

Watch the 2003 Oscar-winning film *The Pianist*, by another Pole, controversial film-maker Roman Polanski (whose own mother died in a concentration camp). The film is based on the memoirs of Polish-Jewish pianist Wladyslaw Szpilman and his survival in Nazi-occupied Poland. Chopin's music forms the soundtrack, even though Chopin himself was shamefully anti-Semitic.

The Pianist won three Oscars: Best Director – Roman Polanski; Best actor: – Adrien Brody; Best Screenplay – Ronald Harwood.

How to be A-list

Getting invited to the Academy Awards (in your own right and not as someone's arm candy) is tough, in fact close to impossible. The event has expanded beyond all recognition, and relocated to the Kodak Theatre to try to squeeze in all the A-listers and Harry Winston diamonds, but there is still only a seating capacity of 3,400 and some 5,000 Academy members. You do the maths. Even at the outset the odds are not stacked in a blagger's favour. But always rise to the challenge.

If you're hell bent on attending the Academy Awards begin by shamelessly pursuing all contacts and connections. Attending drama school or working in the industry (in PR, radio, TV or media-related roles) does help. There are also the lighting and costume designers as well as camera technicians who all need assistants.

Make your wish, and make it come true. Remember making your dream came true can take years, so don't give up the day job. Do pray for a lucky break.

But be careful what you wish for.

Fame is a fickle game and, if this is what you want, you should aim to *earn* fame rather than *acquire* it. Notoriety can be fun but not as satisfying as recognition for being the best in your field, and earnt fame lasts longer. Fame in your neighbourhood, respect in your workplace, recognition for your talents and contributions does not require a ticket to LA. Aim to be the star at your own red-carpet event – make an entrance worthy of an Oscar winner at the supermarket. Show these starlets how it's done.

The Hollywood Hills

Perhaps the nearest thing to mythical Mount Olympus on earth crowns the top of Mount Lee, LA's tallest point – a sign that measures 450 feet long and stands 45 feet high.

'Hollywoodland', as it originally said, was actually nothing more than an estate agent's sign to advertise the 1923 Beachwood Canyon real estate development, but that doesn't have the same ring, does it? As studios and show business took off in the vicinity, the sign became a beacon to all that visited.

In 1945 the 'land' part was removed and Hollywood was truly born.

In 1977 it was burnt to the ground by an arsonist (or an actor who didn't get that part – the identity remains a mystery). The A-list were outraged at the sacrilege and Hugh Hefner hosted a benefit dinner at his Playboy mansion to raise funds to replace the most loved nine letters in LA. Hefner bought the new 'Y' and rocker Alice Cooper made a huge donation and dedicated one of the letter 'O's to his hero Groucho Marx.

> 'I sent the club a wire stating: PLEASE ACCEPT MY RESIGNA-
> TION. I DON'T WANT TO BELONG TO ANY CLUB THAT
> WILL ACCEPT ME AS A MEMBER.' Groucho Marx

The current sign is made of steel and concrete and is protected by 24-hour security and a million-dollar fence. It is the jewel in the crown of Tinseltown, best viewed from a distance, a hillside penthouse, or on a postcard.

The award ceremonies

There is always a reason to dress up and go up the red carpet in the movie business. All the actors and movie moguls want to be on the guest list for these award ceremonies; even more to get a nomination.

The SAGs – The Screen Actor's Guild awards. This is a cool one to win as this is the only award for actors voted by actors and the industry.

The Emmys – The TV awards of America given by the Academy of Television Arts and Sciences. It got the name 'Emmy' as a feminization of an 'immy', which is the nickname for an image orthicon tube. Huh? Basically some inner workings gizmo of an early camera – an insider joke clearly but ignore that, it's now a great red-carpet runway.

The BAFTAs (British Academy of Film and Television Awards) – Billed as London's version of the Oscars. As well as the internationals, it champions British film and TV achievements.

The Golden Globes – Time to get excited as this is considered to be the main indicator for who will win (and wear which designer labels) at the Academy Awards only a few 'what to wear' weeks later.

The Academy Awards – The Oscars and the industry's highest accolade. The Big One. Don't worry about not having a date, if you get one of these golden tickets actors, directors and script writers will be banging down your door. And forget about having a clothing crisis – those invited, let alone nominated, are inundated with designers desperate to dress them.

The Grammys – The prestigious US music awards ceremony that takes place in the same month as the Academy Awards.

The BRITs – the UK pop music awards happen in London the same week as the BAFTAs so there is lots of razzle-dazzle in WC1.

Nowadays, as much as the nomination, what adds shine to the star – and adds to her column inches – is the size of the entourage.

To fit in you will need:

Agent
Publicist
PA
Stylist
Hair/make-up team on call 24/7
Husband/pet/child, depending on space

Personal trainers, chefs and any other 'luxury' hangers-on are up to the individual's budget and status, as are which hotel and whether they fly business or first class. By Hollywood standards it seems best to aim for excess. Less is not more. Now isn't that a pity?

When dressing for a dinner or fancy soirée think 'Would this work on the red carpet?' or 'Is it too much/too little for the Oscars?' Well, if it is too much why worry? Better to be overdressed than underdressed. Undressed? Well, that comes later.

Academy Award trivia

The first Academy Awards of Merit were presented in 1929, at the Hollywood Roosevelt Hotel. Only 250 guests attended and they had to pay $10 a head for the privilege of being there.

Oscar himself is the little statuette. He weighs eight and a half pounds, yet is the heavyweight of movie-world achievement. The knight with a crusader's sword stands on a reel of film – the ultimate doorstop. Buy your own (replica) at *www.ebay.co.uk* or *www.theuktrophy.co.uk*.

As to the origin of his name – as with all the best tales, opinion is divided as to how he got his nickname. Margaret Herrick, the Academy's librarian and executive director, said that he reminded her of her Uncle Oscar, while

Bette Davis said the backside of the statue reminded her of her then husband, Harmon Oscar Nelson.

Maybe it's half and half? Back and front?

The first time the nickname was used was in 1934. Columnist Sidney Skolsky referred to Katharine Hepburn's Best Actress award not as a golden statue, but as 'Oscar', after a vaudeville joke he'd heard, and the name stuck.

With 1,500 press, 41.5 million viewers and 25 awards there are over a hundred parties in the month building up to the big day. Could be worth jetting over and hanging out at the Chateau Marmont but don't clog up the bar, you won't be the only one waiting to be discovered.

The glitziest of all parties is a toss-up depending on who shows up where, but with top billing are: the Governors Ball, the *Vanity Fair* post-awards shindig, Elton John's AIDS fundraiser, and A Night of 100 Stars (a $2,500-a-head dinner with the awards projected an a big screen). Failing that a copy of *Hello!* or *OK*! will keep you up to date on who wore what.

3rd March

The great Hollywood costume designer Adrian Adolph Greenberg was born in 1903. His on-screen credit simply read '*Gowns by Adrian*'. He designed for over two hundred and fifty films, twenty-eight films with Joan Crawford, eighteen with Norma Shearer, nine with Jean Harlow, and Garbo through thick and thin, though somehow he was never nominated for his own Academy Award. He famously remarked, 'It was because of Garbo I left MGM. In her last picture they wanted to make her a sweater girl, a real American type. I said, "When glamour ends for Garbo, it also ends for me." When Garbo walked out of the studio, the glamour went with her – and so did I.'

Watch some of his greatest creations in *The Women*, *The Wizard of Oz* or *The Great Ziegfeld* today.

How to do the red carpet

To dress the winning 'Best Actress' is the ultimate goal for fashion designers. *Who* will wear *what* is a closely guarded secret, and as you know it's a female prerogative to have a last-minute change of heart. It's just as nail-biting for the designer as the actress. Designers, however, are suckers for the glitz so will run the gauntlet on this night, as whoever she wears, she will be the most photographed woman in the world. Whoever gets their creation on a photogenic icon will reach more homes than their advertising campaigns could ever hope to. Yup, worth the gamble.

Favourite designers to wear at the Oscars include:

> Vera Wang – Keira Knightley, Michelle Williams
> Chanel – Nicole Kidman
> Carolina Herrera – Renée Zellweger
> Dior – Charlize Theron
> John Galliano – Cate Blanchett
> Versace – Catherine Zeta-Jones, Jennifer Lopez

Julia Roberts wore vintage Valentino to pick up her statuette in 2001 and Reese Witherspoon dazzled in an original fifties vintage Christian Dior in 2006. One actress who does not bow to designer pressure and remains one of the biggest stars on the red carpet is Sharon Stone. She's so sure of her sex appeal and dazzling presence that she collected an award in a Gap turtleneck one year, and a Vera Wang full satin skirt teamed with her then husband's crisp white shirt another. Proof that you don't need anything other than style and confidence to carry yourself with poise. That or her legs, her smile, her role, her attitude, her talent . . .

For more fashion moments on the red carpet get a copy of Bronwyn Cosgrave's *Made for Each Other*.

How to walk the red carpet artfully

by Sophie Dahl, model and author

As a rather bosomy adolescent I took to it like a duck to water. The red carpet was a bigger version of dressing up and parading in front of the mirror with girlfriends, but much more fun; flashbulbs and cat calls, and that sea of strangers with phallic photo lenses shouting my name with brassy familiarity. Most weird things are fun when you're a teenager; implication and reflection come a bit later. And how! With wanton abandon I set the stage brilliantly to spend my adult life wearily reminded in print of fashion faux pas, angry spots, puppy fat and public inebriation, and the odd caddish boyfriend. I don't have the chutzpah or chest I had then, so walking the red carpet now gives me gnawing anxiety and a quivering upper lip, but just sometimes it has to be done. Here's how you do it:

- Wear knickers. I don't care what kind, just wear them. Unless, of course, you have aspirations towards a career in porn or you get off on that sort of thing.
- Before you leave make sure that your dress which looked so winning and diaphanous in the light of your bedroom is not in fact see-through. If you think it might be, it probably is. Something that has a whisper of sheer to it at home is going to be like an X-ray under the stark light of a thousand flashbulbs. Have done this; not fun.
- In the car quaff some Rescue Remedy, and apply powder to

potentially shiny places. Do not spill powder on your boyfriend's black tie. He will not be pleased.

- Play some good music – Stevie Wonder or some proper solid hip hop. Make sure you are sitting on the correct side of the car for where your red carpet will be, so when you pull up you don't have to walk awkwardly around the car, narrowly avoiding getting run over.
- Take a deep breath. Get out, with your legs together (particularly if you are wearing short) in a sort of reverse bunnygirl bend. Stand up, and discreetly arrange dress.
- Walk slowly, and stop for each tier of photographers, on the left and the right. Try and give them equal time. Don't be compelled to take strange poses copied from a fashion story; no arms in the air, blowing kisses or clutching your cleavage. Simply look up and smile. Bodywise think the poise of Audrey Hepburn, or your favourite old screen siren. Shoulders back, weight slightly on one hip, legs still together. If your dress has a good back, smile over your shoulder as you are walking away; it's good for detail and the designer.
- Don't start chattering with the photographers as they are snapping; you'll have your mouth open in the pictures and look like a freak. Don't say nervous inane things because they will come back misquoted to haunt you, like what began as: 'No, I can't turn around too much, because this dress is slit perilously high and when I move you may see my bottom,' which became in its pitiful printed incarnation: 'Do you want to see my bum?'
- When you and the photographers have given each other enough time, or someone far more famous has come along, say thank you and sail gracefully through the door, as though you were born wearing five-inch stilettos with a slash of red sole.

How to decode dress codes

The Oscars aside, knowing *what* to wear and *when* is not a dilemma solely reserved for the starlets. How to decipher dress codes is an essential skill when deciding what to wear to formal invitations, such as your boss's or boyfriend's ball. Make an impression – the *right* one.

Do you know the difference between a *lounge suit* and a *morning suit?* When is it *black* and when is it *white?*

Note: Formal wear need not break the bank. Formal does not necessarily mean designer. Nice if it can, but you can hire as well as find great suits or dresses at markets if you know where to scour and leave time to do so.

January sales are a great time to look for cocktail or evening dresses or plan ahead for potential summer weddings. Don't be too proud to rummage around for a bargain – and sample sales are not to be sniffed at. Your rule of thumb should be, if it's fabulous – buy it. You can wait for an event to wear it, or if nothing is forthcoming create an occasion!

Wedding invitations, as well as formal invitations, often specify dress codes – you are not required by law to follow them, but nevertheless it's rude to ignore them and they should be respected. (See July for full Bridal Breakdown, page 245.) Usually the wording on the invite will specify the man's dress, and the women's correct 'dress code' can be worked out from this. (Men obviously need it spelt out, women can be relied upon to be creative.)

Casual

This means 'anything goes', but 'Smart Casual' means 'please make some effort, you needn't think you are coming in what you usually just throw on'.

Lounge suit

This is just another way of describing a business suit or a day suit. That said, you shouldn't let him wear one he's had on all day at the office to a glamorous function – make an effort, tell him he needs to be freshly pressed and shaved for a night out. The lounge suit became the height of fashion after Warren Beatty wore one in *Shampoo* (1975), when every man wanted to be a Casanova lounge lizard. The colours might be less garish now but men still want to be a Beatty.

Cocktail

This means wearing something you consider 'one of your best'. This is champagne and nibbles – dressy, but not dinner and dancing. Its precise definition for ladies is usually short to knee-length. Something that you feel is a significant notch up from what you would wear to the office, yet a notch down from what you would wear to a wedding.

Black tie/formal

This, technically, is semi-formal evening dress when men have to wear dinner jackets (see page 394 for its history) and a black bow tie and the women wear long gowns. Save the crown jewels or the total bling-bling look for below.

Morning coat (or morning dress)

This is lovely. It's when gentlemen dress up in tails, usually for a wedding. (That said, an event with a morning coat dress code which begins *after* five p.m. means the event has a White Tie dress code – see below). The man's jacket is single-breasted, the front fastened with one button. If the jacket is black, trousers are usually striped. It is worn with a waistcoat, usually grey, formal trousers, stiff-collared white shirt, black shoes and sometimes – say, for Ascot – a top hat. Most people tend to hire these, from either Moss Bros, Austin Reed, or a local equivalent. Now if the boys are dressing up, girls can do so even more. For daytime, hats with large brims, *à la* Ascot style, gloves and a delicate feminine dress. Time to be a lady.

White tie

This is for a really glittering, special occasion like the one Fred Astaire sang about in 'Putting on the Ritz' or at the White Tie and Tiara Ball Elton John throws each year. This requires the traditional black (white only if you want to really go for it) tux with tails, white shirt, white tie and, if he's perfect, black patent shoes. Women should wear long, full-on gowns. The dress code sometimes refers to this as 'ultra-formal'. This is the Ginger Rogers/MFL (My Fair Lady) moment you've been waiting for. This is a night for marabou feathers.

If your invitation says 'Black Tie Preferred' it is optional – but opt to look smart. Why turn down the dress-up opportunity?

If it says 'Black Tie Invited' that should be interpreted as 'you really need to make an extra-smart effort'. You have to look smart to the *standard* of black tie, even if you haven't gone for the hassle of hiring the full black-tie ensemble (see above).

If it says 'Creative Black Tie' this means you can interpret the rules slightly, but still err on the formal side. Creative does not mean crazy or fancy dress – if unsure ask rather than stand out like a sore thumb.

For ladies there are fewer rules and guidelines. Select a style that flatters you rather than is 'on trend' for the sake of it. Bias-cut might be nice for the slender but a fuller skirt may be preferred if you have more of a curve and don't want to spend the night remembering to suck it all in, or want to go dancing.

Choose a Hollywood icon and use her as your template: Jean Harlow to upstage the bride, Garbo to exit stage left with only a gin for company, Jessica Rabbit to exit stage right with every man trailing after you.

Décolletage can be accessorized with a necklace, throw or delicate cardigan, while length should depend more on whether legs are assets or not than the dress code, but it is common good manners to start below the knee when going to formal dos. Easy as it is, remember there are more colours than black on offer for eveningwear, though black will always be the most slimming and stain hiding.

Hand Luggage

Once you have cracked the clothing, what are the essentials to carry with you? Sirens are rarely seen on the red carpet with anything more than a miniature clutch purse, so where they stow the phone, keys, lippy, etc. is anyone's guess. Perhaps *this* is why the entourage is so essential? The base essentials:

> Tissues for emotional moments
> Lipstick for retouching after all those kisses
> Acceptance speech for that 'just in case' and you need a prompt
> Mobile to call family if you win/text if you lose
> Credit card, so much less cumbersome than cash or notes
> Hotel key card so you can take those wretched shoes off
> Tiny perfume sample bottle
> Mints for aforementioned kissing

Prioritize what you can fit in, then give the rest to your plus one. Also, and most important of all, only take a bag to functions if you have one that goes with the dress. Rucksack and ballgown have not hit a runway with any conviction yet.

Just why is it *a truth, universally acknowledged*, that despite the mounds of tulle and fabric, few of these fabulous dresses have pockets secreted away in them? A modern missed opportunity in many respects, but probably a blessing if at the end of the night you pass out on your bed – only to wake and find you have cracked your camera lens, or worse. Think of David Larrabee in *Sabrina*: he hid champagne flutes in his back pockets and was just off to seduce Sabrina in the way that never failed – until his brother caught him mid-exit and tricked him into sitting down. Glass shattering under your behind is one way to kill a moment.

How to tie a bow tie

For *real* black-tie events it will be necessary for men to wear a black tie and this means a bow tie. You can of course buy ready-made, ready-tied varieties that simply hook together, but this is cheating. Also, let's face it, there are likely to be many hooks and eyes, fiddly fastenings, lipsticks to carry, and little jobs for him to do on your behalf, so it's a nice gesture to show some element of concern over his appearance.

Ready-made also removes the option, as the soirée progresses, of him wearing it untied around his neck, top button casually undone in the style of Clark Gable/George Clooney, and who wouldn't want to leave with either of these icons?

Tying a bow tie is a mix between tying a tie and a shoelace, finished with a bow.

Start with collar up, lie the loose silk bow tie around the neck. Tweak so it hangs slightly longer on one side. Twist the long end under, as if you are going to knot the silk, and bring it up through the centre fold, towards the neck. Then twist this loop to make half a bow on one side, before you cross it with a similar-sized loop on the other. Basically you should have two bunny ears that just need to twist and knot themselves together. This is just like tying a bow – only in slippy silk and with the subject at eye level rather than on the floor. Tighten, don't strangle. Adjust and puff out the ends of bow. It may take a few attempts to perfect. Be sure to practise before the night in question.

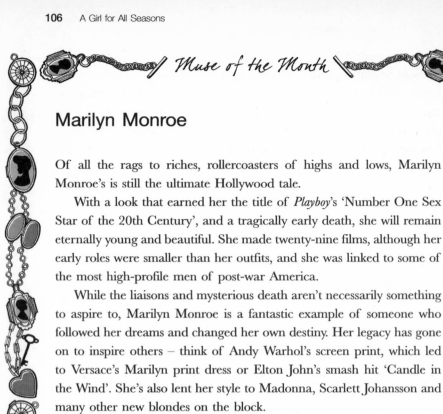

Muse of the Month

Marilyn Monroe

Of all the rags to riches, rollercoasters of highs and lows, Marilyn Monroe's is still the ultimate Hollywood tale.

With a look that earned her the title of *Playboy*'s 'Number One Sex Star of the 20th Century', and a tragically early death, she will remain eternally young and beautiful. She made twenty-nine films, although her early roles were smaller than her outfits, and she was linked to some of the most high-profile men of post-war America.

While the liaisons and mysterious death aren't necessarily something to aspire to, Marilyn Monroe is a fantastic example of someone who followed her dreams and changed her own destiny. Her legacy has gone on to inspire others – think of Andy Warhol's screen print, which led to Versace's Marilyn print dress or Elton John's smash hit 'Candle in the Wind'. She's also lent her style to Madonna, Scarlett Johansson and many other new blondes on the block.

This month when dressing for a black-tie occasion, think Marilyn, with a flick of black eyeliner, bright red lips and a wiggle to celebrate your curves. You could even get the peroxide out (or a good wig) and see if blondes really do have more fun. If this doesn't take your fancy, what about finding out if diamonds can be your best friend?

Her life and times

Marilyn Monroe was born Norma Jean Mortenson in Los Angeles on 1 June 1926 to Gladys Pearl Baker, a paranoid schizophrenic. When her mother was committed, Norma Jean was sent to an orphanage where she stayed until she was eleven, when her mother's friend, Grace Goddard, with her new husband, was able to adopt her. At sixteen, when the

Goddards were due to leave town, they married Norma Jean to a 21-year-old neighbour, Jimmy Dougherty, and the young couple moved to Catalina when he enlisted in the merchant marines. While working on the assembly line at the Radio Plane Company, she was spotted by photographer David Conover, who'd been commissioned to shoot 'morally uplifting snapshots of pretty girls'. When Conover saw Norma Jean he noticed that 'there was a luminous quality to her face, a fragility combined with astonishing vibrancy'. Also she had curves and was dynamite on film. Soon she was the most popular pin-up the Blue Book Modelling Agency had on their books.

By 1946 husband number one was gone, she'd changed her name to Jean Norman and she was reading lines in the office of Ben Lyon, head of new talent at 20th Century Fox. Hollywood here we come. She had the ambition, the pout and hit the peroxide, but the name was all wrong. She adopted Monroe after her maternal grandmother, Della Monroe, and at Lyon's suggestion, took the first name of 1920s starlet Marilyn Miller, whose surname, ironically, she would later inherit herself through marriage. Marilyn Monroe was born.

Her first appearance was in *Dangerous Years*, followed four months later by *Scudda-Hoo! Scudda-Hay!* She bewitched Groucho Marx in *Love Happy*, who said he'd cast her because he needed 'a young lady who can walk by me in such a manner as to arouse my elderly libido and cause smoke to issue from my ears'. Well, luckily that was her speciality.

By April 1952 *Life* magazine declared she was the girl all Hollywood was talking about and in 1953 she eclipsed the more established curves of Jane Russell in *Gentlemen Prefer Blondes*. The film included her rendition of 'Diamonds are a Girl's Best Friend', which was to become something of a theme tune.

Pursued by fans and hounded by the paparazzi, she graced magazine covers and presented Oscars; the inevitable next step was the celebrity boyfriend. In 1954 she married baseball hero Joe DiMaggio but even on her honeymoon newly-wed Mrs DiMaggio went to perform for the troops, stationed in Korea. The artist formerly known as Miss Cheesecake and Miss California Artichoke Queen had become the fairer

half of Mr and Mrs America. However, she was happier in front of the camera acting than she was with her own reality.

'Nobody discovered her, she earned her own way to stardom,' said Darryl F. Zanuck, legendary president of 20th Century Fox. On 15 September 1954 the hard work paid off. In front of several hundred photographers, and 2,000 spectators, his peroxide protégée stood over a subway ventilator while her dress was blown about. No one remembers much about *The Seven Year Itch* except that white pleated halter-neck dress, so when you're cursing a howling wind that is ruining your hair, as well as your look, remember what a wind did for Marilyn. (That, and always to wear knickers you don't mind the world seeing.) Perhaps not surprisingly, Mr America found the attention his wife attracted a little hard to take. Monroe had said, 'I am going to be a great movie star some day,' and she couldn't give it all up now to be the dutiful wife. The timing was terrible so, with regret, marriage number two was over.

Thirty, newly single and having legally adopted her stage name as her own, Marilyn decided she wanted to tackle her crippling stage fright and ditch the 'dumb blonde' tag: it was time be taken seriously. She enrolled at the Actors Studio, to study method acting under Lee Strasberg, who advocated breaking down a script word by word and 'inhabiting' the role. He taught all the greats: Marlon Brando, Jack Nicholson, James Dean, Robert de Niro. On one of the rare occasions he himself ventured in front of the camera (as Hyman Roth in *The Godfather Part II*) he was nominated for Best Supporting Actor, so there was clearly something in it.

The effect Strasberg had on her acting may have been negligible but it did have an impact on her personal life. It was through him that she met Arthur Miller, the older, famous playwright, who made her 'feel giddy'. They married in 1956. On the surface things looked good – she set up her own production company and produced, as well as starred in, *Bus Stop* and *The Prince and the Showgirl* – but behind the scenes there were miscarriages, affairs, abortions. She was also hitting the bottle (and we're not talking hair dye here) as well as the medicine cabinet to cope. Monroe had a spectacularly public affair with Yves Montand, who she

starred with in the appropriately titled *Let's Make Love*, and seemed to want to hit the self-destruct button.

Tony Curtis, her co-star in *Some Like It Hot*, also felt strongly about her – hardly surprising! 'They've taken this woman and kind of blown her into something that never existed,' he told Larry King on the *Larry King Live* show in 2001, which was celebrating what would have been her seventy-fifth birthday. Curtis told how they started out together, and how changed she was when they reunited a decade later to work on *Some Like It Hot*. 'And I never said "kissing Marilyn Monroe was like kissing Hitler",' he said – though it was famously attributed to him. 'Someone got back to her with it and she was offended by it, and I don't blame her. [But] she understood that it was never said by me.' Which is a relief, as such an icon simply *had* to be a good kisser. Billy Wilder however just sighed. 'She was impossible, not just difficult, to work with.' Yet despite the angst she won a Golden Globe for her portrayal of Sugar Kane Kowalczyk. Just goes to show you can't please all of the people all of the time.

Despite this acting accolade it was her off-screen persona that really captivated the world. What script could compete with the reality? Alleged affairs with her co-stars included Charlie Chaplin. There were dalliances with everyone from members of the Rat Pack up to the White House, abortions as well as failed attempts to conceive, depression and dependency. From foster homes to America's idol, her reality – on-screen glamour, off-screen misery – was far juicer than any script.

Her next film was *The Misfits*, written by (fed-up husband) Arthur Miller. But by this time things were really out of hand off screen. Even Clark Gable, a super-loyal fan, said working with her 'damn near gave me a heart attack' – and two weeks after filming wrapped the words came true . . . he died of a heart attack. And *you* thought office politics got you down?

Her marriage to Miller was over and shortly afterwards, on 7 February 1961, she was admitted to a psychiatric clinic. Four days later DiMaggio, her devoted hero, who had never stopped loving her, got her out. A few months later on 19 May 1962, she delivered one of her sexiest (and last) performances when she jetted up to New York to purr 'Happy Birthday (Mr President)' to JFK, live on television. This was rumoured to be near the end

of their affair, but things were hotting up between her and his district attorney brother, Bobby. She was starting to become a political headache.

On 5 August 1962 she was found dead, apparently from an overdose of sleeping pills, but conspiracy theories abounded.

Joe DiMaggio insisted on a small, media-free cremation. He would send roses to the Westwood Memorial Park Cemetery every week for the remainder of his life, and, like the rest of the world, never got over Marilyn Monroe.

Marilynisms

'Being a sex symbol is a heavy load to carry, especially when one is tired, hurt and bewildered.'

'It's not true that I had nothing on. I had the radio on.'

'I want to grow old without facelifts. I want to have the courage to be loyal to the face I have made.'

'Fame is fickle and I know it. It has its compensations, but it also has its drawbacks and I've experienced them both.'

Men on Marilyn

'She seemed very shy, and I remember that when the studio workers would whistle at her, it seemed to embarrass her.' Cary Grant

'Her beauty and humanity shine through ... she is the kind of artist one does not come across every day in the week. After all, she was created something extraordinary.' Arthur Miller

'She has a certain indefinable magic that comes across, which no other actress in the business has.' Billy Wilder

'Marilyn is a kind of ultimate. She is uniquely feminine. Everything she does is different, strange, and exciting; from the way she talks to the way she uses that magnificent torso. She makes a man proud to be a man.'
Clark Gable

Something to aim for even if Hollywood doesn't beckon . . .

How to make an acceptance speech

Though all the excitement seems to be on the red carpet outside, what really matters is on the inside, like beauty being only skin deep. The winners and the losers are what matter now. When you are collecting a glittering prize – Academy Award or third place at the local Bingo – try these tips.

Speeches are ideally prepared in advance, written or learnt. 'Surprise' prizes are a nightmare – if you get more than five calls to casually check that you are attending and why haven't you sent an RSVP, dig a bit and think about preparing a short, heartfelt speech in your head. And very discreet cue cards – keyword prompts and names can be written on delicate little cards, or in a last-minute scribble on the corner of your invite. These are great to prevent you from getting tongue-tied, or waffling, should the occasion arise.

Length

Think: short and chic and most of all succinct. Less is more. Do *not* fall into a convoluted emotional waffle; it will only come back to haunt you. Why, even the super chic Grace Kelly got nervous and remarked on Oscar night in 1954, 'This is the one night I wish I smoked and drank.' She needn't have worried – flawless and faultless she scored Best Actress that night.

The shortest speech award goes to Clark Gable, who collected an Oscar in 1934 for his role in *It Happened One Night*. He simply said 'Thank you'. The longest Oscar acceptance speech (so far) was made in 1954 by Greer Garson. She won Best Actress Award for her role in *Mrs Miniver*, and was still saying her thank-yous five and a half minutes later even though she still hadn't got round to her high school sweetheart, first cat, first kiss, smiling second row of the audience and all the surnames beginning with G in the phone book and . . .

The following year a time limit was set.

'I'm going to spend some time up here,' was how Julia Roberts famously opened her 2001 acceptance speech. The Pretty Woman won an Academy Award for her role in *Erin Brockovich* and though she was true to her word she unfortunately forgot to thank the real-life Erin Brockovich who inspired the film. Oops. Halle Berry, Nicole Kidman and Gwyneth Paltrow were also all suitably choked when it was their turn up there, and Sarah Jessica Parker was so overwhelmed by her Golden Globe she forgot to thank her husband, actor Matthew Broderick. Prompt cards do help.

In 1969 Barbra Streisand tied to win Best Actress with Katharine Hepburn (who skipped the ceremony that year . . . sharing? Yuk). Streisand won for her part in *Funny Face* and opened her speech 'Hello Gorgeous'. (See page 415 for the real Fanny Brice/Funny Face.)

Public speaking back on planet earth

Know *who* (which organization) is giving you the award, *who* you are giving your speech to – and restrict yourself to three key names you want to thank. Do it well and they may invite you again.

Drinking

Back on planet earth, you might want to wind up any kind of speech you're giving – at a wedding, after dinner or at the annual fête – with a toast. Proposing a toast is always a popular punch line as it not only involves your audience, it involves alcohol. Hurrah. You will be doubly popular for *not* making an agonizingly long speech and for getting the glasses refilled. Do not worry if you don't have them rolling in the aisles; at least you didn't bore them to death, and they'll be too schnozzled to care.

However, do not drink to excess before your big moment. A glass of wine is fine for the nerves – but water is better to clear your throat. A bottle of wine is definitely not advised in advance. Alcohol and nerves will not only make it harder to find the podium, focus and stand upright. It will be very tricky to communicate all your musings if every word you utter is slurred.

For more ideas look at *www.speechtips.com*; they practically do the hard work for you.

Ash Wednesday

The first day of Lent; forty days until Easter. When Easter falls is in the hands of your diary – it could be any time between now and April.

In Christian services on this day a cross is marked on foreheads in ash. People today will give up a certain type of food or something they love indulging in – it is, after all, supposed to be a sacrifice. Let's face it, the abstinence involved in forgoing KitKats for forty days is not quite as dramatic as what Jesus went through. This is a serious time of religious thought, prayer and penitence.

Kissing Friday

The Friday after Ash Wednesday brings a custom that was known as Kissing Friday. On this day in Shrove Week English schoolboys were, once upon a time, 'entitled to kiss girls without fear of punishment or rejection'. No wonder it only lasted until the 1940s but you could work out ways to improve and modernize it for today.

Hot Lips

On Kissing Friday celebrate and paint your lips the most scarlet shade you dare. The Ancient Egyptians were fans of painting their lips and Cleopatra's colour came from crushed carmine beetles. Nice. Queen Victoria banned lipstick saying it was impolite, that only prostitutes wore make-up. She decreed that it should not be worn until after marriage in case a woman tricked a man into believing she was more beautiful. But soon, with the rise of Hollywood and Max Factor, the starlets and glamour-seeking girls got their compacts out again, not that they'd ever really given them up.

Max Factor (1877–1938) was the most famous face painter in Hollywood. A Russian who emigrated to America in 1904, Jean Harlow, Bette Davis and all the major movie actresses of the day were regulars at his beauty salon, situated near the Hollywood studios.

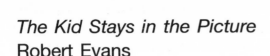

The Kid Stays in the Picture
Robert Evans

Why

If you want sex and scandal and celebrities read *The Kid Stays in the Picture*. It is a riveting autobiography spanning forty years in Hollywood's fast lane by the maverick actor turned film producer Robert Evans who tells of his rollercoaster ride – rags to riches to rags and worse – and doesn't hold back to save face, either his own or that of his associates. Many of the best-known names are mentioned in this fast-paced Who's Who and 'How Not To' of Hollywood. He's been there, done that, been bedded and bankrupted by the best. There's enough drama and name-dropping for several books – it's like an annual subscription to the *National Enquirer* condensed into one blockbuster.

Who

Born on 29 June 1930, Evans started his career doing promo work for his family-run commercial clothing line Evan-Picone (big in the seventies in the US). He went on to become the youngest ever head of Paramount Studios. Evans was the producer behind a string of hits including *Rosemary's Baby*, *The Godfather*, *Chinatown* and *Love Story*, and at the height of *Love Story*'s success he married its star Ali MacGraw.

His meteoric rise began in 1957 when the great Hollywood actress Norma Shearer spotted the pretty boy by a poolside and successfully championed him for the role of (her one-time lover) Irving Thalberg in *Man of a Thousand Faces*. The same year studio boss Darryl F. Zanuck cast him as the bullfighter opposite sultry Ava Gardner in Ernest Hemingway's *The Sun Also Rises*. Evans' star was also very much on the rise.

But acting didn't last long. 'I was sure of one thing,' Evans said. 'I was a half-assed actor.' But Hollywood was his drug (well, one of the

legal ones). He rebranded himself as a producer and moved behind the camera. Friends with Jack Nicholson and Warren Beatty, it's no surprise the guy was trouble. Big trouble. He cast Al Pacino in his first major role, was friends with Henry Kissinger and had a massive cocaine addiction. He's been linked to Ava Gardner, Grace Kelly, Margaux Hemingway and has been married seven times – which makes him even more enthusiastic about going up the aisle than Henry VIII! His wives include Sharon Hugueny, model Camilla Sparv, Ali MacGraw (with whom he had his only child, a son, Josh Evans), Phyllis George, Catherine Oxenberg, Leslie Ann Woodward and most recently Victoria White O'Gara; their marriage ended in June 2006.

His marriage to MacGraw ended with her very public affair with Steve McQueen, who she met while they were filming and Evans was wrapped up in *The Godfather* (Part I) editing fiasco.

Hosting

If ever there was an occasion to try and get a table at LA's The Ivy, (you knew you liked this book for a reason), it is this month's book club. Dressing up for this event is *essential*, either in Oscar-night glamour or as your favourite movie character from one of Evans' films. Get a hair cut *à la* Mia Farrow. If you don't have time to read the book but don't want to miss the discussion, watch the film of the same name, with voice-over provided by Robert Evans himself – but this is a bit of a cop-out and only acceptable if you have to learn an entire script for your own on-screen debut – and no, the school play doesn't count.

Alternatives include:

Sam Spiegel by Natasha Fraser-Cavassoni
Ava Gardner by Lee Server
Goldwyn: A Biography by A. Scott Berg
Laurence Olivier by Terry Coleman
Joan Crawford; Hollywood Martyr by David Bret

Katherine Hepburn by Anne Edwards
Easy Riders, Raging Bulls by Peter Biskind
You'll Never Eat Lunch in This Town Again by Julia Phillips

4th March

The Italian composer, priest and violinist Antonio Lucio Vivaldi was born in Venice, 1678, the same date the city was struck by an earthquake. His father was a musician, and played at St Mark's cathedral and young Antonio, aged only seven, vowed he would too. He entered the Church (good job security) aged fifteen and was known as '*il prete rosso*' (the red priest), on account of his red hair, but had to withdraw from active priesthood due to his chronic asthma and so he concentrated on his compositions. He was a teacher at the all girls *Ospedale della Pietà* and was a prolific composer of over 500 concertos. But it was when a huge catalogue of his work, including his *Four Seasons*, was rediscovered in Turin and Genoa in 1926 that he because famous. Listen to the *Four Seasons*, S*pring*, today to celebrate the season as well as the man.

8th March

French composer Maurice Ravel was born today in 1875. Listen to his most famous piece – *Boléro*.

The original is eighteen minutes long, and set in the unusual 5/4 time. (A piece of music trivia here – another famous piece that used the same syncopated time meter is Mars in Holst's *Planets* suite).

The version of *Boléro* that everyone knows was edited to four minutes and twenty-eight seconds, and accompanied Torvill and Dean on ice.

More than 24 million people watched on 14 February 1984 as the British couple scored a perfect score – the maximum 9 sixes for artistic impression, and 12 of 18 possible sixes for free dance – at the Sarajevo Olympics. They followed this Olympic gold medal with a world record-breaking maximum score at the World Figure Skating Championships later that year.

Go skating today. Aim to mirror their routine, or at least circle the rink successfully, by Christmas. It's all about thigh-burning exercising and most people won't think to do this in spring. It pays to think ahead.

9th March

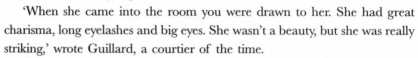

Napoleon married Josephine, 1796

'When she came into the room you were drawn to her. She had great charisma, long eyelashes and big eyes. She wasn't a beauty, but she was really striking,' wrote Guillard, a courtier of the time.

Rose, as Josephine was originally called, was forced into an unhappy marriage as a last-minute substitute for her sister who died tragically en route to her betrothed, Alexandre de Beauharnais. A few years later he met his fate at the guillotine. He left behind a young widow and children and she set out to find a position, or a person to support her. It was around this time that she met Napoleon and knocked him off his feet.

'Sweet, incomparable Josephine, what a strange effect you have on my heart,' he wrote to her. She saved his letters; alas her replies are lost.

He proposed in January 1796 and they were married in March. His wedding present to Rose was a gold medallion inscribed 'To Destiny'. Ahh. He 'renamed' her Josephine so it was a fresh start for them both.

Napoleon eventually divorced her so he could marry another, and produce an heir for his crown. His dying words were for his great love, 'Josephine'.

13th March

In 1905 Mata Hari debuted on the cabaret scene in Paris.

Born on 7 August 1876, her real name was Margaretha Geertruida

Zelle but she changed her name to Mata Hari, meaning 'sun' in Malay, part of the web of intrigue that surrounded her. Her exotic dress and provocative dance style made jaws drop. In reality she was born in Leeuwarden, the Netherlands, not exactly the Orient as she claimed, but she played it well.

Just about everything about Mata Hari made her a man magnet. She attracted very high-ranking military officers, decided to make profit from her pillow talk and was rumoured to have been a French informant.

In January 1917 the French intercepted a message detailing the activities of a German spy, H21, who was revealed to be agent Mata Hari. The Germans knew the message had been detected and simply sat back and waited for the double agent to be 'neutralized' by the enemy.

The French arrested her on 13 February 1917. She was put on trial and found guilty of costing the lives of thousands of soldiers. She was executed by a firing squad on 15 October 1917, at which point she threw her coat open to reveal the words 'Merci Monsieur' scrawled on her naked torso. A performer to the end.

Mata Hari's legend was immortalized in the 1931 film *Mata Hari* with Greta Garbo playing the lead.

14th March

Albert Einstein, the most important scientist of the twentieth century, was born, in Ulm, in 1879.

The German physicist and eccentric figure was the author of the theory of relativity, $E = mc^2$ or E= mass times the speed of light to the power of two (which inadvertently revealed the formula for an atomic bomb. Yikes.) In 1921 he won the Nobel Prize for Physics but all you need to remember is that his name is synonymous with genius.

Today is also the feast of Purim, the Jewish festival to celebrate the deliverance of Persian Jews from the plot of Haman.

This is a good tale worth knowing.

In the land of Persia in 358 BC in the city of Shushan, King Achashverosh held a beauty contest to find a new wife (after he had his former one put to death because she refused to dance nude before his dinner guests. I mean really . . .) A Jewish girl called Esther entered the competition at her cousin Mordechai's bidding and won. He thought that at a time of tense religious relations it would be helpful to have a person on the inside and he was right. When her cousin overheard a plot to have all the Jews put to death, Esther bravely went to her husband unbidden (a penalty for which in those days was death – and you thought your man was moody) and asked him why he was planning to kill her the next day.

He exclaimed that he did not want her killed and why would she think such a thing? He really liked this wife. To which she responded, 'The ordinance of your vasir, Haman, which you are going to enact tomorrow, entails my death. For I too am a Jew.' Furious at his aide and because of his love for Esther, the king hung Haman on his own gallows the next day.

On Purim Jews shout and rattle noisemakers in the synagogue to drown out Haman's name when it is read from the text. They also eat triangle cookies in the shape of Haman's hat to further crush him, and they dress up as the characters of the story.

Today is also the Hindu festival of Holi. This is the festival of colour, where people spray each other with coloured water and make bonfires.

15th March

Emperor Julius Caesar was murdered in 44 BC
Read Shakespeare's version of the tragedy that retells Caesar's final days or enjoy MGM's lavish 1953 production, with Louis Calhern as Caesar, James Mason as Brutus and Marlon Brando as Anthony, which is considered the definitive film version (though John Gielgud and Charlton Heston starred in an equally iconic version in 1970). Today you have to spare a thought for Caesar and let his leadership inspire you.

Shakespeare's play and history have merged into one and there are some famous lines in Julius Caesar that have been woven into contemporary scripts, jokes and drama.

'Et tu, Brute?' are his dying words at the close of Act III, Scene 1 when his inner circle have betrayed him and one by one stabbed him, even those he thought he could trust. Keeping friends close and enemies closer really backfired on this occasion.

'Beware the Ides of March' warns the soothsayer in Shakespeare's *Julius Caesar*, Act I, Scene II.

Shakespeare's original audience, just like the Emperor, would have understood exactly when the Ides fell, as this was the calendar used until the Renaissance era. Over 2,000 years later we don't appreciate how specific and crystal clear the warning was. Caesar was told plain and simple what date to watch out on, and did he?

The Romans organized their calendar around three days in the month – and the days on either side were incidental.
In other words:

Kalends was the first day of the month.
Nones was the seventh day in March, May, July and October, and the fifth day in all the other months.
Ides was the fifteenth day in March, May, July and October and the thirteenth in all others.

No wonder they had to shove an extra day on every leap year to rectify all this confusion. (See 29 February, page 86.)

The remaining days were not given their own title; they were identified simply by counting back from the Kalends, Nones and Ides. It's not as complicated as it sounds. For example, 11 March would be V Ides – in other words, five days before the Ides.

16th March

The Patron Saint of Ireland, St Patrick, was born *c.* AD 389. '*Beannachtaí na Féile Pádraig oraibh*' or 'May the blessings of St Patrick be with you' is what to say, and *the* colour to wear is green. Green will bring you luck and without it you will get pinched (so says Irish tradition) which would be very unpleasant. While garlands of shamrocks swing from most pubs, the official emblem of Ireland is the Celtic harp.

Traditional dishes to try on this day include Irish corned beef (actually bacon) and cabbage, stew, and sweet Irish soda bread. Order a Baileys or a pint of Guinness and settle into your local Irish pub for tales of leprechauns or great men and women, as this is the nation with the gift of the gab.

Famous Irish names include:

Samuel Beckett, George Best, Bono, Kenneth Brannagh, Gabriel Byrne, Daniel Day-Lewis, Colin Farrell, Michael Gambon, James Joyce, Van Morrison, Liam Neeson, Bram Stoker, Oscar Wilde, Terry Wogan.

20th March

English scientist Sir Isaac Newton died in London in 1727 (although other sources say he died on 31 March 1727). And, yes, he is the one who is said to have been inspired to write the theory of gravity when an apple fell on his head. He also came up with the Three Laws of Motion, or the Three Laws of Newton, and invented the Newtonian telescope. Groovy.

Also on this date, in 1815, Switzerland became permanently neutral, and the favourite tax haven for the very rich.

Eat an apple or some Swiss chocolate today.

21st March

The German composer Johnann Sebastian Bach was born in 1685.

Famous for his organ music, as well as the *Brandenburg Concertos, The Art of the Fugue* and *St Matthew's Passion,* his music has stood the test of time and has appeared in over four hundred films which would definitely have got him several Academy Award nominations.

Bach soundtrack appearances include:

The Aviator (2004), *Minority Report* (2002), *Lara Croft: Tomb Raider* (2001), *The Talented Mr Ripley* (1999), *The English Patient* (1996), *Schindler's List* (1993) and his 'Adagio of Viola da Gamba' Sonata BWV 1029 had a starring role in *Truly, Madly, Deeply* in 1991, one of the most romantic tear-jerkers directed by Anthony Minghella, which stars a cello, Juliet Stevenson and Alan Rickman. Watch this film today, as if you need telling twice.

22nd March

Johann Wolfgang von Goethe died in 1832. Get your cultural head on.

Goethe was Germany's greatest poet. His dying words are said to have been 'open the second shutter, so that more light can come in'.

Mozart and Mahler set his poems to music, and playwrights, such as Marlowe, were inspired by his words.

Goethe said:

'A clever man commits no blunders.'
'A person hears only what they understand.'
'Age merely shows what children we remain.'

Which applies to you?

23rd March

Spanish painter Juan Gris was born in 1887 and French painter Raoul Dufy died in 1953.

Artists that have been depicted on film include:

Jackson Pollock, Andy Warhol, Leonardo da Vinci, Artemisia, Toulouse-Lautrec, Vincent Van Gogh, Basquiat and Pablo Picasso.

26th March

Ludwig van Beethoven died in 1827.

The composer spent his latter years totally deaf and was said to have sawn the legs off his piano so he could feel the vibrations better. When conducting, he could never hear the orchestra, let alone the applause. His last words were said to be: 'I shall hear in heaven.'

Listen to his most popular work, Symphony No. 5 in C minor, Op. 67, written between 1804–8. Even if you don't know classical music you will know this – it is the most recognized piece in European classical music.

Mothering Sunday

Mothering Sunday has been celebrated in the UK on the fourth Sunday of Lent since the sixteenth century but celebrations to honour motherhood date right back to the Ancient Greeks as they paid tribute to Rhea, mother of gods and Titan of earth and fertility. The day was known back in Tudor England as 'refreshment Sunday' or 'mid-lent Sunday' and the fasting rules were relaxed so all those children in service – scullery maids, apprentices and those working away from home (and they could be as young as ten; be thankful!) – could go home to see their mummy. So popular was this tradition that it is now celebrated in over forty-six countries across the world, all on different dates, so check where your mother is. This is a good day to make a cake, perhaps digging out one of her favourite recipes. A bunch of daffodils or a hand-picked posy from your garden (yours not hers) and a card will show that you care. *Mommie Dearest*, the 1978 misery memoir by Joan Crawford's adopted daughter Christina, is not a wise gift. Above all, spend the day with her.

British Summer Time begins

It's Daylight Saving Time and the clocks go forward, a tradition observed since 1916 when it was adopted to help farmers by giving them more daylight.

Summer Time begins the morning after the third Saturday in March, or if that was Easter day, the day after the second Saturday, and is now in force until the last Sunday in October.

27th March

The man who redesigned Paris, Baron Georges Eugène Haussmann, was born in 1809. But before you get confused, Haussmann was not an architect – he was Napoleon III's city planner who was employed to ensure that the imperial power was reflected in the design of the city. Haussmann made streets wider, not only to better accommodate the expanding population, but to enable the flow of services and the suppression of violent uprisings by eliminating any spaces for them to brew. He enhanced the city's façade and beauty. His plan was so successful that Paris is still a blueprint for modern cities today. Take the Eurostar and see for yourself.

28th March

Constantinople (which rhymes with 'we-should-be-so-grateful', as Miss Alan gleefully wrote in E.M. Forster's *A Room with a View*) became Istanbul in 1930.

In 1941 British literary great Virginia Woolf drowned herself. She threw herself into the River Ouse, her pockets lined with stones to pull her down to her watery grave.

Woolf was a central figure of London's Bloomsbury literary set, a bohemian, feminist, critic and novelist. Visit her sister's house (see page 314). She began writing for the *Times Literary Supplement* in 1905 and published her first novel, *The Voyage Out*, in 1915. Woolf went on to write *Mrs Dalloway* in 1925, *Orlando* in 1928, *To the Lighthouse* in 1927 and *The Waves* in 1931.

Michael Cunningham's book *The Hours* combines the life of Virginia Woolf with that of two fictional women, and although all three come from different eras (the twenties, the fifties and today), it is about how they are linked. Nicole Kidman played the British novelist and became the first Australian woman to win an Academy Award for Best Actress. In 2003 she was honoured with her own 'star' on Hollywood's 'Walk of Fame' and she remarked, 'I've never been so happy to have people walk over me for the rest of my life!'

The stiletto

When you think of a high heel you essentially think of the stiletto – the ultimate sexy shoe. It first sashayed into view in 1952, and though several claim the spiky four-inch heel as their own, credit should probably go to two great shoemakers, Salvatore Ferragamo and Roger Vivier. Cobblers love stilettos because of the constant upkeep they require, interior designers loathe them as they can mark floors or pierce carpets, while doctors despair and warn their patients of twisted or broken ankles. Madonna, however, commented that Manolos, made by the modern-day maestro of heels and the sharpest stilettos, 'last longer than sex', so who says that diamonds are a girl's best friend? Jayne Mansfield confessed to having over 200 pairs; how many stilettos there are in Imelda Marcos's collection is unknown.

The stiletto was the essential of every sultry sex symbol of the fifties and shows no sign of abating in the modern day (well, only if love and romance fly off the menu, but is that likely? No). The seductive power of the heel is undisputed; the needle and spike of the stiletto is the perfect accessory to bring out the flirty and naughty girls. After domi-nating the fifties it waned in the swinging sixties with bra burning and free love, but with the power-dressing of the eighties it came back with a vengeance. It has stamped its heels and refused to leave ever since, becoming a chameleon to indulge the fetishes and fantasies of all footwear fiends.

April

'Always laugh when you can. It's cheap medicine.'
Lord Byron

Wish You Were Here

Erin O'Connor remembers Wales

I have very fond memories of my parents loading up the lime-green estate car and then squeezing in themselves, my uncle plus the girlfriend of the time and us three kids in the back, and driving to the seaside, for our annual 'break'. Year after year we would drive to the Rhyl Sun Valley Caravan Park in Wales, where everything stood lined up in a concrete row, with the little tin-roofed nightclub at the end. Erasure played on my older sister's cassette player and constantly in the aerobics, disco and bingo hall, competing against the low hum of the electric fires and squeaking plastic corrugated bathtubs . . . I thought this place was heaven on earth.

I remember one particular trip – I must have been twelve – was the time that I first 'fell in love'. I met the most gorgeous boy (or so I thought at the time). For our 'date', I remember, I went to his caravan, and he poured Tesco's undiluted orange squash into a china teacup. It was all so innocent yet one of the most romantic things. I fell totally in love with the moment, though I am afraid not the boy, and sadly can't even remember his name.

I do however remember the ice-cream van, where the older, cooler kids got to eat the Feasts while the younger kids ate Screwballs, 'cos only the older kids could afford the 35p! It was a holiday where you saved up your money to buy your own can of hairspray, Impulse spray deodorant and you'd then keep them all proudly in a newly bought beach bag (with rope handles and 'Rhyl' motif). The day could be spent reading copies of *More* magazine and feeling very grown-up flicking through *Just Seventeen* as we watched the older kids head to the beachfront when it got dark. For seven years I was totally fulfilled, high on 'Poppers', and thought that being in a brown sleeping bag on the brown and beige carpet was a proper adventure as I waited for the chocolate on my Coco Pops to melt. This to me was the only way to holiday, with treats at every turn, such as battered sausage and chips or braving the sea for a swim, whatever the weather – that was what a holiday was all about. To top it all there were the bingo competitions, and in my last year at Rhyl I did bag myself a real boyfriend, called Derek. One night at bingo I just wanted to go on stage so I leapt up and said I had won, when I hadn't, though when they checked my numbers they soon worked this out and the applause turned to shame, and I left with my head down. But then out of nowhere we had our first kiss – that feeling of contentment and escape; I didn't think it could ever get any better.

Discovering something new, or about yourself, is what makes a holiday so exciting. I love to escape the city and I don't think you have to jump onto a plane to find it – just head up the M4 and you can get your fix.

Love, Erin

1st April

Everyone knows there's no fool like an old fool, but today foolery is as hard to avoid as a hangover on 1 January, as April starts with All Fools' Day. Look left, right, up and down – and proceed with caution today.

No one will own up to when and where the folly originated but there are reports of it dating back to 1582 in France. It all came about with the calendar shift. Before the switch to the Gregorian calendar (see February, page 86) the New Year coincided with the start of spring, and was celebrated for eight days, culminating on what is now our 1 April.

When the New Year was moved from April to January there was no television, Internet or text alerts – let alone a daily newspaper – to let everyone know so it took a bit of time for the information to spread. Those behind the times who were caught celebrating the old calendar's New Year on this day were consequently labelled April Fools. Nicer than being called an idiot,

I suppose. If you thought being out of fashion was bad news, April Fool gags had, and still have, far riskier consequences, so if you don't want egg on your face – and lets hope it's only the proverbial kind – be wary and wise.

Over the centuries this date has evolved into the date to pull a prank – from the easy (such as putting all the clocks forward an hour in the office or on a friend's mobile) to the elaborate.

The April Fools' Hall of Fame:
In 1962 Sweden's TV network promise of 'Instant Colour TV' if you twiddled your aerial in a certain direction tricked thousands.

In 1977 the *Guardian* printed a supplement to celebrate the tenth anniversary of San Serriffe (a country they had created). This prompted a deluge of enquiries from curious and confused potential tourists. This set the standard for an annual media obsession to come up with the wittiest gags to fool their unsuspecting readers and viewers. One of the most successful was by *USA Today* in 1998, with a story about Burger King's Left-Handed Whopper. Left-handed food?

However, retaining the crown for number one April Fools' hoax is the (usually) very sensible BBC. In 1957 the respected and highbrow *Panorama* (surely too sensible for silliness) did a special report on the 'Swiss Spaghetti Harvest'. The footage showed locals pulling the fresh pasta off trees as if they were picking apples. The story was so believable that BBC phone lines were jammed by perplexed callers wanting to know if they could grow their own trees.

Accept invitations and proposals with prudence today.

2nd April

The world's most notorious (real-life) seducer, Giovanni Giacomo Casanova, was born in 1725 and though bedding 122 women may seem tame by the standards of some of today's lotharios, he has retained his crown.

'I have had many friends who have acted kindly towards me, and it has been my good fortune to have it in my power to give them substantial proofs of my gratitude,' he said, justifying his ways.

Casanova was intended for the Church, as a clerical lawyer, but then he discovered girls ... Read his scandalous autobiography, *Histoire de ma vie* ('Story of My Life'), or the novel by Arthur Japin, *In Lucia's Eyes*, which tells Casanova's story through the eyes of his first love – the one that set him on the road to ruin.

Make sure any gigolo you might be seeing is giving you their full attention (undivided, *not* shared) today. If alone, single, or having a night in, rent *Casanova* on DVD. Would you really want this drama?

3rd April

On this day in 1721 Robert Walpole became the first prime minster of Great Britain in 1721. Until then the British people had been reliant on the whims of the monarchy. Thank God for the rise of democracy and the right to vote. Check if you are registered on the electoral roll today.

4th April

Today in 1581 Elizabeth I knighted her favourite pirate and adventurer Sir Francis Drake, who had just returned from a voyage around the world. He had managed to sail through the Spanish-controlled Strait of Magellan, south of Chile, had raided the west coast of South America, claimed a slice of California as a keepsake for England and sailed home with enough treasure to pay off the entire national debt (that's some treasure chest).

He certainly was a hero, and though Queen Elizabeth ignored his cheeky marriage proposal, he remained a favourite at court.

Muse of the Month

Elizabeth I

Queen Elizabeth I is still today considered one of the greatest monarchs of English history and she did it all without a man by her side. Known as 'Good Queen Bess', 'the Virgin Queen', and 'Gloriana', Elizabeth was married to England and she reigned for forty-five years from 1558–1603. 'I may not be a lion, but I am a lion's cub, and have a lion's heart,' she said and she meant it.

Her reign was known as the Golden Age, and that it was. The arts flourished, Shakespeare and Marlowe were prolific; Drake and Raleigh discovered the New World, bringing back tobacco and the potato amongst their treasures; and Edmund Spenser wrote *The Faerie Queene* in Her Majesty's honour.

As befits her regal status and dramatic life, she has been the subject of numerous films, immortalized by actresses ranging from Jean Simmons to Bette Davis, Helen Mirren and Cate Blanchett. In 1998 Judi Dench played the role of queen in *Shakespeare in Love*, and won an Oscar for Best Actress in a Supporting Role, despite only being on-screen for a meagre fourteen minutes.

Elizabeth was not only a dedicated leader, she inspired loyalty in her people as well as those at court: a model for aspiring female leaders and thinkers. Why not watch *Elizabeth* or *Shakespeare in Love* on DVD, or go to the Globe Theatre (providing you are in season) and enjoy an evening at the theatre, just as she would have, before you go out and conquer a man's world?

Elizabeth was a monarch who proved pretty dresses, a persuasive manner and power *could* go together, and though she had a queue of suitors no one was ever fully qualified enough for her. God save the Queen.

Her life and times

You can only imagine how furious Henry VIII was when on 7 September 1533 his second wife Anne Boleyn gave birth to a daughter, Elizabeth. After all the trouble he had gone to – annulling his 'political' marriage to his first wife Catherine of Aragon (the first ever divorce in the UK), creating new legislation so he could marry Boleyn (well, she refused to sleep with him until he did), splitting with the Pope, Rome and the Church, all this hell, fire and damnation – she couldn't even provide a male heir. Bother. Little did he know the flame-haired child that he rejected would grow up with his fiery temper and ruthless determination, outstrip his popularity as a monarch and add glory to his legacy.

When Boleyn continued to fail in producing a male heir, and boy was she trying everything, Henry accused her of incest, adultery and witchcraft (all charges were false, but he was the absolute monarch, absolutely fed up and, if truth were told, he was keen to marry his new mistress who was already pregnant, and, fingers crossed . . .) He had Boleyn executed for treason on 19 May 1536. Elizabeth was two years old when she went from being the 'heiress presumptive' to the banished and illegitimate 'Lady Elizabeth'. Though she barely knew her mother she had many of Boleyn's characteristics: she was resilient, charismatic, glamorous, as well as neurotic and flirtatious, all of which would prove useful in politics. Never underestimate the fairer sex.

It wasn't until Henry was married to his sixth and final wife, Catherine Parr, that Elizabeth and her half-sister Mary (from Henry's first marriage to Catherine of Aragon) were reconciled with Daddy and brought back to court. Henry had had a son with his third wife Jane Seymour, so the line of succession was safe and there was no harm in having two daughters as back-up. When Henry died in 1547, Parr became Dowager Queen and (Uncle) Edward Seymour became Lord Protector of England, while Henry's golden child, and Elizabeth's half-brother, Edward VI, grew into his crown. He was only ten years old at the time. Young orphan Elizabeth went to live with stepmother Parr and Parr's new husband

Thomas Seymour (another of Jane's brothers). She had been reinstated to the line of succession in her father's last will and testament which meant favour at court. However, Parr turned against Elizabeth when she discovered her husband had made moves on the young princess. The incident tarnished Elizabeth's reputation – though she was totally innocent – and made her even more mistrustful of men.

Maybe she was too smart or too modern-thinking? Elizabeth was a keen scholar like her father. Though he wasn't a hands-on dad (and didn't allow her in his courtly presence) Henry had at least ensured that she and her sister had an education equal to that of their brother. She could read and speak six languages: English, French, Latin, Greek, Spanish and Italian. Under the influence of stepmother Parr she was raised a Protestant but wisely kept as religiously neutral as possible knowing the trouble this caused.

In 1553 her sickly half-brother Edward VI died, aged only fifteen, unmarried and with no heirs. Problem. In his will he was advised to name his cousin, the Protestant Lady Jane Grey, queen instead of his sisters. Poor Lady Jane was a pawn used by Lord Protector Seymour to try and keep his power but England was not fooled, and her reign lasted only nine days. The two sisters united (a rare occurrence) to claim the throne and rode triumphantly into London, backed by an army and huge popular support.

Mary became Queen, as was her right, and married Philip II of Spain, a strong Catholic political ally. She became known as 'Bloody Mary' for the brutal – and unpopular – way she tried to restore Catholicism to the country; essentially it was a 'disagree and die' method. As the sole surviving Protestant heir, Elizabeth's name was constantly used in plots to overthrow her sister's reign of terror. Mary had no option but to arrest and force her sister to enter the Tower of London, of all places, via Traitor's Gate. Elizabeth was imprisoned in the tower where her mother had been beheaded, but with no heir of her own, even Mary was reluctant to kill her sister. Things relaxed a bit when Mary thought she was finally pregnant and the Catholic line of succession seemed to be assured. Relieved, Elizabeth returned to Hatfield, albeit it under house arrest. But the pregnancy was a false alarm. In fact, it was an ovarian cyst that would eventually kill Mary.

On 17 November 1558 news of her sister's death reached Elizabeth

and she is reported to have said, 'It is the Lord's doing, and it is marvellous in our eyes.' Finally she was in charge, she was her own boss – and she was the boss of England too. The underdog had won against all the odds. England rejoiced. Elizabeth had survived and, aged twenty-five, was Queen of England.

Elizabeth's coronation took place on 15 January 1559. Her first priority was to calm the fraught religious situation, and restore peace and tranquillity amongst her subjects. Top on everyone else's list was the subject of whom she was going to marry – some things never change.

When Catherine Parr died Elizabeth had managed to avoid her arrogant stepfather's lecherous advances, but now she had propositions from her former Catholic brother-in-law, Philip II, to contend with. Perhaps it was the appalling example her father had set, or perhaps it was because the man she really loved was of lower rank; either way she opted out and stayed single.

The man she was said to have been deeply in love with was Robert Dudley, the Earl of Leicester. 'The course of true love never did run smooth', to quote her contemporary, Shakespeare. Dudley was already married (his wife Amy later died in very suspicious circumstances) and the Council would never approve of him, not only because of his first marriage but because of his father's involvement with getting Lady Jane Grey on the throne. 'You are like my little dog,' she told him. 'When people see you, they know I am nearby.' But that was as far as the relationship could go. Duty rather than Dudley. When Dudley died she was devastated and always kept an envelope marked 'His Last Letter' on her desk.

The only other real contender for her hand was Francis Duke of Alençon, later Anjou, but after the disaster of her father's political marriages, and the unpopularity of Mary's foreign union, she decided to give him a miss too. Plus, in a *pre*-pre-nup era, it would have cost her much of the Tudor fortune in dowry had she decided to tie the knot. No, it was just her and England.

Just as it became accepted that she would never marry she caught smallpox, which in those days could be fatal. Parliament freaked out about the lack of an heir and renewed the pressure for her to find a husband, or at least to name an heir. The Queen was furious and all the obvious heirs to her throne also had disadvantages:

Mary, Queen of Scots – a Catholic. England was still recovering from the *other* 'Something about Mary'.

Lady Catherine Grey – had married without her consent. *Nil points.*

Lord Huntingdon – a Puritan who didn't want the job. Hopeless.

The religious issue continued to cause major headaches, particularly when uprisings involved her cousin Mary, Queen of Scots. As the Catholics' last claim to the throne, the young widow of the King of France, Francis II, had once herself been a major contender to marry Elizabeth's brother, Edward VI. They would have united England and Scotland, Catholic and Protestant, job done, but he'd died young and she had gone to France to be married. Since her return Elizabeth had offered Mary countless chances to stop being a nuisance and convert to the Protestant faith, including the opportunity to marry her beloved Earl of Leicester when the young Catholic widow returned to Scotland. Can't say fairer than that, but no, Mary wouldn't do it. Elizabeth was forced to imprison and later execute her cousin. Rivalry is so much easier to deal with when you can behead the opponent, don't you think?

Leaving affairs of the heart aside, Elizabeth achieved much in affairs of State. She wanted to concentrate on building England up, focusing on consolidating its wealth at home rather than warring abroad. Imagine her surprise when her former brother-in-law and ally, Philip II, turned against her, pitting the Spanish Armada against England? Luckily her navy outwitted and defeated Spain, a victory which made Elizabeth even more popular.

To celebrate she commissioned a portrait of herself, hand on a globe, victorious fleet in the background, and wearing an elaborate dress of pearls, pink bows and ruffles. Portraits were the era's propaganda and paparazzi fodder, albeit in oils, and Elizabeth used them to communicate to her country her victories, wealth, success and, of course, incomparable beauty. As she grew older the wigs remained her signature flaming-red colour, her pox-scarred face was painted with white lead

and vinegar, her cheeks rouged with red dye and egg white and, where her rotten teeth had been pulled out, she stuffed rags into her mouth to fill out her cheeks. No wonder she is rumoured to have banned all mirrors towards the end of her life.

She died on 24 March 1603 at Richmond Palace. On her deathbed she named James I (son of Mary, Queen of Scots) as her successor, saying, 'Who but a King could follow a Queen.' Sadly he was no match for her legacy.

Her Majesty's mottos

'I would rather be a beggar and single than a queen and married.'

'I know I have the body of a weak and feeble woman, but I have the heart and stomach of a king, and of a king of England too.'

'I thank God I am endowed with such qualities that if I were turned out of the Realm in my petticoat I were able to live in any place in Christendom.'

'To be a king and wear a crown is a thing more glorious to them that see it than it is pleasant to them that bear it.'

5th April

In 1976 the reclusive billionaire (pioneer of aviation as well as engineer, industrialist and film producer) Howard Hughes died in Houston. He was one of America's wealthiest men. Why not watch one of his films or the story of his life as captured in *The Aviator*?

7th April

The poet William Wordsworth was born today in 1770. Wordsworth, along with Samuel Taylor Coleridge, helped launch the English Romantic Movement in literature.

Born in the Lake District, Wordsworth captured his love of nature, landscapes and England in his verse.

> I wandered lonely as a cloud
> That floats on high o'er vales and hills,
> When all at one I saw a crowd,
> A host, of golden daffodils;
> Beside the lake, beneath the trees
> Fluttering and dancing in the breeze.

Wordsworth was named English Poet Laureate 1843–50.

The post of Poet Laureate was created in England in 1616 by James I for writer Ben Jonson. It is the job of the Poet Laureate to provide a poem for all State and government events plus grand occasions. Past poets who have held this title include John Betjeman and Ted Hughes.

How to recite poetry

There is more to life than reading emails and texts, so go and find some more inspired lines. Whether writing or reading poetry, respect the rhythm as much as the words and meaning. There is a world of difference between reading poems and reading the newspaper and you'll feel much better for a bit of poetic enlightenment.

Poems on the Underground, published by Cassell, offer over ten editions of the most well-loved, well-known verses as well as some nice new ditties. Come on. Poetry is not just a high-school thing. Poetry is perfect for a ride on the District Line or a walk in the park.

Great poets to dip into include:
W.H. Auden, William Blake, Lewis Carroll, Emily Dickinson, T.S. Eliot, Gerard Manley Hopkins, Ted Hughes, John Keats, Rudyard Kipling, Edward Lear, Sylvia Plath, Siegfried Sassoon, Dylan Thomas, Philip Larkin.

Poetry is great for any aspiring songwriters, and romantics should keep a couple of well-known classics up their sleeve as well as learn the secret formulas, so that they can produce their own for the object of their affection and inspiration. Jerry Hall and Sophie Dahl are both examples of beautiful models turned poets and prove that it isn't an outdated hobby only to be pursued once you reach rocking-chair age. Get into it while you still have all your own teeth.

Start your new-found poetic personality by picking up *Catching Life by the Throat: How to Read Poetry and Why* by Josephine Hart. You can get it on CD with poetry readings by names such as Roger Moore on Rudyard Kipling and Ralph Fiennes doing W.H. Auden. Hart says: 'Poetry is a trinity of sound, sense and sensibility [and] gives voice to experience in a way no other literary art form can.' Hmmm. She goes on to say, 'It has never let me down. Ever. Without poetry I would have found life less comprehensible, less bearable and infinitely less enjoyable.'

Well, how can you say you're still not sure you want to give this a try? Come on, get as much culture as you have chic.

Note: Poems are different from sonnets – they are more free flowing and have unlimited verses. For sonnet rules and rhymings turn to Shakespeare, master of the style, on 23 April.

Practise reciting Wordsworth's classic poem out loud. Don't read it, *say* it. Do it in a normal voice, not with an actor-like inflection. Pause where the commas are rather than when the line ends. Poetry is laid out not to throw you, but to encourage the rhymes to stand out (for example notice *cloud* and *crowd* in the Wordsworth poem).

'I wandered lonely as a cloud that floats on high o'er vales and hills.' If you read it without taking a breath at the end of the line it starts to make more sense. A slight pause at the end of each laid-out line (after cloud) gives a subtle emphasis to the meaning and encourages the rhythm to flow. If you still can't imagine anything more excruciating than a poetry recital, watch the 1989 film classic *Dead Poets Society*, where Robin Williams plays the batty English Professor John Keating who inspires students to love poetry and to '*carpe diem*' ('seize the day'). This will be far more poetically inspiring (and uplifting) than the tragic tale of *Sylvia*, the 2003 film based on Ted Hughes' poet wife Sylvia Plath.

8th April

Gautama Buddha, spiritual teacher and founder of Buddhism, was born in 563 BC in what is now Nepal. He was a prince with a life of riches, but he left his privileged background to seek the truth of human existence.

Buddhism is one of the oldest and most widespread faiths in the world. It began in India around the fifth century BCE and is founded on teachings rather than a god or gods. Buddhism aims to bring a person to a closer state of awareness, conquer suffering and distress, and ultimately to reach the 'enlightened state' that was experienced by Buddha himself.

Buddhism teaches morality, enlightenment and practising wisdom. The contemplation/meditation focuses on Four Noble Truths:

1. Suffering exists.
2. Suffering arises from attachment to desires.
3. Suffering ceases when attachment to desire ceases.
4. Freedom from suffering is possible by practising the *Eightfold Path*.

Famous Buddhists include:
David Bowie, Leonard Cohen, Richard Gere, Goldie Hawn, George Lucas, Keanu Reeves and Patti Smith.

Films with Buddhist characters include:
> *The Golden Child*, 1986, starring Eddie Murphy.
> *Point Break*, 1991, starring Patrick Swayze and Keanu Reeves.
> *Seven Years in Tibet*, 1997, starring Brad Pitt.

Easter and Passover

In western Christianity Easter falls on a Sunday between 22 March and 25 April, while eastern Christianity follows the Gregorian date system and it could fall any time between 4 April and 8 May.

Passover and Easter are calculated using a lunar calendar similar to an ancient Hebrew calendar that refuses to conform to modern-day scheduling. You need to check when the date falls in your current diary, or on the Internet, before booking your spring holiday break.

Passover is the Jewish holiday that celebrates the Exodus and the children of Israel's freedom from slavery in ancient Egypt. Passover marks the birth of the Jewish nation. It is one of the most important feast days in their calendar.

Easter marks the end of Lent, which started forty days earlier on Ash Wednesday, and most importantly commemorates the resurrection of Jesus Christ. The Sunday before Easter is known as Palm Sunday, and the last three days of Lent are Maundy Thursday, when the Last Supper took place on the feast of Passover, Good Friday, the day of the Judas kiss, betrayal and crucifixion, and Holy Saturday. This all culminates on Easter Sunday, when Christians celebrate Jesus rising from the dead.

Easter brings many traditions and the best ones are edible. Eggs were originally given as a symbol of rebirth, resurrection and new life, though it could be argued a Cadbury's Creme Egg can give as much pleasure as a new life. How do you eat yours?

Hot cross buns (those sweet spiced buns with a white pastry cross on top) have pagan roots. The Aztecs and Incas considered buns sacred food for the gods and thought the cross represented the four ancient quarters of the moon. Others believed the cross prevented sickness and held supernatural powers. Christians, on seeing the cross, decided to adopt the bun as their own and made it a symbol of the events of Good Friday. The bun-toasting tradition dates back to the twelfth century and is still the most popular thing to eat at Easter time today.

But, as every Judy Garland and Fred Astaire aficionado knows, Easter Sunday is when you can see the Easter Parade (live if you're in New York, on television if not). You can't just let yourself go gorging on eggs, you have to step outside as well.

The New York Easter Parade started in 1870 and all the ladies would don pretty bonnets and gentlemen their Sunday best. Together they would walk from St Thomas's Church to St Luke's Church in their finest. Don't let location or religion stop you from creating your own Easter bonnet.

How to make an Easter bonnet
by Stephen Jones, milliner

'In your Easter bonnet, with all the frills upon it, You'll be the grandest lady in the Easter parade . . .' Irving Berlin's evocative lyrics describe mid-nineteenth-century New York.

This parade is a true red, white and blue occasion, on a par with Labor Day and Thanksgiving, but these patriotic shades are not the colours that you should be wearing for your local Easter parade. Yellow is the symbolic Easter colour, for everything from Simnel cake or eggy trimmings to home decor, but in particular your Easter bonnet. A bonnet should be pretty with a touch of winsome naivety; anything too outré should be remaindered for Halloween.

Start with an old straw hat (men's, women's, children's, holiday, etc.) and then plan your trim, as that's really what an Easter bonnet is all about. You probably have everything at home already but not in yellow

. . . Buy Dylon dyes and overdye fabrics and trims in the microwave (instructions at *www.dylon.com*).

The best yellow dye, according to my assistant Lesley, who has dyed everything from chiffon dresses for Dior Haute Couture to Kylie's feathers, is Dylon's Golden Glow. So that should be your golden hue too.

Try and stick to only a few decorative elements, not a 'more is more' frightmare.

For *eggsample*:

A cute miniature bunny with flowers and ribbons.
Yellow feathers with Smarties (fab for polka dots).
Glam yellow silk and gold sequins.
Yellow tulle with white daisies (for the Lady of the Manor look).

For me the ultimate trim has to be crêpe paper. Today is the perfect occasion to indulge in it. I remember I was first introduced to it by the children's TV programme *Blue Peter*, where a series of improbable toys were fashioned from crêpe paper (along with yoghurt pots and toilet rolls). I have made paper hats for many people including Lulu, John Galliano, Anna Piaggi and *Vogue* magazine. It has a spontaneity which is both charming and dramatic. Crêpe paper can be stuck on card for a complete hat but your bonnet could be just a giant bow or a cluster of paper pom-poms (very Giles Deacon). For trims, expressive crêpe-paper flowers look fabulous if you give them a couture twist, by adding extra petals of tulle or organza to give the paper lightness and delicacy. If you are making crêpe-paper streamers, match them with taffeta, while home-dyed velvet ribbon can look sumptuous contrasting with crêpe-paper frilling. But the real joy is that crêpe paper can be simply glued together, so anyone can do it, and will have the personal charm that I was insisting on earlier. Make something of which you are proud, pin it on your dressing table and on a drab dark November afternoon it will remind you of a sunny Easter morning. Who says bonnets are just for springtime?

12th April

England adopted the Union Jack as its national flag today in 1606.

The flag combined:

The flag of England – St George's Cross, white with red horizontal cross.

The flag of Scotland – St Andrew's Cross, blue with white diagonal cross.

The flag of Ireland – St Patrick's Cross, white with red diagonal cross.

14th April

Classical music composer George Handel died in London, 1759.

George Frideric Handel, son of a barber-surgeon, studied law, at least until his father died. He then became a full-time composer and musician. While living in London he wrote his famous *Water Music* suite, which was no doubt inspired by the English obsession with the weather. Handel loved London and settled here having secured a £200-a-year pension for life from Queen Anne (considered a grand old sum at the time). Following a stroke he went on to publish his greatest musical legacy, his *Messiah*, in 1742.

His influence on Haydn, Mozart and Beethoven in the transition from Baroque to Classical is very clear, so don't neglect him. Make sure you have at least one of his tunes playing on your iPod today.

15th April

You know, of course, the 1997 film, but today is the date the 'unsinkable' RMS *Titanic* did just that – on its maiden voyage to New York in 1912.

At 11.40 p.m. she struck an iceberg 400 miles off Newfoundland, Canada.

There were 2,228 passengers and crew, and 20 lifeboats – the maths was never going to add up. Only 705 were rescued, while the others perished in the icy temperatures, and the cargo of over $600 million sunk in the worst ever transatlantic tragedy.

19th April

'Folly loves the martyrdom of fame,' sighed George Byron, Sixth Baron Byron, the flamboyant Anglo-Scottish poet who died on this date in 1884.

Read his poem *Don Juan*, one of his most famous works about a kindred spirit who remarked, 'truth is always strange; stranger than fiction'.

21st April

On this date Queen Elizabeth II was born in 1926, eldest daughter of Albert, Duke of York, and his wife, Lady Elizabeth Bowes-Lyon. Initially no one would have guessed she would become queen, but no one predicted that her uncle, Edward VIII, would abdicate to marry Mrs Wallis Simpson causing Elizabeth's father to ascend to the throne.

Also on this day in 753 BC Romulus and Remus founded Rome.

According to legend, when vestal virgin and high priestess Rhea Silvia was raped by Mars, god of war, she conceived twins. When they were born she was killed, as having children was against the vows she'd taken, but the newborns were smuggled to safety. The boys were abandoned by the banks of the river Tiber and left to fend for themselves. Legend says a she-wolf found the babies and suckled them with her own milk until an old shepherd, Faustolo, discovered them and decided to raise them.

The boys grew up strong, clever and healthy and decided to build a town on the Palatine Hill, on the site where they had been rescued. On this date they marked out the borders. Unfortunately they had inherited their father's fiery temperament and a bitter argument broke out. Remus was murdered by his brother Romulus who then assumed sole reign and named the city after himself – Roma.

How to be house proud

Wherever you live – whether a dungeon or dormitory or that detached dream home nestled among acres of woodland with a white picket fence – April is the month to look at sprucing things up with more vigour than the usual plumping of the cushions and dusting of the skirting boards.

Setting the scene, keeping it clean and creating the right ambience is one thing but how can you be house proud when everything starts to come crashing down around you?

There are two types of home improvement: those you choose to do and those that choose to happen to you.

The latter can be avoided if you are a builder, a structural engineer, a mind reader, or all three. Acts of God tend to happen when you least expect them, or budget for them. The trick is damage limitation, and that includes everything from neighbours from hell to paperwork.

What are you getting into?

Try and discover problems before you inherit them. Leaks and cracks need to be sorted out sooner rather than later – the saying 'a stitch in time saves nine' really does apply here.

If you are buying a home you'll find it is like a relationship, and requires all sorts of searches similar to a pre-nup. Check how much damage previous owners have done or ignored. Rising damp or rotten floors are never that romantic. Surveyors are there to find all skeletons in the closet, so to speak.

Forewarned is forearmed.

Of course, no one (sane) wants a ceiling to cave in, a radiator to explode or cowboys to install the boiler and then proceed to knock down half the front of the house. That said, it can and does happen. Are you ready?

Check mate

When buying a house/flat/box, make sure you've ticked off everything on the checklist of chores and structural issues before you say 'I do' and sign on the dotted line. A moment or two now will save you a (nervous) break-down in a few months time.

> Do you know where all your paperwork is?
> Do you have your insurance details?
> Who supplies your gas?
> Your electricity?
> Your water?
> Do you know where all the account details are?

Put all these somewhere safe and easy to find. Keep the lease agreement, share of freehold, and communal as well as personal insurance documents here too. Finally, make a note of the names of solicitors, estate agents and any other grown-up details you might need at a later stage.

Get insured

For flats and shared homes you need to have joint building insurance and individual contents insurance.

In a nutshell building insurance applies to the bricks and mortar of the property: the roof, the guttering, the stairs, the walls, the things that stay when you go. This includes windows, central heating, creaking doors and anything structural. In conversions this also involves any communal areas such as stairwells and hallways.

The contents insurance is down to you, and *for* you. This covers the tables, chairs, cookers, shoes – all the things you can take with you if you move.

There are a few grey areas, but check with your insurers before chipping off the pretty cornicing as a souvenir.

The nuts and bolts of the building industry

When talking about builders you need to be armed with the right advice before giving them 'carte blanche' on your home improvements.

Check the following before they so much as pick up a hairbrush (let alone a hammer) in your property.

- Does your builder have valid insurance cover? This is the single most important thing to know before employing a builder. If your builder is not insured for mistakes or accidents then you are liable, and it is unlikely that your house insurance will provide sufficient insurance if things go wrong.
- Do they have any industry accreditations (these will usually be displayed on the letterhead)? Look out for Constructiononline, National Britannia Safe Contractor, QMS (Quality Management Systems) and The Guild of Master Craftsmen. *www.houseprofessionals.com* is an easy way to find vetted and qualified builders, plumbers and electricians. It also offers free quotes.

Note: Only those installing gas and electrical appliances require industry qualifications to work. Electricians must hold an Institute of Electrical Engineers '16th Edition' qualification. For gas or boiler repairs or installation use only a Corgi-registered contractor. For details look on *www.corgi-direct.com* – which also lists those who have been removed from their register. A Corgi certificate is renewed every two years, so check your boys haven't gone past their sell-by date.

- Does your builder work within the constraints of the industry and the law? Is he licensed to carry waste; can he remove your asbestos or any other dangerous waste?
- Does your builder come recommended? Who by?
- Get a quote in writing and in advance. This includes all parts and materials as well as the cost of labour. Ask them to give you a time estimate as well. Don't forget to add VAT into the calculations. Agree this cost in advance. Do *not* let them get creative – washing machines should never go on wheels, grouting is not glue that can do anything other than stick tiles. If they are there to fix

a crack in the ceiling this is a three-day job (tops). Don't let them keep finding opportunities for you to put all seven of their children through school (without at least getting one child named after you). Likewise, if you find a goodie – it's like dating, there is a lot of crap at first – hold onto them, even if they do need constant chivvying and calls to pin them down for a start and finish date. Men – it's always the same.

- Check you're speaking the same language. If picking a builder that doesn't share your mother tongue, check there is a go-between whom you can ask questions and who will give an accurate reply. Understanding each other is tricky enough in plain English when it comes to piping, plastering and plumbing – don't make the agony any worse or more prolonged.

- The customer (you) is always right. Even though they have taken over your home and the rooms are hidden under dust sheets, you are the key holder/bill payer and it is your name on the mortgage – only let them kick you out for an agreed amount of time. It may not feel like you are the boss any longer but you are. If you want psychedelic walls, that's your prerogative. Note: if you are paying peanuts you get monkeys; by the same token do you need Michelangelo painting your ceiling for four years?

- Be sure they use your colour. Even if you're not going to paint your walls yourself you need to choose the colours. There are millions of shades of white – make sure your decorator gets the white with the right hint of whatever you've chosen before the painting process begins. Set up a project where you both know what to expect (more or less).

- Never pay more than half up front. You want them to come back and finish the job, don't you?

23rd April

Today is the day to fly the flag for England with as much gusto as you would for an English World Cup Final, because not only is today St George's Day but on this day William Shakespeare was born in 1564. It is also said he died on this same day in 1616 which was very tidy of him.

St George is the patron saint of England and his shield of a red cross on a white background still makes up the flag of England, and is what all devoted football fans, crusaders and sports fanatics wave about.

St George was a Roman solider who lived in the third century and was against torturing Christians simply because of their beliefs. He became particularly popular and inspiring to the soldiers during the Crusades.

The most famous story about St George tells of his heroic killing of a dragon and saving a damsel in distress.

The Golden Legend describes a dragon that lived near a lake near Silene, Libya. Armies and all sorts were trying to shoo it away to no avail, and every day the dragon came down and would eat two sheep at a time when mutton was scarce. When the sheep ran out, the dragon started to gobble up people, and on the particular day that George rode into town the dragon was about to serve himself up a pretty princess. George crossed himself, rode into battle on his trusted steed and slew the beast with a single blow. The locals rejoiced – as did, I imagine, the princess – and converted to Christianity in honour of the knight and out of respect for his God who had saved them.

How to brush up your Shakespeare

William Shakespeare is arguably the most famous playwright (and poet) ever; his works and words are the most quoted in the world. He is considered to be England's greatest writer; the fact that his work has survived and retained its popularity for some 400 years is proof.

Church records show he was baptized on 26 April 1564 so it is assumed he was born a few days earlier, most likely on the twenty-third (but don't forget this era followed the Julian not the Gregorian calendar so the timing might not be quite accurate).

People often refer to him as 'the Bard', which literally means 'the poet'. In 1769 actor David Garrick wrote: 'For the bard of all bards was a Warwickshire Bard,' and the nickname stuck.

His father, John Shakespeare, was a glove-maker and town official, who rose to Bailiff/Mayor in 1568. His mother, Mary Arden, was the daughter of gentry so clearly this was a love match as it wasn't exactly considered sensible for a girl to marry below her class.

Shakespeare was educated at a grammar school, pretty intense by today's standards. School would start between six and seven in the morning with an hour for lunch, no physical education, and went on until five or six every evening. There were no holidays and no weekends off, and Sunday had to be totally dedicated to church-going. No wonder only the wealthy could afford to let their children study rather than bring home the bacon for their family.

Aged eighteen, Shakespeare married Anne Hathaway, on 28 November 1582. She was twenty-six and three months pregnant with their first child, who was born and baptized Susanna on 26 May 1583. Anne was to be his long-suffering wife who stayed in Stratford while he was up in London seeking fame and fortune (and all sorts, if you believe *Shakespeare in Love*). They went on to have twins Hamnet and Judith, baptized on the 2 February 1585, but Hamnet died in 1596 (and yes, his son's death was a major influence on his great play Hamlet).

His early life is referred to as 'the lost years' as there are very few records of his time in Stratford.

Around 1592 the playwright moved to London and two years later was part-owner of – as well as actor and playwright for – the most celebrated players of the time, 'the Lord Chamberlain's Men'. They were named after their main patron and were a favourite of Elizabeth I who would often insist on attending opening nights for a new Shakespeare play. Such was their success that when James I came to the throne in 1603 he claimed the company as his own, renaming them 'the King's Men'. Well you don't say 'no' to a royal warrant, do you?

In 1599 The Globe Theatre was built as the players' permanent theatrical home. All the groupies knew where to go and ticket sales soared. But disaster struck when in 1613 the theatre was destroyed by fire, due to its thatched roof. The Globe was rebuilt in 1614 but closed in 1642 due to plague, poverty and politics. What remained was finally demolished in 1644.

In 1997 Hollywood actor Sam Wanamaker had finally raised enough funds to orchestrate the renaissance of the Globe and lovingly opened a modern reconstruction. Faithful to the original, with a few extra fire and safety features added, it was built on the exact same site. There is standing room for the 'peasants' and benches for the 'gentry'. Be sure to opt for the gentry option; standing for a three-hour drama might have been how they did it, but the modern-day theatre buff might find this hard to endure.

Shakespeare's plays, though popularly performed in his lifetime, were not edited and published in a full folio until after his death, in 1623. It was John Heminges and Henry Condell, both actors with him in the Lord Chamberlain's Men, who gathered the collection of all his scripts together. The exact chronological order is vague, because he would constantly re-edit and tweak the scripts as they were performed. It wasn't until after his death that a definitive version could be fixed upon. If only he had insisted on royalties for all his descendents.

The works are mainly divided into three groups:

The comedies
A Midsummer Night's Dream
All's Well That Ends Well
As You Like It
Cymbeline
Love's Labour's Lost
Measure for Measure
Much Ado About Nothing
Pericles
The Comedy of Errors
The Merchant of Venice
The Merry Wives of Windsor

The Taming of the Shrew
The Tempest
The Two Gentlemen of Verona
The Two Noble Kinsmen
The Winter's Tale
Twelfth Night
Troilus and Cresida

The histories

The Famous History of the Life of King Henry VIII
The First Part of King Henry IV
The First Part of King Henry VI
The Life of King Henry V
The Life and Death of King John
The Rape of Lucrece
The Second Part of King Henry IV
The Second Part of King Henry VI
The Third Part of King Henry VI
The Tragedy of King Richard II
The Tragedy of King Richard III
Venus and Adonis

The tragedies

Antony and Cleopatra
Coriolanus
Hamlet
Julius Caesar
King Lear
Macbeth
Othello
Romeo and Juliet
Timon of Athens
Titus Andronicus

For sonnet's sake

In addition to writing plays, Shakespeare was also a prolific poet. He wrote 154 sonnets, 26 addressed to 'The Dark Lady' and 126 to 'The Fair Lord'.

As well as people probing into his personal affairs, and trying to identify exactly *who* he penned these sonnets for, some scholars have even questioned if he was in fact the author of all these great works. Conspiracy theories abound, suggesting writers such as Francis Bacon and Christopher Marlowe provided the talent, or perhaps the 17th Earl of Oxford, Edward de Vere, or even Queen Elizabeth I.

A sonnet is a fourteen-line lyric poem written in iambic pentameter following a strict rhyme scheme. The word originally comes from the Italian for 'little song' – *sonnetto*. Eugh. Now, before you drop the book in horror, panic ye not. Keep going. Iambic pentameter is merely the name of the most commonly used meter in poetry, an unstressed syllable followed by a stressed syllable. Put simply:

Da-DUM da-DUM da-DUM da-DUM da-DUM

If this brings on a total wobble replace the da-dums with words. Look at Shakespeare's Sonnet XVIII, which fits the structure perfectly:

Shall I compare thee to a summer's day?
Thou art more lovely and more temperate:
Rough winds do shake the darling buds of May,
And summer's lease hath all too short a date:

Lovely. This is a perfect iambic pentameter masterclass.

The original formula comes from classical Greek poetry but Shakespeare was such the undisputed wizard that once he'd mastered this he pretty much threw the rule book out of the window and started to adapt things to his own needs. It became known as the English or Shakespearian sonnet.

You also have the option of the Italian (Petrarchan) and Spenserian sonnets.

Sign up for a sonnet a day from the Bard at *www.sonnetaday.com* and inject a bit of inspiration and education into your email routine each morning.

Start with Shakespeare and yours will follow; don't always dumb things down – especially not today.

Quoting the Bard

Shakespeare's words remain the most iconic in literature but how many of his lines do you know beyond the immortal: 'Romeo, Romeo, wherefore art thou Romeo?'

Did you know that it was the Bard who first coined these phrases –

'brave new world'
'I'll not budge an inch'
'It's Greek to me'
'We have seen better days'
'Into thin air'

– as well as giving us such sage advice from *Hamlet as* 'Neither a borrower, nor a lender be; for loan oft loses both itself and friend, and borrowing dulls the edge of husbandry.'

And of course the most understated, yet oh-so-true saying: 'The course of true love never did run smooth.'

Rather than running up a phone bill, or watching re-runs on the telly, why not see for yourself why his words have survived and read a play of his tonight? Then you can write a list of your own words of wisdom.

26th April

Lord Nelson's mistress, Emma Hamilton, was born in 1765.

Originally christened Amy Lyon, daughter of a Cheshire blacksmith, Emma went on to become one of the most famous muses, classical beauties and mistresses of her day.

When she first moved to London she earnt her way as a 'living illustration' and her beauty was to become celebrated when she captivated artist George Romney, whom she sat for over a hundred times. When her aristocratic lover Greville palmed her off with his aged uncle, Sir William Hamilton, she called everyone's bluff and married the old guy. They didn't see that coming, but as well as his older partner she'd graduated to an old master of oils too and was painted by the great artist Reynolds.

But it was her passionate affair with heroic Lord Nelson that she is most remembered for. They met in 1793 in Naples and she reportedly fainted when she saw him (not because he had lost an arm and most of his teeth; it was more of a swoon and a 'wow, love at first sight' type of faint).

A hot affair quickly followed and as he was such a war hero everyone politely, and so Englishly, turned a blind eye to this infidelity, choosing to ignore the fact that the two were both married (and not to each other). Emma gave birth to their child, a daughter, Horatia, on 31 January 1801. They lived as though they were married in Merton, South London where many local pubs, hospitals and street names still bear their names.

In 1803 Emma's actual husband, the aged Sir William, died. Nelson returned to sea and Emma was left pregnant with their second child, who died after a few weeks.

It was the beginning of the end.

She distracted herself by drinking, gambling and spending all she had inherited from her husband. In 1805 Nelson died, and the provision Nelson had insisted the government made for his mistress, a last request, was 'accidentally' ignored; they weren't married so there was no legal binding.

Emma Hamilton was reviled in England and was forced to flee to France to escape her creditors, turning increasingly to drink. She was disowned by her daughter, and died of liver failure in poverty in Calais, January 1815.

Page Turner

A Pair of Blue Eyes
Thomas Hardy

Why

First published in 1874, it is one of Hardy's earliest novels, and his most autobiographical. It is the re-telling of the love story that changed Hardy's life, persuading him to leave architecture and become a writer. You'll have to read the book to discover if the love-struck trainee gets a happy ending like the author, who went on to become a writer of enormous repute.

Who

Thomas Hardy (2 June 1840–11 January 1928) was born in the parish of Stinsford, East Dorchester. His father was a builder and stone-mason who loved to play the violin, while his mother loved reading and encouraged her son to continue his studies even after his formal education finished. When he was nineteen he became an apprentice to the architect John Hicks. But he gave this up and went on to become one of England's most beloved writers, taking over Dickens' mantle in writing about morals and respectable family life, and then blowing it by having affairs and divorcing his first wife, who inspired this novel and a collection of poems. His next novel *Far from the Madding Crowd*, published a few years later, secured his popularity and was followed by *The Mayor of Casterbridge* in 1886, *Tess of the D'Urbervilles* in 1891 and his great swansong *Jude the Obscure*, which was dubbed 'Jude the Obscene' in its day as it was considered very racy.

The plot

As a trainee architect Hardy travelled to St Juliot, Cornwall, to plan the restoration of the local parish church. Here he met and fell in love with the rector's sister-in-law, Emma Lavinia Gifford. England was on the brink of industrial revolution, and Hardy, in his thirties, was on the cusp of marriage and a major career change. After the success of his next novel he left the architecture practice and became a full-time writer. The hero of this novel, Stephen Smith, is in a similar position. The young trainee draftsman has been sent to sketch Endelstow rectory so his company can restore it. He travels down from London to the remote sea-swept parish and within moments of arriving he meets the girl with blue eyes, Elfride Swancourt, daughter of a clergyman – and everything changes.

Though Smith is training in a gentleman's position he is socially inferior (as Hardy was to Gifford) and despite being an ambitious man set on a successful career path, Elfride's first love will never be good enough to get her father's blessing. Elfride, like many maids of the time, is stuck – she can either marry for love beneath her status, without her father's consent, or make a union to elevate her familys' status and settle with being content.

Smith leaves, resolved to prove himself worthy, and after the counsel of his mentor, the gentleman and scholar Mr Knight, accepts a position oversees and sets off to make his fortune. Elfride is no help in making Smith's choice easy – one moment she is flouting convention and being reckless and romantic, the next she is sobbing and returning to her father. With Smith off to prove himself in India, and her father newly married, there is little for the educated unmarried lass to do, so she spends her time writing a romance novel for young ladies. The book is published, yet when Smith shows the book to his mentor Knight, a literary editor, he savages it in a review (not knowing the significance of the author). Elfride replies to her harshest critic and, through a mutual family acquaintance, they meet and start to form an attachment. But who will she choose when Smith returns? The architect or the gentleman?

Hosting

Hardy sets all his tales in and around his beloved Dorset. A train ride to Hardyland for high tea could be an appropriate and authentic setting for the book club. Hardy was as passionate about the countryside as he was about his poetry and prose. Alternatively, consider somewhere that is sympathetic to his heroines: a tearoom, a library, or Syon House in Brentford, Middlesex near Richmond, Surrey (go to *www.syonpark.co.uk*). Or lay a picnic in the garden and serve a delicate spread of sandwiches, cordials, pink lemonade and fairy cakes – something ethereal for the Elfrides of the group.

Alternative titles would be:

Middlemarch by George Eliot

A Room with a View by E.M. Forster

Wuthering Heights by Emily Brontë

To the Lighthouse by Virginia Woolf

Brideshead Revisited: The Sacred and Profane Memories of Captain Charles Ryder by Evelyn Waugh

Further reading on Thomas Hardy himself could include *Thomas Hardy: The Time-torn Man* by Claire Tomalin

Foot Note

The wellington boot

Essential for April showers, and anyone living in Britain. The gumboot, the wellie, the rubber boot, call it what you will, is indispensable for the rainy season, and what Gene Kelly should have worn when splashin' in the rain. It's a must-have for this month.

It is so named and famed thanks to Arthur Wellesley, first Duke of Wellington. The duke, clearly sick of battling with wet feet, took his favourite hessian boots to his shoemaker and said, 'There's a good fellow, can you modify this design?' The shoemaker, one Hoby of St James's Street, said, 'Yes, of course, sir, leave it with me.' They got rid of the trim, lowered the heel, fitted and tightened it to the leg. It might not have been a fashion statement, but to the soldiers in the ravages of war it was a godsend, and back home the patriotic were also keen to style themselves on the heroic Iron Duke. Across the land demand rose and the name wellington boot stuck.

Though originally made of leather, in 1852 industrialist Hiram Hutchinson met Charles Goodyear (yes, think tyres) who had just invented natural rubber. Before you knew it, they had teamed up and their boot was a lightweight smash hit. Now wellies are not only a fisherman's and farmer's friend, they are a [wise] festival-goer's essential item. Hunters are the Ferrari of the gumboot gang and designers from Chanel to Pucci have made theirs a must-have, though it would be a shame to let those get muddy.

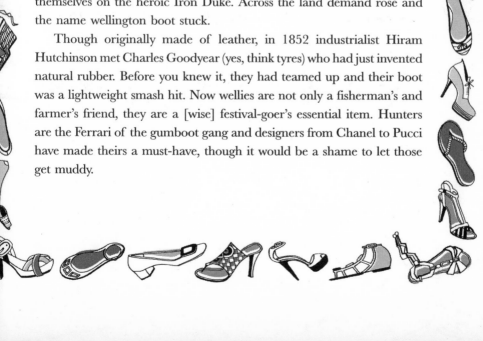

May

'If I could tell you what it meant, there would be no
point in dancing it.'
Isadora Duncan

Wish You Were Here

Giorgio Armani from St Tropez

Thought you'd like a postcard from St Tropez, my ideal Riviera destination. This glamorous, sparkling, sun-drenched port has been home to
so many interesting people over the years – artists and writers in the
thirties and forties (when it was still a fishing village), French existen-
tialists after the war and, of course, the jet set of the sixties and seventies. Mick married Bianca here in 1971 – she wore a white trouser suit
by Yves St Laurent – and the reception was held at the famous Hôtel
Byblos with its pastel-coloured buildings and leafy courtyard and clear
pool. But for me St Tropez will always mean Brigitte Bardot in her
youth, the picture of natural, sensual – and yet somehow innocent –
feminine beauty.

I have a house in St Tropez where I would usually stay. But occa-
sionally I visit St Tropez on my yacht, the *Mariu*, and I sleep with the
sound of the lapping water mingling with the town's own murmurings
– the clinking of glasses and the babble of conversation. My favourite
place for an aperitif is the centrally placed bar, Café de Paris. Alternatively, if I want to do a spot of people watching – always a popular
pastime here – I go to Le Gorille, the bar to be seen at.

Of course St Tropez is all about sun, sea and sand. I like Club 55
– a comfortable central beach club with great staff and service and a
beach restaurant with a simple yet delicious menu. They can even accommodate large groups here. Generally, the best beaches are considered to
be along the coast in the Baie de Pampelonne.

For the evenings it's the famous club, Les Caves du Roy, in the Hôtel
Byblos. This is in the centre of town. It has a great atmosphere and a
disproportionate number of beautiful people and eclectic personalities.

You know, I love this place for all the obvious reasons – the chic prom-
enading visitors, the incredible light, the clear, warm, salty Mediterranean,

the smell of lavender, the bodies beautiful. But I also like it because it is still a little bit bohemian, a little bit wild and mysterious and exotic. I come here to relax and unwind in a beautiful setting. I strongly recommend you join me and do the same.

Lots of love, Giorgio

1st May

May Day – No, this is not a distress signal, but the start of another month with many ways to celebrate. You could dance around a ribboned pole or go to Oxford for a breakfast pint (traditionally pubs open at sunrise to help toast this pagan feast day). In pagan times – a fairly blanket term for 'long, long ago', and an era which lasted until around the eighth century – May Day was celebrated as the first day of spring, but let's face it if the sun hasn't come out by now you really can start to despair. You have two options (no, not with the weather, that is a lost cause): you can either elect a May King and Queen and dance around the maypole (to encourage fertility) or look to another, more black-tie, flash-bulb-popping festival celebrated in May – the Cannes Film Festival.

Also on this day:
  Mozart's *Marriage of Figaro* premiered in Vienna in 1786
  Folies Bergère opened in Paris in 1869
  Citizen Kane premiered in New York in 1941

It's all about entertainment this month.

How to can-Cannes

Those in the movie business will know there is practically a festival for every month, and in every city, so there are ample locations and opportunities to show off your work:

January – Sundance, Utah
February – Berlin
March – Academy Awards, L.A.
April – Festival du Film de Paris
May – Tribeca, New York
June – Moscow
July – Colorado
August – Venice
September – Toronto
October – BFI (BAFTAs), London
December – L'Age d'Or, Brussels

The one they all want to come to and be seen at, however, is Cannes, described as 'the granddaddy of all film festivals' by the *Hollywood Reporter*. If you can get your jet to land in Nice it is but a short jaunt down the coastline.

A brief history

Cannes became host to the film festival in 1939, after the rise of Fascism in Italy put something of a creative gag on the Mostra de Venise (the then Venice film festival). Things really came to a head when the jury overlooked Jean Renoir's *La Grande Illusion* in favour of a Nazi propaganda film made for Goebbels by Mussolini's son, which won the *Coppa Mussolini*, the top prize. It was clear that politics rather than film-making was top of the prize-giving agenda and *La Grande Illusion* was essentially anti-war, so not what the Fascists wanted. Rather than suffer restricted freedom of speech and compromising their artistic integrity at such a sensitive time, a group of key critics and film-makers decided action needed to be taken, and so they headed for the sun and sea of the Riviera.

The affluent town of Cannes was more than happy to host the event, and enjoy the influx of wealthy movie types and their extravagant starry entourages. The film buffs ditched the gondolas and off-screen politics for a bucket and spade, the casinos and all the bling-bling and big bucks that the Hollywood set so love to be around.

Renoir's film, incidentally, became a cinematic smash; Mussolini's vanished without a trace.

While the Oscars give out a little golden man, Cannes is all about the exotic golden palm. The Palme d'Or trophy originated with the Parisian jeweller Suzanne Lazon's interpretation of a sketch done by legendary director Jean Cocteau, and the prize was introduced in 1954.

There was another event that also changed the face of Cannes that year: sex. At a photocall with actor Robert Mitchum and a French starlet, Simone Sylva, the infamous phrase 'get your tits out' was first heckled, and unabashed young Sylva obliged. Now the movie might be forgotten but the technique of securing coverage (through lack of coverage) has become an art form. Mr Mitchum's bemused face was caught in the frame as the first of many men to be upstaged by a pair of the other's assets.

Cannes was soon synonymous with sex, the shocking and scandalous – with a barely bikini-clad Bardot frolicking on the beach much to the delight of all the poised cameras. Girls and good weather (and good films and parties) – how could it not do well?

The Palme d'Or is now regarded as one of the film industry's top prizes, and is one of the highest accolades in film available in Europe, yet since its introduction only one woman has won the top prize so far and that is Jane Campion, in 1993, for her film *The Piano*. In 2006 Penelope Cruz won a prize for Best Actress for her role in the all-female Spanish movie *Volver*. Of course, Best Actress can only be awarded to a female but Best Director and Best Producer are not gender specific so there is definitely room for a female invasion here.

Have you worked out how to write that screenplay yet? Are you ready to show your life on the big screen or press the podcast performance of your life into the palm of someone who can? Press play and pray.

Location, location

Let's start at the top of the wish list when looking for somewhere suitably starry to stay. When you think of Cannes you will probably first think of the iconic Carlton Hotel built along the Croisette. The hotel itself had a starring role as the location for the video of Elton John's 1983 hit 'I'm Still Standing'. It is the hotel along from the quayside where all the yachts of the rich, famous and beautiful can dock. In addition to its pop career it had another major role alongside Cary Grant and Grace Kelly in the Hitchcock classic *To Catch a Thief* and remains, quite frankly, the Ritz of the Riveria – the ultimate address, or picture postcard.

Grace personified

When it comes to Cannes there is one name that stands out as the ultimate icon to emulate. Grace Kelly (12 November 1929–14 September 1982) was a model turned actress whose father was a self-made millionaire, so she was used to the high life but graduated, with honours, to an even more regal status.

While filming *Mogambo* in 1953 she memorably commented, 'What else is there to do if you're alone in a tent in Africa with Clark Gable?' when hounded by the press about her affair with the screen legend. Fair point. The movie earned Kelly an Oscar nomination for Best Supporting Actress, though she was pipped to the post when the award went to Deborah Kerr for her role in *From Here to Eternity* (the one with the famous kiss with Burt Lancaster as they roll in the sand). The affair with Gable was a flash in the pan; her career, however, was on the up and up. She went on to make three films with Alfred Hitchcock (see page 322): *Dial M for Murder*, *Rear Window*, and diamond heist *To Catch a Thief*. She became his ultimate icy blonde.

Kelly starred twice with Bing Crosby, whom she was also rumoured to have had a fling with. They starred in *The Country Girl* for which she won an Academy Award in 1954 and were reunited for what would be her final film, the 1956 musical *High Society*, where they sang the duet 'True Love' that topped the billboard chart. Kelly was major Hollywood A-list – and yes, as well as the accolades and roles, she had a string of A-list lovers, including William Holden and Oleg Cassini, the fashion designer who created Jackie Kennedy's outfits. But despite the glitzy lifestyle she gave up acting and actors in the end – but only because she had found something even better, something even Hollywood hadn't scripted, when she crossed the Atlantic to marry her real life Prince Charming.

On 19 April 1956 she was crowned Her Serene Highness Princess Grace of Monaco when she married the dashing Rainier III, Prince of Monaco. Tragically, though, the fairy tale had an unexpected ending when she died when her car spun off a winding cliff-top road in 1982.

She had become the epitome of royal chic, a real-life Cinderella. She was unforgettable, especially as she had a cult accessory named after her.

The Kelly bag

So named by the French leather luxury goods house Hermès after Grace Kelly appeared on the cover of *Life* magazine in 1956 with the bag. She was not, as it happened, using it as the fashion statement or status symbol it became – she was using it to help conceal the early stages of her pregnancy. The bag was originally created in 1826, but it was so her look, and seemed so chic when she carried it, that the name stuck and all women wanted 'that Kelly bag' so they would own at least a bit of her lifestyle.

The Kelly bag remains one of Hermès' most coveted and sought-after bags, with waiting lists reaching up to two years, and prices starting at a staggering £2,500 for plain leather ... ouch. At least you'll have time to decide which one you want as you save up – they don't offer payment plans. If you really hit the jackpot you can go for styles in excess of £25,000 for exotic skins such as stingray or crocodile. Quality, quality, quality. A man just wouldn't understand the price of being a lady.

Jane Birkin was also immortalized by Hermès in 1981. The actress inadvertently spilled the contents of her too-small bag over the Hermès accessories designer as they were seated together on a plane. The avalanche of its contents inspired the designer to create a big bag with a top flap for added security. This was the start of a trend of iconic endorsements, though these two remain the ultimate in prestige and luxury. On this occasion, a trip to Tiffany's may be cheaper.

2nd May

The great Leonardo da Vinci died in 1519. Legend has it that his last great patron, King Francis I of France, cradled the genius's precious head in his arms as he slipped away.

Born on 15 April 1452, from inauspicious beginnings (he was the illegitimate child of a 25-year-old notary and a peasant girl) da Vinci went on to become an artist, inventor, scientist, architect, mathematician – the ultimate Renaissance man and one of the most exciting minds that ever lived.

If there was ever a day to invent something, today's the day. Da Vinci was said to have invented:

scissors, the stiletto, the aircraft, the bomb, the machine gun, the submarine, and he did several sketches for flying machines, including a very early helicopter.

His paintings were famed for their realism and remain as well known as their creator. *The Last Supper* had a starring role in the film of Dan Brown's *The Da Vinci Code*, which had its world premiere at the Cannes Film Festival on 17 May 2006. The film grossed $224 million on its opening weekend in the US.

His favourite work was the *Mona Lisa* and, though he never signed it, he spent ten years painting her lips just so. It was one of *only three* of his works that he kept, the mysterious eyes privy to all his inventing. The *Mona Lisa*, a teeny thirty by twenty-one inches in oil painted on a wooden panel, has around 1,500 visitors an hour at the Louvre Museum, Paris. The woman's true identity remains a mystery even though she is the most recognized face of her era. Most likely she was the wife of a sixteenth-century Florentine businessman called Francesco del Giocondo and was respectfully called 'Mona', the Italian equivalent of 'Ma'am', but this, like just who her eyes are following, da Vinci never revealed.

If portrait painters are in short supply, the modern-day equivalent in status must be to appear on the cover of a magazine. Who can you get to take your photo today?

How would you want to have your close-up? Shot by whom? How could you capture your spirit in one sitting and sell magazines? Think Princess Diana, Demi Moore and some of *Vanity Fair*'s greatest cover coups.

American's Society of Magazine Editors (ASME's) Top Forty Magazine Covers of the Last Forty Years can be viewed on: *http:www.magazine.org/Editorial/Top_40_Covers/*

How to podcast

A podcast is a bit like iPodding. Essentially it's an audio (and now visual) magazine that you can edit and compile for yourself from radio, live shows, sessions and speeches; from bands to books you create your own repertoire to replay. With the Internet, iTunes and the publishing house in the sky you can compile the playlist of your dreams from TV and radio (with only your favourite bits). Podcasts can play the soundtrack of your mind.

Still not sure? It's really less scary than it sounds. Podcasts play and record what you want to hear. You log on and subscribe to what interests you – like signing up for a newscast to give you bulletins on only the things you want to hear about. All you do is choose whether it is in or out – fashion-wise as much as playlistwise.

Though Apple have adopted the expression, the word 'podcast' actually first appeared in the *Guardian* newspaper on 12 February 2004, and the first ones were available for purchase on 28 June 2005. By December 2005 so many people were curious about them that 'podcast' became a word to be added to the dictionary.

Podcasts are a rapidly expanding field and, just like with the Internet, radio stations and magazines as well as individual authors and musicians are all jumping on the idea, keen to be 'poddy'. By 2010 it's (conservatively) estimated that 45 million people will have listened and subscribed to a podcast at least once, though the figure is expected to be nearer 75 million. Go on – be brave, click on a podcast today. As with things like MySpace and YouTube, once a few people have done it a whole movement has occurred, and before you can say 'pod' there's a new one. Don't be behind on a trend.

Podcasts mean no more waiting for a song you like to come onto the radio. No longer do you have to stay in on a Friday night to see a show you're addicted to, unless you want to, of course. Good grief, you'll have a social life as well as being up to date on all your soaps and songs. Whatever next?

Getting clicky

Are you ready? Firstly, do you want to download an audio or a visual podcast? If you love BBC Radio 4 you could get their podcast, or even be as specific as signing up for one particular show. If you obsess over Harry Potter, he has one, while the National Geographic Channel have done a series called 'I Didn't Know That' which is full of addictive and useless trivia – a worthy first pod-score. Once you've subscribed, every time you click on 'refresh' another ditty downloads.

As for the time limit – there is none. Your options are as big as your hard drive, so, steady on that subscription enthusiasm; leave enough room to store and grow all the goodies. The cost? Well that depends on you – some are free, and some . . . well they are worth the cost.

Once you have mastered downloading it is time to start uploading and creating your own.

Why would you want to upload your own? If you are aspiring to get into the movie business, or to look more techy than your rivals, you should learn how.

You are the author, the editor and the boss – the contents, quotes, interviews and any clips or effects are entirely up to you. Once you have all your content it's easy. The only real 'work' comes before you do the first one and it's plain sailing after this.

Start with setting up an account with iTunes, which you should already have as this is what you use for your iPod purchases. Clear enough computer space to store each podcast – you need megabytes for your brilliance so don't start a stream that you can't finish. Design a logo so you've got a nice image on screen. Image is everything. Think about any special effects and gift-wrapping – cyber style. *Et voilà.*

Once all that's done (which will incur a slight cost) then all you need is a relative who's a camcorder fanatic or a devoted admirer who would be happy to follow you and record your every soundbite. Obviously chop all the crappy bits out and edit it down to a nippy fifteen minutes. (No more Madame Spielberg.) Send it to iTunes and then about twelve hours later, after they do some techy stuff and check the contents are up to scratch, you are live.

Video takes longer to make than audio: you're essentially making a short film, and that means the costs are higher – cameramen, hair, make-up, stylists, more complex editing equipment, image rights, blah blah blah – but even Hitchcock had to start somewhere. Go on, think L'Oréal: 'you're worth it'. Open iTunes, click on iTunes store, then click on Podcasts and have a look at what's around to get ideas. Once you have a film as short as your skirt you can wander around with your latest pitch in the palm of your hand – so much nicer than lugging portfolios and so forth up to town. Just remember, when putting a podcast out on the net, copyright it first as once it's out there any Tom, Dick or Harry can download it. For the nitty gritty go to *www.how-to-podcast-tutorial.com.*

Throwing fabulous ideas onto the web can attract lots of unexpected and new fans, so it is a very handy bit of modern-day PR. The podcast is your entertainment as well as your future: one side is for you to compile your own 'best of' soundtrack; the other is to show off all you have achieved. Off you go, then.

3rd May

Margaret Mitchell won the Pulitzer Prize for *Gone With the Wind* in 1937, a novel very much *not* of podcast length.

4th May

Al Capone found himself in the Atlanta federal penitentiary in 1932 with sadly no iPod to keep him amused. The famed gangster was not convicted for his more gruesome crimes, but got tripped up for tax evasion. Crime never pays and tax returns are internationally a pain.

6th May

Sigmund Freud was born in 1856. He is considered the father of Psycho-analysis, established the theory of the unconscious, pioneered the use of cocaine (as a medical treatment) and encouraged people to talk things through, something women have believed in for years. Why not lie on the leather couch today? And you thought BT came up with the phrase: 'It's good to talk.'

7th May

In 1833 Johannes Brahms was born and in 1840 the composer Pyotr Tchaikovsky was born. Don't worry if you can't spell their names (the second one is clearly more likely to cause problems) as it's their music you need to know.

Brahms was a prominent Romantic composer while Tchaikovsky was famed for his ballet music (*Nutcracker, Swan Lake*) and was the guest conductor for the opening of Carnegie Hall, New York, on 5 May 1891. Tchaikovsky was also the composer of the canon-firing *1812 Overture* playing over the

Russian national anthem 'God Save the Tsar' (sounds very similar to La Marseillaise'). The *1812* was not only in the Beatles film *Help!*, it had a starring role in the 2005 film *V for Vendetta*. Download the original today.

10th May

Today in 1508, Michelangelo started his backbreaking task painting the ceiling at the Sistine Chapel, Rome. It took him years of sitting in hammocks and climbing scaffolding to create, and it was said that for many years afterwards Michelangelo couldn't read anything unless he held it over his head. But when the masterpiece was unveiled on Christmas day in 1541 it was worth all the agony: he had surpassed himself and all his rivals with it. 'The dead seem dead and the living living,' wrote Dante on seeing the work. Today it attracts as many as 19,000 visitors a day.

Tip: if visiting you should bring a mirror and binoculars.

How to dance

It was also on this date in 1899 that possibly the greatest dancer of all time was born: Fred Astaire.

'Can't act. Can't sing. Balding. Can dance a little,' was how RKO Pictures described Astaire's initial screen test. Yet what did they know? When he was paired up with Ginger Rogers it was magic. The duo appeared together on screen for the first time in *Flying Down to Rio*, and their chemistry and dancing skills led to a further nine films together.

'Fred gives Ginger class and Ginger gives Fred sex,' Katharine Hepburn said.

Astaire, being a glutton for punishment as well as perfection, famously insisted his routines be filmed in a single shot, saying 'either the camera will dance, or I will'. But even the super-talented still had to practise, and it was well known that he rehearsed in a closed set, with a security guard on the door.

Once, however, he bent the rules.

A young, eighteen-year-old Debbie Reynolds was exhausted and demoralized working on *Singin' in the Rain* with Gene Kelly, and was finding it hard to keep up with her leading man.

'I was a wreck, under the piano crying, and Fred [Astaire] walks by, and he says, "Who is that under the piano? Get out of there and come on, I'll let you watch me."'

Reynolds describes how she sat there mesmerized, watching him, 'figuring out his steps and throwing his cane, red in the face and just cussin' away. Finally, he looked at me and said, "That's it. You've learned, OK? Out!" [And] that's how you do it – you can't learn unless you sweat and work like a dog.'

Come – Get together
Let the dance floor feel your leather
Step as lightly as a feather
Let yourself go

Music and lyrics by Irving Berlin

A–Z of dance styles

So now you know that all you need is practice and patience, find a class. See which takes your fancy and suits your wardrobe.

Argentine Tango – Sexy stuff from 1800s Buenos Aires.
Ballet – Tutus, pointe shoes and sugar plum fairies.
Bolero – Torvill and Dean Spanish dance with sharp sudden turns.
Cha-Cha – Triple-step rhythmic ballroom dance.
Charleston – Frenetic fast-paced twenties dance characterized by
   energetic kicking.

Disco – John Travolta in *Saturday Night Fever*.

Electric Boogie – Street dance kids.

Fandango – Great word and lively Spanish spin.

Flamenco – Gypsies to goddesses in rigorous routine.

Foxtrot – One of Fred's specialities, slow, complex ballroom number.

Gigue – Triple-time Baroque bop (think Jane Austen).

Hip Hop – Break-dancing to body-popping on the streets of New York.

Irish Dancing – Skippy, leapy folk dance. Fancy footwork, arms slapping at your sides.

Jazz – Black and white rhythm and another Fred or Gene Kelly special.

Jive – Improvised swing-dancing in pairs.

Kathak – Indian classical dance style.

LeRoc –An eighties simplified version of jive dancing, born in France. Le Rock and Roll, baby.

Lindy Hop – Originating in Harlem, New York in the Prohibition era, this is an energetic fusion of swing and African dance moves.

Mambo – Another Latino number to shake to, this is the Cuban cocktail of the Salsa.

Maypole – Skipping round the pole and twisting ribbons.

Merengue – National sultry dance of the Dominican Republic.

Morris Dancing – Men leaping about waving hankies and bells.

Nightclub Two-Step (NC2S) – Invented in the swinging sixties by the King of Swing, Buddy Schwimmer, with a 'quick-quick-slow' pattern.

Odissi – The earliest classical dance style from India.

Paso Doble – The matador and the bullfight in the ballroom.

Pole Dancing – From strip clubs to a recognized form of exercise, no partner necessary.

Polka – Mid-nineteenth-century form of waltz from Bohemia with tempo popular with composers of the day.

Quickstep – Syncopated version of the Foxtrot and Charleston perfect for partners with tails (the tailored variety).

Rumba – Mélange of African and Cuban steps taken to the ballroom.

Salsa – Latin-American hip-wiggling dirty dancing.

Samba – Brazilian hot-blooded wiggle.

Tango – *Scent of a Woman*, rose between your teeth.

Tap – Fred, Ginger, Gene . . . step, ball, change.

Ukrainian Dance – Energetic, fast-paced folk dance.

Viennese Waltz – Cheek to cheek and how Ginger earned her nickname 'Feathers' when Fred swallowed her dress as he tried to serenade her.

Waltz – Originating in Vienna in the 1780s, this was the first time you held your partner tight and swooned if he was Astaire.

X-Step Waltz – Once you have mastered the waltz you can add complex leg-crosses to get the X factor.

YMCA – For the Village People's number-one selling song of 1978 a whole routine was invented. Essential for everyone on the dance floor to learn.

Zouk – Caribbean dance evolved from Merengue. Means 'to party'.

Zydeco – The opposite of swing, this is a Creole dance, a low rather than leg-kicking number born in Louisiana.

11th May

The waltz was introduced into the British ballroom in 1812. It caused a bit of a scandal as it was the first closed-couple dance done by the aristocracy. Until then, all the other dances had been open dances (certainly not cheek to cheek). Finally couples could be close enough to whisper in their partner's ear, or at very least say hello. Oh, to hell with taboo, life is too short – so the dancers held each other so close that their bodies and even faces touched while they danced. Grab a partner.

How to moonwalk the Michael Jackson way

If your dancing shoes are on, the most famous, as well as the most tricky, of all dance moves to learn is the moonwalk.

Fact: This cannot be done in high heels – you will break either your neck or your heel or both.

This move takes a lot of practice, and socks or slippy shoes, preferably suede-soled shoes so that you slide rather than stick. Attempting this on carpet or a shaggy rug is hopeless unless you want to leave with more fluff on your foot than a hobbit or give your feet carpet burns.

The moonwalk craze caught on when Michael Jackson leapt on stage and performed it at the Motown 25: Yesterday, Today, Forever star-studded concert in 1983. Jackson had just released his album *Thriller* and though the sparkling socks and one glove might not work for everyone, he certainly pulled it off. The first moonwalk took place three minutes and forty-seven seconds into his live performance of 'Billie Jean' and started a craze three minutes and forty-nine seconds later.

His moves were so impressive that Fred Astaire and Gene Kelly both phoned Jackson up afterwards to say 'wow'. Once perfected, make sure you have the opportunity to show it off.

Learn the moves by watching Jackson in his prime on *www.allmichaeljackson.com* then follow the simple instructions.

Step 1 Find a pair of low-grip shoes; you could try to do it in your socks to start off with. *As mentioned above, the suede sole – slippy not grippy.*
Step 2 Make sure that the ground you use to practise to moonwalk on is

also not too grippy, such as a polished floor. *So that means not carpet, rugs, splin-tering wood or sand. Marble is ideal but will hurt if you fall, and tiling is hard as your toes could stumble in the grouting grooves.*

Step 3 Stand with both feet close to each other, left foot slightly ahead of the right (toes of right should be in line with half the left foot). *OK, all stages to here are totally do-able, it just sounds perplexing. Deep breath: this is where it's going to get frustrating. Turn the music off and practise without the fast beat to throw you at first.*

Step 4 Now raise the heel of the right foot so that you are standing on the front of the right foot as if you are taking a step. The left foot must stay where it is (take care not to move it). *Easy . . .*

Step 5 As you lower the heel of the right foot, lean all your weight on the right foot. Now drag back the left foot so that its toes are in line with the heel of the right foot. The left foot's heel must be slightly off the ground at this stage. As you drag back, do not push down on the left foot at all or it will not glide. *Concentrate.* Make sure as you lower the heel of the right foot (slowly) the left moves at an equal speed. You will need lots of practice to master the right speed. *Argh . . . read this a few times. Don't panic: if you can walk in high heels this will be a cinch.*

Step 6 Keep practising up to the above steps until you can make the move-ment subconsciously without any difficulty. *OK, so step five is actually the key thing, let's try that again or watch him in action again.*

Step 7 Once you have mastered that, 'kick' outwards with the left foot, although it's not quite touching the ground, make it look as if it is touching. Move it out a foot-size's worth away from the toes of the right. No part of the left foot should be raised higher than another. *Alternatively watch wretched moonwalk video clip again and go back to Step 5.*

Step 8 After you make your left foot move so it is at the starting position, lift up the heel of the right foot once more. Make sure the left leg is bent at the knee. Now repeat Step 5. *Or stick on Step 5 till you know what you are doing.* Keep practising until you have the whole thing figured out, and it has been verified by others, and you feel quite comfortable with it.

Step 9 Once you've figured it out for the right leg bending, switch legs, and try the same with the other foot. Lift heel of left, lower left as you glide right back. Left still on the ground, throw out right foot, lift up heel of left foot, and once again drag right foot back as left heel is lowered. *Good grief.*

If you ever get past Step 5, try it with the music

12th May

'The Lady with the Lamp' Florence Nightingale was born in 1820. She was the nurse who cared for the British soldiers in the Crimean War and worked for other charitable causes.

Also on this day Edward Lear was born in 1812.

> The Owl and the Pussycat went to sea
> In a beautiful pea green boat,
> They took some honey, and plenty of money,
> Wrapped up in a five-pound note.

Born in Upper Holloway, London, Lear was one of twenty-one children. Seriously! Not surprisingly he was sent out to earn his living aged fourteen. Shy and stout, he hid behind his thick milk-bottle-top glasses and hardly looked destined for success. He trained as a zoological draughtsman, and later as a landscape painter, but his imagination had other ideas.

The Owl and the Pussycat is probably his best-known work and was written for three-year-old Janet Symonds, whose family he was spending the winter with down on the French Riviera. Lear wrote this ditty some time between 14–18 December 1867 to cheer up Janet while she was ill in bed with a fever.

Either learn to recite one of his Nonsense Poems or write your own list of nonsense today (not the everyday stuff, but special nonsense). You can never have too much nonsense . . .

13th May

Painter and sculptor Georges Braque was born in 1882. He, along with Picasso, is credited with inventing Cubism.

16th May

In 1770 Louis XIV married Marie Antoinette, and on the same date the great Charles Perrault died in 1703. Great Perrault? Who's that? you might ask. While you may not instantly recognize the name, you do know his work. He was the author behind some of the most loved fairy tales, so you'll never forget him after today. His stories, known to us as *Tales of Mother Goose,* include *Cinderella* (see December's Muse of the Month page 468), *Puss in Boots* and *Sleeping Beauty.*

Once upon a time . . . is the classic opening line for any fairy tale.

For those moments when your fairy tale takes you to other enchanted lands try:

French *Il était une fois* . . . literally meaning, 'There was, once . . .' Common ending: . . . *et se marièrent et eurent beaucoup d'enfants.* '. . . and they married, and had lots of children.'

German: *Es war einmal* . . . 'Once there was . . .' Common ending: . . . *und wenn sie nicht gestorben sind, dann leben sie noch heute* . . . 'and if they have not died, they are still alive today.'

Greek: Μια φορά κι έναν καιρό . . . 'Once, in another time . . .' Common ending: . . . Κι έζησαν αυτοί καλά κι εμείς καλύτερα . . . 'and they lived well, and we [lived] better.'

Hebrew: *Hayo hayah pa'am* . . . (היה פעם ויה) 'Once there was a time . . .'

Irish: Fadó, fadó, fadó a bhí an (agus bhí rí in nGaillimh) . . . 'A long, long, long time ago it was (and there was a king in Galway) . . .'

Italian: *C'era una volta* . . . 'There was a time . . .'

Japanese: *Mukashi mukashi* . . . (昔昔, 昔々, むかしむかし) 'A long time ago . . .'

Mandarin (Chinese): 很久，很久以前 'Long, long time ago . . .'
Spanish: *Había una vez* . . . 'There was a time . . .' Traditional ending: . . .
Y vivieron felices y comièron perdices. '. . . and they lived happily and ate partridge.'

However there are other ways to start a book. Great book openings include:

The Bible
    'In the beginning, God created the heavens and the earth.'
Romeo and Juliet by William Shakespeare
    'Two houses both alike in dignity In fair Verona where we set our scene.'
Peter Pan by J.M. Barrie
    'All children, except one, grow up.'
A Tale of Two Cities by Charles Dickens
    'It was the best of times, it was the worst of times.'
The Metamorphosis by Franz Kafka
    'As Gregor Samsa woke one morning from uneasy dreams he found himself in his bed, transformed into a monstrous insect.'
1984 by George Orwell
    'It was a bright cold day in April, and the clocks were striking thirteen.'

Back to our storyteller and his tale . . .

Charles Perrault was from a French bourgeois family and he trained as a lawyer before entering public service. Perrault initially published his works *Tales of Mother Goose* under his son's name, fearing that his colleagues, indeed most people, would mock him as fairy tales were considered peasant fodder. But the book was a smash, and his re-telling of *Puss in Boots*, *Tom Thumb*, *Cinderella* and *Beauty and the Beast* have become the definitive versions. Well, why be shy now? thought Charles.

The only royalties, however, that Perrault saw were the kings, queens, princesses and prince charmings he wrote about. Authors weren't paid royalties until Frances Hodgson Burnett kicked up a stink (see page 490) and managed to ensure author copyright. Alas Perrault, like so many other artists and authors, had no idea of the legacy he was creating. That's why you need a good agent to get a Happily Ever After.

The bestsellers of all time

The *Diamond Sutra* is the first known printed book – a copy found in China was dated back in AD 868. Later monks produced handwritten and lavishly illuminated manuscripts, but it was the invention of the printing press in Germany in 1436 that can be considered the genesis of modern publishing. It was brought to England in 1486 by William Caxton. According to the latest edition of *The Top Ten of Everything* by Russell Ash, the top five bestsellers are:

The Bible
Quotations from Chairman Mao (毛主席语录)
The *Harry Potter* series (a relatively new entry compared to its rivals, to date it has sold over 300 million copies earning J. K. Rowling an estimated $576 million).
The Lord of the Rings
The Chronicles of Narnia

But just to confuse things there are 548 editions of Mary Shelley's *Frankenstein*, 518 versions of Jane Austen's six novels in circulation, and 510 of Charles Dicken's *Great Expectations*. All publishers like to be able to publish a classic author whose sales are guaranteed, especially one who is dead and out of copyright.

The number of ideas for books is endless. Isn't it time you put a book proposal together? Everyone has a book in them, it is said, but do be warned: to quote Capote, 'Writing is hard and you get depressed.' Or overwhelmed. The choice is yours. For more advice on writing or getting an agent, look at *The Writers' & Artists' Yearbook*, published every year by A&C Black.

Page Turner

Rebecca
Daphne du Maurier

Why

While wannabe Hepburns and Hitchcocks are showcasing their ideas and podcasts at the Cannes Film Festival why not choose a title that has been adapted for the screen?

Daphne du Maurier's novel *Rebecca* was already an international best-seller when, in 1940, Alfred Hitchcock transformed it into an unforgettable Oscar-winning film starring Laurence Olivier as Maxim de Winter and Joan Fontaine as his new bride. Hitchcock was faithful to the novel yet brought the thriller to life and added style and celluloid chic.

Who

Dame Daphne du Maurier (13 May 1907–19 April 1989) combined mystery and romance, sort of Brontë meets Agatha Christie, if you like. The daughter of a successful actor-manager she had an affluent, care-free childhood where her imagination could blossom. The success of her first novel, *The Loving Spirit* (1931), brought not only fame but the attentions of the dashing Major Fredrick Browning whom she fell in love with and married (so often reality can be better than fiction).

Du Maurier wrote this book in 1937, when her husband was posted to Egypt. Unlike other wives she didn't wave him off, she simply packed up and went determinedly with him, leaving their children with the nanny in Cornwall.

Her rich descriptions and strong narratives made her novels appealing for Hollywood. True, *Rebecca* sealed her eternal fame, but her other novels, which include *Jamaica Inn* (1936) and *Frenchman's Creek* (1942), are equally intriguing. The latter pair were also turned into films, as were two of her short stories, *The Birds* (1963) and *Don't Look Now* (1973).

The plot

From a combination of du Maurier's own Cornwall mansion Menabilly and the great mansion Milton in Peterborough, where she had stayed as a child, she created Manderley, and the unforgettably famous opening lines:

> 'Last night I dreamt I went to Manderley again. It seemed to me I stood by the iron gate leading to the drive and for a while I could not enter, for the way was barred to me.'

Rebecca is a reworking of the *Cinderella/Jane Eyre* tale only this time it is set in forties England.

The story begins in Monte Carlo with Mrs Van Hopper and her companion – a shy young girl, whom we instantly empathize with – and she becomes our unnamed heroine. Van Hopper is a ghastly, gaudy American lady who is delighted to discover the eligible English gentleman Maxim de Winter is staying at their hotel. De Winter is there to get over the loss of Rebecca, his first wife, but committed social climber Mrs Van Hopper refuses to leave him in peace until fate steps in and she catches flu and is confined to her room, leaving her employed travel companion and de Winter to explore Monte Carlo together. Showing her a consideration she is not used to, the rich widower inadvertently sweeps the poor, plain(ish) and innocent girl off her feet. He in turn is captivated by this devoted child, and when it is time for their holiday friendship to end he can't bear to be parted from her and wants to save her, so he proposes marriage.

But the happiness of the honeymoon comes to an abrupt end when they return to his family home, Manderley, in Cornwall, and here the twists of the plot really begin.

The omnipresent shadow of de Winter's first wife, Rebecca, threatens to eclipse any hope of happiness for his second wife. To make matters just a little bit worse the terrifying housekeeper Mrs Danvers makes it perfectly clear that she is not even in the same league as the former mistress of Manderley. From beyond the grave Rebecca seems to bully

her nameless new rival, and the more she does so the more helplessly the young bride tries to impress Maxim. Du Maurier said originally the heroine was nameless simply because she couldn't think of a name. She then realized it could be used as a device to illustrate how much Rebecca dominated the house and how insignificant the new wife felt. Well, don't you just hate it when you can't remember someone's name, or worse, when they can't remember yours?

But here's the thing – will the new Mrs de Winter be able to save Maxim from the ghost of his first wife? Can love conquer all? It's certainty a page turner.

Hosting

A forties dress code should be issued with the invitation and the table should be laid for tea. Think about what Rebecca would have served. Which tea, which jam with the crumpets or scones? Would Mrs Danvers approve? For the finale you could watch Hitchcock's stylish classic, or discuss the continuations of the tale, *Mrs de Winter* by Susan Hill, or *Rebecca's Tale* by Sally Beauman.

Other films that began life as books:

The French Lieutenant's Woman by John Fowles
Memoirs of a Geisha by Arthur Golden
Gone With the Wind by Margaret Mitchell
Marie Antoinette by Antonia Fraser
Harry Potter and the Philosopher's Stone by J.K. Rowling

18th May

Peter Carl Fabergé was born in 1846. Yes, think Fabergé eggs. Even though he didn't *actually* create any of the eggs that bear his name, he came up with the design and concept while the intricate construction was done by master jewellers Michael Evlampievich Perchin and Henrik Wigström. Fabergé was 'discovered' by the Russian royal family at a jewellery fair in Moscow where he was awarded for 'having opened a new era in jewellery art'. The Tsar was thrilled as it meant he had the perfect present for his wife for Easter, the most important feast in the Russian Orthodox church calendar: rather than give any old egg, he ordered her a beautiful gold and enamel version with jewels inside – all carats and no calories. So, in 1884, armed with this royal commission the Fabergé egg was created and the tradition continued every Easter. When Alexander III died his son Nicholas II, who turned out to be the last Tsar, continued to commission the precious eggs, these becoming the most famous collection. The Imperial eggs became not only historical works of art but symbols of this pre-revolution grandeur. In total, fifty-six Imperial eggs were made, forty-five of which have been located today. The Queen and Kate Moss are among the modern-day collectors: style and class.

20th May

The man who painted the *Birth of Venus*, Sandro Botticelli, was born in 1444, in Florence. Alessandro di Mariano dei Filipepi was known by his nickname 'Botticelli', which was bestowed on him by his grossly obese brother Giovanni, who was known as 'Bottoicello', basically meaning 'little barrel'. Regardless of their shape, size or stature the name stuck and all of the brothers got landed with the Teletubby nickname from fifteenth-century Italy.

But Botticelli was only interested in capturing beauty, and the model he used for the *Birth of Venus* was Simonetta Cattaneo Vespucci, the Supermodel of the day, who was only thirteen when he painted her. She was known as 'La Bella Simonetta' and dashing nobleman Giuliano di Piero de'Medici commissioned a painting of her by Botticelli to fly on his standard bearer's banner to bring him luck in a joust, and also declare his love for her. She was celebrated by just about every poet, artist and writer; however, she died tragically young nine years later.

21st May

Clara Barton founded the American Red Cross in 1881 after seeing the International Red Cross in action whilst on vacation in Europe. Establishing the same care Stateside became her calling.

What charities do you support and what causes do you believe in? There are around 200,000 charities alone in the UK. See which public figures, charity or social causes motivate you to perform a good deed and do it. You count: *www.icount.org.uk.*

Muse of the Month

Audrey Hepburn

Audrey Hepburn is more than an 'actress' – she's an icon, a brand, an ambassador. Her delicate nymph-like frame, regal air and innocence were a refreshing change to the box-office boom of buxom belles that were the pin-ups of the day, and, even if you haven't seen her in *Breakfast at Tiffany's* you will know what she looked like as Miss Golightly. Despite her success as a Hollywood star, a mark of her character and integrity was that she considered motherhood and her charity work the most rewarding roles of her life.

Hepburn is one of only nine people to have won all the major showbusiness awards. Her awards include an Emmy, a Grammy, an Oscar and a Tony but ultimately it was her sense of style combined with her acting ability that set her apart and made her timeless. Hepburn herself disagreed, saying, 'My look is attainable. Women can look like Audrey Hepburn by flipping out their hair, buying large glasses and little sleeveless dresses.' If only it were that simple.

Watch one of her movies and let her grace inspire you. Let her be the motivation to get to that dance class, do that session at the gym, or follow her example and transform yourself. Either use her *Cinderella/My Fair Lady* style for a pre-date transformation, or do a good deed and polish your halo the Hepburn way. Why not throw a LBD (Little Black Dress) party to raise money for UNICEF (her charity) or host a 'Breakfast in your Ballgown' coffee morning? True Hepburnites know that there are more worthy causes than the 'I want a diamond from Tiffany's' fund; there are all sorts of other gemstones and gift options.

Her life and times

Audrey Hepburn always said that if she wrote about her life she would begin: 'I was born on 4 May 1929, and I died three weeks later.' Let's explain. Born Audrey Kathleen Ruston in Brussels, the baby caught severe whooping cough and her heart stopped. It was her mother who saved her, spanking her newborn daughter back to life, and this mother–daughter bond was to remain intense throughout her life. Hepburn was the only child of the marriage between Anglo-Irish banker Joseph Victor Hepburn-Ruston and the Dutch aristocrat Baroness Ella van Heemstra, who had two sons from her first marriage.

Educated at private schools in England and the Netherlands, she was a shy child who constantly strove to satisfy the ambitions of her mother. Boarding school in England helped her avoid her parents' bickering, but the turbulent marriage ended with divorce in 1938. The baroness then turned her full attention on her children – namely her daughter. Audrey was fluent in English, French, Italian, Dutch/Flemish and Spanish yet was desperately homesick at school.

She was brought back to Holland when war broke out and spent much of her childhood under Nazi occupation. During this time she

adopted the pseudonym Edda van Heemstra, as her mother thought her English name put her at risk. As for her much envied svelte figure, this was a legacy of the war and the serious malnourishment she, like so many, suffered at this time. The stories about her having to eat tulip bulbs are somewhat exaggerated – the bulbs were crushed to make flour then used to make cakes – but you have to admit there's a certain charm and romance in imagining this fairy growing up on flower food. Dancing (rather than acting) was what helped her escape her war-torn reality, though even this was tinged with danger and she reportedly carried messages for the Resistance in her ballet shoes.

At the end of the war Hepburn returned to England, hoping to study ballet having won a scholarship to Marie Lambert's dance school. However, due to lack of funds she wasn't able to travel and accept the place immediately. By the time she had enrolled, her gamine figure had (like Princess Diana's) grown too tall for her to be a prima ballerina. Her career aspirations were dashed – despite her poise she was not going to be the next Anna Pavlova. She set about finding another way onto the stage – in the chorus line, at nightclubs or with a spot of modelling – her mother her ever-present chaperone.

It was in the French Riviera in 1951 that she was truly 'discovered' while shooting *Monte Carlo Baby*. The legendary French playwright Colette was passing through the lobby where Hepburn was filming, when her wheelchair got caught in the film crew's cables. As they untangled her she saw Hepburn and exclaimed, 'There's our Gigi!' Though Hepburn had no formal acting training, Colette was adamant that she play the role of Gigi on Broadway. Before she knew it Hepburn had moved to New York to take centre stage.

The show was a triumph and as soon as *Gigi* closed Hepburn was flown to Rome to start filming *Roman Holiday* with Gregory Peck, who was to become a life-long friend. Peck was blown away by her presence and star quality and (generously) insisted this first-timer on film should share his top billing. He was right. The film was a smash and she won the Academy Award for Best Actress.

Her next film was *Sabrina* and before filming began the studios sent their starlet to Paris to get some French couture pieces made, in preparation for her character's 'transformation'. It was a trip that would transform her life off-screen as much as immortalize her on-screen. Hepburn didn't hesitate and headed straight to the young designer Hubert de Givenchy, whose clothes she had longed to wear but had, until now, been beyond her budget. When Givenchy was told 'Miss Hepburn' had come for an appointment, he rushed down, expecting to meet his idol – Katharine Hepburn. Instead he found this delicate doe-eyed beauty he'd never heard of, but in a few moments he was smitten and she became his muse. Their partnership won an Oscar for Sabrina's costumes and she inspired that unique '*je ne sais quoi*' that had the most glamorous women clamouring for appointments at the house. Givenchy would dress her on and off the screen for the rest of her life. Opera diva Maria Callas even admitted to dieting to try and emulate Hepburn's look. It's not easy being iconic.

While filming *Sabrina* she and her co-star William Holden enjoyed an on- and off-screen romance, despite her mother's protests. But Mummy needn't have fretted as Hepburn herself ended the relationship when she discovered that Holden wouldn't be able to father the children she longed for as he'd had a vasectomy. Idiot.

She was a star, but single; well, that was no good – so in 1954 Gregory Peck introduced her to actor Mel Ferrer at a party. Soon after Ferrer sent her a script, and before long they were starring in *Ondine* together.

It turned out to be quite a year, and while *Ondine* was on Broadway, love blossomed between her and Ferrer. On 25 March 1954 she won the Best Actress Oscar for *Roman Holiday*, and three days later she won a Tony for Best Stage Actress for *Ondine*. 'How will I ever live up to them?' she asked reporters. But, typical of Hepburn, her real happiness came not from the awards, but when Ferrer proposed and she accepted, against her mother's wishes. They married at a civil ceremony on 24 September 1954.

Her career was riding high yet the one thing she wanted most – motherhood – was evading her and she suffered several miscarriages. She returned to Paris to dance with one of her film idols, Fred Astaire,

in *Funny Face* and just carried on acting, until, while filming *The Nun's Story*, she realized she was finally pregnant, and turned down all new roles to concentrate on the one she wanted most. On 17 July 1960 she gave birth to Sean Hepburn Ferrer.

After a year off she was persuaded to return to play 'the role she was born to play'. Though writer Truman Capote would disagree, as he intended Marilyn Monroe for the part and opposed Hepburn's casting, Hepburn made Holly Golightly her own. She earnt her fourth Academy Award nomination for *Breakfast at Tiffany's* and it's widely considered to be the most stylish film of the last century. (See November's Page Turner, page 428, for more on the original novel it was based on).

A few flops followed *Tiffany's* before another inspirational pairing happened when she was cast as Eliza Doolittle in *My Fair Lady*. The pairing in question was not with her leading man, Rex Harrison, but with the eccentric English costume and set designer Cecil Beaton. He was enraptured by her: 'She embodies the spirit of today.' Though her beauty was in no doubt, the film landed Hepburn in the middle of a controversy when her singing voice had to be dubbed by Marni Nixon, plus there had been fierce competition and opposition for the role. Despite playing Doolittle on Broadway, a certain pre-*Mary Poppins* and *Sound of Music* Julie Andrews was passed over for the role, as she wasn't considered 'bankable', but this wasn't really Hepburn's fault. Sure enough Hepburn once again made the role appear tailor-made for her (dubbed or not), so all doubt vanished the moment she walked on set.

Though it had been her husband Ferrer who had encouraged her to go back to work, it was a double-edged sword as the greater her success, the more their marriage suffered. Ferrer started having affairs and was sick of being in his wife's shadow, and they divorced on 5 December 1968. Whether it was rebound or real love, barely a month later she married Dr Andrea Dotti, an Italian psychiatrist she met on a cruise. Four months later she was pregnant and their son Luca was born on 8 February 1970. But Dotti was a womanizer and cheat, and despite her movie-star status and financial security she felt vulnerable and clung on to the marriage for ten years, fearing its 'failure' and worrying about how her sons would cope with a single mother. Finally sick of his philandering she divorced him in 1982.

Her second divorce was finalized as she filmed *They All Laughed* and soon after she met actor Robert Wolder. They both had Dutch roots, he was a widow, she a single mother, and he became her final constant companion. When her formidable mother died on 29 April 1984 Robert moved in to comfort her and, though they never married, he never left her side.

In 1987 she took what she considered to be her most important role as UNICEF's (United Nations Children's Fund) Goodwill Ambassador. It was a cause close to her heart, as in the Second World War food and clothes provided by UNICEF had saved her life and so many others' in war-torn Holland. She relished the chance to give something back. She travelled widely and tirelessly to promote the charity and visited the most deprived areas to highlight where help was needed the most. After a trip to Somalia she and Robert went home via California so she could see her son Sean. Here Hepburn started to complain of stomach pains. She was diagnosed with colon cancer and given less than three months to live. She returned to her beloved home, La Paisible, in Switzerland and died on 20 January 1993. Awards and accolades flooded in and well-wishers mourned the loss of a beloved icon.

Tiffany stores around the world hung her picture in their windows with the sign:

Audrey Hepburn
1929-1993
Our Huckleberry Friend

Audreyisms

'People associate me with a time when movies were pleasant, when women wore pretty dresses in films and you heard beautiful music. I always love it when people write me and say, "I was having a rotten time, and I walked into a cinema and saw one of your movies, and it made such a difference."'

'I was born with an enormous need for affection, and a terrible need to give it.'

'I heard a definition once: "Happiness is health and short memory!" I wish I'd invented it, because it is very true.'

'As a child, I was taught that it was bad manners to bring attention to yourself, and to never, ever make a spectacle of yourself . . . All of which I've earned a living doing.'

'For beautiful eyes, look for the good in others; for beautiful lips, speak only words of kindness; and for poise, walk with the knowledge that you are never alone.'

25th May

In 1895 Oscar Wilde was sentenced to two years' hard labour for gross indecency. Wilde's first love, Florence Ann Lemon Balcombe, jilted him in favour of her childhood sweetheart Abraham Stoker (later to become the renowned Bram Stoker, author of *Dracula*). Thus rejected, he moved from Dublin to London and buried himself in his work. A 'lavender marriage' (marriage of convenience) to Constance Lloyd, on 28 May 1884, may have helped save face and quash a few whispers but he was editing *Woman's World*, wore velvet, and lavender gloves, carried a jewel-topped cane, sported a dyed green buttonhole flower and wrote *The Picture of Dorian Gray* (in which a young man is convinced that beauty can justify anything) for heaven's sake! It should have been obvious. Apparently not.

It was his relationship with the beautiful, yet spoilt brat, Lord Alfred Bruce Douglas ('Bosie'), who was fifteen years Wilde's junior, that really caused the scandal (and his downfall). Wilde and the Marquis of Queensberry, Bosie's dad, waged a very public war of words over the couple's relationship, which eventually led to the trial of the century.

'Wilde wanted a consuming passion,' his biographer Richard Ellmann wrote of the affair. 'He got it and was consumed by it.' Do be careful what you wish for.

Wilde didn't help himself; he couldn't resist. When asked at his trial if he had kissed a witness, Wilde responded, 'Oh dear no, he was a peculiarly plain boy.' And things got worse when, asked if he had ever adored a man, he said, 'I have never given adoration to anybody except myself.' Stop it.

Yet Wilde sacrificed himself to protect Bosie. Love is blind – and sometimes it is insane. Wilde's wife and children disowned him, changed their name and moved to Amsterdam. He was bankrupt and spent six months at Wandsworth and the rest of his sentence at Reading gaol. As he himself lamented 'everything popular is wrong'. Probably, but doesn't that make it all the sweeter?

Watch the 1997 film *Wilde*, with Stephen Fry as the lead and Jude Law as his lover, or read one of his many books, or plays, such as *The Importance of Being Earnest*.

Also on this date in 1977 a sci-fi fantasy, written and directed by George Lucas, opened. It was simply called *Star Wars*.

Set, cue drum roll, trumpets and stirring music. It is nineteen years after the formation of the Galactic Empire, and a deadly weapon – the Death Star – has been constructed and threatens to destroy the Jedi rebels. You must have seen this? If not, try *not* to do so with a boy who can recite the entire script as the action unfolds. Off-putting.

Princess Leia (Carrie Fisher), leader of the Rebel Alliance, steals the plans but is captured; cue damsel in distress. Meanwhile a young farmer named Luke Skywalker (Mark Hamill) buys two droids and gets into a whole heap of trouble when he meets a strange old hermit, Obi-Wan Kenobi (Alec Guinness), on the desert planet of Tatooine who tells him of his destiny. When Luke discovers his home is destroyed (damn droids' fault), Obi-Wan begins Luke's Jedi training as they attempt to rescue the princess from the Empire. Here they hitch a ride with Hans Solo (Harrison Ford) in the

Millennium Falcon and every little boy's dream comes true – good versus evil with light sabers at dawn and spaceships leaping through galaxies.

Produced with a budget of $11 million it became one of the most successful films of all time, earning $798 million worldwide during the original theatre release alone. And it was just the start of the series.

The great British actor Sir Alec Guinness, who played Obi-Wan Kenobi, earnt more in royalties from this film than anything else in his prolific and illustrious career. He also got to be one of the first to say the immortal Jedi greeting, so apt for this month: 'May the Force be with you'.

Today's essential accessory is the light saber, perfect for a futuristic fashion moment. It was invented by Nelson Shin for the Jedi Knights in the first *Star Wars* movie. In 2006 at the US Burning Man festival a record-breaking fight with over a thousand Jedi warrior wannabes took place. Do we ever grow up?

30th May

Joan of Arc was burned at the stake in 1431. Would you die for what you believe in? A very heroic end to the month.

Foot Note

The ballet shoe

There is yet another perk to being a dancer, other than the figure and the bendability – they get the best shoes, with ballet shoes riding top of the list. Dancing is actually the oldest form of the arts and shoes are the tool you will no doubt need for the part (tap shoes, tango shoes, jazz shoes, lots of lovely new shoes!) Ballet shoes come in either leather or

satin, pointe or soft, depending if you are dancing or merely striking a pose. As well as the dance version they can have a flat leather sole added and be worn on the street with Capri pants, dark shades and sixties vibe *à la* Hepburn, Bardot and Fonteyn. Just wearing a ballet shoe gives you membership of the graceful gang.

The word 'ballet' first appeared in 1415. The ballet shoe appeared in the French court when Catherine de Medici arrived in 1533 to marry Henry II with a *ballet de court* on her foot, though it was not until 1581 that a ballet performance was unveiled on the Paris stage (for a staggering five-hour performance). Ballet shoes were the perfect footwear for dancing the night away at court, at masquerade balls and costume extravaganzas. With all the hectic headgear, wigs, corsets and skirts, the dainty shoe was the perfect slipper to dance and be merry in – what else could nice young girls do to have fun in those days? With dancing at the top of the list for all social occasions, in an age of high morals and lovely decorum, this was a polite way to collide, mingle and twirl with strangers and, more excitingly than that, members of the opposite sex. In fact it was from the ballet shoe and the appetite for dance at well-mannered court that the phrase 'minding your Ps and Qs' was derived. Bows and curtsys were as important as the actual moves, and dance masters would scream at their charges to watch their *pieds* (feet) and *queues* (the tails of their wigs) when dancing . . . until the French revolution swept the excess and the heads of the aristocracy away.

In the nineteenth century ballet became more romantic and the pointe shoe for the prima ballerinas got its block. From the professional on-stage shoe of the *belle époque* to 1957 when the capezio became the perfect combo with capri pants, to the ballet-shoe makers in London – Frederich Freed, Gamba, Anello & Davide – it's time to take your places and plié, darlings.

June

'Music and rhythm find their way into the secret
places of the soul.'
Plato

Wish You Were Here

Manolo Blahník from Istanbul

The name of the airport is already intriguing: Atatürk, named after the country's first president, the founder of the republic. I see a picture of him whilst indulging my palate in the most exquisite quince pastry I have ever, ever had. He looks imposing in a suit, hat and silk mouchoir and I am tempted to turn my short trip here into a quest for Atatürk – where he worked, lived, ate. But there is so much to see in Istanbul that Ataturk falls by the wayside, as ghosts from Byzantium and Constantinople take over. What splendour!

Istanbul is a huge city. Vast. Noisy. Busy. Crazy. Get caught in one of its traffic jams and it's a nightmare. When planning social events the citizens allow time for traffic. A gallery opening gets moved by half an hour, because of traffic. My appointment is delayed by forty minutes, because of traffic. Is there no respite?

There is. The secret is to forget all about it and lose yourself in one of the city's many architectural marvels: Justinian's Hagia Sophia, which dominates the city's skyline – so noble, so huge, so spectacular. I have never seen such a beautiful light entering a building. Or the Topkapi – the former imperial residence built by Mehmet II. There are marvels wherever you look.

And it continues: Suleyman the Magnificent's mosque – the Suleymaniye; the Rustem Pasha Camii – tucked away from the crowds, with the most incredible colours my eyes have ever come across; the gardens of the Beylerbeyi Palace . . . Even my hotel, a former prison strategically sited between the Hagia Sophia and the Blue Mosque, is perfection.

Amidst all this is the Bosphorus, lined with *yalis* – the wooden summer houses of the Turkish elite – splitting the city between Europe and Asia. The river crossed by Jason and his Argonauts is as essential to the city today as it has been throughout its history. Ferries go along, transporting the thousands of tourists that add to the city's chaos. And I sit on a terrace, sipping fresh mint tea and raising yet another powdered cube of rose-scented *loukoum* to my mouth.

Love, Manolo

1st June

1967 saw the UK release of *Sgt. Pepper's Lonely Hearts Club Band*, the eighth album by the Beatles. It is described by music aficionados as 'the most influential album of all time'. Recorded over 129 days, it was the longest time the group had been able to spend in a studio for years as they were now the biggest band on the planet, and had only just finished a world tour.

John Lennon had caused a storm in the teacup when he had remarked the previous year – 5 August 1966 – that the Beatles were 'bigger than Jesus Christ', but this album turned out to be a gospel of new ideas, from the technical studio gismo recording techniques (which we won't worry about) to the instrumental arrangements including sitars and symphony orchestras produced by the 'Fifth Beatle' George Martin to, last, but by no means least, the cult cover art. *Sgt. Pepper* was groundbreaking in every sense.

The Grammy Award-winning packaging of *Sgt. Pepper* was created by art director Robert Fraser and designed (under the watchful eye of Paul McCartney) by pop artist Peter Blake. Fraser was a man of many titles in the art world, including being Blake's agent at the time. Together this Swinging Sixties network of friends created one of the most recognizable covers of the century (after Fraser had thankfully talked the boys out of using a hippy trippy design collective called The Fool, which would have been folly itself).

Peter Blake (born 25 June 1932) studied at Gravesend School of Art before finishing at the Royal College of Art, alongside artists Bridget Riley and Frank Auerbach. Blake is considered one of the most important Brits to contribute to the Pop Art movement. His iconic cover not only served to cement his eternal fame, but because of the band's enormous popularity it brought Pop Art to a far wider audience than Andy Warhol and his group the Velvet Underground managed to achieve.

Blake also designed the covers for:

Band Aid's *Do They Know It's Christmas*

Paul Weller's *Stanley Road*

He also created the cover for the Ian Dury tribute album *All New Boots and Panties*, as Blake was Dury's tutor at the Royal College. He has also stayed friendly with Macca and has been seen front row at Stella McCartney's fashion shows.

The cast

Blake's album cover design was simply entitled 'People We Like' and shows a collage of the Beatles in their psychedelic suits waving goodbye to the innocent bowl-cuts of their youth and saying hello to hedonistic experimentation – in music as well as image. The group are surrounded by cut-out images of heroes, friends and icons, all of whom are instantly recognizable: Stan Laurel and Oliver Hardy, Marlene Dietrich and Bob Dylan, Sigmund Freud, Oscar Wilde, Karl Marx plus their one-time band members the late Stuart Sutcliffe and Pete Best (their first drummer) all rub shoulders with each other.

Mae West originally declined permission to have her photo included saying, 'What would I be doing in a lonely hearts club?' What would any of us be doing there Mae? But after the Fab Four themselves dropped her a line, the blonde bombshell relented and agreed.

Blake and his wife stuck the collage together in the last two weeks of March 1967 with the cover shoot for the double-fold album taking place on 30 March 1967. The total bill came in at £2,868 5*s.* 3*d.*, an estimated hundred times the average cost of covers in those days.

In addition to the *Lonely Hearts* album other releases that set the musical tone for the month include, on this date in June 1968, Wings, who released 'Live and Let Die' – yes, the Bond theme, one later covered by Guns N' Roses in 1994. And on the same date in America, Simon & Garfunkel's 'Mrs Robinson' hit the number one spot where it stayed for three weeks. Director Mike Nichols became obsessed with the duo's music while filming *The Graduate* and asked them to write three songs, but due to their touring they only had time for the one. But how could they have topped the song 'Mrs Robinson', named after the character played by Anne Bancroft, the older woman who seduces Dustin Hoffman's character? Pick up a toy boy or at the very least download the theme tune today.

2nd June

The infamous writer the Marquis de Sade was born in 1740. He caused shock waves in his French homeland for his explosive and explicit novels, and Napoleon Bonaparte arrested him for blasphemy, a mild way of describing the obscene novels *Juliette* and *Justine*. Put it this way – the term sadism comes from his name.

He was undeterred: 'Kill me again or take me as I am, for I shall not change,' the Marquis de Sade wrote in his last will and testament, and that may be enough from him, though he is still inspiration for people today, including John Galliano's January 2006 Dior couture show.

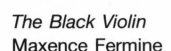

The Black Violin
Maxence Fermine

Why

This is a love story where music is the aphrodisiac as well as the poisoned chalice. Though only a short novel it captures the emotion and the magic of performing. Fermine composes a melancholic tune about unrequited love and finding one's voice, the soloist of course being a black violin.

Who

Not much is known about Fermine himself. He was born in 1968 in Albertville, France, and grew up in Grenoble. He moved to Paris to complete his studies and went on to work in Africa before moving to Tunisia. His three novellas are all inspired by colour, and have been translated across the globe. In addition to *The Black Violin*, he wrote *Snow*, a tale where the words of a Japanese haiku take a poet on a quest for love, and *The Beekeeper*, which is about a painter, very similar to Van Gogh, and his obsession with a girl whose skin is the colour of honey.

Fermine's style of writing is a poetic stream of consciousness, poignant and witty. The stories are tales of coincidence and consequence and all contain a moral.

The plot

The tale begins when Johannes Karelsky is only five years old and he hears a gypsy in the street play the violin. He is so moved by the music that from this moment he knows he is a violinist. He starts lessons and yes, he is a natural. Soon Karelsky and his mother are touring Europe as people applaud and marvel at his virtuoso talent. He is a gifted performer, but sadly his mother is old and cannot take the strain of constant touring. She dies and almost immediately he stops touring, and

the fame and the accolades vanish. Karelsky disappears from the public eye and instead begins to earn a meagre income by teaching music while he dreams of writing a great opera.

In the spring of 1796, however, Karelsky is called up for military service. The lost soul is happy to go and fight for Napoleon and escape his life without music. He gets wounded and, as he lays dying, he hears a woman singing, her voice so pure and beautiful that the music touches his soul and saves him. Karelsky not only lives, he is inspired once more. He wants to capture this mysterious melody and to make the voice speak through his violin and sing of his journey. For the first time in years he takes out his violin and begins to play, but the sweet laments are too much for the soldiers, as it haunts rather than soothes them, stirring up memories of lives they once had.

He wakes to find his instrument smashed. The music stops.

A year later the army marches into Venice and once more fate brings music back into his life.

Karelsky is stationed in the city and given a room at the house of Erasmus, an elderly violin-maker. Erasmus is a lonely figure who trained under the son of Stradivarius, the world's greatest ever violin-maker. There are three passions in Erasmus's life: a chessboard, an ageless bottle of grappa and his black violin.

Cautiously and slowly they start to tell each other of their lives, the violin uniting them. The black violin that hangs ominously on the wall, is never touched, never spoken of, but always present.

Karelsky finally focuses on trying to write the opera he has always had inside him but there are strange spirits at work in the house. Every time he writes the manuscript, by the time he wakes up in the morning the pages are blank. There is no logical explanation, but he suspects the black violin may have something to do with it.

Finally, one evening Erasmus decides to entrust Karelsky with his tale. Erasmus takes him back to his youth, to his apprenticeship, the voice that haunted his dreams, and to the only woman he ever loved. He tells of the quest to win her heart and the challenge behind the black violin. Did Erasmus succeed in his quest? Did he make the perfect violin and what powers were involved to create its song? And more importantly will Karelsky have the strength to break the spell? Will music or man triumph?

Hosting

Live music could be the cultural prelude to the book discussion with the whole group going to see a string quartet together. Is there a festival or event that could set the scene? After the music and the words of *The Black Violin* have been heard, crack open a strong bottle of grappa, and compare tales of lost loves. This could be the perfect book to read around a campfire or in between acts at Glyndebourne.

Alternatively follow these performances:

An Equal Music by Vikram Seth

Music & Silence by Rose Tremain

Mozart's Women: His Family, His Friends, His Music by Jane Glover

Faithfull by Marianne Faithfull

Room Full of Mirrors: A Biography of Jimi Hendrix by Charles R. Cross

I'm with the Band: Confessions of a Groupie by Pamela Des Barres

3rd June

In 1976 Queen's 'Bohemian Rhapsody' went gold.

'Bohemian Rhapsody' is the only UK single to have had two Christmas number ones; once, when it was originally released in 1975, and the second time in 1991 when it was re-released after Mercury's death.

Originally recorded for their 1975 album *A Night at the Opera*, this song is unlike anything heard before – or since. Starting a cappella (unaccompanied) and building up to choirs, crashing choruses and squealing guitars it was originally simply labelled 'Fred's Thing'. Mercury cannily gave a copy to his pal, the equally flamboyant Capital Radio DJ Kenny Everett, saying, 'Don't play it, it's too long, it's just for you.' This garnered textbook reverse psychology success. They then released the single with a promo video, made by Bruce Gowers, so the rock band could stay on the road and simultaneously appear on *Top of the Pops*. It was shot in only four hours on a rehearsal stage. After Mercury's death and the head-banging rendition in the 1992 film *Wayne's World* the band re-edited the video, splicing in footage from their other outlandish videos and tours. The video and song became cult classics and essential to own.

Think you can do any better? (And in four hours?)

You can try bouncing images and sounds off each other but this remains one of the best pop videos of all time.

In a 2006 poll Channel Four revealed people voted the following as the greatest pop videos:

1   Michael Jackson: *Thriller*
2   Peter Gabriel: *Sledgehammer*
3   a-ha: *Take On Me*
4   Queen: *Bohemian Rhapsody*
5   Madonna: *Like a Prayer*
6   Robbie Williams: *Rock DJ*
7   Michael Jackson: *Billie Jean*

How to handle hen nights

As the wedding season approaches it is likely you will be subjected to a few hen nights – either friends' or perhaps your own. For the complete wedding planner's list turn to July, page 251. To commemorate the last moments of singledom it's now tradition for the bride-to-be and an entourage of flushed faces to lurch through the streets sporting pink wings and devils' horns. 'Kiss Me Quick' hats are an optional extra that are worth skipping.

The exact origin of the hen night is as fuzzy as your head the morning after, but it is thought to have come from Holland, where a Dutchman refused to let his daughter marry a poor milliner. But they were in luck, as well as love, as they happened to live in a village that clearly believed in romance at all costs. All her friends turned up with gifts, presents and crafts which softened the blow, and soon it seemed a more favourable match.

Back to the modern-day *miss*-demeanors: on this night any gifts bestowed are more likely to be handcuffs and obscene undies – the tea towels and plates come later, on the wedding list.

The cost of a modern-day hen night varies enormously from the dinner and dancing idea, to high tea, a day at the races or a spa – it can very easily tot up. Mercifully (if you are the hen) this is *one* thing the bride does not have to worry about – when you see her list you'll see she has enough to be getting on with. The hen night is the responsibility of the chief bridesmaid and invited 'bachelorettes', as they are known in America. The head-girl/boss bridesmaid should plan ahead and gather together a posse of the bride's nearest female friends and plot something unforgettable, and, if you like, horribly embarrassing. Note: it is the stag nights that involve strippers or getting the groom shipped to Alaska, but why let the boys have all the fun?

To avoid aching head and additional nausea on the big day, stage this debauchery – and his – more than a night in advance. You don't want the groom Missing In Action or peering through a crashing hangover while the bride tries to remember all her vows and relatives' names.

Once the elected hen-planner has the numbers and names of all the clucky bits of trouble the hen wants to invite, she can plot and budget what to do with the bride-to-be. Rather than going on a bender (so obvious and not that chic) why not opt for something more original and infinitely more memorable? Make her a star.

A popular new way to spend a hen night is as a group – I mean a pop group – and recording your own music video. Try *www.adventureconnections.co.uk*, who have studios in London (Clapham) or Brighton. If you're not based in either of these locations could it be the excuse you need for a night away? When you book a session you will be sent a list of songs to choose from. Email or send a shortlist round to all the attendees (the backing singers-to-be) as to what the hen should or could perform. Want to relive your youth and don a school skirt? Then pick Britney's *Hit Me Baby One More Time*, or is Cyndi Lauper's *Girls Just Wanna Have Fun* the theme you seek?

Now all you need to do is get your victim, I mean lead singer, to the studio. You can do so in a – 'Surprise, surprise' – stretch limo situation, but don't give her too much warning as she could try and leave the country and where would the fun be in that? Stage fright should slip away as Adventure Connections – for example – supply copious amounts of alcohol, as well as a hair stylist, make-up artist, choreography and cameraman. The moves, grooves and general shame/hilarity can now be immortalized on DVD – perfect viewing for years to come; just maybe don't show the future husband until the deal is signed and sealed with a kiss . . .

4th June

Today in England Derby Day rides in. It's time to don your finest finery and, under a wide-brimmed hat, mingle with the well-mannered and well-to-do at the races.

Pronounced with rather a plum in your mouth, Daaaaaaarby Day gallops in as the most famous thoroughbred horse race in the world. From Elizabeth Arden to Her Majesty the Queen, this is where they all want to cheer on the jockeys and back a winner. The Epsom Derby (*www.epsomderby.com*) is the perfect place to mingle with the gentrified social climbers as well as horse and gambling fanatics – you could even leave with some takings in your pocket if you back the right horse.

The first race took place in 1661 at Epsom Oaks and the winning horse, Bridget, was owned by one Edward Stanley-Smith, the twelfth Earl of Derby. To commemorate his win the race gathering was forever named after this first victory, and the race took his name – the Derby – regardless of its Epsom address.

Horses which compete in the Derby will most likely also be riding in the Prix de l'Arc de Triomphe in France and the Breeders' Cup in the US, but this is the one for afternoon picnics, gloves and gentile conversation (Ascot is the one for the hat fashion statement).

Derby day trivia

1884 The race finished with a dead heat between Harvester and Saint Gatien.

1909 Edward VII's horse, Minoru, won and became the first horse owned by a reigning monarch to win.

1913 Suffragette Emily Davison died as she leapt in front of King George V's horse, Anmer.

1854 Lester Piggott, aged only eighteen, became the youngest ever jockey to win the race.

1996 Alex Greaves became the first woman to ride in the race. She came last. Doh.

How to do the season

There are four seasons of changing climes but only one matters to those who have aspirations to socially climb. This is 'the season' – and all the hard preparatory work should culminate in a marriage proposal in June. *Debrett's* remains the bible for the courting calendar. Go to *www.debretts.co.uk* and click on 'the season' if you feel you're posh enough.

But the season is not just for the posh – it's for the cultured, the curious and those seeking some inspiration on what to do when.

There are all sorts of manners and etiquette books that spout rules, and the only reason to study them is so you know how many you can break. In a nutshell, as long as you don't slouch, stand tall, keep your head held high, shoulders back, bust out, tummy in, you'll be fine. Those who are really on the platinum-card-holding husband-hunting circuit are the debs.

A 'debutante', coming from the French for 'female beginner', is exactly that – it is the title given to young girls who are coming out into society for the first time, i.e. ladies from aristocratic/upper-class families who want to present their precious jewel (daughter) to the world (and snare a husband). If only life really was like the nicer parts of *My Fair Lady*, but yes, she too had to undergo training and follow all sorts of ancient rituals, including carrying feathers (an ostrich-feather fan is a smart way of working this stipulation) before she could be presented at court. Being presented to the reigning monarch was the ultimate pinnacle for a deb, but Queen Elizabeth abolished this ceremony in 1958 feeling it had become outdated, and it's just not the same without Her Majesty doing the honours, despite what these new debs might proclaim. The debbing tradition does continue with all the pomp and ceremony it can muster in America, with white gowns, satin or kid gloves, all topped off with the perfect deep curtsy. It's a million miles from the Glastonbury Festival.

To see and be seen at

Put on your best dress and prepare for the champagne corks to start popping.

Here are the key dates to be photographed at, according to *www.hellomagazine.com*

January
London Boat Show. *www.schroderslondonboatshow.com*
National Fine Art and Antiques Fair, NEC, Birmingham: *www.nationalartandantiquesfair.co.uk*

February
Six Nations Rugby Internationals: *www.rbs6nations.com*
Olympia Fine Art and Antiques Spring Fair, London: *www.olympia-antiques.co.uk*

March
Crufts Dog Show, NEC Birmingham: *www.crufts.org.uk* (No place for mongrel mutts.)
National Hunt Festival, Cheltenham Racecourse, Cheltenham, Gloucestershire: *www.cheltenham.co.uk*

April
Oxford and Cambridge Boat Race: *www.theboatrace.org*
Royal Shakespeare Company theatre season starts, Stratford-upon-Avon, Warwickshire: *www.rsc.org.uk*
Queen Elizabeth II's birthday (April 21): *www.royal.gov.uk*
Flora London Marathon: *www.london-marathon.co.uk*
The Gold Cup, Sandown Park Racecourse, Surrey: *www.sandown.co.uk*

May
Polo season starts
Royal Caledonian Ball, Grosvenor House Hotel, London: *www.royal-caledonianball.com*

Royal Windsor Horse Show, Buckinghamshire: *www.rwhs.co.uk*
Glyndebourne Opera Festival, Sussex: *www.glyndebourne.com*
Chelsea Flower Show, Royal Hospital, Chelsea, London: *www.rhs.org.uk*
Hay Literary Festival, Hay-on-Wye, Wales: *www.hayfestival.com*

June

Biggin Hill International Air Fair, Kent: *www.bigginhillairfair.co.uk*
ArtLondon, Chelsea, London: *www.artlondon.net*
Formula One British Grand Prix, Silverstone: *www.silverston-circuit.co.uk*
Stella Artois Tennis Tournament, Queen's Club, London:
www.stellaartoistennis.com
The Royal Academy Summer Exhibition, London: *www.royalacademy.org.uk*
Grosvenor House Art and Antique Fair, London: *www.grosvenor-antiques-fair.co.uk*
Queen Elizabeth II's official birthday (June 17), Trooping of the
Colour, Horse Guards Parade, London: *www.royal.gov.uk*
Queen's Cup Final, the Guards Polo Club, Windsor Great Park, Berkshire: *www.guardspoloclub.co.uk*
Royal Ascot, Berkshire: *www.ascot.co.uk*
Wimbledon Tennis Championships, London: *www.wimbledon.org*
Henley Royal Regatta, Oxfordshire: *www.hrr.co.uk* (More boats – think
palazzo pants.)
Summer Shakespeare season opens, Regents Park, London:
www.openairtheatre.org

July

Red and sika stag season opens in Scotland: *www.basc.org.uk*
Eton and Harrow Cricket Match, Lords, London: *www.lords.org* (Well,
did you really think that you'd find Mr Right at a fashion show?)
RHS Hampton Court Palace International Flower Show, Surrey:
www.rhs.org.uk
Goodwood Festival of Speed, Goodwood Park, Sussex:
www.goodwood.co.uk
Wimbledon tennis finals, London: *www.wimbledon.org*

BBC Proms concert season opens, Royal Albert Hall, London: *www.royalalberthall.com*

Open Golf Championship: *www.opengolf.com*

De Beers Diamond Day at Ascot, Berkshire: *www.ascot.co.uk*

Cowes Week, Isle of Wight: *www.skandiacowesweek.co.uk* (Even more boats)

Cartier International Polo final, Guard's Polo Club, Smith's Lawn, Windsor Great Park, Berkshire: *www.guardspoloclub.co.uk* (Princes and horses.)

August

Red and sika stags and fallow buck season opens in England and Wales; fallow buck season opens in Scotland: *www.basc.org.uk*

Glorious Goodwood, Goodwood Racecourse, Sussex: *www.goodwood.co.uk*

Edinburgh International Festival, Scotland: *www.eif.co.uk*

September

Start of partridge shooting season in England, Scotland and Wales: *www.basc.org.uk*

Last Night of the Proms, Royal Albert Hall, London: *www.bbc.co.uk/proms*

Chelsea Antiques Fair, London: *www.penman-fairs.co.uk*

Salmon and trout season closes in England

October

Pheasant shooting season starts in England, Scotland and Wales: *www.basc.org.uk*

Prix de L'Arc de Triomphe, Longchamp, France: *www.france-galop.com/promo/prixarc.htm*

Horse of the Year Show, NEC Birmingham: *www.hoys.co.uk*

The Cheltenham Festival of Literature, Gloucestershire: *www.cheltenhamfestivals.co.uk*

Red and sika stag season closes in Scotland (Oct 20): *www.basc.org.uk*

Red and sika hind, fallow doe and roe doe season opens in Scotland
(Oct 20): *www.basc.org.uk*

Roe buck season closes in England and Wales (Oct 21): *www.basc.org.uk*

November

Traditional start of the fox hunting season (Nov 1): *www.basc.org.uk*
(Watch *Fox and the Hound* instead)

Red and sika hind, and roe and fallow doe season opens in England
and Wales (Nov 1): *www.basc.or.uk*

London to Brighton Veteran Car Run (Nov 5). Starts from Hyde Park
Corner, London: *www.vccofgb.com*

Olympia Fine Art and Antiques Winter Fair, London:
www.olympia-antiques.co.uk

Lord Mayor's Show, London: *www.lordmayorshow.org*

December

Social season closes in England, Scotland and Wales (Dec 10)

International Show Jumping Championships, Olympia, London:
www.olympiahorseshow.com

NSPCC Cinderella Ball, Savoy Hotel, London: *www.nspcc.co.uk*

Boxing Day Meeting, Kempton Park Racecourse, Surrey:
www.kempton.co.uk

5th June

The nearly US President, Senator Bobby Kennedy, was shot in 1968. He
died early on the morning of 6 June.

His assassination, five years after his elder brother's, shocked the world
as once again it was unwittingly caught on camera. It went on to inspire
Emilio Estevez's 2006 film *Bobby*, starring Anthony Hopkins, Demi Moore,
Sharon Stone, Lindsay Lohan and Martin Sheen. The film follows different
characters at the Ambassador Hotel on the day and shows how they were

affected by RFK's death. When it premiered at the Venice Film Festival in 2005, it received a seven-minute standing ovation.

'Those who dare to fail miserably can achieve greatly,' Robert Kennedy said. He became Attorney General when his elder brother, JFK, was President. With his heartfelt speeches, strong sense of family and charisma he rose from senate to candidate – no longer living in his brother's shadow. He was billed as America's great hope. He famously quoted George Bernard Shaw: 'There are those who look at things the way they are, and ask why. I dream of things that never were, and ask why not?' This was to be used by his youngest brother, Edward, during the eulogy describing the work and life of America's nearly President.

6th June

Coca-Cola registered their label in 1889.

How to break into music.

No, don't be fooled, it's not 'easy', however simple auditioning for *The X Factor* may seem. Nor does it happen overnight.

First things first – are you musical? Honestly? Talented? Then what is your style, inspiration and sound – group or soloist? Once you have gathered your group of like-minded misfits you have to then practise and perfect your sound, style and stage presence. Autograph-signing technique comes later. Once all this is polished and you can successfully and collectively carry a few tunes it's time to test yourselves on a dummy audience (the living and breathing kind, normally friends and relatives). They are bound to be biased but they should also be honest enough to prevent you from making a total fool of yourself. If you don't faint with fright in front of rent-a-crowd you are ready for the next phase. This is performing in front of an audience where members of the public attend, maybe even pay to see you. Just don't give up the day job quite yet.

The fast-forward checklist for a successful ascent to A-list musical status and Billboard fame varies from case to case but it does need harmony on and off stage. You need good tunes, an original sound, and most of all determination and a thick skin – plus a manager or mum. They will be the designated 'driver' to take you to all the gigs and presumably set up your fan base and sort out all the tricky things that rock stars just don't think about such as money, contracts, royalties. Groovy.

If you are good, make a demo, and try and tempt A&R scouts or radio stations (such as the Xfm with their Unsigned session programme) to listen to it. MySpace.com is host to thousands of up-and-coming new names and a hotbed of new stars. No unsigned band worth its encore would be silly enough not to have a MySpace page for the band, with their latest tracks available for potential groupies to listen to and download. Bribery and corruption is fine. Buy them a drink, dinner, or why not add an ironic mince pie and say: 'All I want for Christmas is to be number one.' Do you think you can achieve it in six months? That's something for the diary. Think of an angle that sets you apart.

Muse of the Month

Ella Fitzgerald

'The First Lady of Song', 'Lady Ella' is widely considered to be one of the most influential jazz vocalists of the last century. Fitzgerald had an incredible three-octave range, perfect pitch and a vocal versatility that had never been heard before, but more importantly she introduced a huge audience to the different emerging styles of jazz. Singing was effortless for her; to those who listened, her 'sound' was sophisticated and unmistakable. 'I didn't realize our songs were so good until Ella sang them,' composer Ira Gershwin commented.

We all know that a bottle of wine, a patient friend and a detailed dissection of what (or who) exactly is driving you crazy is one way to make the world feel a better place – but for a different approach, you could try singing. As Vincente Minnelli said, 'If you want to learn how to sing, listen to Ella Fitzgerald.' Shame you can't guarantee the results will be as good. Breathe in deeply, let your chest expand and instead of letting out a scream or counting up to ten, why not grab a mic and put your heart and soul into a song? True, you might not discover a mesmerizing and melancholic voice, but you'll definitely feel great for trying and there is less chance of incurring any physical pain yourself –which you might when kick-boxing or karate-chopping the problem out of your system. Give your neighbours earplugs. If you feel ready to take your sound out of the shower and into the classroom try *www.singers-uk.org* to find a teacher. Alternatively if you notice your audience is still wearing those earplugs, take a hint, sit back and listen to a masterclass from Ella. You could begin with her 1944 million-copy hit 'I'm Making Believe', or listen to her historic scats – such as in the 1947 bebop version of 'Lady Be Good'. Scroll through her song-books for the tunes you know so well – 'Summertime' is perfect for June.

Her life and times

Ella Jane Fitzgerald was born on 25 April 1917 in Newport, New Virginia. Her parents split up soon after her birth as they weren't right for each other; no drama. She was raised by her mother, Temperance (Tempie), in Yonkers, New York. A few years later they moved in with her mother's long-term boyfriend, Joseph Da Silva, and in 1923, when her half-sister, Frances, was born the happy family was complete. Though money was tight – Joe dug ditches and was a part-time chauffeur, her mum worked in a laundry and Ella would run errands for the local gamblers to help ends meet – life was good.

Tragedy struck in 1932 when her mother was killed in a car accident. Ella went to live with her Aunt Virginia (Tempie's sister), and not long after, grief-stricken Joe died of a heart attack, so her young sibling Frances joined her. Ella hated her new surroundings – she was miserable and her school grades plummeted. She went completely off the rails, so much so

that the police took her into custody and she was sent to a reform school. Ella was only fifteen, alone and abused, beaten by her 'carers', while America was in the grip of the Depression. Things couldn't have looked more bleak. But she was independent, determined, and no quitter – so she ran away from her foster home, deciding she would do better on her own. In later life she made huge donations to disadvantaged youth organizations to help provide them with better a start in life than she had.

Shy and self-conscious about her appearance, but desperate for money, she entered a local talent competition hoping to make a quick buck. On 21 November 1934, at the Apollo Theater Amateur Night, she made her (albeit accidental) singing debut. She entered as a dancer, but after the Edwards Sisters' performance, whom she described as 'the dancingest sisters around', she opted for a last-minute rethink. As Ella got on to the stage her knees shook so much there was no way she could dance. She asked the band to play one of her mother's favourite songs, Hoagy Carmichael's 'Judy', originally a hit for Connee Boswell. The audience went wild, so for her encore she sang 'The Object of My Affection'. . . Sometimes you just need to let destiny take a hand. The moment she was on stage singing, she was no longer shy and awkward, and dancing never got a second thought. Who cared if she wasn't a size ten? She had found her calling and was totally alluring. Ella was on top of the world – and yes, just like a great fairy tale, she was the winner of the contest.

Saxophonist Benny Carter was in the band that night and was blown away by her voice. He insisted he introduce her to all his contacts. And Ella? Well, she now entered every talent contest around – she couldn't get enough of the buzz, and if she got paid for it so much the better. Soon she was winning every competition she entered, and in January 1935 she won a chance to perform with the Tiny Bradshaw Band at the Harlem Opera House. Though Chick Webb (the bandleader) had just hired a male singer, he gave her a challenge – if she managed to impress the Yale university crowd she could stay the week. At the end of the night Ella Fitzgerald had secured a salary of $12.50 a week. She was on her way.

In 1936 she made her first recording, 'Love and Kisses'. As the swing band's style evolved to 'bebop', Ella used her voice – like a horn – to improvise, and made 'scat singing' her own. A new craze was born. In 1938, aged only twenty-one, she recorded 'A-Tisket, A-Tasket' originally a nursery rhyme, now a jazz/pop crossover smash that sold over a million copies. It reached number one and stayed in the pop charts for seventeen weeks. Ella was a star.

But with every high there comes a low – and on 16 June 1939 her mentor and bandleader Chick Webb died. Such was her popularity, the band who'd discovered her was now renamed Ella Fitzgerald and her Famous Band.

In the midst of all the glitz, fame and adulation she tried to ground herself so decided to marry a local dockworker, Benny Kornegay. Unfortunately she'd picked the wrong guy – Kornegay was a hustler and a drug dealer. When she discovered his shady side the short marriage was annulled. Ella's other relationship – with her band – didn't last long either as all she wanted to do was sing rather than have all the responsibility that went with the baton.

In 1941 she decided to pursue a solo career, preferring to guest with a variety of touring big-name bands rather than being tied to only one. 'Ella's musicianship is just incredible. Playing with her is like playing with a full orchestra,' gushed jazz drummer Ed Thigpen. 'Ella's voice becomes the orchestra's richest and most versatile sound,' continued musician Arthur Fiedler. 'Man, woman or child, Ella is the greatest of them all,' Bing Crosby concluded. It wasn't until 1946, despite singing about love every night, that Ella risked getting married again. While touring with Dizzy Gillespie's band she met and fell in love with the bassist Ray Brown whom she married. Together they adopted Ray Brown Jr.

Through her musician husband she met jazz impresario Norman Granz and joined his 'Jazz at the Philharmonic' tour. She collaborated with Louis Armstrong, became a TV regular on the Ed Sullivan, Frank Sinatra, Bing Crosby, Nat King Cole and Dean Martin shows. She had never been busier, but the touring and working took its toll on her family life. Ray and Ella divorced in 1952 and her adopted son Ray Jnr sadly would always come second to the schedule.

As well as juggling real life with superstardom, there was another thorn

in her side. Ella had to contend with the ugly truth of racial and sexual discrimination. She was a black woman – in a (narrow-minded) white man's world. On one occasion she and Dizzy Gillespie, plus his band, were arrested and taken to the station under some pretext. When they got there the police 'had the cheek to ask for an autograph' whilst they were detained for no reason other than the colour of their skin. Disgusting. While some couldn't bury their prejudices, there were plenty who saw only her incredible talent. 'I owe Marilyn Monroe a real debt,' she acknowledged. The sexy siren was such a fan she insisted the trendy nightclub Mocambo book Fitzgerald to perform. At first they were reluctant, but Monroe agreed to take a front-row table every night Fitzgerald was onstage. Ella became the first black woman to perform there – and it was a sell-out. '[Monroe] was an unusual woman – a little ahead of her times. And she didn't know it.'

Throughout the sixties and seventies Ella continued to headline around the world. In 1974 she did a sell-out two-week stint in New York, sharing the stage with Count Basie and Frank Sinatra. 'The best way to start any musical evening is with this girl. It don't get better than this,' Sinatra enthused.

In September 1986, aged sixty-nine, she underwent quintuple coronary bypass surgery, and diabetes was diagnosed as the cause of her failing eyesight. Despite pleas from her friends and family to slow down Fitzgerald kept on singing. By the start of the nineties she had recorded over two hundred albums, and in 1991 gave her final concert, at Carnegie Hall in New York.

Though her voice never aged, her health worsened. Towards the end she was nearly blind and was forced to have both legs amputated below the knees.

She died on 15 June 1996 at her home in Beverly Hills. But don't dwell on the end – listen to her legacy.

Ella-isms

'It isn't where you came from, it's where you're going that counts.'

'I stole everything I ever heard, but mostly I stole from the horns.'

'Just don't give up trying to do what you really want to do. Where there is love and inspiration, I don't think you can go wrong.'

'The only thing better than singing is more singing.'

Other iconic jazz singers to listen to include Billie Holiday, who went on to inspire Janis Joplin and Nina Simone. Holiday's life story was captured in the 1972 film *Lady Sings the Blues* with Diana Ross playing and singing the lead role, for which she earned a Best Actress Academy Award nomination. Billie Holiday was the inspiration behind U2's 1988 hit 'Angel of Harlem'. Diana Ross, and the band that started her career, the Supremes, was the inspiration for the 2007 film *Dreamgirls* starring Beyoncé Knowles and Pop Idol reject turned Oscar winner, Jennifer Hudson.

6th June

In 1972 *The Rise and Fall of Ziggy Stardust* was released by David Bowie.

Where did the glamming-up come from? Marc Bolan and producer Tony Visconti paved the way but Ziggy Stardust, the blue martian, who had come down to earth disguised as the ultimate rock star, was where it all went wild. Ziggy was in search of peace and love and a lot of sex, and initially Bowie concealed his true identity and lived the part to the full. He fused the names of two of his (conveniently iconic) friends, Iggy Pop and model Twiggy, and came up with the only name he could think of beginning with 'Z'.

Originally Ziggy's album was going to be all about clothes; well, what else would a glam martian with a penchant for dressing-up sing about? But the quest for love took over, and the album charted his adventures on planet earth.

The album was a smash. Ziggy/Bowie became a megastar. Style worked in tandem with sound, and the pop stylist's role was born. Just remember it's fine to have an alter ego but make sure the real you is the *best* you.

7th June

In 1937 the original blonde bombshell, actress Jean Harlow, died from a gallbladder infection aged only twenty-six.

Though only briefly in the limelight, her magnetism and on-screen presence has endured. From the moment she smouldered onto the screen in *Hell's Angels* to her appearance in *Platinum Blonde,* her on-screen and off-screen bad girl personality was mesmerizing. Her affair with Clark Gable, as well as her acting accomplishments, ensured her lasting fame and her last film with him had to be completed by a double as she died before *Saratoga* finished shooting, a macabre twist guaranteeing a cinema smash. See if you can work one of her classic quips – 'I like to wake up each morning feeling a new man' – into your schedule today.

8th June

Nancy 'these boots were made for walking' Sinatra was born in 1940. Why not treat your feet to a pedicure or a day in super-comfortable shoes?

9th June

Composer Cole Porter was born in 1891. Porter wrote hits including 'I've Got You Under My Skin', 'Kiss Me Kate' and 'Night and Day'. Definitely worth adding to your cabaret medley in preparation for festival season.

Two films were made about his life: *Night and Day* in 1946 with Cary Grant as Porter, and in 2004 *De-Lovely* with Kevin Kline as the lead. Only the latter mentioned his more colourful private life.

10th June

Judy Garland was born in 1922. Born a star, to paraphrase one of her later films. Garland signed a contract with MGM when she was only thirteen and made forty-three films. Most famous of all her songs was her rendition of 'Somewhere Over the Rainbow' by Harold Arlen, which was named Song of the Century by the American Film Institute. She sang it in *The Wizard of Oz*, one of the first big Technicolor movies. But what really stole the show was her ruby-red glitter shoes. The silk and sequin-covered shoes, finished with flat bows, lined in white kid leather, came in a size 5 $^1/_2$, and looked their best when she clicked them, saying, 'There's no place like home.'

In 1970 a pair sold for what was then a record sum of $15,000 before it was discovered that there could have been as many as seven pairs made in total, though only four were used. In the original book, written in 1900 by L. Frank Baum, Dorothy was actually given silver shoes, but the 'red slippers' in the 1939 MGM version have become the most recognized shoe in history (after Cinderella's glass slipper). They were the jewel in Minnesota's Judy Garland Museum's showcase – and were insured for $1 million, but on 28 August 2005 they were stolen, a story which made headlines all over the world.

How to wear red

Red shoes traditionally symbolize a wild party girl, though obviously not in Dorothy's case – clearly the block heel and sequins cancelled this out. Red lips, red nails, red shoes – how hot can you handle it? Red shoes seem to always dance towards the fierce and feisty.

Other famous red shoes feature in the 1948 ballet film *The Red Shoes*. The film follows the ballerina Moira Shearer as flame-haired Vicky who dances her way into the prestigious Ballet Lermontov (run by the ferocious yet debonair Boris Lermontov, played by Anton Walbrook). It's not Walbrook but the young composer of the company that she falls in love with and she has to choose between her love for him and her love of ballet. It's like *Phantom of the Opera* except Walbrook is not ugly just moody, and this is ballet not opera.

Of course she chooses love, so *The Red Shoes*, the ballet written for her, is banned. But the lure of the dance is too strong and some months later she is convinced by Lermontov to perform the ballet one last time. Her now husband is furious; once again it's an ultimatum – him or the ballet. This time she chooses the ballet, but at the last moment she changes her mind and runs to her husband, though just like the Hans Christian Andersen tale the film is based on, the dancing shoes lead their leading lady and she has to dance to the tune they choose.

Shoes can get you into terrible trouble.

The tale was also turned into a song in 1993 by Kate Bush and sold over 3 million copies worldwide, making the story part of pop culture as well as folklore.

12th June

On this day in 1942 Anne Frank began her diary. This is a timely reminder to check you have read and replied to all your emails, and to update your blog and MySpace pages while you spare a thought for Frank.

13th June

In 1967 *You Only Live Twice* premiered in the US – the twelfth novel in the Ian Fleming James Bond series, the fifth adapted for the screen, with screenplay by Roald Dahl, and the fifth appearance of Sean Connery as Bond.

To date there have been twenty-one Bond films charting the affairs and adventures of British secret service agent 007. They are the second highest grossing film franchise of all time (after *Star Wars*).

As well as Bond himself, what makes them so instantly recognizable is the signature theme. The 'James Bond Theme' was written by Monty Norman and performed by the John Barry Orchestra, while the title track is traditionally written and performed by a popular singer of the time. The linking of music and film, generating Bond success in the singles charts as well as the movie ratings, has been key to its eminence.

Best-known Bond tracks include:
Tom Jones, 'Thunderball', 1965
Carly Simon, 'Nobody Does It Better', 1977
Duran Duran, 'A View to a Kill', 1985
A-ha, 'The Living Daylights', 1987
Tina Turner, 'Golden Eye', 1995
Madonna, 'Die Another Day', 2002

But the reigning queen, so to speak, is Shirley Bassey who has performed three Bond titles : 'Goldfinger', 1964; 'Diamonds Are Forever', 1971; and 'Moonraker', 1971.

How to grab a graduate

Around the mid-June mark come the graduate shows in all subjects. You should particularly keep a keen eye out for the arts graduates with end-of-degree art and fashion shows providing an ample opportunity for you to find the 'next big thing' as they launch themselves into the big wide world.

Sites to keep an eye on for emerging stars include:
www.gfw.org.uk
www.goldsmiths.ac.uk
www.rca.ac.uk
www.csm.arts.ac.uk
www.ucl.ac.uk/slade
www.art-graduates.com
www.britisharts.co.uk/artistsavailable.htm

16th June

Gilbert & Sullivan's *HMS Pinafore* debuted in 1879, the Victorian music hall duo's first international hit. They went on to pen *The Pirates of Penzance* and *The Mikado* together. Have a sing-along today.

17th June

Russian composer, conductor and pianist Igor F. Stravinsky was born in 1882. Stravinsky was one of the most influential composers of his day, and principal composer for Sergei Diaghilev's Ballets Russes. While in Paris he collaborated with Picasso and Jean Cocteau and had an affair with Coco Chanel. His most famous compositions are *The Firebird* and *The Rite of Spring*.

18th June

In 1935 the Rolls-Royce trademark was registered and would become the iconic car for the seriously wealthy and successful to drive.

Owners include: Fred Astaire, Brian Jones, Elton John, Lady Penelope.

How to Wimbledon

An occasion for wearing whites – well, that means we are certainly not at Glastonbury yet – is the tennis. Tickets for Wimbledon are so hard to get hold of you have to enter a ballot – which makes you want to go even more.

The SW19 tournament has been taking place every summer since 1877, and happens in the last week of June and first week of July. It has been at its current address at the All England Lawn Tennis Club (AELTC) since 1922. Yet despite all the pomp and pride, no Brit boy has managed to win since Fred Perry in 1936, and no woman since Virginia Wade in 1977, unless you count the 2004 film *Wimbledon,* starting Paul Bettany, when he gets the girl *and* wins Wimbledon. You can't be serious.

Back to reality. On court there is all sorts of etiquette to observe. Players have to bow or curtsy to the royal box if it holds a member of the Royal Family (usually only on Finals Day). They have to wear white (the line judges and ball boys and girls have recently been given navy and white uniforms designed by Ralph Lauren), and of course they must remember good manners, which is why McEnroe and his volatile behaviour became so infamous.

Love and serve

This is the only time that you really want to avoid love. Love is the equivalent of a zero score in tennis.

The player who is serving for the game will have their score announced first – whether winning or losing. Keep your eye on the ball and when you work out who is serving then you can work out which way the points are going. You get two attempts to get the serve in and then it's a double fault and a score to the other side.

The points rise from 'love' to 15, 30, 40 and then it gets more heated. The player has to score two points ahead to win a game, so there is often a struggle between deuce (40 all) and 'advantage' before it's a clear game, set and match. (A set comprises the first player to win six games, but with a two-game or tie-break lead; three sets for women, five for men in the grandslam tournaments). Above all you must eat strawberries and cream (it's fine – you burn 100 calories in fourteen minutes of vigorous tennis playing). 28,000 kilos of strawberries and 7,000 litres of cream are consumed within the championships fortnight.

22nd June

The doughnut was created in 1847.

The original ingredients that first brought the doughnut into existence may be lost in myth, but Captain Hanson Gregory is thought to be the man who brought it to America. During a ferocious storm Gregory impaled his doughnut on the spoke of the ship's wheel, so both hands were free to control the ship and steer it to safety through treacherous waves. Not only did he prevent the boat becoming shipwrecked, Gregory also created the doughnut's signature hole, for which Homer Simpson will be eternally grateful.

24th June

Midsummer or the summer solstice occurs on this day at the end of June. Though many days may feel like the longest days of the year, if not your life, today is the official one to own the title. It's all downhill after today, with the sunlight hours getting shorter and shorter.

You can celebrate midsummer in various ways. You could take your yurt and incense sticks down to Stonehenge and party like a pagan, dance with the druids or play with the fairies.

A Midsummer Night's Dream

Written around 1595/96, this is one of Shakespeare's earliest comedies. It is thought to have been written as the entertainment for a real wedding feast (they didn't have DJs at the time).

The plot involves a complex weave of characters around the theme of unrequited love, donkey's ears and fairy mischief. In brief there are two couples: Hermia and Lysander, Helena and Demetrius. Hermia loves Lysander but is meant to marry Demetrius, whom Helena is in love with. Things are complicated further when they enter the fairyland woods where the king and queen of the fairies, Oberon and Titania, are quarrelling.

The tangle all stems from headstrong Hermia refusing to marry someone she doesn't love, but rather than risk being sent to a nunnery she decides to run away. Helena tries to win Demetrius for herself but, when she tells him of the planned elopement, her plan backfires and he runs off after Hermia – the object of his unrequited love. Oberon witnesses poor Helena desperate to please her man and decides to send his page Puck to sprinkle some love-at-first-sight potion over the foursome to help her out. The trouble is that when they wake up they see the wrong people. Chaos. Meanwhile Titania, who has also received Puck's potion, awakes. As a joke her husband has arranged for Bottom – an actor wearing an ass's head – to be the first thing she sees and consequently he becomes the apple of her eye.

How Shakespeare, or indeed Oberon, remedies the love-struck group should ideally be seen at an open-air performance on this magical date when the spirits are said to wander the earth.

The most famous open-air theatre is in Regent's Park, London; it opened in 1932. The play has been performed and linked to this date ever since its debut. Go to *www.openairtheatre.org* to book your Midsummer Night.

Find a local performance today or brew your own magic to ensure the right guy gets the right girl.

How to have a midsummer's night picnic
by Michael Howells, set designer

Take one enchanted isle . . . well, are you going to do this properly? The best would be in the middle of a beautiful lake in Shropshire or Hertfordshire, a secret find somewhere very English, rural and magical. Light Chinese lanterns in the trees and line the paths, and if you are really going for it you could import fireflies, or at least use tea lights and candles to help set the scene. If you do find that little isle, hopefully it is lost in a lake or lagoon and your guests have to take a little boat, and row or be rowed by very pretty oarsmen, maybe nymphs or sprites as the fairies will be out tonight. Purcell's 'Fairest Isle' could be sung as the boats swim the guests over to the picnic. Don't worry about rain; that's not allowed – though being England, make sure you have a back-up plan and a stash of parasols or pagodas as a standby.

If there is no island, create your own kingdom with rugs and fabric remnants, with hammocks, cushions and even little tents to conjure up your own 'Field of the Cloth of Gold' feel for one of Titania's feasts. But as much as *setting* the scene, all these details have to also appear in the food, which you want to be bewitching. Have violets tossed in the salads; petals and posies should be as much part of the menu as they are the decoration. Have elderflower water, pink champagne and roses as well as delicate sandwiches, jellies, fairy cakes and fairy food. Keep the food relatively simple so it's easy to transport and so you don't have to worry about cooking, serving and so on. As for plates, cutlery, cups and glasses, a mishmash of old plates from willow prints to chipped floral porcelain found at bric-a-brac stores are so much more inviting than papers ones – although they do mean washing-up will be needed. See what you think will suit your feast best as you scatter the ground with found objects, flowers, food and cushions for your guests to relax among and let the enchanted evening begin.

26th June

In 1977 the King – Elvis Presley – gave the last performance of his career in Indianapolis. Also on this date Cher divorced Sonny Bono in 1975: 'I Got You Babe' no more.

How to have festival chic

From feeling like a whiter-than-white washing powder advert during Wimbledon to wishing you were as you wallow in mud – festivals are the rock 'n' roll way to spend the summer. Glastonbury is the largest music festival in the world and happens every other year, partly to let the land recover and partly to let the other music festivals try and catch up. This is the haute couture of all festivals. Go to *www.glastonburyfestivals.co.uk*, Not to be confused with the opera festival Glyndebourne, *www.glyndebourne.co.uk*, which runs from May until August with three-course picnics and a much less muddy menu.

Other music festivals of note to pitch your tent at include:
Early June – Isle of Wight festival: *community.isleofwightfestival.com*
Late July – Secret Garden Party *www.secretgardenparty.com*;
    Cambridge Folk Festival. *www.cambridgefolkfestival.co.uk*
Early August – The Big Chill: *www.bigchill.net*
Mid-August – V Festival: *www.vfestival.com*
Late August – Reading Festival: *www.readingfestival.com*
End of August – Creamfields: *www.cream.co.uk*
Early September – Bestival: *www.bestival.net* (Features the biggest fancy-
    dress party in the world.)
Mid-March – The Green Man Festival: *www.thegreenmanfestival.co.uk*

There are also all sorts of international ones including Burning Man at the end of August, in the Black Rock desert, Nevada, US. Perfect for the crazy hippy in your life: *www.burningman.com*.

Mud, mud, glorious mud

While the debs are coming out, others are knee-deep in mud. There are so many different ways to 'come out'. In music festival terms Glastonbury is the 'big one'. Big in every sense of the word – the acres are as extensive and diverse as the band line-ups. If serious about this, make sure you make a note and get your ticket the moment they go on sale in March/April as this festival sells out faster than you can say 'mud'.

Founded in 1970, the first gathering took place only two days after Jimi Hendrix died – he would have surely been an ideal headliner. Marc Bolan was among the first ever headline acts, and 1,500 people attended. It is a very different story and scale today although the original spirit survives.

When going to a festival it's best to go in a group – and here I mean an assorted group of fellow audience members, not as in drummer, guitarist, backing singer, etc. When buying your ticket get your friends organized and aim to buy in bulk (and no, this doesn't guarantee prime location or better tent pitches, but it means safety in numbers and someone else to carry and assemble said tent).

Glastonbury now has over 2,000 performances (not including all the off-stage ones like: 'How do you put up a tent?', 'Who stole the guy ropes?', and in at number one, 'Come with me to the portaloo, I'm scared'). There are over thirty-eight stages, pitched over fields of 700 acres (with a perimeter of eight and a half miles). With not a taxi or road in sight, it's all *à pied* so don't lose your way as it takes about four hours to walk the entire perimeter.

So, why are you doing this? What are you letting yourself in for, Little Miss Dry-Clean Only? Well, at a festival everything is live and on tap right in front of you. Rather than change radio stations you just wander a few steps to the left or right to see what's happening in another field. Everyone has different tastes in clothes and shoes so, similarly, people's taste in music differs widely. Try and pack a good cross-section of people as well as shirts. Music is much more personal than clothes – you can live with colour clashes, but discord or techno squeals that hurt your ears could have you heading for the hills. Anyway, there will be so many thousands of people milling around, chances are you'll lose whoever you came with. Be a social flutterby and mingle through the tents, fields and twilight hours, find new friends and new bands to download and impress those who didn't come when you go home.

Play your cards right and maybe you could end up inspiring a rock god to pen a classic (see page 241). Hopefully there will be some gallant gent, complete with torch, happy to check your guy ropes won't become a death trap once the lights go out. If nothing else, it will make you really appreciate all your creature comforts when you get home.

Have a heart

Love is in the air – and that's nothing to do with the cocktails of sounds, spirits and so on. As well as the music there is a good cause at the heart of Glastonbury. Michael Eavis, the man who really brought this festival to life, always donates a percentage of the profits to charity. The three main charities now supported are Oxfam, Greenpeace and Water Aid, plus a 'gift' to the nearby town of Pilton, the lives of whose inhabitants presumably have to go on hold for this week of invasion.

What to wear

The big question is what groups you should watch but, frankly, a lot harder to get right is of course what the heck do you wear? Kate Moss single-handedly brought the waistcoat back into fashion when she wandered around Glastonbury in 2005. Then again, she has the ability (however unfair) to look perfect in anything. Probably even a binbag. She's a hard icon to live up to. Just how can you make a fashion statement in a cagoule and wellies?

Know your pain threshold. Watch Julian Temple's doc-film *Glastonbury* from the comfort of your sofa to get an idea of what to expect.

Don't go out and buy an entire new wardrobe; similarly do not pack all your favourites – the couture, the vintage, the priceless. Get a balance. Don't pack clothes so grim you can't bear to leave the tent. Cheap, cheerful and, frankly, chuckable.

Do not even consider wings, costumes or any other such frivolity. They can be chaffing, uncomfortable and take up valuable luggage space.

The *chic* list

Bikini (hope for the best)

Cagoule (be realistic, come prepared for the worst)

Vests (small and easy to pack)

Cut-off jeans/skirt (legs permitting and easier to dry)

Jumper (it does get cold when the sun goes in; you *are* in England and this can also double as pillow)

Jeans (as above, and you will want some 'civilian' type of gear to arrive in)

T-shirts (hope for good weather, but all sorts of band T-shirts and merchandise will be available on site so you could hold on to see who you want emblazoned over your chest. Alternatively you can model one you've customized for yourself.)

Make-up bag (though keep it minimal: sunscreen, lip-balm, mascara, the basics)

Flip-flops

Trainers (good for the travel look too)

Hunter wellies (the best, let's have at least *one* designer label)

Toothbrush

Pocket mirror (you will want to try and keep up appearances)

Plasters and painkillers (let's be realistic)

Obviously, the fine-tuning of underwear-count, shoes and so on is down to you but keep things minimal and disposable. You have to carry everything and wheelie cases get horribly stuck as they drag through grass. Also, as much as 'love is all around', generally speaking a tent makes safe-guarding your stuff difficult. Leave any diamonds, heirlooms and Manolos (sob) at home. Hunting 700 acres for a dropped contact lens is bad, but a lost diamond will be as infuriating as it is close to hopeless.

The hottest two accessories you can hope for are wellies (see page 163) and a backstage pass.

As much as you may want to look stylish, you'll appreciate feeling warm and dry more. This is a very New Look for the fashiony and worth embracing. Clean? You'll have to fudge that one. You'll have to make up for it by soaking in a hot bath for a few days when you get home.

Also in the packing you will need to remember tents, toilet paper and so forth. There is no room service here – cater for survival. Fully charged phone, torches, matches, sense of humour all go without saying.

Plan your packing with sober, military precision from sunglasses to shelter. Rather than pack your perfume bottles, try and get sample sizes. Antiseptic wipes or Wet Ones will also help life feel less revolting. Socks are a must, while hairdryers and straightening irons do not work in a field.

Rock chick royalty

If you are going for a rock-chick look the ultimate muse is Patti Boyd. Super-model of her day, she modelled for Ossie Clark and Mary Quant, and was a photographer and the inspiration behind two of the greatest hits of the twentieth century.

George Harrison of the Beatles was crazy about her after spotting her in their 'A Hard Day's Night' video, where she played a naughty schoolgirl (years ahead of Britney). They got together, got married and he went on to write 'Something' for her, which Frank Sinatra called the 'greatest love song ever written'. Boyd cast a spell on the leading icons of the day – with Mick Jagger and John Lennon also trying, and failing, to catch her eye.

But broken-hearted and fed up with his rock-god philandering ways, Boyd left Harrison. After years of chasing her, Eric Clapton finally won her heart. He had even written 'Layla' about his frustration over his unrequited love, and later wrote 'You Look Wonderful Tonight' to describe his date with her at the McCartneys' annual Buddy Holly Party, on 7 September 1976. That must have been some dress. From compliment to chart classic.

Boyd divorced Harrison in June 1977, then divorced Clapton in June 1988 after eleven years of marriage to each man. She has vowed never to marry again. (What do you go for – the better man or the better song? And what has *your* boyfriend written for you lately?) Read more about her in *Wonderful Today: The Autobiography of Patti Boyd* by Patti Boyd and Penny Junor.

How to customise your T-shirt for Glastonbury – or Glyndebourne

by Amanda Harlech, fashion designer

You will probably need a parka not a T-shirt in the rain – but if the sun shone I would do my own slogan T-shirt along the 'Drop

Beats Not Bombs' line. Rip the sleeves and the hem of the neck off for starters and then draw your own idiosyncratic doodle tattoo with a black marker-pen – strategic placement is essential. I had an old Verbier T-shirt with a mountain which had evaporated into incandescent snow spume on the flat of an iron, so I wrote 'Tinkerbell' (Peter Pan's not Paris Hilton's) across the snowline. I was finally the evil fairy – perfect!

Panos, one of the greatest stylists on the planet, uses safety pins – lots of them – on a black shredded T-shirt (not a new black one; it must be washed to a soft virtual grey). With patience you can achieve a chain-mail look – and add a bit of black lace at the shoulder or across the breast for a chivalric flavour. A destroyed wisp of a Victorian silk bodice could be pinned or crudely tacked (visible stitching is good – use red thread like blood!) onto your T-shirt for a romantic look with cleavage coverage.

And then there's always your boyfriend's contribution – why not get him to print 'You Are Mine' in finger-paint. Whatever you do, make it as original, fun and unpredictable as you can manage.

28th June

In 1902 Richard Rodgers was born – one half of the Rodgers & Hammerstein team that composed, amongst other things, *The Sound of Music*. Ideal to sing in those green fields while you build up your trendy new playlist.

But for real random trivia to discuss around the campfire, did you know that on this date in 1820 the tomato was proven non-poisonous? How different life would have been, and how different pizzas, spaghetti bolognaise, salad and, of course, ketchup would have become. Far-out, man.

 *Foot Note*

The wedge

What is the difference between the platform and the wedge? To many people not a lot. To the wearer it is perfectly clear: one hoists you in one direction, the other elevates you in another. A wedge is a more delicate platform, and essentially lifts just the heel to give you all the height yet none of the hassle. The advantage over a stiletto is that there is a much more generous centre of gravity, so you can run around all day. The effect of the wedge style is like walking on a block of cheese, rather than a stiletto's bread stick, if you want a foodie analogy.

The wedge was invented in 1936 by Salvatore Ferragamo. When Brazilian bombshell Carmen Miranda exploded onto the Hollywood scene, the diminutive diva made her entrance in glittering wedged shoes and put the idea on the map. Miranda, a mere five foot in height but so much more in melodrama, went on to record 'I Like to be Tall' in 1955 as she stood singing in eight-inch wedges. The wedge is considered the more seductive of the blocked heels, as the curve of the wedge can accentuate the curves it carries. When it was first carved, wood and leather were being rationed and in short supply so an alternative had to be found fast. Ferragamo found cork, waxed its surface, and a very successful lightweight lifter was born; well, you wouldn't want bricks on your feet. In the seventies the company Kork-Ease launched an entirely cork-soled line which inspired espadrille weavers to work an extra cushion into their heels. Though little can topple the appeal of the heel, a wedge can give all the illusion and stature without any of the disadvantages, and can navigate many tricky surfaces, such as cobbles, grass (festival-tastic!) and gratings. It is an ideal extra for the high-heel devotee's trousseau.

'Lovers don't finally meet somewhere,
they're in each other all along'
Rumi

Wish You Were Here

Matthew Williamson from India

I'm writing to you here from my houseboat in Kerala, while taking in the stunning backwater scenery! It is so relaxing here and the massages are amazing.

Before I arrived in Kerala I was working in Delhi. From old Delhi I took a cab to Rajasthan and stopped off along the way at Neemrana Fort Palace. This place was amazing. An old crumbling fort on top of a hill with a tiny village beneath. The rooms were 'beautifully distressed' and quite inspiring. I could hear chanting from the village and see parrots in full flight, circling the fort as I looked out of my arched windows to watch the sun go down.

My favourite place in India has been Udaipur in Rajasthan – the perfect combination of the picturesque, the romantic and the mystery that makes India such a unique experience. It is really worth visiting the Lake Palace there.

Also, definitely important to make the trip to Jodhpur. The vegetable thalis at the roof-top restaurant of the Haveli Inn are probably the best in India. Elsewhere, I've been writing my diary and reading Alastair Sawday's *Special Places to Stay – India* which is the ultimate guidebook for those wishing to wander off the beaten track.

Will make sure I bring you back some lovely silver costume jewellery and fabulous patterned lightweight fabrics.

Lots of love, Matthew

1st July

In 1930 Imelda Marcos, the world's most famous shoe collector and former First Lady of the Philippines, was born.

'I did not have 3,000 pairs of shoes, I had 1,060,' she commented in 1987. It is not known how many pairs she has accumulated since then. 'I was born ostentatious,' she said. 'They will list my name in the dictionary some day. They will use *Imeldific* to mean ostentatious extravagance.' This is the perfect word to have in mind during the month for planning a wedding.

How to get a ring on your finger

The origin of *tying the knot* stems from Sweden where, long ago, illiterate sailors and soldiers would send a piece of rope to their sweethearts as a marriage proposal. The rope was sent with two ornate knots and if it came back with the two twisted and tied together this would mean 'yes'. The knotting crossed any language or literacy barriers. If, however, the maid preferred to be wooed with flowers and pretty verse, a piece of rope was not likely to win her (and quite probably the only rope tying she'd be doing would be making a noose. A noose should be taken as a very bad sign by any knot man).

Fortunately, things have moved on, and now an engagement is symbolized by a ring on the left hand. Back in 1856 the glimpse of a glove-free hand could tell you everything you needed to know about a man or woman. An article called 'Love's Telegraph' in the first edition of etiquette manual *Enquire Within* explained:

> If a gentleman wants a wife, he wears a ring on the first finger of his left hand; if he is engaged he wears it on the second finger; if he is married, on the third; and on the fourth if he intends never to be married.

When a lady is not engaged she wears a hoop diamond on her first finger; if engaged, on her second; if married, on her third; and on the fourth if she intends to die a maid.

If you think a proposal is imminent you can casually discuss the options. You can either:

1 Choose the ring together (combining your taste + his credit card + your finger)
2 Inherit an heirloom of great beauty and value (or, if it's not very nice, feign that it doesn't fit and resort to option 1)

Without sounding like too much of a brat you want to end up with something you love as you'll (hopefully) be wearing this ring for ever. Look at the site *www.engagement-rings-guide.com* for a few starter tips or turn to *How to pick a diamond* on page 435. (Note: this section refers to the rock rather than the fiancé though both will need polishing.)

Diamond is the most popular choice of stone for an engagement ring – with good reason. In medieval Italy a diamond was called the *pietra della reconciliazione* (the stone of reconciliation) and wearing them was thought to prevent squabbles – definitely a good move when planning your wedding. But then again, when has giving a girl a diamond not produced a positive reaction?

How to get hitched

Once all the tears of joy/relief and congratulations have subsided there is not a moment to lose.

Now you have got him to commit you need to:

Set a date

Book a venue

Draw up a guest list
Send out announcements and invites
Find/order/design the dress

Does he know what he has let himself in for? More to the point – do you?

With all that is involved in pulling off a big white wedding the planning usually takes about six months, so have this as the minimum length of your engagement. November engagements for a summer wedding are ideal – unless you get chronic hay fever in which case you might want to think of another time of year for your do. When you accept his proposal, casually calculate how much planning you need to do before you'll be ready to go up the aisle. A run, a sprint or a leisurely stroll – it's up to you, but see the checklist on page 252, for what you need to cross off to achieve perfection on your big day.

Before you throw away your independence for love and invest everything in a joint bank account, take stock of 'what's mine and what's yours'. It's grown-up, cards-on-the-table time. Talk future and finance as well as flowers and fairy-tale endings. (Sorry.) Do you want to be a stay-at-home mum? Would you be happy as the woman who lived in the shoe, or are five children enough? Are you the breadwinner or the housekeeper? Good gracious, this *is* grown-up. Prenups might not be for everyone but, without meaning to throw cold water on the moment, think of the trouble the wagon-wheel coffee table caused Marie (Carrie Fisher) and Jess (Bruno Kirby) in *When Harry Met Sally*. Establish who owns what now: the mortgage, the cat, the larger bank account, etc. Things can be split fairly at this pre-entanglement point. It should also prevent gold-diggers taking you for everything – heart *and* bank balance. A stitch in time . . .

Consider this contract now while you're in the flurries of choosing engagement rings, setting dates and are so deliriously in love – and accommodating – that the idea of breaking up seems ludicrous. Hopefully the prenup will be one of those things that is never seen or thought of again. It's a bit like making a will – yes, it's dull, but it saves hassle in the long term.

Back to the bouncy side of things: nowadays engagement parties are more popular than printing a formal engagement announcement in a national newspaper (yes, it's optional, but friends, relatives and exes you've lost contact with will love this; it also exonerates you from forgetting to tell anyone). Phone or email the preferred newspaper and ask for their deadlines and rates. For weddings and engagements some papers insist on signatures from both parties or a trusted parent or third party to avoid being responsible for printing an elaborate joke. Keep your text short and snappy (you pay by the word). You don't need to mention your 'pleasure' and 'delight'. But with email and text making it possible to convey all your news to your entire address book in an instant, you could ditch this tradition and spend the money on champagne instead.

Before throwing your party and announcing your glad tidings to the world, try and decide, even if only vaguely, when you want the wedding to take place. It is a fact universally acknowledged that the moment you get engaged you will become an object of curiosity that inspires only two questions:

Have you set the date?

Can I see the ring? (Regular manicures are clearly essential at this time in your life as the left hand will take centre-stage.)

Avoid dragging the engagement out for too long after you've found the dress as it will be hard to resist showing your husband-to-be for so many months.

Whatever you read there is no right and wrong way to plan a wedding, there are just things to consider – if you want to get married in a hot-air balloon or at a music festival, just find one that has the licence to do so. Whether you want the big church wedding or to run away to a tropical island, now is the time to action all those plans that have been simmering – consciously or not – ever since you performed your first Barbie and Ken wedding ceremony at playschool. Discuss these plans with your betrothed – the current plan, not the playschool version.

Are you planning on inviting all and sundry or are you thinking small and intimate? Will you be on horseback, in Elvis get-up or do you fancy having more bounce to the day, because you can get married in an inflatable church. Seriously: *www.inflatablechurch.com.*

Whether you want the full-on *Four Weddings and a Funeral* white wedding with all the trimmings or not, use the skeleton of the traditional and edit to fit your requirements. Here comes the checklist. Basically, you can get married once you have achieved everything on this list.

Decisions

Once you've got the all-clear – or at least told the families – it's time to choose Best Man, Bridesmaids and Maid of Honour. (Note: before going wild with the number of bridesmaids remember it's the bride who has to dress them.)

Make an appointment to see your local priest/vicar/rabbi/registrar or whoever will be conducting the service. Agree on the venue (*you* agree, not the parents; it is *your* wedding, but don't snub them totally as this is something they will have dreamed of too). Will it be religious or not? What order of service and style do you want? Book the time and date. Start the paperwork; if you are Catholic this can be as time-consuming as doing a tax return. For better, for worse really starts now.

Call the General Register Office to check that the venue you want to marry in is licensed to legally host the ceremony. Check also that your chosen registrar is licensed to perform it. The first is more necessary when wanting to marry on unicycles, motorways or on Centre Court and is not necessary for usual places of worship as they come fully consecrated, but it would be a drag, to say the least, to host the knees-up and have no legally binding paperwork for your efforts. Call 0151 471 4817 or go to *www.gro.gov.uk/gro/content* for the full list of approved places to marry in England.

Legally you need to give at least fifteen days' notice of a marriage in England while three months is preferred in Scotland, but finding a venue that isn't booked up for months in advance anyway tends to be the date-deciding factor. Church of England weddings can only take place if the 'banns' have been called on three successive Sundays in advance of the marriage. It announces an intentended marriage and allows the congregation to object if they know of any reason why the wedding can't go ahead. No news is good news. This comes prior to the bit in the actual wedding ceremony when everything has already been paid for and they ask: 'If anyone here knows of any lawful impediment . . .' In the best romcoms, someone will always burst in and punch someone at this point. In reality this is not to be encouraged; it can be a real mess and no one likes to spoil the big day; and, frankly, what will you do with all those guests? A note of caution if you are planning on being the one to object to the nuptials: if you don't have *proof* that the wedding should be called off, and your objection is unfounded, you're liable to pay for the whole thing!

When you book a venue for your wedding it's generally recommended to choose a nearby location for the reception or party – you don't want to lose key guests en route.

Setting the budget

Before you book the caterer/DJ/band/photographer/someone to do the video, shop around, ask friends for recommendations as well as look online and in magazines. Get a few quotes. If you want the works it may be worth seeing if you can hire a professional, like Jennifer Lopez in *The Wedding Planner* (just hope that it isn't actually someone as beautiful as her as she ends up with the groom in that film). Allocate any bonuses and savings to a wedding fund. Remember summer is the peak period so the best places do get booked up months, sometimes years in advance, and they often charge more at this time of year. Only book friends and relatives if you *know* they can do a good job (i.e. they have a proven track record); what you might save in cost you could gain in stress. Why add drama to the day?

Sit down with parents from both sides (hopefully they have met before this occasion and can politely get on). Discuss the size, style and scale of wedding you are planning. Draw up a guest list – and debate just how many relatives you've never met actually need to come. Keep remembering this is *your* wedding. If it's getting too out of hand you can always run away and elope – just do something that suits you.

'Budgeting' and the 'big day' are not two things that happily go together but forewarned is forearmed. If you do your guest list alongside catering quotes and budget planning this will help you keep a reality check on the numbers to invite. Now is also the time to find out how much, or how little, the parents on both sides want to chip in.

This is the biggest day in a girl's life, so even if you don't have *Hello!* or *OK!* clamouring to cover your nuptials you'll still be the centre of attention, so hang the expense (as far as possible)! Pull out all the stops to make sure this is the best day ever. But becoming a Bridezilla is something to avoid.

Worry Not Dot Com

Websites that are *invaluable*, as well as compulsive reading for all brides-to-be as well as invitees, include: *www.confetti.co.uk*, who have also published a series of manuals for all concerns connected to the big day, and Condé Nast's *www.bridesmagazine.co.uk*.

Costs can be controlled by culling the guest list down to the essentials, combining wedding and honeymoon, or buying a dress off the rack rather than a couture number spun from pure gold.

The Budget Planner

Key: FOB = Father of the Bride

Get FOB a strong drink before discussing this with him, as (traditionally) he gets to pay for all this. These prices are approximate and there are plenty of ways you can pay less. You need to look at your entire wardrobe before choosing what to pack or what to wear; similarly, here you should see all the options and possibilities before editing them down to the things you can't live without on the day. Can your brother double as photographer? Can you persuade your closest friends that they don't need food? Can some of your aunties make sandwiches if you organize a fun evening with fish paste and DVDs? Indeed, why not spend your wedding night in a tent?

OK, that might be taking things too far, but be sensible too. If you know a famous photographer, now would be the time to call him up and ask if he's free on this date, and if he'd like to be more than a guest. If you know a chef, ask if they have ever catered private family events (and would they like to do yours instead of a wedding gift), and so on. DJs, dress designers, flower arrangers, drivers, ushers, waiters, contacts, contacts, contacts. Really, as long as the bride and groom are there, what else really matters? How many extras do you really need?

According to figures suggested by *www.bridesmagazine.co.uk*, this is going to add up. Deep breath – here we go . . .

The must-haves	Average cost	Who pays
Engagement ring	£1,180	Groom
Press announcement	£100	FOB
Wedding rings	£600	Groom
The dress	£2,000	Bride
Shoes	£150	Bride
Veil/accessories	£250	FOB
Hair (and trial)	£200	Bride
Make-up (and trial)	£200	Bride
Lingerie	£200	Bride
Groom's outfit	£400	Groom
Ushers' suits	£300	Groom
Bridesmaids' outfits	£500	Bride
Going-away outfit	£500	Groom
Licence fees/bann/reg.	£500	Groom
Invitation and printing	£300	FOB
Flowers	£600	Groom
Wedding service details	£200	FOB
Hiring organist	£100	FOB
Hiring choir	£100	FOB
Hiring celebrity guest	£500+	*Hello!/OK!*

Reception venue	£2,500	FOB
Catering and food	£3,500	FOB
Drink	£1,000	FOB
The cake	£800	FOB
Band/DJ	£1,000	FOB
Photographer	£2,000	FOB
Professional Video	£2,000	FOB
Transport	£500	FOB
First night hotel	£500	Groom
Honeymoon	£3,000	Groom
Happily Ever After	Priceless	Happy Couple

The dress

Well, this is a *whole* crisis in itself so turn to the dedicated section, just after couture, on page 265. A made-to-measure number takes four to six months, so allow time for your Cinderella creation to come to life when planning this option. Do you want to wear something white or something more suited to you, the venue, your life, your man? Little Bo Peep is fine but if you're saying 'I do' at a registry office you might prefer cocktail and smartest Sunday best over trying to squeeze a big mound of meringue through the fast-turning municipal doors.

If this is your wedding and dilemma, go to the Designer Wedding Show in London – *www.designerweddingshow.co.uk* – where there are often catwalk presentations of the top styles and designer names available. Any wedding events or trade fairs you can get to are helpful so you can see all the hot new names. Companies with all the best dress, cake, shoe, catering and associated essentials will be at these events to help you, and hopefully get your custom. Yes, you can take your cheque book, but go for ideas as much as solutions. Find out what you *do* want as much as *don't*. Go with a friend, not the groom – a) he's not meant to see the dress in advance, and b) this will terrify him, so who knows how much therapy he'll need afterwards?

Staying with the traditional, after the dress you now need to think of:

The suits

Men may *think* they have this under control but the women need to keep a close eye on this. Ensure that if he's hiring the morning suits, they are in fact hired. If buying them, make sure the correct sizes, shirts and so on are purchased. This needs to happen for the groom as well as the best man, ushers and fathers. Check they coordinate on this.

Rings

His and hers. Welsh gold is in rare supply and reserved for royalty, but whatever you choose, ensure you have matching bands of gold/white gold/platinum/silver to complete your big day. The wedding band symbolizes the never-ending circle (two halves equal a whole). Ancient Egypt and Rome believed a vein from the fourth finger led straight to the heart so the ring is placed on a direct path to the heart – if you are wearing one why shouldn't he? Make it clear he's taken. And don't let the best man lose them; that's a very old gag.

The flowers

These include the bridal bouquet, flower girls' posies, buttonholes and church flowers. You cannot rush out the day before and hope for the best.

Invitations

You can put a bit of your own stamp on these and design them yourselves. For instance, take a favourite book cover or CD artwork for 'your song' and adapt it using a photograph of the two of you together or an illustration that means something special to you. Be sure to send them out at least six to eight weeks in advance. Create or supply a specific email address for the RSVP in addition to a postal address. It's very nice to supply addressed and stamped reply cards, which also act as a nudge for invitees to reply. Try to avoid any excuses that leave your caterers guessing on the numbers to expect. It's very simple – no RSVP, no place on the seating plan.

If you are one of the invited and you haven't RSVPed, shame on you – karma will catch up with you and haunt you when it's your turn. Don't even think about dragging along a plus one for company without getting the nod from the wedding couple. Similarly, babies need to get the all-clear – those teething and nappy-wearing might not take much of a bite out of the catering budget, but a crèche is preferable to having a screaming child drowning out the vows.

Remember your Ps and Qs on the wedding invitations as they go out for scrutiny to all your friends and relations. Traditionally the bride's parents are the hosts, so they do the inviting. Nowadays the bride and groom often organize the wedding themselves, which simplifies things incredibly.

Sticking with tradition it should read something like this:

Mr and Mrs John Spencer
request the pleasure of
your company at the marriage
of their daughter
Diana
to
Mr Charles Windsor
on Saturday, 29th July
at 3 o'clock
at St Paul's Cathedral
and afterwards at
Buckingham Palace, London.

If, however, as in the case above, the bride's parents are actually divorced and the mother has remarried it should read: 'Mr John Spencer and Mrs Frances Shand Kydd', while if the parents are divorced and she hasn't re-married it reads: 'Mr John Spencer and Mrs Frances Spencer'.

If you are marrying royalty, or indeed you come with a title, say as the daughter of 'the Viscount and Viscountess Althorp, the (8th) Earl Spencer and the Hon. Mrs Shand-Kydd, daughter of the 4th Baron Fermoy', crikey you're going to need some help. Did you allow room for their royal highnesses, titles and any coats of arms? You may need a bigger invite.

Order of service

A printed programme of the day makes a nice memento as cake can go mouldy.

Will you have a procession? Who is giving you away? Do you want any readings? Who is going to witness the marriage – friends, family or passing strangers? Think about the vows (this bit is essential), the exchanging of rings, signing the register, lighting a unity candle, the declaration of marriage. Do you want music to walk in to? Or music to keep the crowd entertained while you think about walking in, music to sign to, music to walk out to? The kiss – will it be a blush-saving peck or a full-blown smooch? Inside or outside? At home or abroad? Or in mid-air?

Transport

You should organize this not only for the wedding party but also for the guests (a minibus is always fun). And don't forget a car to whisk the happy couple away at the end of the evening – it's not the night to be waiting around for the night bus.

If the wedding is taking place in a foreign country it's perfectly acceptable that guests who make the effort to come pay for their flights and accommodation. When organizing this, try to block-book and get cheaper deals for everyone, and give advice on accommodation and other local information they'll need.

Wherever the island of love might be, transport there is only a cost to be picked up by the newly-weds if they offer and they happen to have recently won the lottery. If it's small and intimate, or you are attending one involving a very A-list celebrity, there's a chance you may be escorted onto a private jet to whisk you to a secret destination. As the bride, make sure you invite as many photogenic friends as possible, as well as your nearest and dearest – think of the albums in the years to come.

If the wedding is in your homeland, there are still many things to consider. That countryside chapel is still miles away from where the majority of the guests live (it is traditional to have it in the town the bride is from), so the couple should suggest local hotels or B&Bs so revellers don't have far to stagger. The to-be's should try and help keep the guests' costs down – you will ensure not only a better turn-out and calibre of guests, but better gifts. A happy guest is a generous guest.

Honeymoon

Book it and don't let him be stingy (see page 285).

Once you've ticked off all of the above, tried on your dress, worked out how you're going to do your hair, whether you'll change your name or not, now *at last* you are ready to say 'I do'.

2nd July

Butch Cassidy and the Sundance Kid robbed a train of $40,000 in 1901. Perhaps they too had a wedding to plan.

The Great Gatsby
F. Scott Fitzgerald

Why

With summer holidays and summer weddings beckoning, you won't need much encouragement to think about romance. Do you ever? This is the month to read about matters of the heart, rekindle old flames, or find new fancies.

Who

Francis Scott Key Fitzgerald (24 September 1896–21 December 1940) was a dashing American whose novels perfectly captured the jazz age in Prohibition America, and reflected his decadent lifestyle.

Born in St Paul, Minnesota, to an affluent Roman Catholic family, he started writing in the First World War when he enlisted in the US army. Luckily the war ended before he saw action; unluckily, his first novel *The Romantic Egotist* was rejected. But it wasn't time completely wasted, because during his training at Camp Sheridan he met and got engaged to Zelda Sayre, who was considered the most beautiful girl in her home state of Montgomery, Alabama. She was a bewitching natural blonde, with flawless skin and striking dark eyes. Undaunted by his earlier rejection, and empowered by love, he re-edited his novel, renamed it *This Side of Paradise* and it was published in March 1920. The following week he and Zelda were married.

The Fitzgeralds were New York's golden couple who split their time between America and Europe. Their only child, a daughter, Frances 'Scottie' Fitzgerald, was born on 26 October 1921. 'Sometimes I don't know whether Zelda and I are real or whether we are characters in one of my novels,' he commented.

In 1922 *The Beautiful and Damned* was published, followed by *The Great Gatsby* in 1925, which he considered his greatest work, and in 1934 *Tender Is the Night*. Zelda was his muse but her kooky, erratic behaviour was later diagnosed as schizophrenia, as captured in *Tender Is the Night*. Sadly her mental illness got worse, and the couple became estranged, eventually separating. She claimed he took pages from her diary and used them for his novels. In 1932 she published her own autobiographical novel, *Save Me the Waltz*. It was said to have been written in six nights, in between her attacks of insanity, and gives her side of the story portrayed in *Tender Is the Night*. In 1948 Zelda died tragically in a freak fire that burned down the hospital where she was committed. Though overshadowed by her husband, her life has been turned into a play, *The Last Flapper* by William Luce.

Whatever might be happening in his private life, Fitzgerald was embraced by Hollywood and went on to sell the film rights to his novels, write short stories, and work at MGM on screenplays, including some scenes for *Gone With the Wind*. Fitzgerald kept writing, and took out loans to fund his lifestyle. Towards the end of his life he moved in with his lover Sheila Graham and wrote seventeen short stories under the pseudonym Pat Hobby. He suffered two heart attacks in 1940, the second proving fatal, and left his final work *The Love of the Last Tycoon* unfinished.

The plot

Some guys are hard to get over, others are impossible to forget. Take Jay Gatsby – a wealthy, dashing bachelor with a penchant for throwing wild parties. No chance.

When Nick Carraway, a New York bond dealer, befriends his new neighbour it seems Gatsby has it all. But Gatsby is unlucky in love – or, more accurately, still heartbroken over the one that got away: Daisy Buchanan.

As luck would have it Daisy turns out to be Carraway's second cousin, married to one of his old Yale classmates, Tom Buchanan. Gatsby can't resist getting Carraway to do some investigating and they discover her husband is having an affair. Gatsby sees his opportunity and he begs Carraway to help him meet Daisy. It's five years since he last saw her

– he's fought in the war and made his fortune. Daisy (very much like Fitzgerald's own wife) is hypnotically beautiful and was inundated with alternative offers when Gatsby proved too unreliable in his youth. Although married, sparks fly from the moment they are reunited and the sexual tension is palpable on the page.

The obvious ensues, but does she love Gatsby or her cheating husband? She thinks she loves both. Problem. There is the confrontation, the getaway and the consequences as the decadence of the jazz age comes crashing down around them.

Hosting

For this meeting why not throw a garden party with a twenties theme or issue a flapper dress code? Watch the film starring Robert Redford as Gatsby and Mia Farrow as Daisy for costume inspiration. Why not learn to Charleston, play poker, tiddlywinks or cards before debating the pros and cons of old flames and *www.friendsreunited.com*?

Alternative reads for long summer nights:

Guilty pleasures like a Jilly Cooper or Joanna Trollope.

Meaty classics such as *Vanity Fair* by William Makepeace Thackeray.

Female psyche and desire are explored in novels like *The Prime of Miss Jean Brodie* by Muriel Spark or A.S. Byatt's *Possession*.

Novels such as *The Diary of a Manhattan Call Girl* by Tracy Quan or the translation of the infamous *Story of O* by Pauline Reage give a different view from the fast lane, and the content is enough to make the blue-rinse brigade's hair stand on end.

4th July

Independence Day is celebrated on this day in America. On this date in 1776, the Declaration of Independence, written by Thomas Jefferson, was signed. It marked America's break from British rule by the Continental Congress.

While America won the battle against English taxation and for freedom on this date, David and Victoria Beckham got married in 1999. Groan – doesn't the wedding planning ever go away? No, and the same day the Beckhams' fairy tale came true Lewis Carroll invented the story *Alice in Wonderland* in 1862 for Alice P. Liddell, and she begged him to write it down.

How to be Posh

This is the month to obsess about weddings, and this one was out of the ordinary. The location was the medieval Luttrellstown Castle, on the outskirts of Dublin, and the wedding of the England footballer to the Spice Girl was billed as the Wedding of the Year. *OK!* magazine paid £1 million for exclusive coverage. All guests were tagged, including their baby Brooklyn, and the reception cost in the region of £500,000, plus security. 437 staff served sticky toffee pudding (keeping it real), accompanied by an eighteen-piece orchestra (Elton John had to pull out of his performance due to 'heat exhaustion'). Victoria wore a Vera Wang dress that cost £60,000 but made her look, and feel, a million dollars, and party outfits for the newly-weds were made to measure by Antonio Berardi. As they were pronounced man and wife a single dove was released. All food for thought. Do you need all sixteen bridesmaids? Will white doves flying over the church really make your entrance or do you risk them fouling things up – or on you? And finally, does it really have to be a sit-down dinner for 500?

5th July

In 1955 Disneyland opened in America. One idea for the honeymoon?

How to haute couture

The beginning of July is when the crème of the fashion industry flock to Paris to see the haute couture (whose collections take place twice a year). The January haute couture shows are filled with the Hollywood elite shopping for their red-carpet appearances at the Golden Globes and Academy Awards, but haute couture shows in July are pure heaven-sent inspiration. Ideal to help set the standard for your wedding dress creations, even if it is 'look, don't touch'. Artists go to galleries, foodies to restaurants, fashionistas to the shows – or at least vicariously via *www.vogue.co.uk* or *www.style.com*.

A brief history

The location, and all the 'frills' and 'flouncing' that accompany the modern haute couture system, was established by an Englishman based in Paris – Charles Frederick Worth (13 October 1825–10 March 1895). *Quelle horreur*!

Worth went from working as a bookkeeper, to opening his own dress boutique, to securing the fashion-conscious patronage of Empress Eugénie of France and Empress Elizabeth of Austria.

Worth was also the first person to show, not on the rails or in a sketch, but using live mannequin models. He pioneered the way for the rise of the fashion show and became the first 'name' designer, sweetie. And yes, though we have already mentioned this, it *is* important to know that he was English – so when Paris claims the title of fashion capital of the world, remember that the English have always been feeding the French ideas and innovations. Fast-forward to John Galliano at Dior and *plus ça change*.

Along with leading the way on how to present haute couture, in 1868 Worth founded the *Chambre Syndicale de la Haute Couture*. Something of a mouthful, but the important aim behind this group was to stop couture designs being copied. (Yes, there were problems with rip-offs and badly made imitations even in the old days.) This organization has continuously evolved to protect the design houses in Paris as well as structure the show schedules and decide who can (and cannot) be part of the fashion weeks – *prêt-à-porter* (ready-to-wear) and haute couture.

In 1946 there were 106 fashion houses producing haute couture. In 2006 only seven big names survive on the schedule, and only three from the great era of Parisian haute couture: Chanel, Dior and Givenchy (though Givenchy was a later addition). This is not to say the art is dying; no – it's just there are very strict rules about how to qualify as a couture house including:

– A couturier must produce fifty original designs of day and evening-wear each season for two collections a year (shown in January and July).

– A couture house must employ a minimum of twenty full-time technical staff in at least one purpose-built atelier/workshop.

There are lots of smaller, one-on-one type designers, but these are classed as dressmakers rather than couturiers as they operate on a different, more economical scale.

Worth's system worked beautifully until Yves Saint Laurent shook things up and modernized fashion even further with the Rive Gauche rebellion (see 1 August for his biography (page 296).

How to choose a wedding dress

This is the most important dress you will ever wear – so once you've got the right guy, proposal and date you have to focus on the biggest 'what to wear' crisis of your life. No pressure, but all eyes are on you.

Try on all styles, makes and names to be sure you find the dress for you, which, like so many things, you will know the moment you clap eyes on it.

From empire line to mounds of meringue, satins to sequins and the wedded white style (which dates back to the Victorian era), whatever type of ceremony you go for this is the day to look your best. Colour is not too prescribed now – although Queen Victoria chose white, at the time blue was considered to symbolize purity; the only thing that is universally agreed on is not to wed in black. Find out what happened to Mary Queen of Scots (page 67) in case you are considering it. White is a symbol of purity and (virginal) innocence, but there are other options apart from a dress – a bikini worked for Pamela Anderson. You don't have to change your personality to suit tradition – although before going too wild, you might want to look at this old rhyme:

Married in white,
You've chosen all right.

Married in green,
Ashamed to be seen.

Married in grey,
You'll go far away.

Married in red,
You'll wish you were dead.

Married in blue,
Love ever true.

Married in yellow,
Ashamed of your fellow.

Married in black,
You'll wish yourself back.

Married in pink,
Your spirits will sink

The best names are led by the undisputed queen of wedding dresses, Vera Wang (Jennifer Aniston wore her when she married Brad), followed by Jenny Packham, Amanda Wakeley and Collette Dinnigan.

Look on *www.morgandavieslondon.co.uk* or *www.le-spose-di-gio.it* for initial inspiration. There is also Browns Bride (*www.brownsfashion.com*) who recommend Monique Lhuiller (Britney Spears), John Galliano (Sofia Coppola), Rochas and Alaïa. Many high-end designers produce exclusives for Browns and, ultimately, you.

In addition to these websites, go to department stores with bridal departments, such as Liberty in London, Selfridges, John Lewis. Back on budget with a bump, Marks and Spencer and ASDA both do wedding dresses so there really is a style and dress for all shapes, savings and seasons.

Tip: look in evening-dress departments and the January sales as well as vintage stores and eBay.

Go shopping

It's never too early to decide how you want to look on your big day – anything from aged four onwards is considered the norm. From haute couture to the high street your dress is out there; you just have to find it. (Don't worry this will be easier than finding the man.) Know what styles suit you by trying a few on. You have to do a try-on – when else do you wear creations like this? Specialist bride shops and stores keep several styles and sizes for this very reason. Wherever you go, just be sure to wear good underwear as assistants will be helping you into the dresses – no greying, sagging bras or neon knickers today. Do you want traditional tulle or to slink up in silk? Innocent maiden or seductress?

If going on any bridal boot camp or crash diet, factor this into any fittings. Do not aim for the impossible, nor lose the figure they fell in love with. If you are a curvaceous pale brunette who decides to crash-diet, work out and tan yourself to become a stick-thin peroxide blonde, your groom would be well within his rights to ask, 'Who are you?' at the altar and run in the other direction. Sure, he's not meant to see your dress beforehand, but give the bloke a fighting chance – come as someone he will at least recognize.

8th July

The world's richest man, John Davison Rockefeller, was born in 1839.

> If I never have a cent
> I'll be rich as Rockefeller
> Gold dust at my feet
> On the sunny side of the Street
>
> Lyrics by Dorothy Fields

The industrialist and philanthropist's fame was such that his name became synonymous with wealth. Rockefeller played a key role in establishing the American oil industry – a real-life J.R Ewing – and was valued at $200 million, yet always gave at least 10 per cent of his profits to the Church. He also had four daughters' weddings to pay for (and one son to carry on his name and legacy).

12th July

In 100 BC the greatest emperor of the Roman Empire Julius Caesar was born. His leadership was legendary but it was his love affair with the most exotic leader of Egypt that made him immortal.

Muse of the Month

Cleopatra

Before you reach for the kohl eyeliner and play the Bangles' 'Walk Like an Egyptian', what do you know about Cleopatra beyond the bewitching eyes, pretty nose and that she bathed in asses' milk? Well, not only did she seduce two of the greatest Roman leaders, she was a powerful leader in her own right and remains one of the most iconic women in history. She is proof that you can have brains *and* beauty, and that it's only a man's world if you let it be.

Intelligent and feminine, femme fatale and pharaoh – Cleopatra had it all, and was doing it BC. The philosopher Cicero wrote, 'Her character was utterly spellbinding.' She always got what she wanted, and knew how to mix business with pleasure. She was a feminist long before the title was even invented, juggled childcare and a career, and had a name that purred seduction.

Her ambition: to rule the world. The result: eternal fame.

In her lifetime she was a revered queen and exotic beauty. Sixteen hundred years later she was still talked about and her affairs were immortalized, first in Shakespeare's *Antony and Cleopatra* and later in *Caesar and Cleopatra* by George Bernard Shaw. The most glamorous actresses have queued up to portray her, including Sarah Bernhardt, Claudette Colbert, Vivien Leigh and, unforgettably, Elizabeth Taylor.

Her life and times

Born around 69 BC in Alexandria, Cleopatra VII ascended to the throne of Ancient Egypt aged eighteen, following the death of her father, Ptolemy Auletes. Berenice IV had, conveniently, been beheaded after an argument with Daddy and Cleopatra VI had died, so that took care of the older sisters. Unlike other royal lines of succession this crown passed not to the male heirs – she had two younger brothers – but to the pharoah's favourite. Such were the benefits of having supreme rulers. Indeed, Cleopatra means 'father's glory'; her full name, Cleopatra Thea Philopator means 'the Goddess Cleopatra, the beloved of her father' – a daddy's girl indeed. Egyptian law, however, did insist that she have a male consort, so to deal with this formality she married her twelve-year-old brother, Ptolemy XIII. Once this was done she pretty much had free reign to rule as she pleased – and began by having her face emblazoned on the local currency.

But her little brother/husband, Ptolemy, and their senate-appointed guardian, Pompey, wanted a male-dominated reign, i.e. theirs, so Cleopatra had to fight to maintain her position. One thing that set her apart from any of the other rulers in this dynasty was that she was genuinely interested in her subjects and their welfare, and was the first of her line to actually learn to speak Egyptian, in addition to eight other languages, which, unusually for the time, didn't include Latin. She was known as a 'virtuoso scholar', and devised the Alexandrian canals and water system, though literature and legend has tended to sideline her achievements with focus falling instead on her infamous bedroom conquests. You *can* be good at more than one thing.

On 28 September 48 BC Pompey was murdered, but no sooner had one problem been dispensed with than another appeared. Four days later Caesar arrived in Alexandria. The Roman emperor declared himself their ruler, and had 3,200 legionnaires and 800 cavalry with him who agreed. Doh. Things were not stacked in Cleo's favour. Her brother Ptolemy XIII fled but was captured. Cleopatra was ignored – and furious. Determined to get an audience with Caesar, she famously smuggled herself in to his private quarters by hiding in a carpet, appearing as the gift was rolled out in front of him. Quite an entrance. The next morning, when the siblings were scheduled to meet Caesar, she already had things under control. Ptolemy stormed out and was arrested, again. Caesar was delighted at the way things seemed to be working out: the brother was weak and he had an exotic nymphet he thought he could put on the throne as his

puppet. No. He'd picked the wrong queen. She might have been his lover, but Cleopatra was no pushover, and her loyalties lay with her country.

A bad case of sibling rivalry followed – the Alexandrian War. Ptolemy XIII raised an army and surrounded Caesar in Alexandria with 20,000 troops. Cleopatra's younger sister Arsinoe fled to Achillas in Macedonia and headed up their mob as queen. Cleopatra sided with Caesar to defend herself. Arsinoe was murdered and Ptolemy XIII drowned in the Nile. Finally Cleopatra was the sole ruler of Egypt. To celebrate she married her surviving little brother, Ptolemy XIV, and promptly set off on a two-month cruise up the Nile with her lover, Caesar, to celebrate. Their son and heir Caesarion (Ptolemy Caesar) was born on 23 June 47 BC.

In July 46 BC Caesar returned to Rome, his Egyptian queen following a few months later. But she wasn't popular with the conservative Roman republicans, especially when she started to refer to herself as their new Isis (the Egyptian goddess of magic and life). There was talk that Caesar intended to marry her – to hell with the small question of bigamy and the Roman law that banned marriage to foreigners. But 'happily ever after' evaporated when, on the Ides of March, 44 BC (See 15 March, page 120), Caesar, Cleopatra's intellectual soul mate, was murdered. She and her son fled.

Utterly fed up with men by the time she got home, she had her brother/husband Ptolemy XIV assassinated, and made her four-year-old son co-regent instead. But in her absence Egypt had been suffering too. She returned to a country beset by plague, famine and poor harvests. Mean-while in Rome there was political chaos as different successors tried to lay claim to Caesar's empire and crown. Cleopatra decided that the four legions he had left in Egypt should drum up support for her son to inherit Caesar's mantle. Unfortunately the army was captured. Antony, Octavian and Lepidus were victorious. Cleopatra retreated while they fought amongst themselves, and then set about selecting and seducing a new ally.

Roman politician and general Mark Antony was invited to Tarsus. As one of Caesar's most trusted supporters, Cleopatra wanted him onside. Making another spectacular entrance – her boat rowed in on silver oars, with purple sails, and Cleopatra was dressed as Aphrodite – her intentions were obvious. Sure enough, they became lovers, which no doubt thrilled Fulvia, his wife. Cleopatra pulled out all the stops to keep Antony spellbound. At one of their lavish dinners she bet him she could spend an obscene ten million sesterces on a dinner. Antony mocked the queen as she served up a fairly ordinary-looking meal, until the second course arrived – a cup of vinegar. She then slipped off one of her pearl earrings, dropped it in the vinegar and once it had dissolved, drank it. Take that. But when his wife died, Antony had to stop flirting and return home. He married Octavian's sister, Octavia, in a bid to restore peace and his position, leaving Cleopatra to give birth to their twins, Alexander Helios and Cleopatra Selene. To celebrate he gave her land, which she used to build a fleet and arm her defences. What a woman. When Antony was defeated in a campaign against the Parthians, despite him marrying another she came to his aid, just after having had their third child.

In early 35 BC, Cleopatra returned to Egypt with Antony, while his loyal wife Octavia remained in Athens with troops and reinforcements. Emperor Octavian was not impressed with the way his sister was being treated and wanted war, but Cleopatra ignored his grumbles and threats and concentrated on establishing political and domestic harmony in Egypt. She was indeed the new Isis, and now Antony was the new Dionysus. They paraded around the streets like crowned deities. What more could a femme fatale, mother and monarch want? Her dream of becoming empress of the world looked like being realized. Antony got a divorce and by 31 BC the Western world was forced to recognize Cleopatra.

Understandably this was all too much for the ex-wife, Octavia, to bear. She declared war on Cleopatra, literally unleashing armies and legions – hell hath no fury like a woman scorned, indeed. Her navy defeated Antony in Actium, Greece, on 2 September, 31 BC. On his way back to Cleopatra, he was informed that his queen was dead. Grief-stricken he committed suicide. But Cleopatra was not dead – though when she discovered the death of her lover and learned that Emperor Octavian was victorious, and not interested in negotiating, she too chose death rather than becoming his slave. She gathered her servants together and tested on them which poison would be the most effective and painless.

Cleopatra died on 12 August, 30 BC, aged thirty-nine, when an asp (an Egyptian cobra) was brought to her in a basket of figs. Her death marked the end of the Egyptian monarchy and the Ptolemy dynasty, but only the start of the enduring fascination with the ruler. In Egypt death by snakebite is thought to make you immortal, and in this case it seems to have done the trick. 'Eternity was in our lips and eyes.' *Antony and Cleopatra*, Act I, scene iii.

In 1963 Elizabeth Taylor signed up to play the title role in *Cleopatra*. She was the first artist to earn a $1 million fee, making her the highest-paid actor in the world. 'I don't really remember much about *Cleopatra*,' Taylor later admitted. 'There were a lot of other things going on.' How true. The real Cleopatra would have been thrilled by the $40 million budget that famously bankrupted 20th Century Fox, and the on/off screen affair between Richard Burton (Antony) and Taylor. Taylor declared, 'I am ruled by my passions . . .' a sentiment Cleopatra would have undoubtedly recognized and applauded.

Cleopatra's quips

'Be it known that we, the greatest, are misthought.'

'Celebrity is never more admired than by the negligent.'

'My honour was not yielded, but conquered merely.'

'Fool! Don't you see now that I could have poisoned you a hundred times had I been able to live without you?'

'I will not be triumphed over.'

13th July

In 1985 Live Aid, the 'Global Jukebox' rock concert, took place in Wembley Stadium, London, JFK Stadium Philadelphia, Moscow and Sydney – its aim: to 'Feed the World'. Organized by Bob Geldof and Midge Ure, it was the largest satellite link-up and music concert of all time with 1.5 billion viewers (95 per cent of all televisions in the world at that time tuned in to it). It helped raise £150 million for the famine victims in Ethiopia. What have you done lately? Isn't it time to think of others? Go to *www.oxfam.org.uk* or into one of their shops, or visit *www.unicef.org.uk* and do something to help make a difference today.

14th July

Today marked the start of the French Revolution in 1789 with the storming of the palace at Bastille. France was practically bankrupt due to the excesses of the aristocrats ruling the country and the corrupt political system. The peasants were starving, the middle class felt powerless, and the monarchy was out of touch and ignoring a reality that didn't effect them. On this day it all came to a head when a group of Parisians stormed Bastille and freed the prisoners inside.

By 16 July King Louis XVI and his wife Marie Antoinette recognized the severity of the situation and fled to Versailles. The king's power was no longer absolute and although only seven prisoners were released it was recognized as a symbol of the French regaining their liberty. The French tricolour flag symbolized the republic's three ideals: *liberté, egalité*, and *fraternité*. The revolution marked the end of the monarchy, the birth of the sovereign nation, and, eventually, the creation of the (first) republic, in 1792.

One much-maligned figure in all this was Queen Marie Antoinette. She wasn't entirely innocent, but was effectively a pawn in eighteenth-century court politics – albeit a highly bejewelled and well-dressed one.

Let's clear this up: she did not say 'Let them eat cake' as has been claimed. Biographer and historian Antonia Fraser explained: 'It was [actually] said

100 years before her by Marie-Therese, wife of Louis XIV. It was a callous and ignorant statement and she [Marie Antoinette] was neither.'

'Cake' is also a mistranslation: the original proposed they eat brioche, much more nourishing. Marie Antoinette was decadent, frivolous and enjoyed a life of luxury – she *was* Queen of France – but she should not be blamed for instigating the revolution with this line. Nor, while clearing up the smear campaign against her, were her breasts what the great Sèvres used to mould his porcelain teacups on. Another figment of a vicious imagination.

Read Antonia Fraser's book, or watch Sofia Coppola's 2006 film *Marie Antoinette* to get an idea of her character. Don't forget her greatest gift to France, the croissant (see page 56).

How to get gifts – the wedding list bonanza

Once you've worked out the cost and expenses you're going to tot up for this day, and so has the FOB, it's understandable to get the jitters. Not only is this a big commitment, but this is the biggest single expense you are ever likely to incur – bar buying a house.

So, while your non-wedding life has been reduced to baked beans on toast to cut some costs, there is one tradition that the bride and groom hit the jackpot with – the wedding list.

When sending out the invitations the couple should take this opportunity to enclose details of their wedding list. Though the couple may already be living together, wedding guests traditionally buy something for the new Mr and Mrs' marital home. Rule: do not pick something random, buy something they want or need – they will be broke after the wedding and will have compiled a wish list of what they need; it's up to the guests to make the gifts come true.

Guests, don't be stingy – remember whatever it's costing you, it's costing them a lot more!

Rather than risk receiving 500 saucepans, or 500 phone calls asking if you want a Le Creuset saucepan, register your wedding-list choices at department stores. It's not greedy – it's practical. Go round the store and select the china set, cutlery, bed linen that will accompany your married life. When composing your list, be sure to put in a variety of prices – ranging from DVDs and sugar bowls to the fantasy plasma screen TV (that is unlikely to be in anyone's budget – you can but hope!) Ask your guests to choose from this rather than make a wild guess at something exotic – of course, some will always go off-list.

In England the most popular places to hold wedding lists are John Lewis, Harrods, Fortnum & Mason, Habitat, Debenhams, with Barneys and Bloomingdale's further afield (where there's a Visa Card sign there's a way). Websites such as *www.confetti.co.uk* and *www.theweddinglist.co.uk* can do all the work for you. Even *amazon.com* has got in on the act. The trick is to make your list with a popular store that has everything you want and is painless for your generous guests to access over the Internet.

The couple can be kept up to date as their wish list gets ticked off and items will be removed as they are bought (thus avoiding multiple saucepans and sugar bowls). They will all be delivered, with notes explaining who bought what, at a date convenient to the newly-weds after the wedding, and usually after the honeymoon.

16th July

Kissing was banned in England (to stop germs spreading) in 1439. The ban was not popular and didn't last long.

Also on this date in 1911 Virginia Katherine McMath, better known as Ginger Rogers, was born. The fairer half of Fred Astaire was also an Oscar-winning actress in her own right, for *Kitty Foyle* in 1941.

Her nickname originated when her younger cousin couldn't pronounce her name so called her *Ginja*, and it stuck.

'My mother told me I was dancing before I was born,' Rogers said. 'She could feel my toes tapping wildly inside her for months.'

She first partnered Astaire in *Flying Down to Rio*. It was her twentieth film – his second. 'When two people love each other,' she said, 'they don't need to look at each other, they look in the same direction.' Sadly, romance didn't blossom off-screen as easily as the dance moves did for the perfect pair (apart from one rumoured hot dinner and dancing date; shame). Turn to Fred's birthday, 10 May, page 178, for a list of dance styles and start thinking about what song you will pick for your first dance.

How to do the ultimate aisle glide

If you've decided to make the folks proud and do it the traditional way, forewarned is, as always, forearmed. At the church the bride's family should traditionally sit on the left and the groom's on the right. There will be plenty of time for mingling later, so stick to the rules at this point.

The groom and best man should arrive thirty minutes before the service (which will give them time to work out a contingency plan for any forgotten rings or last-minute nerves).

Once everyone is seated the bride's party will arrive. The bride does *not* have to rush today (within reason).

When the bride's car arrives at the church the bride's mother is shown to the front pew while the bridesmaids will do last-minute dress fluffs and tweaks. The bride and her father (after all, the poor blighter is paying for most of this so he should get a starring role) will then slowly glide up the aisle, with the bride on the right side of honour (literally as well as metaphorically) as the father prepares to give his little girl away. If your father is not giving you away you can turn to a guardian or other family member such as mother, uncle, brother, friend, etc. Elizabeth Hurley had Elton John do the honours at her 2007 wedding. However independent the bride may be, she cannot walk up the aisle alone – just as Tracy Lord needed help off her pedestal in *High Society*, it's best to have someone to lean on for the walk towards married life.

Top tunes for the I-do aisle glide.

5. Verdi's 'Grand March' from *Aida*
4. Handel's 'Arrival of the Queen of Sheba'
3. Abba's 'I Do, I Do, I Do, I Do, I Do'
2. Van Morrison's 'Have I Told You Lately'
And, of course, in at number one –
Wagner's 'Bridal March' (yes, the 'here comes the bride' one).

But what about considering Mozart's 'Wedding March' from *The Marriage of Figaro*, Pachelbel's Canon in D? Or go for the more contemporary – this is a modern-day match after all – such as Norah Jones' 'Come Away with Me', Etta James' 'At Last', Nat King Cole's 'Unforgettable'; or do you have a song you both love that is suitable to share here? Or is that to be saved for the first dance later?

How to say something meaningful

If you're getting married the readings are up to you (obviously) but here's the thing – if it's in a church they need to be religious, or at least have a slant in that direction, while if it's in a registry office they don't allow religious readings. Shakespeare is a popular choice but it's worth looking through well-loved poetry anthologies too. Try to be original rather than cheesy – everyone uses 'love is patient, love is kind'. Find something more memorable and tailor-made. What about Hemingway's *Farewell to Arms*? (See page 281).

The most successful hymns are usually the old school favourites such as 'Jerusalem' and 'All Things Bright and Beautiful'. Choose something appropriate for the time of year as well as ones that everyone from your granny to your naughty little nephew can belt out every word to. Remember there is nothing more annoying than singing a solo; go for hymns or carols for the masses.

Vows

You can stick to the book or personalize. Sure, everyone knows the punch line, but you might want to refine things to make them all about you. How do you feel about committing to 'obey' your partner? Mrs Beckham whipped that line out. The vows are the magic, binding bit. Try to put your reasons for doing so into your own words.

OK – finally, after this bit, it's time to celebrate with speeches, champagne and dancing in your big white dress. It's a showstopper and it's unlikely you'll ever wear it again, so work it!

18th July

William Makepeace Thackeray, author of *Vanity Fair*, was born in 1811. The novel tells of the social-climbing Becky Sharp who was based, in parts, on Thackeray's grandmother, and was played by Reese Witherspoon in the 2004 Hollywood version of the tome.

19th July

Neil Armstrong and Edwin Aldrin become the first men to walk on the moon in 1969. As he stepped out of Apollo 11 Armstrong said the famous line: 'That's one small step for man, one giant leap for mankind.' But he later said, 'I blew the first words on the moon,' having left out the 'a', changing it from 'one small step for a man'. 250,000 miles from Earth he probably had other things on his mind than his speech, whereas at a wedding you can be sure the groom and best man won't really be able to relax until these are done (see page 284).

21st July

Ernest Hemingway, author, novelist, Nobel and Pulitzer Prize-winner, was born in 1899.

He said that his first job at the *Kansas City Star* taught him to: Use short sentences. Use short paragraphs. Use rigorous English. Be positive, not negative.' His style was born.

On 8 July 1918, while serving in the Second World War, he was wounded saving an Italian soldier. It earned him the Italian Silver Medal for military valour. It was while he was in hospital recovering from his injuries that he met, and fell in love with, the Red Cross nurse, Agnes von Kurowsky. He never forgot her and *Farewell to Arms* is a fictionalized account of the affair. In 1996 the film *In Love and War*, starring Sandra Bullock and Chris O'Donnell, directed by Richard Attenborough, retold the real love story. You may want to consider a passage from *Farewell to Arms* at your wedding.

> At night there was the feeling that we had come home, feeling no longer alone, waking in the night to find the other one there, and not gone away; all other things were unreal. We slept when we were tired and if we woke the other one woke too so one was not alone. Often a man wishes to be alone and a woman wishes to be alone too and if they love each other they are jealous of that in each other, but I can truly say that we never felt that. We could feel alone when we were together, alone against the others. We were never lonely and never afraid when we were together.

25th July

James I, son of Mary Queen of Scots, was crowned, uniting England and Scotland in 1603. Elizabeth I was a tough act to follow, and he didn't do anything that special but will be remembered for thwarting the 1605 Gunpowder Plot – see 5 November, page 437.

26th July

Irish writer George Bernard Shaw was born in Dublin in 1856. He wrote, amongst other things, *Pygmalion*, and directed its first production. It opened at His Majesty's Theatre on 1 April 1914, starring Mrs Patrick Campbell as Eliza Doolittle. The play was transformed into the film *My Fair Lady*, starring Audrey Hepburn, and inspired the later film *Educating Rita*, starring Julie Walters.

'Fashion is nothing but an induced epidemic,' Shaw said. 'I often quote myself. It adds spice to my conversation.' Read the play, rent the DVD, or do something ladylike today.

28th July

Beatrix Potter, the most popular Potter before Harry, was born in 1866. The children's author wrote the tales of *Peter Rabbit, Jemima Puddle-Duck, Tom Kitten* and many others. When she died she left her house, along with its 4,000 acres of land, to the National Trust to help preserve the landscape in her beloved Lake District.

The 2007 film *Miss Potter*, starring Renée Zellweger and Ewan McGregor, tells the story of Potter and her publisher and their doomed and forbidden affair.

29th July

When thinking of weddings and blushing brides, there are few more beautiful than the one that took place on this date in 1981, when Lady Diana married the Prince of Wales. 'It was like watching a beautiful butterfly emerging from a chrysalis,' said Elizabeth Emanuel, the wedding dress designer Diana chose.

Born on 1 July 1961, Diana Frances Mountbatten-Windsor was to go on to become the most iconic and photographed woman in the world – so her dress on this occasion was going to have to be spectacular. 'She was like a silent movie star who used her clothes to speak for her,' Galliano said. With 3,500 invited guests and 750 million watching the wedding across the world it's only natural she wanted to get it right. 600,000 people lined the streets to watch her and her father travel from Clarence House in a glass carriage to St Paul's Cathedral, and her ivory taffeta and antique lace dress had a twenty-five-foot train. Read *A Dress for Diana* by David and Elizabeth Emanuel for a taste of the magic moments from 1981.

How to party on the big day

Once the ceremony is over and all the angst and military planning has paid off, you can start to relax and enjoy yourself.

Warning : Do not watch any *Weddings From Hell* TV episodes in the run-up to yours. If you have:

Something Borrowed
Something Blue
Something Old
Something New

NOTHING will go wrong.

In fact, just both of you turning up is reason enough to celebrate, as it's not just the man who gets scared by weddings. Remember you are doing this because you love each other and want to. You're not surrendering your freedom – you're just entering a different phase as a team or partnership.

Top table

Other than the happy couple, top of most people's list at this point is the food. Serve champagne and nibbles while the newly-weds get the photos done (best to do this while still sober and red wine has not been thrown down the pristine white dress).

To avoid squabbles, the top table and seating plans can be pre-planned to mix and matchmake relatives and guests nicely. Usually both parents and the couple will take the top table but if there are family feuds, tensions, divorces and dilemmas, divide things up for the most harmonious results.

Between the initial toasting and before everyone tucks in, it is time for the speeches (or, if your guests look starving, feed them and do the speeches just before dessert). The bride traditionally doesn't have to worry about this part – the groom, however, does. A lot.

Order of speeches

Traditionally first up is the father of the bride (or whoever gave the bride away). He formally introduces the bride to the groom's family, welcomes the groom into the bride's family and tells endearing stories. Remember the bride should always be portrayed in a good light. This is followed by a toast.

Note: It's probably best not to drive to a wedding, as even a teetotaller will seem churlish turning down a toast, and it might be seen as bad luck for the wedding.

Next is the groom. He should thank the bride's family, the guests and his bride for marrying him. Another toast. Gulp.

Some brides do in fact like to make a speech to thank everyone who has helped her, as much as to declare her love in return – she should probably leap in before the best man's speech in case it causes her to retract any affection: *You've been married how many times? And what was that about the pole-dancing troupe?*

Now we come to the best man's speech. This is notorious and its intent is to shame and embarrass the groom as much as possible – lovely – though hopefully not enough to cause a divorce. The contents should be chosen with extreme care as any revelations are best mentioned in private – and any in-jokes should be funny for everyone. This will be followed by a toast (and relief all round that that bit is over).

Now it's time to eat – buffet or sit-down. This is why getting everyone to RSVP is essential. You will want to know how many cheesy hedgehogs or sausages on a stick to have at the ready. Buffets are easier on the budget and a good way of dealing with fussy eaters with exotic allergies.

The cake is the grand finale of the feast. You can cut this either at the start of or alongside the speeches, but be sure to allow enough time for it to be sliced so every guest can have a piece. Pass the knife to someone who can do the numbers and equations. Number of tiers and style of cake is up to the budget again. Fruitcake might be the most popular but if the bride has a wheat allergy or the groom a penchant for chocolate these can also be catered for. Look at *www.thecakestore.com* or *www.jane-asher.co.uk* for some suggestions.

How to honeymoon

If they survive the big day and party into the small hours, the newly-weds will have most certainly earned their honeymoon. Every Bridezilla needs a holiday to recover before she comes back to reality. This is traditionally paid for by the groom, so even more reason to enjoy it.

The top honeymoon destinations are usually secluded, exotic, white sandy beaches, floating around Venice on a gondola or five-star room service in Paris. However, if you met hiking, camping, at a grand slam or festival, do you want to go back to where it all began or find a new adventure together?

Try not to skimp on the honeymoon, as this is the corner that research shows many newly-weds regret cutting the most. Learn from their folly – cut a few relatives you've never met from the guest list and upgrade the getaway. Caution: it's very nice if your groom wants to surprise you but ask for some hints, as well as dropping your own – you need to know what to pack. You don't want to bring a bikini if you'll be starting married life on the ski slopes, even though it would undoubtedly add spice to the honey part of the holiday.

A brief history

Ignore any nonsense Hugh Grant's character said in *Four Weddings and a Funeral* (men can be very inventive and say anything to impress the ladies) – it has nothing to do with the moon, or honey, though it will of course be sweet. The origin of the word 'honeymoon' is not as romantic as the word implies – it comes from the Norse word *hjunottsmanathr*. Try saying *that* after a glass of bubbly. The tale goes that in Northern Europe a new bride was abducted from the neighbouring village. In order to keep his bride the groom/abductor took her to an unknown hiding place, had his wicked way and waited till the bride's family gave up the search.

How to mark the milestones

If you make it to the first-year anniversary it's reason to celebrate. You've survived the hardest year

So, what to give? As well as exchanging a card and a kiss a married couple should celebrate each anniversary with the appropriate gift.

Anniversary	Traditional Gift	Modern Gift
1st	Paper	Clocks, Plastic, Gold jewellery
2nd	Cotton	China, Cotton, Calico, Garnet
3rd	Leather	Crystal, Glass, Pearls
4th	Fruit, Flowers	Appliances, Linen, Silk, Nylon, Blue topaz
5th	Wood	Silverware, Sapphire
6th	Sugar, Iron	Wood, Candy, Amethyst
7th	Wool, Copper, brass,	Desk sets, Onyx
8th	Bronze, Pottery	Appliances, Linens, Lace, Tourmaline jewellery

9th	Pottery, Willow	Leather, Lapis jewellery
10th	Tin, Aluminium	Diamond jewellery
11th	Steel	Fashion, Turquoise jewellery
12th	Silk, Linen	Pearls, Jade
13th	Lace	Lace textiles, Furs, Citrine
14th	Ivory	Ivory, Gold jewellery, Opal
15th	Crystal	Crystal glass, Watches, Ruby
16th		Silver hollowware, Peridot
17th		Furniture, Watches
18th		Porcelain, Cat's eye jewellery
19th		Bronze, Aquamarine
20th	China	Platinum, Emerald
21st		Brass, Nickel
22nd		Copper
23rd		Silver plate
24th		Musical instruments
25th	Silver	Sterling silver
26th		Original pictures
27th		Sculpture
28th		Orchids
29th		New furniture
30th	Pearl	Diamond
31st		Time pieces
32nd		A car
33rd		Amethyst
34th		Opal
35th	Coral, Jade	Jade
36th		Bone china
37th		Alabaster
38th		Beryl, Tourmaline
39th		Lace
40th	Ruby	Ruby, Garnet
41st		Land
42nd		Property

43rd		Travel
44th		Groceries (sexy)
45th	Sapphire	Sapphire
46th		Original poetry tribute
47th		Books
48th		Optical goods
49th		Luxuries, any kind
50th	Gold	Gold
55th	Emerald	Emerald, Turquoise
60th	Diamond	Gold, Diamond
75th	Platinum	Diamond-like stones, Gold
80th		Diamond, Pearl
85th		Diamond, Sapphire
90th		Diamond, Emerald
95th		Diamond, Ruby
100th		Ten-carat diamond

30th July

Emily Brontë, author of *Wuthering Heights,* was born in 1818. Her only novel tells the story of Cathy and Heathcliff – the lovers that can't live with each other and can't live without each other.

> Catherine Earnshaw, may you not rest so long as I live on! I killed you. Haunt me, then! Haunt your murderer! I know that ghosts have wandered on the Earth. Be with me always. Take any form, drive me mad, only do not leave me in this dark alone where I cannot find you. I cannot live without my life! I cannot die without my soul.

So says Heathcliff – crikey! He was famously played by Laurence Olivier in the 1939 film version of the novel and the role earned him a Best Actor Academy Award nomination. What has your Heathcliff said to you lately?

'If he loved you with all the power of his soul for a whole lifetime, he couldn't love you as much as I do in a single day.' Go Heathcliff. Watch the film or read the book today. Check your other half is as devoted, if not slightly less obsessive.

How to admit defeat

Some are not marriages or men made in heaven – and sorry statistics say half of all marriages will end in divorce. Sad but true.

Even Las Vegas has scaled back its twenty-four-hour shotgun wedding chapels to help keep divorce costs down. When you marry it should be for love not liquor. Tequila slammers can lead to many things – but remember an impromptu wedding is harder to annul than a hangover; think of Britney Spears or Ross and Rachel in *Friends*.

If it's a drunken jolly then you're both to blame. For irreconcilable differences – such as playing away from home – people often call it a day.

70 per cent of divorces are filed by women: 27 per cent due to extra-marital affairs, 6 per cent for being married to workaholics.

Divorces are the most traumatic period in a person's life – unless you are as canny as Ivana Trump, who turned tragedy to triumph and her greatest claim to fame. She received a settlement of $20 million in one of the most written-about divorces of the eighties, divorcing tycoon Donald Trump when he wandered.

The fashion model and ski enthusiast, who famously had a limo to ferry her poodles to their daily grooming appointments, realized she was going to have to start earning again. She turned herself into a brand – founded jewellery and fashion lines, wrote bestselling novels – *For Love Alone* and *Free to Love* – as well as the bestselling self-help books *The Best is Yet to Come: Coping with Divorce* and *Enjoying Life Again*.

Ms Trump even played a cameo role in *The First Wives Club* with the line: 'Remember, girls, don't get mad, get everything.' Sage Advice. Princess Diana and Prince Charles divorced on 20 December 1995, with the decree nisi being issued on 28 August 1996. For his second marriage to Camilla Parker Bowles he invited only thirty guests to the ceremony.

Foot Note

The slipper

This did not start life with the 'granny-doing-her-knitting-in-a-rocking-chair' connotations that it has today, and it would no doubt be appalled at how its fortunes have fallen. Slippers started off as the total opposite of functional – they were so fancy, so thin soled, so elegant that they only lasted one night. They showed the wearer had wealth, style and could afford this fine slip of a thing that barely covered the foot, let alone served a purpose. These were shoes so delicate that they were only seen in the boudoir – eek; how did you end up in such close proximity? In ancient Rome women wouldn't be seen outdoors without their *socci*. Empress Josephine was said to own in excess of 521 pairs, and Marie Antoinette had a maid whose sole, pardon the pun, role was to care for her slipper collection. Novelist Gustave Flaubert sighed, 'I'll take a look at your slippers, I love them as much as I do you . . .' But somehow they faded from naughty to fuddy-duddy. Today the slippers that are truest to their original art form are the soft satin shoes most often worn under wedding gowns. Like the dress, the wedding slipper is only intended to be worn once. Some use the slipper to follow the Anglo-Saxon tradition of the father of the bride giving the groom one of his daughter's shoes (brave) to symbolize the transfer of authority. But this seems very outdated. Would you let your father give away one of your Manolos? For the modern-day madame who wants to keep warm and stylish indoors, the only slipper to consider is the marabou mule (if carpet and sense of balance permits), *à la* Marilyn Monroe and Betty bo-bo-be-do Boop. That said, if you're sure you're alone, Garbo, those fluffy moccasins and a cup of cocoa seem very tempting.

August

'I have not told half of what I saw.'
Marco Polo

Wish You Were Here

Christian Louboutin from Egypt

I think this is a great civilization – I mean, the people are super nice plus there is incredible beauty all around you. It's an amazing country – as well as the *Pharoah-ific* architecture there is so much history and culture, past and present. There is so much imagination here that to me it always surpasses what you have seen before and you can turn a corner and never see the same thing again.

I first went to Egypt when I was fifteen years old, and I did the classic tour – the Pharaohs, Cairo, Luxor, the pyramids and the great temples at the epicentre of it all. I think it's very normal for a French person to go as it's such a big part of the history lesson we are taught – I think every little French person has this thing to go to Egypt at some point. Now I go at least every two months for a few weeks as I have my house there. I draw all my shoes there as it's really peaceful and very inspiring to me. I like knowing a place and not having to do the 'tourist' thing every time, and worrying I might not see something, might not have time as I know I will be back and there is not a view I will miss.

I feel totally relaxed here. My house takes its style from the Egyptian architect Olivier Sednaoui; it looks at the shade and the absent shadow and cuts rounds and circles. I am near the Temple Medinet Habu on the West Bank of Luxor and from the house I can see the sacred mountain of Theba on one side and an all-green oasis on the other. For the last seven years my Christmas tree has been a green palm tree.

There are so many places to see, so many sites that you have to visit to taste the richness of the area – just get there and take a ride. It's a funny civilization – funny interesting. I love the way the children react, from amused to shocked, to the arts of the ancients, the cartoon-like quality of the imagery; it is very interesting to see. Yes, there are bazaars, markets, as well as the views along the Nile but if it is your first trip take the classic tour – sample just what Egypt can offer. There is so much. Go to the pyramids but maybe go to Dashur or one a bit away so you can experience it by yourself, not with a million visitors. Take the tour at lunchtime when everyone else stops to eat, and when all the tour guides take a break, or time your visit for the afternoon when it is hot but empty and then ride through the dessert and let the sand take you back to another age. Egypt is an adventure that must be taken.

Love, Christian

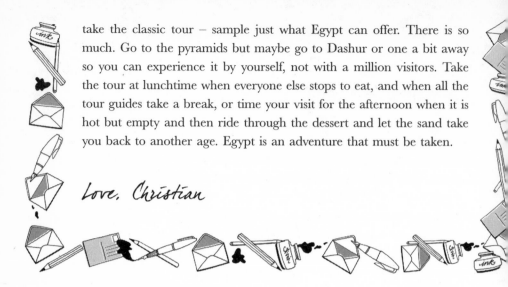

1st August

In 1976 Elizabeth Taylor divorced Richard Burton for the second time. It was the sixth of her eight marriages. But don't let this put you off embarking on a holiday fling . . .

Also on this date in 1936 fashion designer Yves Saint Laurent was born. Shy, yet with a formidable talent, it was not long before not only Paris but the world knew his name. He inherited the mantle of designing for Dior at twenty-one, when the house's founder unexpectedly died of a heart attack. He ensured the house survived and started to inject 'youth' into his designs. When war broke out he was ripped from the charmed life of a couturier and drafted into the army, which led to a nervous breakdown. When he returned to health and Paris with Pierre Bergé, his business partner as well as his rock, they found backing and went on to launch his own label in 1961. Yves Saint Laurent became the name synonymous with liberating women from the couture salons when he decided to bring 'ready-to-wear' to the forefront of fashion with his Rive Gauche collection.

He hung out in Marrakech with the rich and famous and his muses included Catherine Deneuve, Betty Catroux and Loulou de la Falaise. He designed some of the most iconic looks of the era, including *Le Smoking* tuxedo pant suit – think Mick and Bianca Jagger's wedding outfits. He was inspired by art, Africa, the Ballets Russes, the streets rather than the salons. At the same time he launched his own line of scents and cosmetics. Business was booming, so, not surprisingly, the Gucci Group purchased it in 1999. Splash out on some Opium, Champagne or Jazz, all his bestselling scents, or read about the fashion icon in:

Yves Saint Laurent: A Biography by Alice Rawsthorn
The Beautiful Fall: Fashion, Genius and Glorious Excess in 1970s Paris by
   Alicia Drake
Yves Saint Laurent: a memoir by Pierre Bergé
YSL: Universe of Fashion by Pierre Bergé

Yves Saint Laurent timeline

1936   Yves Mathieu Saint Laurent is born on 1 August in Oran, Algeria.

1953   YSL wins prize in International Wool Secretariat design competition – Karl Lagerfeld is another of the prizewinners.

1955   Gets introduced to Christian Dior by Michel de Brunhoff, then editor of French *Vogue*.

1957   Takes over after Dior's death.

1958   Debuts the Trapeze line for Christian Dior. Meets Pierre Bergé.

1960   His Dior Beatnik collection features a motorbike jacket in black crocodile with mink trim. Is drafted into the French army and suffers a nervous breakdown. Marc Bohan takes over at Dior.

1961   Sets up Yves Saint Laurent couture house with Bergé.

1965   Debuts his Mondrian shift dresses with abstract geometrics, using the artist's work as a print basis for his design.

1966   Designs the first tuxedo for women. Rive Gauche ready-to-wear boutique is launched on Left Bank in Paris.

1967   The African collection is unveiled; beaded lattice dresses, Out of Africa and the Safari are put on the runway for the first time. He designs the costumes for Catherine Deneuve in *Belle de Jour* and she is to remain a close friend and confidante.

1971   Beautiful YSL himself famously poses nude for the photographer Jean Loup Sieff to advertise the launch of his men's fragrance.

1974   The couture house moves to 5 avenue Marceau.

1977   Launch of Opium fragrance.

1983   The Yves Saint Laurent show at the Metropolitan Museum in New York, curated by Vreeland, is the first museum exhibition devoted to a living designer.

1989   YSL goes public on the French stock exchange, Paris Bourse, valued at $500 million.

1996   YSL turns sixty.

1998   YSL 'retires' and hands over ready-to-wear to Albert Elbaz.

1999   François Pinault buys YSL for $1 billion, selling the company to Gucci Group and closing the famed couture part of the house to focus on expanding and evolving the ready-to-wear line.

2000   Tom Ford launches his first collection for YSL. YSL archive institute set up in Paris.

2002   23 January, YSL celebrates forty years of his couture house with a spectacular retrospective of all his great models, with all his greatest muses, at the Pompidou Centre, bringing Paris to a standstill.

Bergé and Saint Laurent weren't seen at any of the YSL ready-to-wear shows while Tom Ford was the design director; Saint Laurent became more and more of a reclusive figure. They were seen at Hedi Slimane's Dior Homme debut, and Bergé returned to sit front row at YSL when Stefano Pilati replaced Ford as the head of design in 2004, giving him the ultimate seal of approval.

When heading off to the sun, pack a book to match your sunglasses. Whether you're modelling Dior or Chanel, there's a biography to complement your accessories. Try:

Christian Dior, The Man Who Made the World Look New by Marie-France Poncha
The World of Coco Chanel: Friends, Fashion, Fame by Edmonde Charles-Roux
Galliano by Colin McDowell
The House of Klein: Fashion, Controversy, and a Business Obsession by Lisa Marsh
The House of Gucci by Sara Gay Forden

3rd August

Just as you should be setting off for a summer holiday, Christopher Columbus set sail in 1492.

Christopher Columbus is regarded as the most famous explorer in history – a visionary, a national hero – as well as being a rather ruthless and greedy imperialist.

Born in Genoa, Italy in 1451, Columbus grew up alongside the Mediterranean coastline. He dreamed of becoming a sailor and seeing the world. Unlike other little boys this was more than a daydream – he was determined to do it. He was twenty-five when his first voyage to England ended in disaster with him overboard, clinging to some wood, after the ship was attacked by pirates. Not how he'd envisaged his great adventure beginning ... But Columbus was not to be deterred. Back in Genoa he opened a shop selling maps and books and, after reading Marco Polo's work, he became obsessed with sailing to the Indies, but rather than following the established route he wanted to sail into the unchartered West and get to it by another route – he just hadn't figured on the continent in his path.

No one was that keen on giving him the ships, crew and capital he needed for the voyage; many still believed that the world was flat. Was he crazy? Who would risk sailing a fleet off the edge of the world? Finally King Ferdinand and Queen Isabella of Spain took a gamble and agreed to back the adventure – provided they got a cut of any treasure or discovered land he claimed.

Columbus set off with a fleet of three ships – the *Niña* and *Pinta*, with a crew of eighteen men in each, and the *Santa Maria*, with a crew of fifty-two adventurers. They didn't sight land for seventy-one days. And you thought long-haul flights were bad.

Sailor Juan Rodriguez Bermejo spotted land (finally) just after 2 a.m. on 12 October 1492. They all thanked God.

They christened the island San Salvador but this was *not* the Indies – this was the West Indies (i.e. the other side of the world), the Bahamas to be precise. Columbus had indeed found the New World – he'd stumbled on this little place called America.

As the Jets sang in Leonard Bernstein's *Westside Story*:

I like to be in America!
Okay by me in America!
Everything free in America
For a small fee in America!

Columbus went on to discover Cuba before returning triumphantly to Spain to tell of his finds. Emboldened and greedy for more, his second voyage took him to the Canary Islands and Dominica (Dominican Republic), and he sighted the Virgin Isles and Puerto Rico before going back to Cuba. His third trip took in Cape Verde, Tobago, South America and Grenada, which he assumed must hang below China, which would have made the world pear-shaped. (For a navigator his map reading was *very* off-kilter.) His fourth and final voyage explored the Indian Ocean to the Moroccan coast, Costa Rica and Cuba. But before you get too envious, here they encountered a violent storm that few survived, and which left them shipwrecked on Jamaica for a year.

Columbus Day is celebrated in America on 12 October – the date he landed in the New World.

Wish You Were Here

Heidi Klum's wonders of the world

I think that as hard as we all work, and how busy life is, it is super important to be able to take some time to relax, be with family and friends, and just get away from it all! One of my favourite getaways is to our vacation home in Mexico. It is absolutely beautiful there – and we do absolutely nothing but eat, swim, hang out and relax, which is heavenly! And because it is where we got married, it is a location that has a lot of sentimental value to me.

I love travel – it's nutritious for the spirit to try things that may seem (at first) weird or difficult. I always want to discover more about myself, and the only way that happens is if I expose my mind (and senses) to things it's unused to, and I like to explore and savour another culture, and to feel what a welcoming place the world can be. I've been to lots of breathtaking, 'the-postcard-doesn't-do-this-place-justice' destinations in my life, but these romantic, beautiful, and fascinating spots are among my all-time favourites:

Malaysia – For a *Sports Illustrated* shoot, I had to ride an elephant with no saddle, wearing nothing more than a bikini (nobody told me that elephants are nearly as prickly as porcupines).

Egypt – Marvelling at the Great Pyramids – truly wondrous!

Bali – I went to Bali thinking it would be all empty white beaches, sarongs, and flip-flops. It had all that but so much more. I was shocked at the diverse beauty of the island: the lush terraced rice fields with the mist lifting off them, the palaces and volcanoes, temples and crafts villages. You can smell paradise from the moment you get off the plane.

The Tyrol – Growing up, my family and I vacationed every winter in the Alpine region of northern Italy (bordering on Austria), and I dare you to name anything more wonderful than being stuck inside during a heavy mountain snowfall – you can't ski, you can't even get out, you're up so high that there's not much to do except drink hot chocolate and watch huge winter-wonderland flakes come down.

Paris – It's glamorous and romantic, with those exquisite yellow limestone buildings bathed in light. I love sitting in cafés drinking café crème, watching the chic ladies pass by or discovering tiny, out-of-the-way patisseries and boutiques. The stores on the grand boulevards are incomparably stylish, but I always score something unique at the gigantic and historic flea markets on the outskirts of the city.

The African savannah – I've been on many safaris – in Kenya and in Tanzania – and it's such an overwhelming sensory experience, especially the natural music: outside your tent at night you hear hippos munching on grass, hyenas laughing, lions prowling. The abundance of wildlife is surreal – I saw buffaloes, elephants, giraffes, crocodiles, gazelles, a cheetah with five of her babies, and the very rare (so I was told) sight of twelve lions eating a zebra, bloody carnage and all. One tip learnt at the Grumeti River: never get between a hippo and the water.

Hong Kong – The city still has a British-inspired elegance – the fancy old hotels, high tea service – but the underworld is what makes it riveting: pigs and chickens hanging in restaurant windows, not to mention some rather peculiar aphrodisiacs on the menu and at night, the lurid little alleys and nightclubs. The view from the peak of the city's gleaming high-rises is jaw-dropping, and the shopping (including the huge jade and pearl markets) is overwhelming (in a good way). It's a modern bazaar.

Venice – I love old things, so I fell hard for the city's ancient streets, old restaurants, rustic gondolas, endless history. Sure they have Prada and Gucci and lots of modern chain stores and conveniences, but not every-thing there is straight and new and perfect, and you can find delights like stunning gold-leafed doges' palaces, frescoes, churches, masterworks of art, and antique shops.

The Mongolian Desert – There's nothing there. No cars, no congestion, no white noise, practically no trappings of civilization. And never has that word trappings seemed so apt. Almost nothing that seems to matter here – how you look, what brand you wear – matters there. The people could not be friendlier, and if you have a chance to stay in a yurt, do it.

Tokyo – It's so clean, chic and sophisticated. The Japanese attention to detail is inspiring, from the elegant presentation of the food down to the heated toilet seat in my hotel. I couldn't stop studying the crazy outfits and hairstyles worn by the city's fashion-forward kids, and I was awed by the beautiful wooden temples and palaces.

New York – There's no place like it anywhere in the world – crazy, dirty streets giving rise to soaring silver office towers, European-style cafés and shops in SoHo contrasting with the wide, elegant boulevards of the Upper East Side. From the yellow cabs and 24/7 delivery options to the melting-pot citizenry and New Yorkers' brusque, efficient energy, it's my kind of city, my kind of home. Right now, it is home. Every spot in the world has something about it that sticks with me and compels me to return.

And some travel tips:

- DON'T BE A PACK RAT. For some ten years (and counting), there's one companion I will not travel without: my Samsonite hard case, covered with stickers from all over the world.
- People often suggest bringing things – a favourite pillow or candles – to personalize your hotel room and make yourself feel cosy, but I am a minimalist. Try not to carry your entire home with you; otherwise, you might as well just stay there.
- For up to a week, I bring two cute outfits – a little black dress and a nice pair of jeans, maybe a jean jacket (which you can wear with the black dress). They all adapt nicely to dressy or casual situations. I also stuff in a great purse, shoes that go with both outfits, and a wrap that can be worn with anything.
- For make-up, I forgo all the colours and steps and just pack a little bag with bare necessities: gloss, lipstick, concealer, sunscreen, and mascara.
- Don't forget those adapters for international outlets!
- I leave room in my suitcase for new purchases . . . or I pack an empty bag or knapsack. (If I buy a lot of clothes and there's no room in my bag, I just wear lots of layers on the flight back.) The combo of suitcase-bursting-at-seams and stern-looking-suspicious-customs-officer makes for an unpleasant re-entry.

Love, Heidi

How to get your sea legs

The last-minute deals will be at fever pitch, so whether you have left it late deliberately or not, you might just snag an adventure or bargain of a life-time. Time off work should be all booked; you just need to set sail. Look on *www.lastminute.com* or *www.expedia.co.uk*.

Whether it's a book, a painting, a postcard or Columbus that has inspired you to journey into the unknown, as well as your passport you need to pack your sea legs.

There is no telling who will or won't get seasickness, or indeed if Columbus suffered, but if you've had it before, buy some tablets in advance, and avoid rich or spicy foods, alcohol and apples – ginger root could be your saviour.

Seasickness has always been a part of sailing because of the unpredictable bounce and roll of the tide and waves. The word 'yacht' comes from the Dutch word *jacht* meaning to throw up violently, which you hope will not be the case.

Basically sea or motion sickness is caused when things become unstable, causing headaches, dizziness and nausea. It's like a fear of flying – once your brain tells you that you're not in control, that you can't get off, that there is no accounting for all of the strange noises, lurches and lack of oxygen, the panic – and turbulence – kick in.

Stay calm. Easier said than done. When in a boat, try staring at a stationary point ahead or, if everything seems to be moving too much, shut your eyes, tight, and if there's room, lie on your back. Another option is to do the exact opposite – keep busy, very busy, which is easier on a ferry than a small boat. Why not see if you can have a go at steering the wheel? Not that this will help anyone else's nerves. Don't do this during a storm; stay below deck and let the experts steer it onto smoother waters.

Unfortunately the only way to see if you have sea legs or not is to go to sea, but every journey has alternatives. If you can't cross the Channel by water take the Eurostar or fly. If you have an overpowering fear of flying – well, do you need to do this trip, or can you enjoy something with a shorter flight? If not, there are courses, fear of flying CDs and all sorts to assure you it is statistically the safest form of travel. Try a short haul before going around the world, or check out the courses offered by the airlines you are considering.

For seasickness, take the tablets, wear the wristbands and don't eat before boarding so you have less in your stomach to lose.

Keep your taste for adventure and indulge it, and take comfort in how things have advanced since Columbus' days – and he did the trip three times.

If curious about Cuba – or you have a yen to indulge your inner-Columbus – head to Havana. You don't need sea legs to get there, just several good films to help you pass the flight. Since he hit the Caribbean island it has become a mecca for writers (Hemingway), gangsters on the run (Al Capone), revolution, and the odd hurricane. Ramon Grau, Ernesto 'Che' Guevara and of course Fidel Castro, president since 1959, have been key in shaping the country. If you visit you can expect to enjoy old Havana and cadillacs, fifties nightclubs and carnival; or sit back and watch the world pass by as you roll a cigar and order a mojito.

How to make a mojito

A mojito is the oldest Cuban cocktail, made up of spearmint, rum, sugar (traditionally sugar cane), lime and club soda. The sweet sugar disguises the alcoholic kick but, as the word itself is derived from the word 'mojo', African for 'little spell', there can be no doubting its potency and intentions.

Ingredients:

12 fresh spearmint leaves
2 tablespoons of syrup (i.e. one part sugar, one part water)
1 $^1/_2$ ounces of light rum
Half a sliced lime
A dash of club soda.
Ice

To make:

Crush the mint leaves and sliced lime (be sure to use fresh, not cordial), add the syrup, ice, rum, shake it all together and serve. Or simply catch a barman's eye and order . . .

Alternatively, if tequila is your tipple and you've got a penchant for wildly coloured woven ponchos, head to Mexico – home of Frida Kahlo.

Muse of the Month

Frida Kahlo

Kahlo's blue house is nestled in a quiet street in Mexico City's Coyoacan district. This is the house where she was born, lived, worked and died – it has been preserved just how she left it, a living memorial to her. It's the ultimate August pilgrimage for the Kahlo fan.

Revolutionary, romantic, raw and unashamed – Frida Kahlo's distinct portraits are expressions of her life and the politics of the time. Her primary subject was herself (fifty-two self-portraits in total). She emerged from a deeply dysfunctional marriage as a feminist icon, and expressed her voice through her art as she captured her life evolving on canvas. Many of Frida's paintings feature her magnificent unibrow and the definite suggestion of a tash, as well as her rich and ornate style of dressing. Be inspired by Frida and get in touch with the real you. Celebrate the things that make you unique, don't airbrush out your character. Dress to please yourself and remember that beauty is conviction – not the cover of a magazine. Alternatively, knock back a margarita and paint a wall cobalt blue or a defiant shade of red.

If you can't make it to Casa Azul in Mexico, rent the 2002 film *Frida*, based on the biography by Hayden Herrera. The film was co-

produced and brought to the screen by another strong Mexican woman, Salma Hayek, who was nominated for a Best Actress Academy Award for the role she was born to play.

Her life and times

Born on 6 July 1907 in Coyoacan, she was named Magdalena Carmen Frida Kahlo y Caldéron. Not only did she shorten this to Frida but she always insisted that she'd been born in 1910. This was not for vanity – she wasn't interested in pretending to be younger than she was, but she liked to claim that her birth coincided with the Mexican revolution which saw an end to the thirty-one-year dictatorship of President Porfino Diaz.

Her father was nineteen when the Hungarian Jewish family emigrated from Germany to Mexico. Her mother was of Spanish and Native American descent. This mix of cultures and looks is discernible in Frida.

It was a second marriage for both her parents – her father's first wife had died in childbirth and her mother's first love committed suicide – but it wasn't the happiest union, being second choice for both. Frida was the third of four daughters and was particularly close to her father who, himself an important photographer and amateur painter, recognized and nurtured the artistic side of his favourite child.

At six, Frida contracted polio, which left her with a limp. Despite her poor health her father instilled in her a spirit of survival. Feisty, determined and clever, by 1922 Kahlo was enrolled at Mexico's top school, but fate dealt her another blow as three years later a tram collided with the bus she was on. Her injuries were horrific (skip this if squeamish) – broken spinal column, collarbone, ribs, pelvis, eleven fractures in her leg, a dislocated shoulder, crushed right foot and, if that isn't enough to make you feel faint, the iron handrail lanced her abdomen, piercing her uterus.

Not surprisingly, after the accident she'd had enough of hospitals and she abandoned her plans for a career in medicine. Her injuries meant prolonged periods confined to her bed, which were made bearable by the easel at her bedside. It's not surprising that many of her most well-known works are self-portraits. 'I paint self-portraits because I am so often alone, [and] because I am the person I know best,' she said. The portraits often refer directly to her disabilities. In one her face is imposed on a deer's body which has been pierced by arrows. She was described as a surrealist but she disagreed, saying, 'I only painted my own reality.'

In 1928, through her friendship with photographer Tina Modotti, Frida caught the eye of Mexico's celebrated muralist, and lothario, Diego Rivera. She was a member of the Young Communist Party, which he'd founded, and had long admired his work, which was at the forefront of Mexico's cultural and political revolution. Her mother was sceptical of the relationship and described the couple as 'the Elephant and the Dove' due to their physical differences – he was twenty years her senior, six foot one to her five foot three, three hundred pounds to her ninety-eight. But you know what they say about opposites attracting . . . Sparks flew and he divorced his wife. Within a year Frida was installed as wife number three, even though Rivera's own doctor remarked he was 'unfit for monogamy'. What is it about great women getting such a raw deal in their love lives?

Kahlo and Rivera had a tempestuous relationship and, once he began having affairs, she did too. She was openly bisexual, and her lovers included the flamboyant entertainer Josephine Baker. Rivera didn't mind her affairs with women, but other men made him ferociously jealous. Frida was more specific: she hated all his affairs and the ones he had driven her to. She especially resented Rivera's choice when he embarked on an affair with her own sister. 'I suffered two grave accidents in my life,' she once said, 'one in which a streetcar knocked me down – the other accident is Diego.'

While her husband enjoyed international accolades, initially Frida worked quietly in the background. But as the pain of their fiery marriage and several failed pregnancies made it onto her canvases the critics began to take her seriously. In 1932, with *Miscarriage in Detroit*, Kahlo proved she was an artist in her own right and her reputation would go on to eclipse her beloved husband's career.

They divorced in 1939. Only to remarry in 1940. Urgggh – some people don't know when to quit. She described him as 'my child, my lover, my universe'. It was as destructive as it was addictive. But despite

the quarrelling, their art and their admiration were irrevocably bound up with each other – truly the agony and ecstasy. They needed the torture.

In later years, the couple befriended political asylum seeker Leon Trotsky, who, escaping Stalin's totalitarian state, came to Mexico. Trotsky and Kahlo had a brief affair. It ended when he (and his wife) moved out, and he was later assassinated (this was nothing to do with his wife). It was obviously a passing fling as she later praised Stalin and referred to Mao as the 'Great Socialist Hope'. Politicians and power can be a great aphrodisiac.

Though she lived in constant pain, Frida Kahlo loved to party and was a heavy drinker and smoker. A tomboy in her youth, she went on to express her individuality as well as solidarity with her country by dressing in native clothing – often plaiting her hair on top of her head and adorning it with flowers. She was always her own walking work of art.

In 1953/4 she was finally honoured with her first solo exhibition in Mexico (the only one held in her lifetime). She wasn't going to miss this, so arrived by ambulance to be transferred to a richly decorated four-poster bed where she could enjoy her great moment of triumph. A local critic wrote: 'It is impossible to separate the life and the work of this extraordinary person. Her paintings are her biography.'

In 1954, to prevent gangrene, Kahlo had her right leg amputated below the knee. In true Kahlo style she learned to dance with an artificial limb, but the rejoicing was not for long. Her last public appearance was at a communist demonstration. In her last diary entry she wrote: 'I hope the end is joyful – and I hope never to come back – Frida.' She'd had enough. She died in her sleep on 13 July 1954 of a pulmonary embolism, though some suspect suicide.

Fridaisms

'My painting carries with it the message of pain . . . Painting completed my life . . . I believe that work is the best thing.'

'I never knew I was a surrealist till André Breton came to Mexico and told me I was.'

'I leave you my portrait so that you will have my presence all the days and nights that I am away from you.'

'I cannot speak of Diego as my husband because that term, when applied to him, is an absurdity. He never has been, nor will he ever be, anybody's husband.'

How to be an artist

Feel like getting in touch with your inner Frida? Why not combine your holiday with learning how to paint? Italy is a popular destination where the galleries, food and lessons are rolled into one just like being in a real-life *Room with a View*. Look on the sites *www.paintinginitaly.com, www.studio-paradiso.com, www.art-holidays.com* and choose a destination that suits your style (of painting rather than swimsuit, but consider both).

Start carrying a sketchbook and pencil everywhere with you. An A5 note-book is perfect as it's small and innocuous. People are naturally nosy and will not be able to resist looking over your shoulder, so at the early stages keep it discreet while you find your feet.

Start with pencil as:

a) Charcoal/pastels are very messy
b) Paints are cumbersome to carry around
c) You will already have a pencil

You don't want to shell out for all the tools and equipment until you decide that this is going to be more than a passing fad or you have some degree of talent.

Pencils are good for details – buildings, people, landmarks – but you need to get softer than the everyday one for landscape shapes. Pencils come in a variety of leads from H (hard) to B (soft), HB being the happy medium. The softer they are the better they are for shading, which you can use to add shapes and texture. It might be an idea to work from a photo or through a window if tackling a big landscape as the composition can take longer than the light and the weather permit.

When drawing people observe your subject before making a mark. You want someone who is as still as a statue. See if there is someone asleep on a bench or lost in a daydream who doesn't look like they're going anywhere soon. When starting, it's nice to draw anonymous subjects so there's no pressure to capture any likeness or show them the result. If you enjoy sketching people you might decide to graduate from drawing the scantily clad on the beach to the totally naked at life-drawing classes – Toulouse Lautrec hung out at the Moulin Rouge and the brothels with his sketch book; well, that was his excuse.

If all else fails, do a Frida Kahlo and set yourself up next to a mirror. Fruit bowls are also popular.

Composing your masterpieces

Look on *www.learnhowtodraw.com* for technical tips, but don't forget there is no real right and wrong in drawing – though if doing a portrait of the Queen a likeness, or at least a kind interpretation, is preferred.

David Hockney's portrait of *Mr and Mrs Clark and Percy* is the Tate gallery's most popular postcard. It captures his friends, the sixties fashion designer Ossie Clark with his then wife, textile designer Celia Birtwell, and their cat. Hockney was the best man at their wedding and based this portrait on the famous *The Arnolfini Portrait* by Jan van Eyck and *A Rake's Progress* by William Hogarth. The lilies symbolize purity and the annunciation, which tied in nicely as Birtwell was pregnant at the time. The cat on Clark's lap is a symbol of infidelity and envy (Clark was gay and continued to have affairs and lead a heady lifestyle – the marriage collapsed in 1974). The cat in the picture is not in fact Percy, it's another of the Clarks' cats, but Hockney thought Percy sounded better despite the real McCoy's stage fright and reluctance to be caught on canvas.

Some students practise drawing people by doing lots and lots of short sketches, allowing about thirty seconds per pose. This focuses the eye and gets the hand to coordinate (hopefully). When doing this, don't work on the face – eyes, nose, mouth – until you have the torso properly placed. Draw an entire silhouette without taking your pencil off the page.

Plot in the head, the angle of the body and then the angle of the upper torso, waist and limbs – legs and arms come later. Fiddly details such as fingers, features and clothing come much later.

Landscapes are slightly trickier in pencil, especially if your view is of endless rolling hills and dales. Here you may prefer to try adding a bit of colour with watercolours or pastels.

Though you might not immediately land an exhibition of your own at a major gallery (and remember even Van Gogh was only recognized posthumously), if you have a piece of work that you are particularly proud of the Royal Academy of Art's Summer Exhibition has an open admission policy so this could be your moment to rub shoulders or frames with your artistic heroes.

Established in 1769 in Pall Mall, the Summer Exhibition is one of the gallery's most popular annual events and is the largest open contemporary art exhibition in the world. It was first held in its current home, Burlington House, in 1869, and over 150,000 people come to see who's hanging and who's hanging out. Go to *www.royalacademy.org.uk/summer-exhibition* to see how your doodles can find fame, though be prepared – as with all things, one man's meat is another man's poison. In 1959 *Reynold's News* ran the headline 'This is not art – it's a joke in bad taste' about Jackson Pollock. What would they make of the Turner Prize entrants today?

If fine art isn't your thing, maybe illustration could be your creative calling. Go to Quentin Blake's Illustration Academy, or visit his touring Magic Pencil exhibition: *www.magicpencil.britishcouncil.org* to get your illustration career started.

'Most people who write about art don't really write about it [illustration]

– I think they're a bit embarrassed,' he says. 'Illustration is not a watered-down version of painting. There is an instinct within us to tell stories with pictures, and illustration is the vernacular expression of that.'

Blake brought Roald Dahl's books to life. He set up his school to encourage young illustrators and is the first ever Children's Laureate. You can read more of his tips on his website: *www.quentinblake.com*, or in *Drawing for the Artistically Undiscovered* by Quentin Blake and John Cassidy.

Where to find inspiration

While it's the weather to be outside, let the Impressionists, Fauvists or Pre-Raphaelites encourage you to add another artistic string to your bow. Of his garden Monet said 'I am in raptures', so get out either the watercolours or the lawnmower.

If your pot plants look as if they have seen better days and the hosepipe ban is playing havoc with the lush lawns you wanted to paint, head to Monet's garden at Giverny, France, *www.giverny.org*, which he considered heaven on earth. 'All my money goes into my garden,' he said, and it features in many of his most famous paintings. Impressionism may look like clusters of splodges and blurs close up, but at a distance the colours become waterlilies, landscapes, bridges. Let the season, the view as well as style and ability inspire you.

Closer to home you can begin with a trip to the hidden treasure of Charleston (*www.charleston.org.uk*), home of the Bloomsbury set, to get you in the mood. Charleston was the country home of Vanessa Bell (sister of Virginia Woolf) and Duncan Grant, and where they invited all the writers and intellectuals of the Bloomsbury Group (Virginia and Leonard Woolf, E.M. Forster and Clive Bell) to live, paint, write, create and debate with one another.

The house itself is a work of art. Inspired by Italian frescoes and the Post-Impressionists, every surface has patterns and colours dancing over it. From the backs of doors to the skirting boards, wardrobes to window frames, even the often-neglected corners are decorated with the Bloomsbury set's watery shades, as the Art Deco swirls through the house. And we haven't even touched on the garden.

In addition to their own murals and mosaics, paintings by Renoir, Pisarro and Delacroix hang on the walls, gifts from past visitors.

Visit Charleston to get a taste of the era or, if you can't make this journey, pick up one of the Bloomsbury set's books, such as *A Room of One's Own*, by Virginia Woolf, or *Notes on Bloomsbury*, by Vanessa Bell to inspire a bohemian streak in your home.

Should the urge take you, stencil your bed frame, or embellish your mantlepiece, or, if this seems too bold (or it's not your house to go wild with a paint brush in), practise on a chair from a car-boot sale or bric-a-brac market. The advantage of objects such as chairs, table tops, trays, vases and lamp bases is that they can be worked on outside – minimizing spillages and giving you a chance to get some fresh air. Doors, walls and floors all have to be done in situ and are less easy to hide if a creative disaster, so make sure you have permission, Picasso.

4th August

In 1792 English romantic poet Percy Bysshe Shelley was born. His first wife Harriet Westbrook committed suicide following her discovery of his affair with Mary Godwin, whom he later married. She became Mary Shelley, author of *Frankenstein*.

6th August

The pop artist Andy Warhol was born in 1928. One of his most famous subjects, Marilyn Monroe (see page 106), was found dead on 5 August 1962.

> 'In August '62 I started doing silk-screens. I wanted something stronger that gave more of an assembly-line effect. With silk-screening you pick a photograph, blow it up, transfer it in glue onto silk, and then roll ink across it so the ink goes through the silk, but not the glue. It

was all so simple, quick and chancy ... When Marilyn Monroe happened to die that month, I got the idea to make screens of her beautiful face – the first *Marilyns*.'

The Monroe portfolio consists of ten fluorescent prints and is considered to be one of the most iconic images of the pop art era. In 1998, *Orange Marilyn* sold for more than $17.3 million, five times the estimated price and a record sum for his work. If that is a little beyond your budget, a tin of Campbell's soup, another of his subjects, costs approximately fifty pence.

Warhol promised we would all be famous for fifteen minutes; his own fame far exceeded that. His celebrity status almost equalled that of his subjects, who included Elvis, John Wayne and Jacqueline Kennedy Onassis.

The Andy Warhol Museum in Pittsburgh, Pennsylvania is one place to go for a Warhol experience. Failing this, go and party in New York. Studio 54 may be gone but the duo behind this infamous nightclub, Steve Rubell and Ian Schrager, went on to introduce the concept of boutique hotels, opening Morgans in New York in 1984. Assemble your best Edie Sedgwick look, taking your lead from Sienna Miller in *Factory Girl*, and take a seat at the bar at one of Schrager's hip hotels: 40 Bond, Grammercy Park, The Royalton and Paramount in New York, St Martins Lane or the Sanderson in London. See *www.ianschragercompany.com* for more details.

Failing all this, at least buy the latest issue of *Interview*, the magazine Warhol founded.

7th August

In 1876 Mata Hari was born. Read about her colourful life in *The Red Dancer* by Richard Skinner or practise your burlesque routine (see page 388).

How to have a retro holiday at home

There was a time when the Redcoats and knobbly-knee competition were the height of holiday entertainment. Now it has undergone something of a facelift and with this revamp the updated 'Carry On' and 'Kiss Me Quick' chalet holidays are back in favour.

Carry on Butlins

William Edmund Butlin was born in South Africa before his family moved to Canada. After serving in the First World War, the holiday-resort promoter worked his way to England where it became his mission to revolutionize the British vacation: well, you had to do *something* to make up for the unreliable weather.

The first Butlins opened on 11 April 1936, offering a self-contained holiday with three meals a day and free entry to all entertainment for 35 shillings a week (£1.75). Bargain.

It became *the* place to get a summer job. Ringo Starr was all set to become a Redcoat at Skegness, but went off and became the drummer in a band called the Beatles instead, while Catherine Zeta-Jones is listed as winning one of the legendary Butlin's talent shows – very *Darling Buds*.

What a *Carry On* – but now as well as the talent competitions and the *Hi-De-Hi* moments there are discos, karaoke and all the entertainment that you may feign to dread, but secretly have been bursting to have the excuse to try. What about considering their sixties-themed weekend as a raucous and unforgettable way to spend a hen night?

If having Gladys greet you with a cheery 'Morning, campers' brings you out in a cold sweat but you don't want to do the long haul, why not follow Erin O'Connor's footsteps and put up a tent? When was the last time you visited London Zoo? Went up Blackpool Tower? Along Brighton Pier? To

Syon Park Butterfly House? Played a game of crazy golf or took a pedalo out for a ride?

How to write a postcard

Yes, this should be a perfectly obvious skill, but with email booths in every coffee shop in every town the picture postcard is getting much neglected. But why? Nothing beats receiving a postcard from some far-flung corner of the globe.

While you are off wrestling snakes (human or reptile), bartering in the local flea markets, or sleeping on the beach under a blanket of stars, send a postcard home to tell of your adventures.

1. Do not risk bringing your little black book with you. There will be nothing more infuriating than leaving this on a beach in the Bahamas – your social life (or you) may never recover. Scribble down, text or commit to memory the key addresses and postcodes you need.

2. When choosing and purchasing postcards, buy stamps at the same time. Try to locate a postbox. Posting at the airport is a cop-out.

Look up the key phrase you will need to say at your chosen destination. French. *Est-ce que je peux acheter des timbres pour Angleterre, s'il vous plaît?* German: *Ich Möchte Briedmarken nach England Kaufen.* Italian: *Vorrei comprare francobolli per l'Inghilterra, per favore.* Spanish: *Puedo comprar estampillas para Inglaterra, por favor?*

3. Pick a postcard that shows off where you are. Pick one with blue skies, long beaches, great views. 'Wish you were here' is actually 'Bet you wish you were here'. Package it as a bestseller.

4. Postcards have a deceptively small amount of space for you to write in. Keep your news short and succinct, i.e. Sunshine. Scuba Diving, Fawlty Towers, Italian stallion next door. There isn't enough room for the whole saga – save that anecdote for when you are safely home.

A postcard is like a movie trailer – sell the teaser so they will want to sit through all 900 photos and the 30-minute DVD. Entice your audience with promises of what's to come.

8th August

'Itsy Bitsy Teeny Weeny Yellow Polka-Dot Bikini' hit the number one polka-dot spot in the charts in 1960. The bikini design celebrated its fiftieth anniversary in 2006. There wasn't much to unveil but it made its debut in July 1946 at the Piscine Molitor in Paris, designed by French engineer Louis Réard and fashion designer Jacques Heim. It was an instant sensation, perfect to aid that all-over tan whilst upholding a modicum of modesty, depending on the wearer.

How to have fun in the sun

'Only Mad Dogs and Englishmen go out in the midday sun,' said Noël Coward, but why not sink your toes in the sand rather than a mound of overdue bills or deadlines?

Should the sun break through, seize the moment to build a sandcastle or bathe in the sea. Go further than a paddle – go in up to your knees, shudder, then your waist; now look, everyone's watching so you have to just leap in.

Sandcastles are less painful, and can go from being a hobby to an artform. You can compete in the World Sand Sculpture Festival *www.wssa.info* or even study at their academy. For enthusiasts there is *www.sandcastlecentral.com*

There are no rules as to how to build your sandcastle though you should try and position yourself not too far inland – too-dry sand is hopeless – and not too near the sea as you don't want the tide to destroy your handiwork. Shells and seaweed add a certain *je ne sais quoi* to the creation, and don't forget to dig a moat to protect your castle from invaders, crabs and such like; your home is your castle, after all. If a sandcastle isn't what you want to toil over after a paddle, you could always write your name in the sand. Practise your hand prints and signature and then turn to page 325 to see how the stars immortalized theirs outside Grauman's Chinese Theatre.

10th August

Artist Jackson Pollock, one of Peggy Guggenheim's protégés (see page 402), died in 1956, and on 12 August 1988 Jean-Michel Basquiat, the graffiti artist in Warhol's circle, died of a drug overdose. Look up their work, watch the films depicting their life stories – or read about a female artist instead.

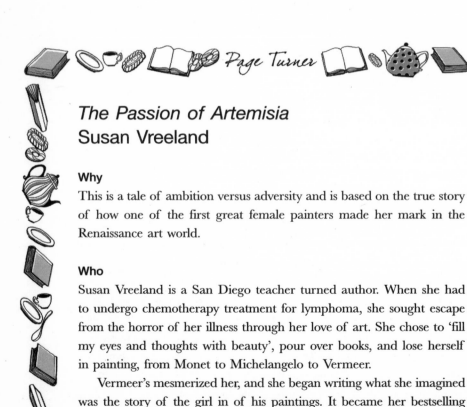

Page Turner

The Passion of Artemisia
Susan Vreeland

Why
This is a tale of ambition versus adversity and is based on the true story of how one of the first great female painters made her mark in the Renaissance art world.

Who
Susan Vreeland is a San Diego teacher turned author. When she had to undergo chemotherapy treatment for lymphoma, she sought escape from the horror of her illness through her love of art. She chose to 'fill my eyes and thoughts with beauty', pour over books, and lose herself in painting, from Monet to Michelangelo to Vermeer.

Vermeer's mesmerized her, and she began writing what she imagined was the story of the girl in of his paintings. It became her bestselling

novel *Girl in Hyacinth Blue*. The next artist she stumbled across was Artemisia
Gentileschi and Vreeland couldn't believe her story had never been told.
As Vreeland wrote she went into remission, and believes writing gave her
the strength to survive the cancer.

The plot

Artemisia Gentileschi (8 July 1593–1653) is a real-life heroine, and her
work survives to this day. She was the daughter of a well-known Italian
baroque painter, Orazio Gentileschi, and went on to be the first woman
admitted into the prestigious *Accademia dell'Arte* in Florence. Despite the
'novelty' of her female status she was acknowledged as being a talented
artist.

Artemisia had to overcome many obstacles. At seventeen she was
raped by her father's collaborator and had to suffer a public trial,
examination and scorn before finally proving his guilt. Her luck with
men did not improve; she was too modern-thinking for most of the
men on offer, and ended up married to a jealous philandering brute.
Despite the suffering in her personal life she continued to paint and
develop as an artist, and even attracted patronage from the great
Cosimo de Medici himself. But could her talent outweigh the disad-
vantage of her sex?

The story follows the strained and competitive relationships between
daughter and father, husband and wife, and later between mother
and daughter – while Artemisia struggles to gain recognition for her
work.

Hosting

For your meeting why not invite your group over to showcase a piece
of your own art, your latest home improvement *à la* Bloomsbury, or an
art acquisition? Perhaps you could set up easels and an impromptu
painting evening. If this sounds too terrifying, many galleries have fabulous cafés and teashops – so you could take in the painters of the period
before tucking into a slab of thought-provoking coffee cake. For ultimate authenticity hold the meeting in Babington's in Rome (well, it's a

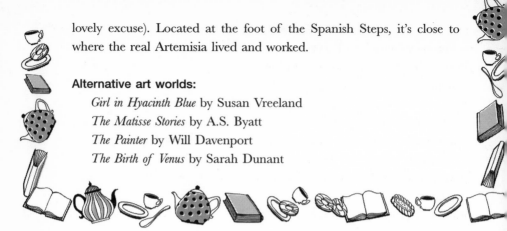

lovely excuse). Located at the foot of the Spanish Steps, it's close to where the real Artemisia lived and worked.

Alternative art worlds:
> *Girl in Hyacinth Blue* by Susan Vreeland
> *The Matisse Stories* by A.S. Byatt
> *The Painter* by Will Davenport
> *The Birth of Venus* by Sarah Dunant

13th August

Alfred Hitchcock, one of the most influential film directors and producers, was born in 1899.

Hitchcock's career spanned six decades from silent to talkies, black and white to colour, and all drew on fear, fantasy and suspense – although, ironically, he never dealt with his own phobia: a fear of eggs. Forget *Psycho*, his fear came with a yoke and a shell. It takes all sorts.

Hitchcock was master of the unexpected, with one element that was always expected – if not anticipated – and that was his own cameo appearance in all his films. Whether boarding a bus, standing in a courtyard or even appearing in a brief shot of a photograph, he didn't miss a film.

His films include: *Psycho*, 1960; *To Catch a Thief*, 1955; *Notorious*, 1946; and, of course, *Rebecca*, 1940 (see May page turner, page 188). His favourite blondes were Ingrid Bergman, Joan Fontaine and Grace Kelly (see page 171).

If you don't fancy Hitchcock, you've seen *Grease* just a few too many times and already been on a *Summer Holiday* with Cliff Richard, another English director, who hasn't enjoyed the same level of success as Hitchcock but is nevertheless perfect for this time of year and the afternoon movie siesta, is Ken Russell. Watch *The Boy Friend* to get you in the mood for a summer fling. His 1971 musical extravaganza, set in the twenties and starring Twiggy as poor little rich girl Polly Browne, with Vidal Sassoon haircut and Bibaesque wardrobe, won two Golden Globes that year (Best Newcomer and Best Motion Picture Actress in a Comedy/Musical).

Either learn the dance routine to 'Sûr la Plage', go to the beachfront for real, or see if Sandy Wilson's original is playing at an open-air theatre.

A holiday romance might be the perfect distraction while waiting for exam results, or getting a tan the traditional and highly factored way. But be warned: statistically, Danny and Sandy are in the minority of success stories. The tan may prove to last longer.

Rather than worry about how to get sand out of your shoes, why don't you think about the big picture and go green?

How to go green
by Anya Hindmarch, accessories designer

I am certainly not the greenest person around but, like everyone else, I am trying to work out how I can live more respectfully for the planet whilst not making life unbearable. Honestly, I've always been a bit more Margot than Barbara when seeking 'The Good Life'. I have a big car because I have five children and I fly a lot because I have to for work. However, I've become a lot more aware of what I do since working on the 'I'm Not A Plastic Bag' campaign which was launched in March 2007. This project has really opened my eyes to the amount of packaging we all waste. I think that fashion can play a huge part in influencing people's behaviour and this is what I tried to achieve with this project. You have to work out how you can help, how you can make a difference and I wanted to get people to think about their actions and try to make it fashionable not to use plastic bags, and create an alternative that inspired them to stick to this. Clearly this bag won't solve the problem alone but I hope it has made a lot more people aware; it seems that the considered opinion is to reduce, reuse, recycle. It's amazing how many plastic bags you can smugly refuse on one shopping trip when you have a reusable bag with you.

All of this recycling and environmental awareness is pretty new to me and, like most people I know, I am still learning. I do think that everyone can do their bit and there are many simple things that can be done as part of everyday life: look on *www.wearewhatwedo.org* and you will see how easy it is. If we all make these small changes together, collectively we can make a huge difference. It's amazing how quickly we adapt to change and how new behaviour soon becomes habit. I remember when I would sunbathe covered in baby oil – now I would never even think of wearing less than 30 SPF (at least for the first week of my holiday). I've become the same now with my washing machine; setting the temperature at more than thirty degrees seems as sinful as eating carbs after 6 p.m.! Work out what you can do and start today!

You know that sick feeling you get when you're on your way to dinner and you suddenly panic and go back home to check whether you've left the iron on (even though you know you checked it twice before you left)? I now have a new phobia – I obsessively check I've turned the lights off, and not left my TV on standby. Little things = big difference! I drive my family mad turning everything off every time I leave a room. But, like manners, it really does matter!

We all just have to think and be aware. For Christmas last year I planted a tree for each member of my team and my suppliers in a local woodland as their Christmas present. I hope that one day we will all be able to picnic under them. Trees are pretty amazing when you think about it – they absorb carbon dioxide which we don't like and give us oxygen in return. Wow! Nature is brilliant . . . let's look after it and help it continue to do its magic.

15th August

10,000 spectators turned up to see Judy Garland and the munchkins follow the yellow brick road at the *The Wizard of Oz* premiere at Grauman's Chinese Theatre, Hollywood in 1939.

Grauman's Theatre (movie theatre rather than the thespy type) is a spectacle in itself and opened in 1927 with the premiere of the silent movie *King of Kings*. Grauman had built the Million Dollar Theatre and the Egyptian Theatre but he longed for his dream theatre – and this was to be the jewel in his crown. Temple bells, pagodas, stone dogs, forty-foot-high curved walls and gigantic red columns crowned with wrought-iron masks travelled from China to LA. With architect Raymond Kennedy, the Chinese actress Ann May Wong drove in the first rivet. The venue soon became *the* most sought-after place to hold a Hollywood premiere – maybe a bit OTT to unveil the holiday home video there though.

The theatre has even played a starring role in its own right, including an appearance in the opening sequences of *Pretty Woman*, *Speed* and *Singin' in the Rain*.

It is now known as Mann's Chinese Theatre after it was bought and renamed by Ted Mann in 1973, although it was originally jointly owned by Sid Grauman, Mary Pickford and Douglas Fairbanks. It was Grauman's idea to capture the stars' footprints outside the venue in wet cement, including those of Monroe, Brando and Loren. This is still considered the ultimate accolade in Hollywood, and space is limited, although a star (and there are over 2,000 of these) on the Walk of Fame is a good second.

16th August

Rock and roll legend Elvis Presley died in 1977. You can make a pilgrimage to the King's fourteen-acre ranch Graceland – a shrine to his memory, music and blue suede shoes.

If in London at this time, Buckingham Palace opens its doors to the public, *www.royal.gov.uk*, until September though the Queen is not in residence. Decide which side of the pond, or which 'royal' family, you want to get closer to.

17th August

Mae West was born on this day in 1892. One of the first and most controversial sex bombs of the silver screen, Monroe and Madonna owe this woman a drink or a diamond or two. As West said: 'I never worry about diets. The only carrots that interest me are the number you get in a diamond.'

'Goodness, what lovely diamonds,' exclaims the hat-check girl in *Night After Night*.

'Goodness had nothing to do with it, dearie,' West's character drawls, and this went on to be the title of her 1959 autobiography. As she famously remarked: 'I used to be Snow White, but I drifted.'

If summer romance is proving problematic, remember Mae's words of wisdom:

'A man can be short and dumpy and getting bald but if he has fire, women will like him.'

'A man has one hundred dollars and you leave him with two dollars, that's subtraction.'

'A hard man is good to find.'

'I only like two kinds of men, domestic and imported.'

'Don't marry a man to reform him – that's what reform schools are for.'

'Good sex is like good bridge. If you don't have a good partner, you'd better have a good hand.'

'I only have "yes" men around me. Who needs "no" men?'

'You only live once, but if you do it right, once is enough.'

19th August

While the boys are still cowering, another feisty woman, Coco Chanel, was born in 1883. Wear palazzo pants and pearls or No. 5 perfume on the beach in her honour today. See February's Muse of the Month, page 75.

22nd August

Right at the height of the summer sun, impressionist composer Claude Debussy was born in 1862. The Frenchman's most famous works or 'tone-poems' include *La Mer, Children's Corner Suite* and *Clair de Lune* – the last on the list being a particular on-screen favourite. In *Casino Royale* James Bond set aside time each day to play it, while in *Frankie and Johnny* Al Pacino and Michelle Pfeiffer's characters fall in love 'to the most beautiful song in the world'. Have you fallen for its charms?

Another art-meets-music collaboration to listen to is Mussorgsky's *Pictures at an Exhibition* which takes a walk round a museum describing the paintings not in shades but in tones, where different timbres paint a view.

If you fancy being a music rather than artistic maestro, download the music programme Sibelius from *www.sibelius.com*, which produces, scripts and then performs the melodies you plot in – no formal music training required.

23rd August

Gene Kelly was born in 1912. Though Astaire and Rogers remain the ultimate partnership, Kelly was an equally virtuoso dancer, particularly in tap. Take a salsa, rhumba or flamenco dance class to spice up the summer moves. For the A-Z of dance see May, page 179. What is the dance of the city you'd most like to be in? Explore the globe through the dance floor.

Kelly starred in *An American in Paris* and, of course, *Singin' in the Rain*, which contains probably the most famous of all dance sequences on film; it's only right to mention it again on the late dancer's birthday.

In reality, when filming this scene Kelly had a fever of 103, and it wasn't rain, it was milk (nice and sticky) to help it show up better on celluloid.

It has been imitated on screen countless times and Kelly himself 'danced again' from beyond the grave through the magic of technology in a 2005 Volkswagen advert. The footage was remixed and updated with a backbeat on the soundtrack. The set was replicated for a trio of street dancers to break-dance and body-pop their way through the routine, with Kelly's face digitally superimposed on the close-ups.

Debbie Reynolds later admitted that making this film and surviving childbirth were the two most difficult experiences of her life (see page 179). Being a good sport she left out Elizabeth Taylor running off with her husband Eddie Fisher not long after she'd given birth to their daughter, Carrie 'Princess Leia' Fisher.

24th August

Brontë sister Charlotte finished writing Jane Eyre on this day in 1847. *Jane Eyre* was to be the most critically successful of the Brontë trio's works. 1847 proved to be a milestone year for the family of writing sensations, as it was in this year that they managed to secure a publisher not only for *Jane Eyre* (Charlotte), but also for *Wuthering Heights* (Emily) and *Agnes Grey* (Anne), all of which you should aim to have read by this time next year.

25th August

Today, in AD 79, some people thought it was the end of the world. It wasn't, but it was certainly the end of Pompeii.

Pompeii, in southern Italy, was a Roman town nestled between Naples and the fishing resort of Sorrento. It was built at the foot of the volcano Mount Vesuvius, believed to be extinct, but on this date the volcano proved everyone wrong, and erupted. Ash and molten lava poured over the city at an alarming rate, killing around 2,000 people and leaving few survivors. In nineteen hours the entire city had vanished.

'You could hear women lamenting, children crying, men shouting,' wrote Pliny the Younger, whose Uncle Pliny, ever the inquisitive writer, had run back into the city to see what was happening for himself (and perished).

It was not until 1594 that traces of Pompeii's buildings were discovered. In 1710 the smaller Roman site of Herculaneum was unearthed and in 1748 archaeologists decided it was time to start the major excavation to resurrect the lost city. Under nine feet of volcanic ash the digging eventually revealed that Pompeii had remained perfectly preserved and everything, like Sleeping Beauty, was frozen in time.

Pompeii is now a major cultural tourist attraction and gives a first-hand feel of a Roman town, from mosaic entrances warning *Cave Canem* (Beware of the Dog) to ceramics. There are even ghostly casts of people, as well as paintings and traces of the dress of the time.

In England, if you feel like exploring the past and digging for your own artefacts why not visit Lyme Regis in Dorset? Read *Mary Anning's Treasures* by Helen Brandon Bush which tells the true story of Mary Anning. Lyme Regis is famous for its fossils, as well as its iconic 'cob' which was the setting for *The French Lieutenant's Woman*. Anning, however, like many visitors here, combed the beach for fossils. She lived in the early nineteenth century and was the only one of four siblings to survive being struck by lightning (very Harry Potter). She started to collect curiosities and fossils to help her widowed mother make ends meet and made some very important finds on her wanderings along the beach, many of which are in museums over the world today. The rhyme 'she sells sea shells on the sea shore' is said to be based on her.

The reason you can 'hear' the sea in your seashell is not because it has trapped the sound in the twists of the shell, but because it captures different frequencies that resonate near your ear. It actually also works with a glass or cup held at different angles, but stick with the more magical theory and take your bucket and spade to see what you can uncover – or purchase a fossil in the local curiosity shop before settling down to a cream tea.

During the last weekend in August the Notting Hill Carnival takes place in London.

The festival first took place in 1964, started with the energy and enthusiasm of the Caribbean families who had roots in the tropics and a home here and wanted to celebrate their cultural sunshine with London. From steel bands to floats to all-night partying, even if the weather lets you down, it brings tropical colour and sounds to the streets. It also coincides with the last bank holiday weekend of the summer, so is the perfect excuse to throw your own street party, join the carnival or have one last escape before September kicks in. Their motto is: 'Every spectator is a participant – Carnival is for all who dare to participate.' Are you game enough?

29th August

The United Kingdom took Hong Kong in 1842 and it became part of the Commonwealth, until its return to Chinese rule in 1997.

Also on this date in 1964, Walt Disney's *Mary Poppins* was released, a perfect reminder that holidays are drawing to an end and, as the tan fades, it's time to get organized and ready to go back to school, college, work, real life. As the last carnival float goes by it's a signal that the season is changing once more.

 Foot Note

The flip-flop

If you want to talk about the first ever shoe – not your first baby shoe – the first shoe in history would have to be the sandal, which dates back as far as you like, and can be traced to when the ancient Chinese upgraded their footwear from the animal hides the cavemen and tribesmen had been wrapping around their feet. The Romans covered their versions in jewels, the Chinese brought in the reinforced sole while the Egyptians introduced the thong – shoes were status symbols and sexy right back in BC. Aphrodite, the Greek goddess of love, was usually depicted wearing only her sandals; well, what else could be as beautiful?

From Franciscan monks let's leap to the flip-flop and the cheap plastic thong that clip-clops its way into the sunshine. This design actually originates from the Japanese zori sandal and has been the top beachwear in New Zealand since the thirties. Flat, backless, ideal for the sand to slide out, and with a sole to protect you from pebbles and shells, they are perfect once you've got used to the thong that rubs between your big and second toes. (The French are so distracted by this feature of the design that they are called 'tongs'.)

Flip-flops were patented in 1957 in Auckland, New Zealand, by Maurice Yock and remain a popular accessory for the beach belle. They are the cheapest footwear available, apart from the giant chaise-longue version that carried mini-Miss Kylie Minogue into the stadium for the 2000 Sydney Olympics. The rise of the Brazilian Havaiana brand once again made flip-flops a fashion statement – and pedicures an everyday essential. However, if you can't bear a thong between your toes, only sand and sea, pack some jellies, sandals, espadrilles or Birkenstocks instead.

September

'Power is the great aphrodisiac.'
Henry Kissinger

Wish You Were Here

Stephen Jones from Tokyo

Having a lovely time. Tokyo still is the most intriguing city in the world and is as inspirational as when I first visited it over twenty years ago. Now as then, I recommend you head for the Harajuku district which is the hub of Tokyo fashion and design (just ask the doorman of your hotel to direct your taxi. Do you know that Japan doesn't have a proper street-numbering system?!) Here you will find the greats of Japanese fashion: Comme des Garçons, Issey Miyake and Yohji Yamamoto jostling with the upstarts of innovation like Undercover and designer shops like Loveless.

I would pass on any of the cathedrals of international fashion on Omotesando (Harajuku's main drag) and explore the narrow streets behind them, where the ultra-stylish passers-by are as much of an attraction as the various tiny Select Shops (boutiques) selling great T-shirts, customized jeans, crazy accessories and the best of avant-garde designers from Japan and around the world. However, for me, fashion – smashion. What *I* make a beeline for is Kiddyland, Japan's ultimate toy shop. Here you will find seven floors of ninjageishamangabarbierama in Day-Glo colours in a background of techno music and flashing lights. My fave is the stationery department where you can buy pencil cases shaped like cartoon gherkins and pencils that play a tune and light up when you write (or sketch Dior). Another local favourite in the nearby Shibuya district (you can walk there in fifteen minutes, checking out the fabulously dressed groovy fashionistas) is Tokyo Hands, life goods store, a fabulous emporium of hardware: paint, plastics, rubber, glitter, fabric, silk flowers, wood and lightbulbs, in fact everything for a Stephen Jones hat. Even if I go to Tokyo for one day, which has been known, I'd rather go to Tokyo Hands than have dinner.

That's the thing about Tokyo – you don't need a guide or a schedule or even a point of view; just keep your eyes open and your creative juices will go bananas!

Lots of love, Stephen

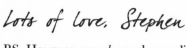

P.S. However, you *do* need a credit card (with a healthy spending limit)!

1st September

In 1985 the wreck of the Titanic was found, seventy-three years after it sank.

2nd September

The Great Fire of London started on this date in 1666. What started as a small fire at a baker's in Pudding Lane (see Samuel Pepys' diary, page 5) gathered momentum at an alarming pace and soon the blaze engulfed London. The fire raged for four days and destroyed 80 per cent of the city, though thankfully only sixteen people perished. One figure who rose like a phoenix from the disaster was Christopher Wren, who built the Monument to commemorate the date that changed the London landscape as well as his most famous legacy, St Paul's Cathedral. The Monument stands 202 feet high, crowned with a flaming urn, and is the same height as it is the distance from Thomas Farriner's bakery, where it all began. Make sure you blow out all the candles before you leave the house today.

First Monday of the month – Labor Day (US)

This began in 1882 as a day off for the working man. Americans celebrated the 'last fling of summer' and threw parades in the streets, a tradition which continues to this day.

There is an old custom linked to this date that says you mustn't wear white (especially not white shoes) after Labor Day. This is sensible given the rainy, dirty, sludgy weather at this time of year. But don't worry too much as every rule is made to be broken; it's like all things – dress appropriately and you'll be fine.

How to get a job

If you want a job, a promotion, or to win a pitch then you have to make sure that you give yourself every advantage to shine above all competition. As well as sharpening up your presentation skills, you have to tighten up your CV. The perfect version should see all your achievements, aspirations and ambitions condensed into a single page – two at the most.

Your vital statistics

There is no such thing as a blanket curriculum vitae – so you cannot simply copy one. You have to tailor yours to each situation. *Tailor* not lie. Update it throughout the year and make sure that even if you're not looking for new work you have new achievements to add.

Your CV should give the key facts about you, your education, qualifications and job experience to date. Highlight your best bits, which will not be in short supply when you are as accomplished and fabulous as you are, but think of the competition. Keep the information succinct and your achievements will stand out. As with all first impressions, this really can be make or break.

There are two main types of CV:

The chronological CV is the most common/practical. This lists all employment and educational dates and achievements. Edit this information to keep it current as well as relevant; tweak to highlight all the skills that make you perfect for this opportunity.

The functional CV highlights skills within a job. It describes what you actually did in your previous position, rather than letting the job title sell you short. Fashion Assistant, for example, could denote anything from Tea Maker to Chief Ironer to Stylist to Editor to Interviewer to Therapist to General Dogsbody. You can explain your role in more detail in a functional CV – functional not fictional – though you can always fill in any gaps come interview time.

Mission statements can be added at the start or end of either CV if you feel your pitch is still a bit lacking – but you don't need to include one if you have completed an application form. Keep a mission statement (which says how focused, determined, perfect for this job you are) up your sleeve in case you still need to add more bumpf once you've edited your CV.

Got it covered

The CV is only half the project – you can't simply send this folded in an envelope and hope for the best. All CVs and job applications need a covering letter. This is where you can make your one-page pitch specific to the job. If you are given an application form to complete and return, which is common nowadays, always remember to photocopy it before you start. Practise before attacking the master copy with a biro smudge. This will later prove invaluable when you want to review it before the interviews.

Don't beat about the bush. State in black and white:
– what job you are applying for
– your contact details

– that your CV is attached

– that you hope to hear from them soon

Type the letter on plain white paper and sign it at the bottom (no kisses, however desperate you are). Save coloured, perfumed paper for other occasions; it could send a confusing message.

Keep it clear and simple. Check for grammar and spelling.

How to be in business
by Mrs Joan Burstein, founder of fashion emporium Browns

My husband and I opened Browns in London back in 1970. We were one of the first multi-brand boutiques, and we wanted to mix names, labels and find new choices for fashion. I remember we were one of the first stores to really travel when we were buying. We would go to Italy, Paris, Tokyo, all over the world to find new names to sell at Browns.

That search continues today, and in fact even more so as it is much more competitive, but now, as then, what I'm looking for above all when we are buying is something individual. It has to be original, attractive and arresting – mad as well as beautiful, something that comes from the designer, from within, I suppose. What matters most of all to me is that the idea is unique. I think standing out is essential in any business, not just fashion; you have to search for the original and the excellent. Yes, you have to look for quality, but above all a designer has to have quality ideas. I love anything that is lovingly made, with a story behind it so you know how much time and care has gone into it. It's not about how a business is structured or if it has a fancy office or studio, it is the ideas and raw talent that count. It doesn't matter where you go – a good collection in a grotty studio will always be more inviting than one with all the trimmings and none of the substance. Don't worry, you don't need to have the whole concept exactly worked out at the beginning. When a label, brand or company is young they need energy and encouragement while they find their feet. It's wonderful that the high street is now doing so much to encourage young designers.

When buying fashion, or anything else, making sure they can deliver is important, but I believe in nurturing new talent and think it's possible to turn a blind eye to the finer details of structure until a designer is slightly more established.

In 1984 I saw the graduate show of John Galliano – it was a once-in-a-lifetime experience, and something I will never forget. There was a real sense of excitement around it. Here was something that was so different to anything else, so original, so confident and it sold in no time. We put his collection into the window at Browns immediately. John was an exception; magic like that doesn't happen every season but once you have found someone like him it inspires you to keep searching, hoping that you'll experience this feeling again. My only regret with this collection is that I didn't keep a piece for myself.

When looking at collections, go without preconceived ideas – this is necessary as a shopper as much as for a buyer. But remember that while searching for something new you always need to remember your client. Who are you looking for, what do they like and appreciate? You have to understand them and listen to their needs – this is true of any business; clothes are the language of fashion but empathy and understanding are key in every industry. The Browns' client is interested in fashion, appreciates craftsmanship and likes to be surprised and inspired, as much as they are loyal to the names they know and trust. As a buyer you have to learn to really focus your eye and think about your customer as well as the designers. You must always keep in mind who you are buying for, and what will suit them. You want to see the right dresses go to the right people. You want to match the perfect person to the perfect design for them as much as the dress! Ultimately, fashion is about giving people confidence, clothing their characters, making them look good and feel emboldened. I want to find the clothes that make people feel as if they can conquer the world, and so with my team of buyers we go to every fashion capital to see everything and find clothes that will 'speak' to you – crazy as that sounds. You have to learn to go with your gut instinct, which comes with experience, I suppose, but I do always like to gently encourage people to try the unexpected and venture into something new, as well as what they know. That is something I think should apply to life and business as well as style!

How to set up your own business

September is the time to stop dreaming about being your own boss and make it happen.

Before starting your own business, clear your desk, and mind. Get rid of the clutter and chaos and work out what you have always longed to do – and then think what's stopping you?

What gets you out of bed in the morning? What excites you? What is your burning passion? Come on, be honest, what are you good at? Great at? Brilliant at?

Work out your motives – saving the world or making your first million?

Start an idea/mood board – keep adding to it and see which are the strongest elements to emerge. Don't be afraid to throw anything into the mix – but be brutal about letting go of things that don't fit or that you aren't completely convinced by. If you don't believe in it, you won't be able to sell it.

Plot how to make things happen, how to budget, what you need to budget for, where the money is going to come from to get things started and where the money is going to come from to keep things going. Does the bank manager like the idea? Can you butter up some private investors?

Once your plan is formulated (and patented if an incredible invention), start talking – networking, darling: work those contacts, listen, learn, come up with a snappy name and make an idea a reality. There are plenty of wheels to be invented and pies to have a piece of.

For an insight into how others have done it, read Anita Roddick's *Business as Unusual: My Entrepreneurial Journey – Profit, with Principles*, Richard Branson's autobiography *Losing My Virginity*, which details his journey from market stall to millionaire, or, for a quick rundown of the lessons Branson swears by, try *Screw It, Let's Do It* or *Tycoon* by Peter Jones, a millionnaire several times over by his early thirties.

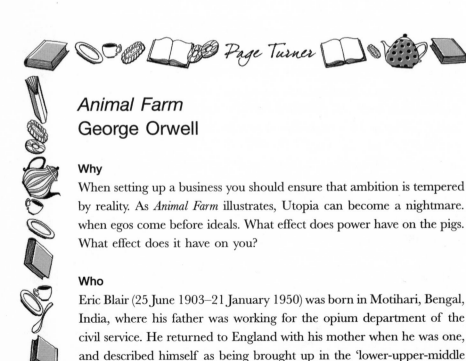

Page Turner

Animal Farm
George Orwell

Why
When setting up a business you should ensure that ambition is tempered by reality. As *Animal Farm* illustrates, Utopia can become a nightmare. when egos come before ideals. What effect does power have on the pigs. What effect does it have on you?

Who
Eric Blair (25 June 1903–21 January 1950) was born in Motihari, Bengal, India, where his father was working for the opium department of the civil service. He returned to England with his mother when he was one, and described himself as being brought up in the 'lower-upper-middle

class'. After completing his scholarship at Eton he joined the Indian Imperial Police in Burma but resigned and returned to England in 1928, decidedly anti-imperialist from the experience.

In 1933 he adopted the pen name by which he is remembered – George, after St George and George V, the then monarch for his beloved English roots, and Orwell after the River Orwell that flowed through a spot he loved in Suffolk. But writing was not paying the bills. He captured his impoverished lifestyle in *Down and Out in Paris and London*.

He fought in the Spanish Civil War but was sent home wounded, and began writing book reviews for the *New English Weekly* where he stayed until 1943, when he became the literary editor of the *Tribune* in addition to being the *Observer*'s war correspondent. *Newsweek* described him as 'the finest journalist of his day and the foremost architect of the English essay since Hazlitt'. Yet it is not for his journalism but his novels that he is remembered.

In 1944 he finished *Animal Farm*, his anti-Stalin allegory where he used farm animals to represent the key characters in the Soviet Union's totalitarian state. The book was a smash hit and for the first time he was able to stop worrying about making ends meet. Orwell's next novel, *Nineteen Eighty-Four*, was published in 1949, not 1948 as he had hoped (and reflected in the title). It was written during a bleak time in his life, just after his first wife had died on the operating table, and while his own health was seriously deteriorating. The book was his prediction about the way he feared the world was heading, and phrases which he coined, such as 'cold war' and 'big brother', have become part of our language. He died of tuberculosis, aged forty-six, unaware of the great impact this prophetic book was to have.

The plot

Depending on how you choose to read/discuss this book *Animal Farm* can be either a farmyard fable or a political allegory. Old Major, the farm's prize-winning pig, is a socialist, just like Lenin, and sets out his vision of a more equal community and the benefits of life without the tyranny of humans. Such is Major's charisma and powerful rhetoric that

the animals believe him and can envisage his new world (Aldous Huxley's *Brave New World* is a novel that Orwell's *Nineteen Eighty-Four* was often compared to). A revolution occurs at the farm and Animal Farm is created.

At first the animals achieve efficiency and all is going well. It promises greater harmony, just as Thomas More dreamed in his *Utopia* and indeed Karl Marx proposed in *Das Kapital*. The only difference is that this state is run by animals not humans.

Only three days after the coup Old Major dies, leaving joint leadership to be assumed by two pigs, Snowball (based on Trotsky), who educates the animals and teaches them to read and think for themselves, and the bullish Napoleon (based on Stalin), who is power-hungry. Napoleon sets the dogs on Snowball (literally) and assumes sole leadership, creating a totalitarian state far, far from the ideals of Old Major. Are they better off now than they were with Farmer Jones? Things become more and more distorted . . .

The pigs learn to walk and dress like humans, and Napoleon's taste for power rather than enlightenment and harmony leads him to make an alliance with the humans. During a game of poker with Farmer Pilkington (Orwell's Hitler) the animals realize there is no difference between the humans and what they have become. Even loyal Boxer, whose motto is 'I will work harder', is betrayed.

Fiction is used as a tool to explain Orwell's view of the revolution and his socialist ideals. In this way he was able to say what politicians dared not, using allegory as his weapon. In the preface to the 1947 Ukrainian edition he explained how he found his inspiration for the novel: 'I saw a little boy . . . driving a huge carthorse along a narrow path, whipping it whenever it tried to turn. It struck me that if only such animals became aware of their strength we should have no power over them, and that men exploit animals in much the same way as the rich exploit the proletariat.'

Ironically his preface was censored in England and, until the war ended, he struggled to get this work published.

Hosting

Obviously going down to the farm and wallowing in mud is out – but mud baths and face packs are not. Why not book a day at the spa and discuss this book while being pampered and pummelled? Unveil your five-year-plan with your friends while your body gets an MOT. Help perfect each member's business pitch and make a pact to start the assertive season in style. Book that hot new restaurant, try that trendy new bar, and taste the high life – indulge in your own Utopia and serve with Champagne and truffles as the mind, body and soul are invigorated.

Alternative visions of society:

Utopia by Thomas More

Paradise Lost by John Milton

The Pursuit of Happyness by Chris Gardner

Mrs P's Journey: The Remarkable Story of the Woman Who Created the A-Z Map, by Sarah Hartley

Wu: The Chinese Empress Who Schemed, Seduced and Murdered Her Way to Become a Living God by Jonathan Clements

Lord of the Flies by William Golding

6th September

In 1664 England (technically) took over New York – and this is not in sheer number of tourists, but rather a full-on conquest-type situation. The state was originally established as New Amsterdam, but when the British came over they decided to scrap that and rename the area after King Charles II's brother – James, the Duke of York (later James II). If you want to split hairs and heirs, Manhattan is still technically in Her Majesty's portfolio of properties. In fact, when the American government asked for a bit of a break over the increasing rent at their embassy in London, it was rumoured that the officials replied that they would be more than happy to try and help if they could – in exchange for the outstanding amount owed to Her Majesty for the long-term stay on her land.

No problem – we can sort that out. What is the address?'

'Manhattan. The island of . . .' And to avoid a diplomatic coup the line went dead.

'Hello? Hello?'

7th September

Singer-songwriter Charles Hardin (Buddy) Holly was born in 1936. He was one of the key founding figures of rock'n'roll. His hits included 'That'll Be the Day' and 'Peggy Sue', and he had a huge influence on other musicians, including the Beatles – named partly in homage to Buddy's group the Crickets. It was at the McCartneys' annual Buddy Holly Party, held on this date, that Eric Clapton was inspired to write a song about his girlfriend: 'You Look Wonderful Tonight' (for full story see page 241). McCartney is such a Holly fan that he bought the publishing rights to the Buddy Holly catalogue.

On 2 February 1959, however, fate decided to change the face of music.

Moments after a plane bound for Fargo, North Dakota took off it crashed, killing three of rock'n'roll's biggest stars: Buddy Holly, Ritchie 'La Bamba' Valens and that Big Bopper' J.P. Richardson. As Don McLean wrote in his 1971 ballad 'American Pie', this was 'the day the music died'.

9th September

Another music legend, Otis Redding, was born in 1941. He too died, aged only twenty-six, in an aeroplane crash. His posthumous hit ('Sittin' on) the Dock of the Bay' would be his first number one and first million-copy seller. Download his hits today.

10th September

Italian Elsa Schiaparelli was born in 1890. She was a fashion designer cum surrealist artist who took on the world of couture with a sharp cut and even sharper wit.

Schiaparelli began her career in America as a scriptwriter and translator before moving to Paris in the twenties where she opened her own design-boutique. From her signature shocking pinks to shoe hats she was the leading female fashion designer of the twenties and thirties, after Coco Chanel (see page 75).

What set Schiaparelli apart was the way she combined art and fashion. She teamed up with Salvador Dali who did some fabric designs for her, including his famous lobster print. It was printed on a silk dress and worn by Wallis Simpson. Schiaparelli also introduced the shoulder pad, fur bed-jackets and rhinestone-trimmed lingerie. She also dressed Daisy Fellowes, Zsa Zsa Gabor in *Moulin Rouge* and Mae West – whose torso inspired the bottle for her bestselling perfume Shocking.

Muse of the Month

Elizabeth Arden

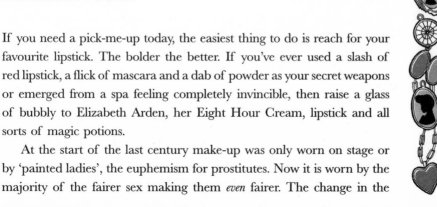

If you need a pick-me-up today, the easiest thing to do is reach for your favourite lipstick. The bolder the better. If you've ever used a slash of red lipstick, a flick of mascara and a dab of powder as your secret weapons or emerged from a spa feeling completely invincible, then raise a glass of bubbly to Elizabeth Arden, her Eight Hour Cream, lipstick and all sorts of magic potions.

At the start of the last century make-up was only worn on stage or by 'painted ladies', the euphemism for prostitutes. Now it is worn by the majority of the fairer sex making them *even* fairer. The change in the

reputation of cosmetics was something of a PR coup and the two women who deserve the credit for putting make-up on the map are Elizabeth Arden and Helena Rubinstein. Their rivalry was infamous, and made Bette Davis and Joan Crawford look like best friends.

At a time when women had only just won the right to vote, Elizabeth Arden was miles ahead of the rest. She was a workaholic and global business mogul who became the richest self-made woman in America. When she was born, fewer than 16 per cent of American households had electricity, and revealing much more than your ankle was a scandal. By the time she died not only did everyone know her name, but most women followed her cleansing routine.

As Coco Chanel commented, 'There is only one Mademoiselle in the world, and that is I; one Madame and that is Rubinstein; and one Miss and that is Arden.' What a pity they couldn't stand to be all in the same room.

While strategizing about the best way to develop your own business empire, don't neglect pampering yourself. Take the night off and paint your toenails. Get creative and instead of serving up a culinary delight, whip up your own organic face pack or potion for radiance inside and out. If you'd rather stick to something tried and tested, smear yourself with Arden's miracle Eight Hour Cream, beauty secret of all the stars, and read about the Rubinstein–Arden rivalry in Lindy Woodhead's aptly titled *War Paint* which is littered with tales of their accomplishments and point-scoring against 'that other woman'.

Her life and times

A lady should always be discreet about her age – especially one in the beauty industry – so the exact year Florence Nightingale Graham was born is slightly open to debate. It is thought to be 31 December 1878. She was born in Woodbridge, near Toronto, the daughter of Scotsman William Graham and Susan Pearce Todd from Cornwall, who had eloped together to Canada. Her mother died when she was six, leaving her father, a market gardener, to raise the children. This softly spoken child, who was terrified of the dark and being alone, would grow into one of America's greatest exports. Her high-school ambition was to be 'the richest little woman in the world'. And she was. It pays to think big.

As a nod to her namesake (Nightingale) she dallied with nursing, but her real passions were horses, flowers and, above all, perfection – she just had to figure out how to turn this into a lucrative career. It was while working as a nurse that she spotted the potential for making beauty products from burn creams and skin salves. Using her medical training she started to test her own formulas at home. The experiments weren't immediately successful and her neighbours were subjected to some pretty foul smells that led them to assume the Grahams were either a) the worst cooks in town or b) so poverty stricken they had to cook rotten food.

In 1908 she moved to New York to seek her fortune. She was struck by how groomed everyone was. She went to work at the popular Eleanor Adair salon and quickly moved from receptionist to beautician and soon clients would ask for 'that nice little Canadian girl'. Adding under-standing of beauty treatments to her medical training, she now felt ready to try and create her own complete skincare regime. She approached cosmetic companies to see who could blend her idea for a light, fluffy yet luxurious face cream. A. Fabian Swanson was the only chemist who was successful at rising to all her challenges. Together they perfected and established the products that would become the heart of Arden's product range, while she developed the ritual of cleanse, tone and nourish. Her quest to package eternal youth and beauty in a cream had begun.

After a brief salon partnership with Elizabeth Hubbard, she wanted to go it alone. She borrowed $6,000 from her brother and promised to repay him within the year (she succeeded in six months). She renamed herself Elizabeth Arden. According to her own legend she took Eliza-beth from the book *Elizabeth and her German Garden* by Elizabeth von Arnim, not her former employer, and Arden after Tennyson's poem *Enoch Arden*. Elizabeth Arden the brand and the entrepreneur was born and soon the

name hung above her salon entrance. The door was painted red, inspired by a traffic light, to make people stop, look and come to Arden.

In 1912 *Vogue* suggested a dab of discreet colour could enhance a lady's face, and no one needed telling twice: it heralded the start of make-up becoming acceptable for everyday use. Arden soon had a palate of new rouge shades available for the newly curious. Two years later, in the name of research, Arden went to Paris and road-tested every salon (nice work if you can get it). By 1917 she had opened her own salon there, which was set up and run by her sister Gladys. It was in Paris that Arden first encountered the name Helena Rubinstein – which was to become the bane of her existence. As Arden crossed the Atlantic one way, Rubinstein, her nemesis, was making a counter-attack and brought her brand to America in 1914.

On her voyage home Arden met banker Thomas J. Lewis. He had once turned down her request for a bank loan, but she was now an affluent and successful businesswoman, and with little else to do on the cruise, romance blossomed and they married the following year.

Back home business was booming – all women wanted Arden. Recognizing that there were many women who couldn't get to one of her salons, Arden cannily made her products available at top-end department stores, maintaining the brand's exclusive image and causing the cosmetics industry to explode.

The following year, 1918, all the profits and income caused terrible trouble with the taxman and, although she had sworn she would never trust a man with her accounts, she hired a man she knew she could trust – her husband – to handle the books. In 1919 Harrods placed a small order for her products. Two years later she packed her husband off to London to build the first Elizabeth Arden factory to keep up with demand.

Above all, Arden's greatest weapon was herself – she had an inherent understanding of her product, was a PR innovator and wordsmith, often firing her advertising designers and copywriters and writing the text herself, and was the first person to tap into 'lifestyle' promotion. Telling women to 'feed the skin', and using the fear factor ('my dear, she looks so much older'), she was the first to explore the power of subliminal product branding with her revolutionary Arden Skin Tonic. Despite the rapid growth of her empire, she insisted on signing off and testing everything personally. In addition to this she had a daily beauty regime involving a long list of treatments, including twice-weekly manicures and daily yoga. In 1929 she opened the first exercise room above a salon where she introduced the forerunner of aerobics. She was a walking endorsement of all she stood for – she had to look good.

In the 1930s it was said that there were three American names known in every corner of the world: Singer sewing machines, Coca-Cola and Elizabeth Arden. Despite the Wall Street crash, the Depression and the war, she kept morale beautiful; whatever was going on in the world, women liked to 'keep face'. In 1932 she introduced the concept of colour to eye make-up, rouge and tinted powder. This was truly revolutionary as make-up was until then only available in light, medium or dark. The make-up bag was booming.

But she didn't have it all – behind the flawless face and army of red doors her marriage became a casualty of her workload, and in 1933 she discovered Lewis was having an affair with one of her treatment girls. Arden divorced him in July 1934 after fifteen years of marriage. They had no children but her company had grown from under $200,000 a year to over $5 million a year. Lewis settled for only $100 – yes, you read right – and was forbidden from working in cosmetics for the next five years. That must have been some divorce lawyer. The following year she opened the first American spa, Maine Chance in Maine, offering head-to-toe pampering for an A-list clientele. It seemed she could do beauty but not marriage. A large part of her success can be attributed to her ability to adapt to the times and create trends that were in step as well as ahead of them. During the war she recognized women's needs; Arden had made beauty an essential for all situations. Yes, there was rationing and restrictions, but she developed Montezuma Red, a lipstick that perfectly matched the military trim of the American Marine Corps Women's Reserve.

Arden was a patron of the arts and her Fifth Avenue apartment was hung with Chagalls and Georgia O'Keeffes from her private collection.

But above all, her greatest passion was racehorses. With the Arden empire at its peak with over 100 salons and 300 products, she was able to invest in her childhood dream of stables, horses and jockeys. Proving that money just makes more money, she made an additional fortune.

Arden felt horses were more beautiful than humans and she was known to massage them with her bestselling Eight Hour Cream (to heal bruising). *Time* magazine put her on the cover on 6 May 1946, celebrating her success in the beauty industry and at the races. But the same month that the article was published, she was devastated when a fire destroyed her Arlington Park stables. As always she bounced back and in 1947 Jet Pilot, one of her surviving horses, won the Kentucky Derby. It was another first – she was the first woman to own a horse that won this prestigious race.

With the beauty industry and racing trophies under her belt, the post-war years saw Arden expand her empire into fashion, launching a lingerie range in 1944 before going into her own ready-to-wear line to complete the Arden lifestyle. While clients were wrapped in towels or hiding behind face packs, house models would waft around the salon in puffs of chiffon and entertain their captive audience mid-treatment with 'impromptu' shows – far more entertaining than thumbing a pile of old magazines. One of the designers who worked on her label was a young Oscar de la Renta. Arden devotee the Duchess of Windsor was even 'persuaded' to wear one of his creations to a gala in 1953 in return for an ongoing complimentary tab.

In 1965 the faces of the day were all Arden models: Jean Shrimpton, Lauren Hutton, Candice Bergen and Veruschka. Arden had achieved global fame with her products.

On 18 October 1966 Elizabeth Arden died and was buried at Sleepy Hollow, New York. She had sacrificed a private life for career success and made women more beautiful. Instead of children she left behind seventeen different corporations, forty worldwide salons and no one obvious to succeed her. In 1971 Eli Lilly acquired the company, it was bought by Fabergé in 1987, and in 1989 by Unilever. In 2002 Oscar-winning actress Catherine Zeta-Jones became the house 'face', and with her as ambassador, Arden's secret of eternal youth is in safe hands.

Ardenisms

'To be beautiful is the birthright of every woman.'

'I pick good women, but I haven't had any luck with my men.'

'I'm not interested in age. People who tell me their age are silly. You're as old as you feel.'

'There's only one Elizabeth like me and that's the Queen.'

'Dear, never forget one little point. It's my business. You just work here.'

'Treat a horse like a woman and a woman like a horse.'

'I only want people around me who can do the impossible.'

How to make a face pack

Next time you aisle-glide your way round the supermarket, why not pick up some ingredients for some home-made beauty remedies? Restore your glowing complexion and gather compliments, as well as a reason to use the whisk in your kitchen – perfect if you are feeling too poor or exhausted to drag yourself to a salon. All you need for this is a blender, a bowl and a deadlock on the front door.

Here are some of the essentials for your supermarket sweep:

Honey – a powerful antioxidant, it helps the skin retain its moisture.

Avocado – packed with protein.

Cucumber – lovely astringent elements to help tighten the pores. Chilled slices can reduce swelling and dark circles under the eyes faster than you can say Touche Éclat.

Bananas – great for the skin and the hair. Old-school movie stars were said to smear ripe bananas over their bra cups to perk up their sagging bunches of coconuts.

CAUTION: If allergic to any of the ingredients or if you have sensitive skin, be careful with the first attempt; it might not be wise the night before an interview or important evening out.

For normal skin

To prevent wrinkles and tighten pores you need vegetables. So if you can't face eating them, blend fifty grams of cabbage and some water in your juicer. Apply this cold, directly onto your face. Paint it on with fingers or a basting brush. After this has dried (despite the smell you have to let it), wash off with water and douse yourself in perfume to recover.

If, quite understandably, the cabbage idea is too much to contend with, why not beat an egg and smooth this over the skin rather than scrambling, frying or boiling (the egg, not the skin). Apply this in the bathroom as it is very messy, and also make sure your hair is securely tied back. It's soldiers you dip into egg, not your locks. Once it has drip-dried you can then splash it off – just don't lick your lips: salmonella poisoning is not a good look.

When next eating an apple – which you should obviously be doing once a day (keeps the doctor away . . .) – peel it and keep this as a skin cleanser (blender job again). Alternatively take an ice cube and smear it all over your face to tighten the pores, in a very *9 ¹/₂ Weeks* way.

For oily skin

Blend half a cucumber and apply to your face while you snack lightly on the rest. Let it dry, and rinse off. Your skin will feel tight and refreshed.

For dry skin

Mash a very ripe banana – you know, the ones with all the black bruises that you don't want to eat but it seems crazy to chuck? Add a teaspoon of honey and beat it into a paste. Yuk, yuk, yuk. Now apply the mush to the face and when it is dry, wash it off. Your skin will be moisturized as well as tight.

Pimple prevention

OK, the million-dollar question – how do you avoid a breakout? No stress, no pollutants and water, water, water, and more boring water. That is what they all say, but if the damage is already done what then? (Other than vowing never to leave the house until after dark.)

You want to loosen and lessen the damage of those pesky blackheads, and some brands can be slightly over zealous and abrasive on the more sensitive souls. D.I.Y. by combining an equal shake of baking powder and water and rub it in circular motions over the face. This will get rid of dead skin and the aforementioned blighters.

Or squeeze half a fresh lemon (add the other half to boiling water and drink – great for detoxing the digestive system). Take the juice and, disgusting as this sounds, pour into a cup of freshly boiled milk. Don't think about it. Leave the room (and the concoction) for a cooling-off period and then apply to your face.

For breakouts when you can't get to a professional, Elizabeth Arden or otherwise, try:

a) Rubbing a slice of lemon over the face and letting it dry overnight. It should dry out the situation and restore the skin's softness as well as give the complexion a glow.

b) Apply a thimble of toothpaste to the problem area and leave to dry.

c) Cry.

d) Swear.

e) Eat what's left over from your experiments.

For more home-made facial recipes look at *www.ultimate-cosmetics.com* or *www.ayuvediccure.com*

13th September

Writer Roald Dahl was born in 1916. Like many writers, Dahl thought writing was a hard gig to get into. 'A person is a fool to become a writer. His only compensation is absolute freedom.'

He wrote (amongst others) *The Gremlins*, 1943; *James and the Giant Peach*, 1961; *Charlie and the Chocolate Factory*, 1964; *Fantastic Mr Fox*, 1970; *The Twits*, 1980; *The BFG*, 1982; *The Witches*, 1983 and *Matilda*, 1988.

He wrote the screenplays for *You Only Live Twice*, 1967; *Chitty Chitty Bang Bang*, 1968; *The Night Digger*, 1971; *Willy Wonka and the Chocolate Factory*, 1971.

He said, 'Nowadays you can go anywhere in the world in a few hours, and nothing is fabulous any more.' So why not travel to one of his lands? Let the BFG blow a dream into your room or take off in the Giant Peach? After all, leaving him the last word, 'a little nonsense now and then is relished by the wisest men'.

14th September

On this date in 1927 the ballet dancer Isadora Duncan, the pioneer of modern expressive dance, died. She styled herself on the ancient Greeks and offstage her life resembled a Greek tragedy. Though her career was celebrated, in 1913 her two children drowned when her car rolled off the road into the Seine. Fourteen years later she tossed her long signature silk scarf over her shoulder and cried, '*Adieu, mes amis. Je vais à la gloire*,' ready to speed off in her lover's sports car in the fashionable French Riviera, when disaster struck. The scarf became caught in the wheel and she was choked instantly. Not the stylish exit she'd planned.

15th September

English novelist and playwright Agatha Christie was born in 1890. To date she has sold over two billion copies, and has been translated into over a hundred languages. Agatha Christie wrote crime fiction, and even if you haven't picked up one of her books you cannot fail to have seen one of her stories on television, at the theatre, or on the big screen as her popularity is second only to Shakespeare. Rule Britannia.

'The best time to plan a book is while doing the dishes,' Christie observed. Given how prolific she was, Christie's house must have been spotless. This could be used as a prompt when you need help around the home.

Hollywood clamoured to adopt her novels for the screen and Christie's detectives, Poirot and Miss Marple, had many faces playing them. Christie, however, preferred books. Her favourites were said to be *Crooked House* and *Ordeal By Innocence*, so add these to your library list, along with a DVD copy of *Murder on the Orient Express*. Alternatively log on and book a ride on the real McCoy at *www.orient-express.com* or travel down to Torquay to visit the museum dedicated to Christie: *www.torquaymuseum.org*, or for a theatrical Christie fix book to see *The Mousetrap* at the St Martin's Theatre in London, which is the longest running stage production in the world. The contract stipulates that no film can be made of it until six months after this production closes – so you'll be a long time waiting for that.

16th September

In 1924 American actress Lauren Bacall was born. Well, that isn't *totally* true – she was born Betty Joan Perske, but they wiggled her name about, as she would her hips, and *voilà* – a siren was born. She became an actress almost accidentally after Howard Hawks' wife spotted the beauty on the cover of *Harper's Bazaar*. Hawks was a big-shot producer, liked what he saw, and a few screen tests later cast her in *To Have and Have Not*. She was an overnight sensation. When Bogart met her he told her, 'I saw your screen test; I think we're going to have a lot of fun together.' 'Little did I know . . .' Bacall laughed.

Sparks flew on and *off* screen, and they married in 1945.

Her other films included *How to Marry a Millionaire* with Monroe, *Key Largo* and *The Big Sleep*, once again with Bogart. They made a cameo appearance in the closing scene of the 1946 film *Two Guys from Milwaukee*, which starred Dennis Morgan, Jack Carson and Joan Leslie. Morgan's character boards a plane and finds two unexpected passengers. 'Aren't you Lauren Bacall?' he asks as he sits next to the siren. Moments later Bogart appears and tells him to move out of his seat.

How to make an impression

If you have survived public speaking – whether a wedding toast, bingo calling or launching your manifesto – you might think that one-on-one interviews should be a doddle and far less nerve-wracking. Wrong. This time the eyes of your audience will be even more intensely trained on you, and they will be sober.

The interview is a legal form of torture and serves to prove whether you can think on your feet, react and respond to various situations. If you're really unlucky, you could be asked to do a role-play.

Interview times vary and remember, it's not the length of time you're stood before the Spanish Inquisition, it's how you interact with them and survive that matters.

It might take the form of a 'good cop/bad cop' interview – i.e. with one nice interviewer, one tough one; one stroppy and dismissive, and the other sympathetic. If you're really unlucky both could have got out of bed on the wrong side, and you'll be dealing with two psychos. How much do you want this job? How well can you perform? Take a deep breath and quietly count to ten. Don't let them rile you – that is what they're testing. Stand up for yourself and show them how it's done; fight back by turning your research into articulate ammunition. If you don't get the gig you will never have to see them again – and if you do, well, they will know you're not a pushover.

Read up on the job that you've applied for and the company before you go to your interview. The night before is perfect for revision, but shouldn't be the first and only time you prep if it's something important. Know the company and what they stand for. Do you believe in their ethics, their vision? Plan how you can fit in.

Research what to ask, and think about what they could ask you. Be sure this is the right place for you. Visit *www.howtointerview.com* for ideas on how to help soothe any last-minute nerves.

Look at your CV. This is all they will have to go on.

If you have talked about your passion for computing, do you know the latest developments and advances, and if not, good heavens, why did you say this? Look it up immediately.

If you have said that you are fluent in another language, be prepared for some bright spark to try and conduct the entire interview in this language – knowing how to order a coffee may not be enough.

Be up to date on current affairs, both general and specific to your industry – knowing that Kate Moss is designing for Top Shop is valuable when applying for a job in fashion, but less so if trying to clinch the deal at the law firm of your dreams. Look at the bigger picture come interview time, which means knowing more than the latest soap opera scandal or who is on the cover of the tabloid glossies. *The Week* is a brilliant digest of world news, arts and reviews – read this and you'll be able to talk about everything from farming in Nicaragua to nudity at the National Theatre.

If going for an interview at a magazine or newspaper, read some back issues, as well as any current ones, plus their rivals. Informed opinion is what they are after. For a restaurant, know the food; if at a store, know the style and product.

Don't wear fur to Stella, or a rival designer to anyone known to be 'sensitive'. Respect them and think ahead.

If small talk is necessary it is far safer to chat about them, how long they've been there and – thank goodness for the all-time English favourite – the weather, rather than what happened in the pub last night. But nothing should or can be generalized, and every case is unique, so your preparation needs to be tailored accordingly. For example, if you are going for a position at the pub, ignore the above – you most definitely do need to know the ins and outs of your local and you should be sure to know all the products, football scores, how to pull a pint, as well as the best tops to wear to attract lots of attention (and tips).

Remember, you can only make one first impression so it has to be better than good – it has to be great. You are a one-off – let them see you sparkle.

Do a trial run

It can be very hard to judge just how others will perceive you, so ask a willing friend/family member/flatmate if they can help. Do a dummy run and ask for constructive criticism on how you package and present yourself. They have to be honest and you have to listen.

The Look

As much as how you present yourself in words, the interviewer will be judging your appearance. You need to be well groomed, pressed and presented. Today you are giving the performance of your life. Can you afford the time and the cost to make a trip to the hairdresser's or have a manicure before the big day? (Don't stress about a pedicure, though if that will make you feel slick, get one.) What about pushing the boat out – can you get a new top/shirt/outfit? At the very least make sure the ensemble you choose is freshly washed, ironed and pristine.

You should wear a formal, smart, 'I mean business' version of your look, and one that fits with where you are interviewing. Skirts can be short – but not too short; you don't want to sue them for sexual harassment this early in your career. Like a CV, leave something to their imagination. Show potential, not suspenders. You want to look like you will fit in as much as creating a positive upgrade on your current look. Do not turn up in overalls, even when going for a position as a grease monkey, unless you know there is a practical side to pass. Dress to impress.

You need to master the following:

- Tall and proud – not arrogant – posture
- Look attentive and alert
- Confident – not cocky – eye contact
- Hold eye contact without psychotically staring them out
- Clean and well-presented clothes, hair and make-up
- Be interested and engaged in the conversation, without seen. like a sycophant

The night before the interview aim to get an early night; this is most definitely not the night to go partying. Instead lay out your clothes, work out your route to get there, have a bath and try to relax. Do you need a portfolio, a laptop, any examples of your work? Scan through your notes, then sleep, or at least try.

D-Day

Be punctual and polite, and have good breath – clean your teeth, have a stick of gum (to be carefully and discreetly removed before you arrive at your location).

Allow plenty of time so you don't have to worry about traffic, the bus breaking down or any act of God. Arrive early and you can sit and catch your breath.

Into the lion's den

Sit straight, do not fiddle with keys, purses, pens – leave them in your bag, for goodness sake. Try to keep your body language open and friendly.

When standing in the line of fire, ask a few of the questions you've prepared as well as answering all of theirs. This not only shows that you are interested, it shows initiative (and courage) as you bat things off you for a moment. Question asking is a great way to steer yourself into safer waters.

As well as understanding what your would-be employer wants, be able to articulate what you want.

– Make them like you, admire you, hire you.
– Get on the payroll before you start playing up and taking time off.
– Remember even the dream job can become a nightmare – it's called 'character building'. Just decide how much extra character you want.

How to hold their attention

From an interview to a presentation, or even limbering up for a pay rise, it's all about the way you execute it, rather than what you say. Think this through.

Know your:

• Purpose – why do this? Why?
• Audience – who are you aiming this at?

- Any other hurdles – how long have you got? Do you need any props or presentation aids or do you merely need a slick of lipgloss?

Another key thing to remember is timing. You are neither a comedian nor launching into a Shakespearean soliloquy – you are in the boardroom. Keep your audience interested and alive.

Pack in as much information as you can while you have their full attention. If you end early it's fine, especially if you have covered everything – if you end two hours late you'll be lynched, so have an escape car waiting.

Know when to send in the dancing girls, the clowns as well as the tissues. Give it the right razzle-dazzle, but keep it relevant.

Shuffle shuffle

Organize your notes.

Little cue cards can help keep things on track. Make concise and legit notes and use as required. Winston Churchill always carried notes, but seldom ever referred to them. He said, 'I carry fire insurance but I don't expect my house to burn down.' Not only does the researching, editing and writing of them help your brain absorb the info, it's often comfort enough to know you have a life jacket safely tucked in your pocket. It's always nice to be prudent and prepared, just like the Girl Guides said.

18th September

In 1851 the first edition of the *New York Times* was published – nice bit of interview-friendly trivia should the subject ever arise – and on the same day in 1905 a real headliner, Greta Garbo, was born.

In the posters for the 1935 film of *Anna Karenina* the advertising screamed 'Garbo Talks!' Talks? It was more like a purr. From the moment this mysterious figure appeared through a cloud of steam, Garbo mesmerized Hollywood.

She first appeared in silent movies but made the transition to black and white talkies. Garbo's timing was as perfect as her poise, and she always left with an air of mystery, and before colour became mainstream.

Born in Sweden on 18 September 1905, she left school at fourteen when her father died leaving her family penniless. She went to work in a department store, and ended up modelling in a few of their advertising campaigns for the local newspapers. It was nothing glamorous, but then as luck would have it a film director, Eric A. Petscher, saw her in one of the store's TV adverts and cast her in a small part. It was all she needed to inspire her to pursue her dream.

In 1924 she was pulled from drama school and cast by the famous Swedish director Mauritz Stiller in *Gösta Berlings Saga*, and the following year they were both signed by MGM. Hollywood here we come. Her first role was in the silent flick *The Torrent*, and the first lines she spoke, thick with her sultry accent, are the now immortal 'Gimme a whiskey, ginger ale on the side. And don't be stingy, baby', in *Anna Christie*.

Other great Garbo quotes include:

'Life would be so wonderful if we only knew what to do with it.'

'There is no one who would have me . . . I can't cook.' (There is hope for the mere mortal, then.)

Finally, she cleared up her most famous quote/misquote of all time: 'I never said "I want to be alone". I only said "I want to be left alone". There is a whole world of difference.'

Isn't misquoting a bind? Be careful of what you say in interviews, in work and play – and especially on camera.

Watch *Camille*, the 1936 Garbo classic, which she considered her favourite performance.

20th September

Alexander the Great was born in 356 BC, and a more modern-day legend, with legions of followers, was born in 1934: Italian actress Sophia Loren.

The Roman-born, Academy Award-winning actress rose from poverty to become the most recognized Italian movie star in the world, and she is still the ultimate sex siren. Loren, who claimed that pasta was the key to her success, said, 'You have to be born a sex symbol. You don't become one. If you are born with it, you will have it even when you are a hundred years old.' She proved this theory by appearing in the 2007 Pirelli Calendar, aged seventy-one, wearing nothing except a large pair of earrings. She out-dazzled the A-listers decades younger.

Although she remained married throughout her career to producer Carlo Ponti (1957–2007), that didn't stop Cary Grant and Peter Sellers being just two of the high-profile men who lost their minds over this beauty. Time to serve yourself up a large spag bol today and don't be shy. Stop counting the carbs – handbags, diamonds, shoes are non sizeist, just elitist, and yes, you're so worth it.

The Pirelli Calendar was first printed in 1964 as a promotional calendar produced for the Italian tyre company – it was not sold, and was very limited in edition. It has risen to being the most prestigious girlie calendar in the world (and just about manages to stay on the tasteful side of porn). Other than Loren, models who have graced its monthly spreads include: Gisele, Jennifer Lopez, Kate Moss, Selma Blair, Naomi Campbell, Cindy Crawford, Heidi Klum, Milla Jovovich. It has been shot by the world's greatest photographers: Herb Ritts, Bruce Weber, Nick Knight, Mario Testino, Richard Avedon, Peter Lindbergh and Terence Donovan.

How to make your boss love you

- Don't waste their time.
- Probably best *not* to sleep with them, especially if married.
- Use your head as well as your initiative.
- Don't ask questions all the time, you can often find the answers for yourself.
- Find solutions rather than highlight problems.
- Learn how they achieved their goals and ambitions.
- Don't keep apologizing – learn from a mistake and move on.
- Don't blame inanimate objects such as computers, photocopiers or printers unless you are sure you are not responsible for the smoke that is rising from it.
- Go beyond the call of duty. 'It's not my job' is the most unhelpful thing you can say. It might not be your job, but it's a route up the career ladder if you put yourself out. Prove yourself and your capabilities. That said, value yourself – don't be a total doormat.
- Dog walking is for dog walkers not paralegals. Accept menial tasks with grace but only if there is a clear indication of improvement on the horizon. Respect yourself as much as them and you will feel as well as see the difference.
- Stay late if you can see the benefit. But sleeping under your desk doesn't enhance your image or result in better work.
- Watch *The Devil Wears Prada*. Are things at this stage? Not even close? Are you really giving it your all?

How to manage yourself

- Be tough yet fair; you will probably be your harshest critic.
- Aim for perfection. Anything less, hit the drawing board again.
- Learn from those at the top and always be gracious to those below you. You never know who you'll bump into on your way up or on your way down.

- Keep a diary – whether it is on your phone, Blackberry, in your Filofax, blog or calendar, you have to have one. This is not an option. This is for your appointments, deadlines, schedules and getting all tasks organized. This is for professional purposes – not the narrative type in which you dissect hot dates and discuss all the gory details; this is the one to be left on your desk, to help with the planning (and is OK for others to see). This is the agenda bible, your way of preventing or preparing for a meltdown or heart attack.

- Watch your time keeping. A relatively new phrase but a very old problem. There is never enough time so at least use what you've got wisely. Less bitching and more pitching. Focus and fast-track your future on millionaire's row, or your own desert island.

- Tick things off. To-do lists not only help you prioritize, they help you see all that you've achieved.

- Organize. Keep it all together and it will keep *you* together rather than cause you to tear your hair out (which will be a waste of all the thousands spent on highlights and haircuts). A Post-it Note in time will prevent the need to turn the entire office upside down hunting for a phone number, document, earring. (If in doubt try the fridge, the photocopier, the bin.)

- Do not disturb. Put the phone on voicemail, on silent, out of sight if you are on a deadline: Distract Me Not. Focus. You can always call them back.

- Use time wisely. There's no point wasting good lipgloss on a meeting you don't need to be at.

How to know your rights

Come on Arethas: '*R.E.S.P.E.C.T.*, find out what it means to me . . .'

Are you employed or self-employed?
Are you entitled to a pension?

Do you have a written contract or just a golden handshake?

What are your obligations?

What is your starting/leaving date?

What is your holiday allowance?

And clothing allowance, if relevant?

What are your minimum working hours?

Do you get any perks?

How much notice do you have to give?

Are you up on the racial and sexual discrimination policies they have?

Are they equal opportunity employers?

What is the pay packet?

Is that guy single?

Just don't be a total pain . . .

For more information on how to get ahead read *Tough Talk Made Easy* by Jenni Trent Hughes or look on *www.fawcettsociety.org.uk*

How to strike the right work/life balance

If you have a problem, talk it through with someone. The moment your job encroaches too far into your home life or weekends, weigh up the pros and cons of making a bid to run up that career ladder – a gentle jog could be more effective. Avoid burnout. Do you really need to take a laptop to bed with you? Keep your eye on the goal but be wary of too many sacrifices and casualties along the way.

Make sure you:

Take a proper lunch break every day – eating a sandwich hunched over your desk is so not a good look, never mind the fact that bits of cheese inevitably end up dropping into your keyboard.

Leave the office on time humming Dolly Parton's '9 to 5' at least three times a week – arrange to meet people you don't work with to ensure you don't spend after-hours dissecting the horrors of the day in minute detail.

Wear high heels on Friday – dress-down Friday is a terrible idea. Dress up and leave an impression that lasts over the weekend.

Ball breakers are so last season – particularly the femme fatale kind.

Turn the work phone off at the weekend.

In a lifetime it is believed that on average women vacuum the equivalent distance of London to New York. Think of the time that will take. Keep a balance. Yes, be the youngest ever CEO by all means, but have you allowed time for all your chores and do you have anyone to share the success with (of life and the hoovering marathon) apart from your cat and the Chinese takeaway delivery guy?

Yes, women have more to prove than men – but they also have more options. Irritatingly the UK still has the worst pay gap between the sexes in Europe, though this is changing. Wimbledon champions now get equal pay but that's only good if you want to take up tennis. According to the Fawcett Society it will be eighty years before we fully catch up, although we are still on target to have more female millionaires than men by then (and this is not all thanks to great divorce lawyers).

Remember job satisfaction is just as important as the pay packet. Consider all the cards you are dealt and play things to your advantage.

22nd September

In 1692 six women and one man were hung in Salem, America. These witch hunts and trials inspired Arthur Miller to write *The Crucible*.

The play begins with a girl's whisper that grows into accusations and, before you know it, the gossip spirals out of control and hysteria grips the community as 'witches' are being sentenced and hung.

Miller wrote this play as a thinly veiled attack on the McCartney administration (just as Orwell used *Animal Farm* as an attack on Stalinism). In Miller's case the 'witch hunts' were for the communist supporters. Miller, who won a Pulitzer Prize in 1949 for *Death of a Salesman*, and married Marilyn Monroe in 1956, was one of the most respected playwrights of the era and one of the many high-profile names called in for questioning about communist sympathizers in the 1960s. Read his play today.

23rd–24th September

Rosh Hashanah, the Jewish New Year, falls 163 days after Passover is celebrated according to the Hebrew calendar. It commemorates the Creation of the World and the Birth and Binding of Isaac. Food traditionally served includes apples, honey, sweets and the pomegranate.

24th September

Jim Henson, American puppeteer and father of the Muppets, was born on this day in 1936 and he shares his birthday with his most famous creation, Kermit the frog, born in 1955. 'You know, as a tadpole in the swamp, I had 3265 brothers and sisters,' his green friend commented.

Kermit's first appearance was in the TV special *Hey Cinderella* in 1969 and he's been the leading Hollywood frog ever since. The prototype was created by Henson using a green ladies' coat that his mother had thrown out, with two ping-pong balls as eyes, rather like Maria creating outfits for all the Von Trapp children out of curtains in *The Sound of Music*. Be creative today and who knows what you will end up with.

Kermit has hosted *The Tonight Show*, starred in his own movies, fronted *The Muppet Show*, was a contestant on *Who Wants to Be a Millionaire?*, sang a duet in 2001 with Kylie Minogue and has valiantly fought off the advances of his very glamorous leading lady – Miss Piggy. Well, like he said, 'It's not easy being green.'

26th September

The English poet T.S. Eliot was born in 1888. Almost a century later Andrew Lloyd Webber set Eliot's anthology *Old Possum's Book of Practical Cats* to music, and the musical sensation *Cats* was born. *Cats* opened on 11 May 1981, was nominated for eleven Tony Awards in 1983, has been translated into over twenty languages, and ran in London for over twenty-one years. From 'Macavity the Mystery Cat', to 'The Naming of Cats', 'Grizabella' and the 'The Song of the Jellicles', Eliot's verse survived in its original form while Lloyd Webber added the music and leotards.

28th September

From dancing cats to a pussy cat – the animal rights activist and sex kitten Brigitte Bardot was born today in 1934. As film critic Ivor Addams wrote in 1955: '[Bardot] is every man's idea of the girl he'd like to meet in Paris.' Practise your pout and backcomb your hair in homage to Bardot the Patron Saint of Bikini Wearers; just make sure you check the weather report or dress code before stepping out in one.

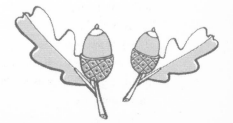

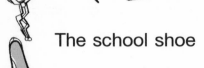 *Foot Note*

The school shoe

The T-bar, the round toe, the width fittings and the Mary Jane – what you hated in childhood becomes a classic and a favourite when it's no longer compulsory. Evoking memories of Shirley Temple on her 'Good Ship Lollipop', the Mr Men and Charlie Brown, brogued, laced or buckled, polished or scuffed from the playground, the school shoe is part of the preppy-style uniform. From the Mary Jane to Clarks, it has always stepped out with all ages, albeit with lemon drops and a large dose of nostalgia. From sensible shoes worn with white knee-high socks to the high-heeled version by Manolo Blahník as worn by Kate Moss, any age, any style – there is a school disco for us all.

The original Mary Jane was the sister of Buster Brown, a popular comic series in America (think the *Beano* of the US). At the 1904 'Meet Me In Saint Louis' world fair its creator and cartoonist Richard F. Outcault sold the name to the Brown Shoe Company, the Clarks of America, and what Mary Jane had on her feet in the cartoon became the girls' bestseller of the day.

Act your age not your shoe size? No chance.

October

'Society is a masked ball, where everyone hides his real character, and reveals it by hiding.'

Ralph Waldo Emerson

Wish You Were Here

Antonio Berardi from La Serenissima, Venice

I dreamed of Venice as a child. It was a place I secretly visited (resplendently masked and decked out in the finest silk damask that would have made Casanova proud) in the music box of my mind. This was courtesy of hand-tinted postcards I had found in my mother's ebony escritoire, and a plastic gondola inlaid with mother-of-pearl that strangely enough played neopolitan music (an unloved gift that had been relegated to my toy box). Venice, the first step to Christendom, gateway to the orient and home of the very same merchant that is my namesake.

Entering La Serenissima is the most exhilarating yet most bizarre experience one could ever imagine. Was this the fabled Xanadu or some crude fairy-tale joke of a place you win tickets to with a Big Mac? It was all this and a whole lot more. A city of light and shadows, of love and death, of music, art and literature, all reflected in the mirrors it is famous for, and the reason for my visit.

I had come to find a master glass-blower who could make my dreams come true. I wanted glass corsets, mirrored, engraved and where the colour would change from the palest skin tone to the most violent of orange. Thanks to my dear friend Giordana (a Murano native and antique dealer) and her friend Chicco, a handsome playboy with a speedboat and a love for the high life, I managed to get what I wanted.

Of course, when you are in this chocolate box of a city, one chocolate is never enough. I wanted to live out my fantasies, and gorge myself as my heroes of yesteryear had, and you will find that, in Venice, you can, can, can-can, can!

From espresso in the piazzetta at Florian's, wandering through the Palazzo Venier dei Leoni, (now home to the Peggy Guggenheim Collection and once to the notorious Marchesa Luisa Casati (where if you let

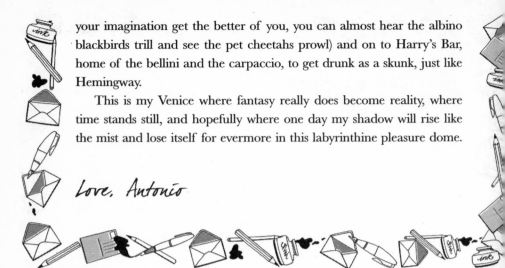

your imagination get the better of you, you can almost hear the albino blackbirds trill and see the pet cheetahs prowl) and on to Harry's Bar, home of the bellini and the carpaccio, to get drunk as a skunk, just like Hemingway.

This is my Venice where fantasy really does become reality, where time stands still, and hopefully where one day my shadow will rise like the mist and lose itself for evermore in this labyrinthine pleasure dome.

Love, Antonio

1st October

The first McDonald's opened in England in 1974 – while in 1066 a more notable invader – William I – was gearing up to conquer Britain. Rather than celebrate these English invasions at the Golden Arches, this is the month to feed your cultural appetite, and where better to have this renaissance than in Venice? October should be about taking a well-earned mini-break after all your career plans have been put into action and your creative side remains hungry.

 *Page Turner*

Miss Garnet's Angel
Salley Vickers

Why

When prepping for a trip to Venice you could watch Visconti's *Death in Venice* or read about Venice's favourite one-time resident, the romantic Casanova, but perhaps the pensioner Miss Garnet is the perfect character with whom to begin your briefing.

The novel takes a strange blend of characters who all fall in love with Venice, and coming to the city helps them find parts of themselves they thought they had lost. After only a few pages this book is hard to put down, and it'll be even harder to stop yourself getting on the next plane to the city.

Who

The author's first name, Salley, is not a typo. It is spelt with an 'e' as it comes from the Irish for 'willow', as in the W.B. Yeats poem, 'Down by the Salley Gardens'. Vickers trained as an analytical psychologist and was a university lecturer, specializing in Shakespeare and the ancient world, before her writing career took off.

Vickers was seduced by Venice 'when it captured my surly teenage heart'. All that obligatory angst melted the moment she first walked round St Mark's Square. It was this feeling of getting lost in a city while also discovering yourself that she drew on for her first novel. *Miss Garnet's Angel* became a huge word-of-mouth hit. Vickers' other novels include *Instances of the Number Three* and *Mr Golightly's Holiday*. She is the perfect author to take on a plane journey – either a real one or in your mind.

The plot

The novel begins with the death of Miss Garnet's friend, Harriet Joseph. So closes a chapter of thirty years as Joseph was her tenant as well as her only friend and companion. Rather than grieve, she feels regret for the way in which she's lived her life up until now and decides to make radical changes. She is suddenly aware of all the things she has never done, and now intends to do them before it's too late.

Empowered by this strange new independence she decides to rent out her house and move to Venice. Not just for a holiday – for six months. Well, why not? This is the most rash thing she has ever done, but with no family, no friends and no love affair, what reason is there to mope about at home? She has never been to Venice before, she knows no one there, she speaks no Italian – it sounds perfect.

Miss Garnet settles into her new apartment and begins making new friends, including the football-mad local children whom she helps with their English, and the twins who are working on a restoration project at the nearby church. The church contains Guardi's painting *Tobias and the Angel*. Miss Garnet finds the depiction of the angel incredibly moving, and her story and that of the painting become woven together.

How can an angel, a pensioner and the young twins affect each other and what can they add to the magic of Venice?

Slowly but surely Miss Garnet starts to live. For the first time the spinster dares to fall in love, albeit with the local lothario, but at least she gets taken out and about and meets a few new friends. Will six months be enough for Miss Garnet and how can the angel from another era save the twins?

Hosting

Find the image of *Tobias and the Angel* (*www.galleriaborghese.it*) or perhaps decorate the room with maps of Venice to set the scene for an Italian-themed evening. Have Vivaldi playing in the background, either on CD or find a willing live string quartet. Serve Prosecco (it's much cheaper than champagne and very Italian as well as delicious) or imitate Caffè Florian's speciality hot chocolate – or is this the excuse you needed to hail a gondola and float under the Bridge of Sighs?

Alternatively you can explore Venice through:

> *The Merchant of Venice* by William Shakespeare
> *The Story of My Life* by Giacomo Casanova
> *A Venetian Affair: A True Story of Impossible Love in the Eighteenth Century*
>   by Andrea di Robilant
> *Death in Venice* by Thomas Mann
> *Venice: Tales of the City* by Michelle Lovric
> *A Thousand Days in Venice* by Marlena de Blasi
> *Francesco's Venice* by Francesco da Mosto

Caffè Florian is *the* place to have coffee in St Mark's Square. It was opened on 29 December 1720 by Floriano Francesconi, and originally called Venezia Trionfante 'Triumphant Venice'. It is where the Bellini was invented and where Don Juans, the well-to-do and tourists come for the rich thick hot chocolate. Oh yes, and the classical music. Both Caffè Florian and the café on the opposite side of the square host live string quartets. For a view of St Mark's cathedral, a culture fix and a free performance, take an ice cream and stand in the middle of the square.

2nd October

While Venice has the *vaporetti* that chug from stop to stop, and the gondolas act as private (and pricey) taxis, on this day in 1925 the first London Red Bus went into service.

It was also on this date in 1890 that the American comedian Julius Henry Marx, aka Groucho Marx, was born.

The stand-up siblings, the Marx Brothers, graduated as the biggest comedy stars to emerge from the Palace Theatre and went on to conquer Hollywood.

Groucho's unmistakeable 'look' of glasses and moustache have been imitated again and again – well, they say imitation is the sincerest form of flattery.

Some of his most well-known quips to toss in today include:

'I never forget a face, but in your case I'll make an exception.'

'Anyone who says he can see through a woman is missing a lot.'

'I find television very educating. Every time someone turns on the set, I go into the other room and read a book.'

The last one is particularly good advice.

Marx was famously well read, far more so than many of his high-profile, highbrow friends. Read a book, toast him at your book club, go to a comedy show or watch a re-run of Marx himself to help sharpen your own comic timing. *Very* useful when telling your friends how awful your boss is or just how bad your date was – particularly if the guy in question turned up with a Groucho tash . . . now, really, does that go with those new Manolos?

Today is also a day for reflection, as the great statesman and spiritual leader Mahatma Gandhi was born in 1869. Trained in England as a lawyer, he campaigned tirelessly for India's independence through non-violent campaigns, and inspired many subsequent leaders, including Martin Luther King (see page 33).

Gandhi was shot on his way to prayer on 30 January 1948. Watch Ben Kingsley in the 1982 award-winning film *Gandhi* based on his life and times.

4th October

Back to the gags. Comic actor, film-maker and director Buster Keaton was born in 1895. 'Think slow, act fast,' he said.

Joseph Frank Keaton Jr grew up on the stage and earned his nickname when he performed with his parents, aged three, in *The Three Keatons*. In 1917 he moved to New York and was soon set up with his own production unit, the Buster Keaton Studios.

Unlike many stars who didn't manage the transition from silent to talkies (subject of debate in *Singin' in the Rain*), Keaton would have done just fine had the switch to talkies not coincided with his loss of independence as a film-maker. Keaton had signed a disastrous deal with MGM that effectively gagged him at the time when he needed his voice most. Keaton quit the limelight and got lost in an alcoholic blur. He sobered up with his third wife and made a few later appearances on screen – including in *The Playhouse*, 1921, which told the story of vaudeville, with another silent great, Charlie Chaplin.

Vaudeville comes from the phrase 'voice of the city', *voix de ville*, and it took its first bow in the 1880s in Northern America.

The evening consisted of a variety of acts – comics, dancers, acrobats and singers – all considerably politer than the music hall acts that preceded them. The new 'clean look' was revealed on 24 October in 1881, by Tony Pastor, and the craze spread like wildfire. Smartening up really was a smart move, as the more respectable the place became, the more the ladies flocked to the auditorium and with them the men.

The evening would start with the 'dumb' act, allowing latecomers to crash in and not ruin the plot or muffle any crucial lines. Things would crescendo up to the penultimate performance – the crowd-puller and the 'headliner', which would feature the star of the show. Then, interestingly, rather than end on a high the theatre would take no chances and send on the 'chaser' – a tough act as it had to be good enough to warrant being on stage, but boring enough to (subliminally) persuade the punters to get their coats and make their way home.

Charlie Chaplin, Judy Garland, Adele and Fred Astaire, Vernon and Irene Castle, Bob Hope, Harry Houdini, Gypsy Rose Lee, Rudolph Valentino and Mae West all learned to do it the vaudeville way but were lured away by the bright lights of Hollywood, which signalled the end for the movement.

5th October

In the same decade that the Eiffel Tower was completed, another hot spot was added to the Parisian skyline when the red windmill of the Moulin Rouge lit up the red-light district of Pigalle in 1889.

At the foot of Butte Montmartre the Moulin Rouge was a music hall that wasn't remotely bothered about keeping it clean, or performers keeping their clothes on. *Ooh la la!* From the moment *le Premier Palais des Femmes* opened its doors others simply had to try and keep up with this high-octane, high-glamour sensation. The Pigalle Club was the original location for the high-kicking, bloomer-flashing dancing girls, and was where the cancan made its debut.

The Moulin Rouge was 'a delirium of feathers, vulgar painted lips, eyelashes of black and blue', wrote Audrey Bely in 1906, and not a lot has changed. Forget Halloween – here is where the *real* extremes of naughtiness and misbehaving happen. There's 'naked feet, thighs, arms and breasts being flung at me', our man continued. From Josephine Baker to Frank Sinatra, burlesque to bustiers, the Moulin Rouge had it all. Six movies were named after and inspired by it, including the 1952 version starring Zsa Zsa Gabor and the 2001 musical version, with added exclamation mark (!), starring Nicole Kidman.

From the 1955 film *French Cancan* by Jean Renoir to the works of Toulouse Lautrec, every artist was desperate to capture the decadence and debauchery that went on behind its doors. Today it is alive, kicking and upgraded so you can choose between the French Cancan Menu, Toulouse Lautrec Menu or the top of the range Belle Époque Menu with your bottle of champagne and seats for the show. Go to *www.moulinrouge.fr* and book an evening to check out the bright lights of the *Bal du Moulin Rouge* for yourself.

The undisputed star of the Moulin Rouge, and figurehead of the French cancan, was the famous 'Goulue'. There was also Jane Avril, known as Crazy Jane or Jeanne la Folle; la Mome Fromage; Grille d'Egout and Nini Patte-en-l'air (legs in the air). The 'Rouge' ladies took stage names to conceal their true identity – though they weren't too worried about concealing their assets!

You can work out your porn star name by taking the name of your first pet as your first name, and using your mother's maiden name as the surname – *et voilà*!

How to dress burlesque
by Liz Goldwyn, author

My fascination with burlesque began with collecting costumes. I found my first two pieces at a flea market in 1995; one of nude fishnet with black lace overlay trimmed with jet beads, and the other of hot pink lace lined with rhinestone piping and fishnets attached at the hips. Examining the interiors of these treasures, I saw handiwork much like that of couture; each stitch sewn with sure hands, every rhinestone, sequined paillete and bead perfectly in its place.

A standard elegant burlesque costume was incredibly complicated to put on – and to take off. Some had as many as ten pieces, which included an outer garment designed to resemble a floor-length evening gown, covered by a long cape or opera coat. Beneath these layers were panels (a strip of fabric worn low around the hips, with chiffon streaming to the floor in front and back), an inner and outer bra, outer 'pants' cut like bikini bottoms, and finally, the ever important g-string and pasties (the proper name for the nipple tassels). It required enormous dexterity to remove so many pieces with ease, for five shows a day, seven days a week.

Through the costumes and the glamorous 8 x 10 black and white pin-up photographs of the greatest burlesque queens, I fell in love. These early strippers were broads in the truest sense of the word. They had class, skill and attitude. Their sex appeal was undeniable as they posed on a chaise lounge, or draped against velvet stage curtains, teasing the camera with come-hither stares. At once they appeared seductive, yet in complete control of their posturing – and herein lies the power of the tease. The tease is the key to the stripper's control; the audience can look, but they cannot touch.

I think the best definition of the tease I've heard came from Zorita, a famous queen well known for her provocative nature and routines (which included performing with two eight-foot-long boa constrictors). She told me that it was part of the fun to give 'everyone a hard-on but they can't have it . . . you give them a peek, you give them a flash . . . but you don't give it all'.

Although burlesque as it existed in its glorious heyday of the early twentieth century has long since passed, there's a lingering feeling of nostalgia among our generation, much due to the legacy the original burlesque queens left behind. We gaze at their glossy photos and study their wardrobe, looking for ways to emulate their style and bravado.

So ladies (and gentlemen), may I recommend a few tricks of the trade, so to speak. High heels make you walk with a little bounce in your step, all the better to stop traffic with a few well-timed 'bumps'. Lipstick – particularly my personal favourite, fire-engine red – can give the plainest of faces a bit of instant glamour, and false eyelashes complete a siren's look. The best burlesque standards, like 'Lament' and 'Blues to Strip By' are available on compilation disks, so put on your favourite tune, fasten up your garter belt and stockings, and practise your sultriest poses in front of the mirror. After all, the best lesson I learned from the last of the great burlesque queens is that a little personal confidence goes a long way towards establishing your sex appeal.

How to burlesque

Burlesque cabarets with their mix of dancing girls, chanson singers and striptease artistes shimmy within an air-kiss of the censors and have recently enjoyed a revival with Immodesty Blaise leading the troops in London, and most famously in the (perfectly formed) form of Dita Von Teese.

There are classes and clubs springing up all over the place. Dress up, practise your wiggle and celebrate being a woman. Look at the Ministry of Burlesque *www.ministryofburlesque.com* or book yourself in on a course at the London School of Striptease (yes, there is such a place) – *www.lsos.co.uk*. 'I never kept up with the fashions,' said Bettie Page, an iconic burlesque babe. 'I believed in wearing what I thought looked good on me.' If these classes can make feathers and balloons look as good with heels as they did on her, what are you waiting for?

Before taking the plunge you could sample the delights at a burlesque night out. The best in London are the Hurly Burly Show, featuring Miss Polly Rae and the Hurly Burly Girls, at Volupte Lounge: *www.myspace.com/hurlyburlyuk*; the Whoopee Club: *www.thewhoopeeclub.com*; the Flash Monkey: *www.theflashmonkey.biz*; and in Scotland the biggest and best burlesque club is *www.clubnoir.com*.

Pretty Things: The Last Generation of American Burlesque Queens by Liz Goldwyn is also worth a look.

How to tease
by Dita von Teese, dancer

I have always been interested in the glamour of the thirties and forties period. I was so enamoured with the women of this time, that by my late teens I was dressing in vintage and imitating their style. I loved finding out about every aspect of their fashions, from the designer gowns right down to their stockings, stilettos, underwear, and the makeup . . . the picture perfect finish. I looked at the pin-up photos of the time and, when I found out that many of the best models of the day were also burlesque dancers, this prompted me to learn about this art and bring it back into the mainstream. I was a dancer, but I wanted to be one of these pin-ups and capture this nostalgic elegance, their poise, their pout, and of course their sex appeal.

I was inspired by Sally Rand, Lili St. Cyr, Gypsy Rose Lee, and as a little girl I watched Natalie Wood playing Gypsy Rose Lee and later on studied up on her life and career. I was really introduced to burlesque by the film and later read about her and watched Gypsy's films and footage – it wasn't her dance style I wanted to emulate but her spirit and attention to detail, to fashion: she wore couture on stage! My favourite movie star was Betty Grable, because many of the Second World War era films she starred in combined beauty, glamour and dance, all things that influence my own style of burlesque. I was inspired by the whole era as much as the burlesque dancers – I loved the opulence, the art, the beauty of their bodies and the costumes, but as much as I wanted to emulate them, I wanted to make my moves suit my own personality and my own ideas of modern burlesque. Burlesque in the forties was considered an art form but it was also risqué, and not every dancer was as revered as Gypsy and Sally, there were many big high end shows, but there were also many 'sleazier' theatres and shows . . . like strip clubs today, some are beautiful, some are not. But the true burlesque was an art form that was stylish, sometimes had a sense of humour, and also had a spirit of smouldering seduction. These strippers were sirens – and I wanted to continue their legacy.

When I perform I like to get up there, have fun, and tease with even just a wink of the eye. Burlesque lets you be a different character. For me it's not so much being this mantrap, it's more about having fun – being a minx. There are no set routines, no rules, and no reason why anyone can't try it, not necessarily on stage but at home perhaps? Work out the size of your stage – from the Crazy Horse in Paris, to The Palace in Vegas, to the bedroom, there are all shapes and sizes and all sorts of routines perfect for every audience.

Before you begin, size up the situation – did you know the runway was actually first built for Minsky's burlesque in New York City *not* a fashion show? It's the ultimate platform to show a grand burlesque strut-off on, and there's nothing quite like performing with a live band. I like all types of music, but I think big band best fits with the style and the routines I perform. Find music that you love – I do not like anything with vocals to perform to, I think lip-syncing is so distracting (unless you are a Crazy Horse girl and then it's specific to the act) but you have to find what works for you. Like everything it's all about attitude, whether you're removing a stocking or showing off a gown – yes, there is a formula to getting undressed as much as there is to dressing. Work with the music, the stage, the setting and situation and don't be shy. My gowns usually have about twelve pieces but I like to start with the gloves – so innocent, yet some kind of promise of what's to come, it shows nothing yet is so evocative – think of that scene with Rita Hayworth in *Gilda*. It's all in the mind – to tease the imagination.

Sometimes I think women get self-conscious, not of seduction but they worry about appearing as if they are trying too hard – they don't want people to think that all they care about is looking good. Of course image is not all I care about – but equally you should remember if you take time before you leave the house I *promise* you will have a better day. The day you don't make an effort, I can guarantee that will be the day you run into your ex! Dress up for yourself as much as for someone else. Keep your nails manicured, rouge your lips, do your hair and you will feel a million times better, sexier. Perhaps even finish with a hidden satin garter-belt? Don't get me wrong, I do my own nails, colour my own hair and if my hair needs a trim I will have a friend cut it. You can be pampered but enjoy learning to do it yourself, enjoy the ritual, care for your body and about how you look, what you wear, how you act. How far you want to go – in the style stakes – is up to you, in America you still have to be a brave girl to wear a hat as you will turn heads. I think hats command attention so you have to take a look that will enhance your day, hats make you glamorous, make everyone want to know you, look, admire, comment – how is it for you?

Dressing up, dressing down, down time and being on stage, I don't have a set routine. I dance, but I also travel a lot and want to live and have fun. I do pilates, yoga but most of all one of my favourite things is to play dress-up and just prance around at home. I love to test looks out, try out different outfits, and this way you can work out not only what works but what order to take things off. Play dressing up as well as dressing down and live with a bit of fantasy. I am not saying that you should be stripping everyday – but that you shouldn't be afraid, you should feel empowered by your body and your sexuality. I think that women should be women – elegant and playful and dressed to impress – nearly every woman likes that candy coat. Perhaps the grass always seems greener for everyone else but just work out where you want that picket fence, what your ideal perfect life is, the look, the success and go get it. Don't WISH to be that girl – be that girl – be the librarian by day, the burlesque star at night – be liberated with this feminine freedom – pick your own theme tune, each and every woman should have their own routine and then they can shake it up.

6th October

In 1927 *The Jazz Singer* opened and made cinematic history as the first talkie. In reality there were only two on-screen minutes of synchronized talking in total, but that, combined with Al Jolson's electric personality, meant it was a box office smash. The takings – double that of the silent flicks – said it all, and audiences could not get enough of him singing 'Mammy'.

8th October

St Mark's Cathedral was consecrated in Venice in 1085. The Basilica of St Mark's Square is considered the most spectacular surviving example of Byzantine architecture in the world. The cathedral was built on the site where, in AD 828, Venetian merchants were said to have built a shrine to house the relics of St Mark the Evangelist.

As well as the churches, the art, and the passageways where Vivaldi's music was composed and Casanova chased girls, Venice is also the home of the mask and the carnival.

The Venice Carnival might have first taken place in 1162, but there are no records of masks being worn until 1268.

It hit its peak of peek-a-boo popularity in the eighteenth century, and mask makers would pull out all the stops at carnival time. But the carnival dwindled out of favour and was banned altogether by Mussolini in the 1930s. Party pooper. It wasn't until February 1979 that the carnival was revived and now it's an event not to miss.

How to mask yourself

Where can you find a mask for your masque? One of the best mask shops in Venice is the Carta Alta. Their website *www.venicemaskshop.com* not only tells you the history of the mask, it shows you how to make one of your own.

But if a trip to Venice or an online purchase through their website is out of the question, try Hamleys, or your local haberdashery for your netting and feathers – and get plenty of UHU glue or spray mount. Isn't that what Blue Peter, Tony Hart and all those childhood craft lessons were for? Sequins can be fiddly, while fabrics with glitter are a godsend. If you feel claustrophobic at the idea of your face being totally covered, angle some netting or a veil over your eyes instead. And decide whether you want to have your mask held with an elastic band around your head or for it to be mounted on a stick so you can waft it on and off your face (very good for initial entrance but will get exhausting to hold all night).

How to throw a masked ball
by Nick Knight, photographer

When Moët & Chandon presented me with their Fashion Tribute idea I didn't want to do the 'expected' event. I came up with the idea of throwing a *bal masqué* as it's different, a bit of fantasy, and I could create a world where one could escape. I read *Beau Brummell: the Ultimate Dandy* by Ian Kelly and I loved reading about how the gentlemen met their courtesans, yet kept their honour as they hid behind masks, and this was my starting point. With a mask, immediately things are not what they seem, and I could slightly destabilize things.

I played with different plots, undercurrents and made reality and fantasy blur. The evening itself layered many different ideas, and was filmed and broadcast for my website *www.showstudio.com/projects/balmasque* I think the reason I was so interested in this idea was realizing this type of ball would free people of their jealousies, insecurities and preconceptions. A bit like photography: everyone would be presented in a very subjective and raw way and show off the character they wanted to create.

We searched high and low for a venue. I wanted something that was dilapidated, lived-in, and where people hadn't been before. When we went to Strawberry Hill House I knew straight away this was the place. I think if you are going to do something like this you have to think of all aspects, so I had one room with a monitor looped to play two guys punching the crap out of each other all night, in another live wolves grazed, an ice-cream van was brought into another room. There were so many ideas and nothing was what you expected. Illustrator Julie Verhoeven worked images of real-life cosmetic surgery onto a collaged form as an installation and there was a 'Cinderella' who at midnight changed from her Galliano couture gown into rags and started to mop the mirrored floor . . . it was total escapism yet everything had a macabre twist.

The rooms created different scenes and ultimately brought together different elements from my life: there was a fencing tournament as I have always wanted to learn how to fence, a dance hall, with underlit flooring and proper ballroom dancing. Learning to dance was something I had always wanted to do and we even held Regency dance classes at the house the week before for any guests who wanted to prepare for the night. I liked the idea that anything seemed possible in a mask – from dancing to fencing – and that was very liberating as everyone explored this strange new world.

It was a really special evening, particularly as everyone made so much effort with their masks and what they wore. I think there is a real desire to take part in something spectacular and be intoxicated by imagination and the evening averaged four bottles of champagne a person, so you get an idea of the heady environment as people quizzed each other to find out just who was under the mask. I was determined the masks had to always stay on – unlike at Capote's where they soon came off. If it's a masque, keep it a masque – from the waiters to the bouncers (even though they refused to wear menacing clown masks) I wanted the illusion to stay intact. I guess I hoped it was a party worthy of a modern-day Gatsby and all the glamorous and the good came out on this night.

9th October

The composer of another carnival, Camille Saint-Säens, was born in 1835.

Carnival of the Animals was only performed twice in his lifetime – once for the Mardi Gras celebration of *La Trompette*, and the other time for his friend Franz Liszt. His last will and testament was fairly fierce:

'I expressly forbid the publication of any unpublished work, expect *le Carnival des Animaux* which may be issued by my usual publishers.' Who was to argue with a man's last request? It is now the most performed of all of his works.

Each of the fourteen movements captures different animals' personalities in tone of timbres rather than colour, from the turtle who does a slow-motion version of Offenbach's *Cancan*, to the elephant taking Berlioz's *Danse de Sylphines* at his own (slow) pace. The most graceful and only animal published as a solo during his lifetime was the beautiful cello solo of *The Swan*.

Download it and press play. As you do so, position your pen at the top of a blank piece of paper. Listen to what shape the notes draw. It is said Saint-Säens wrote this melody so the tones would gracefully rise and fall so, if you use your imagination and a creative squint, the shape your pen makes as it follows the notes should create the outline of a swan.

10th October

In 1886 the dinner jacket made its debut – and no doubt there were plenty in evidence in 1935 at the opening night of Gershwin's *Porgy and Bess* on Broadway. Think about slipping one on for a night at the theatre. Tonight you can celebrate the 1813 birth of the great Italian composer Giuseppe Verdi, the perfect excuse to go to the opera or the Teatro la Fenice in Venice, where Verdi, aged forty-two, debuted his most popular opera, *Rigoletto*, in 1851.

Hang on – how can a dinner jacket have a birth date? you ask. Well, it was the date it first stepped out in America, but you will be pleased to learn that black tie, like Bond, has its origins very firmly in Britain.

Beau Brummell (1778–1840) is often credited as the dapper gent who made dressing for dinner de rigueur, and for generally smartening up the gentleman's dress code, so it was *the thing* of the nineteenth century. The DJ came later. Brummell preferred to come dressed in monotone shades of chic black and white and let the ladies and conversation provide the colour. How gallant, how stylish! This idea stuck from Regency to stylish Regents-to-be. Fast-forward to the dashing Prince of Wales, Edward VII, whose Savile Row tailor Henry Poole and Co. noted he was the first to order a short smoking jacket back in 1865 – years ahead of it becoming in vogue. A proper Prince Charmant.

After the would-be king appeared in black bow tie and cropped jacket it was an instant must-have and *all* the gents were on the phone to their tailors the next morning to order their new-look DJ. One such man was on the other side of the globe – it was on this date that he first wore his scarlet smoking jacket with satin-faced lapels to wow the ladies. The gentleman debutante was a tobacco manufacturer and thoroughbred horse owner called Pierre Lorillard, and he wore his jacket to the Tuxedo Park Country Club. The name of the venue stuck to the look. So the tuxedo/dinner jacket was launched stateside today, in 1886, and though technically it was actually a man named James Brown Potter, a friend of Edward VII's, who first wore the ensemble in America, after dining with his royal friend, he was far too much of a gentleman to say so.

How to get a taste for opera

First things first – get rid of that clichéd image of the busty woman with horns on her head. This Viking stereotype comes mainly from Bugs Bunny cartoons and not opera; well, maybe Wagner, but steer clear of him at the start if this image scares you.

Live opera, rather than watching it on DVD or just listening to the music, will bring the full package to life. Don't forget that these classics were written to be seen *and* heard, and so this is when they are at their best. Pop music can work without visuals but opera without full scenery is a bit like hearing a film without seeing any of the action sequences. If you've ever tried watching *Grease* with a blindfold on, or without the sound, you will understand.

Many operas are written in Italian, French and German (thanks to a big push by Mozart and Beethoven) rather than plain old English. But however proficient/dreadful your language skills, even if you go and see a version 'translated' into English it's often easier to *look* and *listen* to the action than to try and decipher words or pick out familiar sentences within an aria or recitative.

Anyway, it is far better to see the work set in its original, and intended, language as the libretto and text will fit the music with more accuracy.

The Marriage of Figaro – Le Nozze di Figaro – is considered the best opera to start with if you are a novice. Not only is it one of the most widely performed of Mozart's operas, it was groundbreaking in its day. This is the opera you are most likely to have heard the music of or know some of the story of. Look up online where it is being performed.

The Marriage of Figaro opens with Figaro measuring the floor to check that his new marital bed will fit. Another Mozart opera, *The Abduction from the Harem,* is set in a brothel, so don't be fooled into thinking this will be a boring evening. There might be the trilling sopranos warbling their way through scales and screeches, but once you get past this there is a lot more sex and scandal than your average rock 'n' roll story of today.

It is definitely worth a try – think how much Julia Roberts's character in *Pretty Woman* enjoyed her first opera experience, and what a great excuse she had to dress up. Just see if you can get Richard Gere to get a private jet to take you to see Verdi's *La Traviata.*

Other plotlines in a nutshell:

'Summertime' comes from Gershwin's operetta *Porgy and Bess.*

Madame Butterfly is all about a geisha girl and her affair with a lieutenant (well, all nice girls like a man in uniform).

La Boheme is about being down and out in Paris.

Don Giovanni is loosely based on Mozart's tricky relationship with his
patriarchal father.

Die Zauberflöte – The Magic Flute is the one with the Lady of the Night.

Carmen is about a hot-blooded woman at the time of revolution – if
only Maria Callas was still belting it out on stage.

Figaro is about a valet getting married and trying to prevent his boss
from having his way with his new wife.

Opera houses tend to be important landmarks and meeting points in capital cities. Some of the most famous opera houses include:

Teatro la Fenice, Venice: *www.teatrolafenice.it*
La Scala, Milan. *www.teatroallascala.org*
Royal Opera House, London: *www.royalopera.org*
London Coliseum: *www.eno.org*
Manchester Opera House: *www.manchestertheatres.com*
New York Metropolitan Opera: *www.metoperafamily.org*
Lyric Opera, Chicago: *www.lyricopera.org*
Paris Opera Garnier and Bastille: *www.operadeparis.fr*
Staatsoper, Vienna: *www.viennaconcerts.com*
Salzburg: *www.viennaclassic.com*
And, of course, the Sydney Opera House: *www.sydneyoperahouse.com*

A brief history of opera

Opera began around 1600 at the height of the twisting and trilling baroque era, its elaborate style suiting the architecture and mood of the decade. Italian composers wanted to bring the style of their heroes, the ancient Greeks, to the stage, and when they found out they sang rather than spoke on stage, the composing began. They had actually got this 'singing Greek' fact wrong, but no matter – the opera was evolving as a high-end evening out and soon the compositions would divide each of their acts into:

Recitatives, which are the talky-singy bits where lots of dialogue and action is crammed in as a sort of aside or information filler. The music in this section is usually fairly monotone and it's more about the words than the harmony, with a harpsichord or simple keyboard accompaniment.

Arias, where the performers get to shine and show off their skills and training with elaborate melodies that stretch and exploit their vocal range to the full. Arias can range from solo to full chorus.

By 1700 the style of opera was divided again into Opera Seria – serious, grand stuff, and Opera Buffa – comic lighter fare that led to a new genre of the operetta, including works like *The Mikado*.

The big guns of the romantic period, however, were not big on comedy.

Wagner and Verdi, for example, excelled in dramas and tragedies and wrote roles that only real divas could take on.

Warning: Verdi is considered more accessible than Wagner.

An evening at the opera

You *can* find tickets to the opera that don't cost a king's ransom. For your first opera experiment sit in 'the gods' (the cheap seats) because:

1) If the soprano is akin to nails on a blackboard to your ears it's a lesson learned and not too much lost, or cost.
2) The seats are steep and hard so there will be no room to wriggle about and no chance to fall asleep.
3) You get a great aerial view of the orchestra pit and conductor as well as seeing the entire stage from high up. (This is all ideal providing you don't get vertigo.)

As well as opera indoors there is also opera outdoors – though not at this time of year. If you're over Glastonbury you could spend a lovely summer night with a picnic at Glyndebourne. Look on *www.glyndebourne.com* to research what's showing next season.

How to love opera
by Christian Lacroix, fashion designer

Above all you have to feel cool, fearless and open-minded with opera, which is often seen as too serious, too boring or too intellectual, snobbish, difficult or old-fashioned. But opera is a true pleasure, especially now when everything is 'canned'.

The best CDs or DVDs never match the intensity and quality of a real orchestra, a live voice, a set and costumes.

Being born in the South of France, with an Italian influence, I must say that for me the opera was normal, not banal but part of a popular culture, a way of life, of our everyday pleasure, through records, radio transmissions or festivals. *Carmen* of course was the 'hit', and when I decided to be a stage designer one day, it was because of the media success of Raymond Rouleau's production with Lila de Nobili's costumes. Besides Gounod and Bizet (Massenet, paradoxically, is more appreciated and performed in Great Britain and the USA than in France), we all loved Verdi and Puccini, and Mozart of course. And later, Richard Strauss overwhelmed me when I discovered *Ariadne auf Naxos*.

Travelling abroad in the sixties, seventies and eighties, my friends, wife and I would rush to the booking offices in Covent Garden, at the Scala or the Met, to get tickets for the same night. As students in Paris, we would queue very early in the morning to get boxes no. 24 or no. 27 (rear seats) which had a good view at a cheaper price, even for the big galas. At that time (mid-seventies), the crowd for this kind of event would of course be clad in black tie and haute couture 'big entrance' dresses from the most famous houses. What a feast it was! Since we had already spent such an amount of money, I managed to provide my wife and friends with dresses from our own confection, or from vintage or customized sales, or even metres of silk or jersey to sophisticatedly drape around their bodies, attached only by a brooch from my grandmother. I remember one of our very beautiful friends terrified by the fear of sneezing, and ending up stark naked when the brooch popped open.

Alas, I only listened to Callas on records or on the radio. In the fifties I remember my family religiously listening to the classical music radio station providing news about the feud between Tebaldi and La Callas. As a very young child, I remember her voice pouring into my soul, spirit and body like a warm overwhelming liquor from hell or heaven. But I have been lucky enough to attend some of the best performances: Caballé, Vickers, Jones, Domingo, Te Kanawa and Pavarotti. I also attended some of the most historic nights and prestigious productions of the mid-eighties, with Countess Marina de Brantes who was back in Paris after having spent years in New York, and who brought to France a new kind of fundraising association, the AROP (Association pour le Rayonnement de l'Opéra de Paris), which organized the most incredible galas at a time when the quality of the music, voices and productions was as high as the dinners, clothes and fun. I must say that I'm a little disappointed now when, even at the big galas, people in the audience prefer a casual attire over glamorous, sophisticated clothes which, according to me, forms part of the pleasure of this experience, and has since the seventeenth century. In those days, they even ate, drank and flirted in their boxes, often not even listening to the poor singers and musicians. That fortunately no longer happens, but I would rather that the modern audience, through their behaviour, be more daring in sharing such a pleasure. Feeling as 'dramatic', powerful and great as the heroine onstage with a spirited and individual look can add to the pleasure of going to the opera, since every man and woman is a character of his/her own life. So, if not a huge ballgown, why not get the best hair-do ever, something festive, even with a pair of jeans? Wear something with a little bit of glitter or sparkle, a cheap but fun garment in sequins or gold or silver lamé, a fake but playful piece of jewellery, maybe something from your mother, grandmother or the flea market. And don't forget to prolong such an evening with a nice dinner or a party in order to stay in the mood of such an exceptional moment.

11th October

First Lady and mother figure to America, Eleanor Roosevelt, was born in 1884.

'Beautiful young people are accidents of nature, beautiful old people are works of art.'

In 1905 she married her distant cousin Franklin Delano Roosevelt and together they had six children (one died in infancy). Her husband rose from

Senator to Governor to President in 1933. As Aretha said, 'Behind every man there has to be a great woman.' Well, that was Eleanor, who stood by his side as she raised their family and nurtured America.

Live by her example and beliefs. As she said: 'Great minds discuss ideas; average minds discuss events; small minds discuss people.' Ain't that the truth?

13th October

In 1925 another formidable woman was born. She would become Britain's longest serving Prime Minister – the Conservative MP Margaret Thatcher.

Thatcher served as Prime Minister from 4 May 1979 – 28 November 1990, entering parliament aged thirty-four. She decided to challenge the Tory Party leadership in 1975 and when she went into Edward Heath's office to tell the then party leader, he didn't even have the good grace to look up. 'You will lose,' he said. 'Good day to you.' How wrong he was. With a string of pearls and her famous handbag, the Iron Lady had arrived at Westminster.

'Being powerful is like being a lady – if you have to tell people you are, you aren't.'

'Any woman who understands the problems of running a house will be nearer to understanding the problems of running a country.'

'If you want something said, ask a man, if you want something done, ask a woman.'

Muse of the Month

Peggy Guggenheim

Peggy Guggenheim, the Mistress of Modernism, was born into one of America's richest families: her surname was synonymous with wealth as much as it would be with art. Before World War I, the Guggenheims controlled 80 per cent of the world's copper, silver and lead mines. She could have easily spent a lifetime attending parties and shopping, but instead of a weakness for shoes this heiress developed a taste for art.

Peggy Guggenheim will be remembered as the most important collector of modern art in the first half of the twentieth century, with a few famous flings along the way.

At first Guggenheim tried to be an art dealer, but as she only liked art that didn't sell, she became a collector, and only parted with pictures when confronted with major financial problems. While other collectors played it safe she shopped with spontaneity and reckless passion and ultimately was able to exhibit work from all the major new movements. She bought art that reflected her personal taste rather than paintings that promised to be sound investments.

Read her scandalous 1946 memoir *Out of This Century: The Informal Memoirs of Peggy Guggenheim* if you want to hear the tale in her own words. It wasn't all recklessness – when she died her collection was valued at in excess of $30 million.

Her life and times

Marguerite Guggenheim (though she was always known as Peggy) was born on 26 August 1898 in New York. She was a product of 'two of the best Jewish families'; her mother, Florette Seligman, came from a leading banking family and her father, Benjamin, was part of the Guggenheim dynasty. Aged five she was painted by fashionable portraitist Franz von Lenbach. Aged seven she was sent to bed early when she exclaimed, 'Papa, you must have a mistress as you stay out so many nights!' Every summer her father took her to Europe, until 1912 when he died on the maiden voyage of the *Titanic*. (He took the *Titanic* because he was rushing home for his daughter Hazel's birthday, something Hazel would always be haunted by.) Legend has it that Mr Guggenheim was the passenger who put on evening clothes and resolved to die on board dressed like a gentleman. Peggy idolized her father's decadent ways ('economizing' to him meant perhaps cutting the number of servants or trips to Tiffany's), though when he died her mother and two sisters, Hazel and Benita, each inherited $450,000 – which was considered small scale by her other relations.

In 1916 she made her society debut and moved to Park Avenue where the suitors (and gold diggers) soon came knocking. But, as you know, money can't buy happiness and struggling to make ends meet sounded far more appealing than dealing with the family and fortune she had been 'cursed' with. In her memoirs she omitted her early years, noting only that 'my childhood was excessively unhappy. I have no pleasant memories of any kind.' Poor little rich girl.

In 1919 she came into her fortune, and like Paris Hilton, she instead wanted to taste the 'simple life'. She learned shorthand and had a stint as a dentist receptionist but it was her cousin's bookstore, Sunwise Turn, that really excited her. Here she encountered a new world – a bohemian and bisexual artistic community. Their extravagance and exhibitionism seemed the perfect place to hide her low self-esteem and botched nose job and she had a wonderful time. Although she was 'technically' engaged, Peggy had an affair with novelist Djuna Barnes. That was all great fun for the short term but soon she was bored and ditched the fiancé and the flings and, in 1920, moved to Paris seeking real adventure.

In 1922 she married the writer and Dadaist sculptor Laurence Vail, whom she refers to in her memoirs as 'Florenz Dale', loving his impoverished lifestyle as much as him. Though she called him the 'King of Bohemia', in reality he was a burden and a bully, and they were always having explosive rows, which sometimes erupted into violence. They had two children

together, Michael Cedric Sindbad and Pegeen, who became part of Peggy's nomadic, artistic life and baggage. Sadly Peggy found it easier to show affection to her pet dogs than her children.

In the midst of marital feuds she was a great hostess and her parties brought together the most creative and brilliant minds of the century. Man Ray photographed her while James Joyce, Truman Capote, Cecil Beaton, Brancusi, Marcel Duchamp, Andre Masson and Isadora Duncan were all regulars chez Peggy. Vail was divorced after he had an affair, but she wasn't too heartbroken as she too had enjoyed a string of glamorous liaisons including one with a man she called Oblomov (Samuel Beckett), and one with Douglas Garman who insisted she prove her love by becoming a communist, which she did, though she cancelled her membership as soon as they split up. In 1928 she met and fell in love with the English intellectual John Holms. He was to be her great romantic love but the flirtation ended tragically when he died in 1934.

By 1938, in between affairs, she focused on her art and opened her gallery, Guggenheim Jeune in London, dedicated to modern art. She exhibited Jean Cocteau and what had been a hobby now became her career. She started to collect abstract and surrealist art in earnest and became the ultimate celebrity art collector. While her uncle – Solomon R. Guggenheim – invested in old masters, she wanted to stick with the new and decided to make her mark as the self-styled patron of the surreal. The more unsaleable the work, the more she wanted it. The art world's respect and curiosity grew as she set out to buy the most uncommercial pieces of her generation and her collection started to grow.

When she met and fell in love again, with artist Yves Tanguy, Peggy decided to give up her gallery in London. She hired critic Herbert Read as her director and started plans for a museum, but all this was scuppered when the Second World War broke out. Mrs Guggenheim (as she liked to be called even though technically that would be her mother and she was, if anything, Mrs Vail) came up with a unique war effort. She famously decided she would 'buy a picture a day' to keep her spirits up, help the artists and snap up some wartime bargains.

She followed Mr Read's advice and compiled a list, which was refined by her friend Duchamp, and followed it as religiously as others would a recipe:

10 Picassos
8 Miros
4 Magrittes
3 Man Rays
3 Dalis
1 Klee
1 Chagall

Not your usual supermarket sweep.

There were also the Cocteaus, Braques, and the exhibition of British surrealist John Tunnard. But where her enthusiasm really overflowed was for the German-French artist, Max Ernst, and in the flesh the feeling was mutual and soon they became a couple.

By 1941 the Nazis were advancing on Paris. She, her ex-husband, lover, children and a merry band of artists were forced to flee. She tried to persuade the Louvre to look after her art, 'but they decided my collection wasn't worth saving', so she shipped the entire lot to America as 'household goods'. She also helped many artists get out of occupied Europe, providing them with money as well as assisting with papers.

In New York she and Ernst finally married, as she 'didn't like living in sin with an enemy alien'. But marriage number two was doomed as they were incompatible opposites: she was a social butterfly while he liked to be solitary and lost in his work. Ironically, he left Peggy for one of the 'Thirty-one Women Artists' whom she had featured in an early show at her new gallery – Art of This Century.

They eventually divorced in 1946 but Peggy's passion for Ernst's work remained – she amassed forty of his paintings and hopefully got a good 'family and friends' discount. Peggy 'the art collector' revelled in the reflected glory of discovering a new wave of talent. She was the first to stage solo shows for sound-poet Ada Verdun Howell as well as artists Motherwell, Baziotes, Clyfford Still, David Hare, Mark Rothko

and Jackson Pollock. Watch Peggy depicted in *Pollock*, the 2000 film about one of her great protégés.

When the war ended she returned to Europe and moved to Venice, as 'I have always loved it more than any place on earth'. In 1948 the Venice Biennale returned the compliment and honoured Peggy by allocating an entire pavilion for her collection. The following year she finally found a home for herself and her art, on the Grand Canal. The Palazzo Vernier dei Leoni – an unfinished eighteenth-century palace – was perfect. The cellar, servants' quarters and even the garden were converted into the gallery. Her Pollocks were stored in the basement, some works gathered moss or crawled with slugs in the garden, while she slept in a bed with a specially handcrafted silver Alexander Calder headboard.

The Venetians adored the extravagant eccentric lady who had adopted their city, and called her the Last Duchess.

In the 1960s she stopped buying and concentrated on presenting what she owned. She loaned her treasures to galleries across Europe and America, including some to 'My uncle's garage, that Frank Lloyd Wright thing on Fifth Avenue' (The Guggenheim, New York). She would eventually bequeath her beloved collection to him, on the condition it stayed in Venice. After 1973 she made no more 'significant' purchases, and chose to live quietly, riding about in her private gondola and dodging the tourists, while her gallery became one of the city's main tourist attractions.

She died in Padua, Italy, on 23 December 1979. Her ashes were scattered next to the graves of her beloved dogs.

Peggyisms

'I try to avoid fools.'

'If Venice sinks, the collection should be preserved somewhere in the vicinity of Venice.'

'I was still told to my face that modern art can only be loved . . . by Jews'.

How to be a collector

Peggy's privileged background may have given her a head start with her art collection, but if you have an eye or passion for art, why not use her, or indeed a trip to Venice, to inspire you to start your own collection?

Fair enough, it's unlikely that your budget will be in the same league as hers, but this is not to say you can't become a collector in your chosen field – whether it's teapots, 70s bri-nylon, 50s Bakelite phones, paintings or photography. If you have passion (and storage) you can start collecting anything. Work on innovative ways to display things you already own several of. Shoes don't need to be kept shrouded in their boxes under your bed – they can make fabulous bookends and doorstops as well as nice adornments on shelves.

Refine your taste, read up on your subject and learn what to look out for and where to go – whether it's the best car-boot sales, artists' open studios, new galleries or graduate shows.

If you're not sure what to collect, go to the RCA's annual Secret Exhibition (keep an eye on *www.rca.ac.uk* for details), where all the postcards are a fixed price (approx £35) and displayed anonymously. Take a punt – you could end up with a postcard from Damien Hirst or Nan Goldin or the next big thing. One way to start a collection.

Next decide whether you want to be a collector or a curator. Yes, you can be both, but for now just see what the two roles entail.

A collector has the passion and several pieces of art. If hanging art in your house, ideally it should be framed, for its protection as well as to add to its value. Respect it. More than five works is considered a collection – and you have to start somewhere.

Private collectors are more low-key about what they have, and might make anonymous loans to galleries when not enjoying the work themselves – but you have to have a fair few really big names to not want to shout about it.

Essentially the passionate collector's job is threefold:

1) To support (financially as well as in admiration) the artist/apple of their eye.

2) To share, promote and 'big up' the genius they have just put down a small fortune to own a piece of (the more attention it gets the more value is added to the purchase).

3) To have a genuine enthusiasm and passion for the work they are supporting. You have to like and believe in what you are buying – art is not for art's sake. Do not succumb to snobbery or peer pressure – if you don't think a framed photo of a mango is for you, keep your art deco poster where it is. Art is like food, or lovers: you want to see what's on the menu before making your final choice.

How the collection starts and who it features is up to you. You might be lucky enough to meet a modern-day Picasso, but be careful before falling in love with him as well as the work; he didn't treat women as well as he did his art (see page 413). It's far safer and more profitable to keep a safe distance. You can be a muse/patron like the Mona Lisa if you want to be captured in art, but the investment aspect tends to be on collecting rather than featuring in art. Moreover, geniuses can be very hard to live with. Have the work hanging in your home, not the hassle hanging round your neck.

Go to the main art fairs such as Frieze, Miami, Basel as well as scouring elsewhere around the globe and trawling the graduate and young fine art shows. If you enjoy this, a Peggy would try and snag a bargain or two at those events or at the Summer Exhibition or the forementioned Royal College Postcard Exhibition. It's like planting seeds – given the right encouragement and watering, they are sure to blossom into something.

If you are serious about adding value to your collection, look at Sotheby's and Bonham's for their upcoming sales; well, 'you can't beat an old master'. Posters and prints, old magazines, illustrations and movie memorabilia are also becoming hot collectors' items. The chances of coming across any undiscovered da Vincis or Picassos on eBay or at a flea market remain few and far between, but you can hope.

The curator is the person who puts on the show and brings the group or collection together, i.e. the organizer. They ensure the venue shows the show at its best, writes a fascinating introduction to the catalogue of works, decides who and what goes where, and accepts compliments as they drift around the private view (the launch party/opening night of the art world).

14th October

Winnie the Pooh by A. A. Milne was first published in 1926. Alan Alexander Milne (the names behind the initials) was encouraged by his friend, teacher and mentor (and another twice-initialled star) H.G. Wells to study and become a writer.

The book was inspired by Milne's son Christopher Robin and their trip to London Zoo – where he first saw the bear Winnie, who became the 'bear with very little brain'.

The series has sold in its millions, and, as Milne wrote, 'whatever happens to them on the way, in that enchanted piece on top of the forest, a little boy and his bear will always be playing'. Go and play Pooh Sticks today.

Also on this day in 1066 the Battle of Hastings was fought. Poor King Harold II lost his crown (and his eye, according to the Bayeux Tapestry) and then his life to William, Duke of Normandy. The Norman Conquest and Norman reign over England began.

15th October

Encouraged by her Uncle Leopold, Queen Victoria proposed to her cousin, Prince Albert, in 1839. Clearly she was allowing enough time to find the ring, book the church and get the dress and guest list just right for a summer wedding. However, in the case of royalty, there is never really a budget or-waiting-time issue: Victoria didn't have a six month engagement – she was Queen after all – and was married on 10 February 1840.

16th October

It was 'off with her head' as Marie Antoinette, Queen of France, was guillotined in 1793 in Paris at the height of the French Revolution (see page 275). To achieve her look (with the head, obviously) why not try Her Majesty's Own Home-made Face Mask? It is believed to have been the secret behind her legendary beauty and is still used by Parisians today, so now you don't have to always hide behind your Venetian mask.

Marie's Mask

Ingredients:
   1 egg
   1 juice of a lemon
   4 tsp of non-fat dry milk powder
   1 tsp witch hazel

To make:
   Put all of the above into your blender and mix at top speed. Yes, you can use a whisk or fork, but think about it – the sooner it's on the sooner its magic can begin. Apply to face, neck and décolletage, lie back and let someone peel you a grape or do something very regal. Fifteen minutes later, or when it feels dry to the touch, wash off using the remaining lemon pulp as your cleanser (in other words, don't feel pressured into slapping all the goo onto your face – save some for later). Rinse, pat dry and moisturize. Long Live the Queen.

17th October

In 1979 Mother Teresa was awarded the Nobel Prize, while in 1918 Rita Hayworth – actress, dancer and the 'Love Goddess' of the forties – was born.
   'A girl is – well, a girl. It's nice to be told you're successful at it,' she said. Successful turned out to be something of an understatement.

Margarita Carmen Cansino was another entertainer who began her career with her family in their vaudeville act. As she developed her moves as well as her curves, she caught the eye of film-makers and transformed from Rita Cansino to Rita Hayworth (her mother's maiden name was Haworth). From minor roles to MGM, add a bottle of hair dye and soon the dancer was not only cast opposite Fred Astaire, she was Hollywood's hottest property and on the cover of *Time* magazine (10 November 1941). Thanks to a later shoot for *Life* magazine where she knelt on a bed in her negligée, she became the most popular wartime pin-up of all (with over five million posters of the print being sold). It *so* pays to get on with photographers and play the part.

Off screen Hayworth was married four times, including to film director Orson Welles, and in 1948 quit the movies altogether to marry Prince Aly Khan, leader of the Shia Muslim', inspiring the film *The Barefoot Contessa* starring Ava Gardener.

In reality she was shy and self-deprecating. 'Every man I knew went to bed with Gilda and woke up with me,' she said. Yet her starring role in the 1946 film noir *Gilda*, and her famous one-gloved striptease (that was *all* that came off), would make many men hope for the chance.

20th October

In 1973 the Sydney Opera House, designed by Danish architect Jørn Utzon, was finally opened by Queen Elizabeth II. Also today in 1968 former First Lady Jacqueline Kennedy married Greek shipping magnate Aristotle Onassis. Read about her on page 443, or download a Maria Callas opera in honour of both the Opera House and the broken heart of Mrs Onassis that never was.

24th October

Today in 1929 came the Wall Street Crash. Forty years later, in 1969, Richard Burton was clearly not short of cash when he bought his wife, Elizabeth Taylor, a 69.42-carat diamond. At over a million dollars, it was an expensive token of love by any standards. See page 425 for how to pick your own diamond.

In 1964 *My Fair Lady* had its world premiere. But the real *My Fair Lady* transformation was not the work of Professor Higgins but that of Cecil Beaton.

Born 14 January 1904, Cecil Beaton was Society's favourite photographer. From the Queen's 1953 coronation to Marilyn Monroe, to the wedding of the Duke and Duchess of Windsor, he was the man they all wanted. Beaton captured the era in photographs and his costume designs transformed many a fair lady, and immortalized Audrey Hepburn. In addition to this, Beaton later 'claimed' Greta Garbo as a lover (before she wanted to be alone) as well as 'Super Duper' Gary Cooper – the latter being more likely.

Beaton's achievements ranged from *Vanity Fair* to *Vogue* to the Academy Awards, where he won two for his costume designs – *Gigi* in 1958 and *My Fair Lady* in 1964. Let him inspire you when dressing up or stepping out this season.

25th October

Two months until Christmas and – yippee – a reason to act like it has come early, as today is St Crispin and Crispinian's day, the patron saint of cobblers, tanners and shoemakers. The shoe twins lived in AD 3 in Rome, but fled to avoid religious persecution and ended up preaching Christianity to the Gauls, but were tortured and beheaded around AD 286. A church was built in Soissons in their honour around the sixth century, but far better to honour them by making a pilgrimage instead to Manolo Blahník or at the very least wearing a pair of your favourite high heels today.

Yet despite their important footwear position, the saintly twins are best known for lending their name to Shakespeare's Henry V in his speech before the Battle of Agincourt: 'hold their manhood's cheap while any speaks that fought with us upon St Crispin's day'.

There is another important event on this day. In 1881 Pablo Picasso was born. Any art collector, indeed anyone with a brain, should know the name of the most prolific (according to the *Guinness Book of Records*) and innovative artist of the last century.

The Spanish painter and sculptor was born Pablo (Diego Jose Francisco de Paula Juan Nepomuceno de los Remedios Cipriano de la Santisima Trinidad Ruiz y) Picasso! However, he produced even more works (100,000 prints; 13,500 paintings; 34,000 book illustrations; 300 sculptures) than he had names.

There is a story of a man once daring to criticize Picasso to his face for his 'unrealistic' art. Picasso reportedly asked him to show him some realistic art. The man pulled out a photograph of his wife. Picasso observed 'so your wife is two inches tall, two-dimensional, with no arms and no legs, and no colour but only shades of grey?' The man's reply was not recorded. Walk round one of Picasso's sculptures or watch how his cubist work jumps off the canvas showing every angle of his subject.

Picasso and his women

Born in Malaga, Spain, Picasso's father was an artist and soon it was clear the young Picasso had inherited (if not exceeded) this talent, and spent his youth gathering inspiration between Barcelona and Paris.

However groundbreaking a painter, Picasso was a nightmare with women – a rock star philanderer before his time; yet ladies were like moths to a flame where he was concerned. First came his relationship with Fernande Oliver whom he left for Marcelle Humbert (known as Eva in his paintings). Mistresses continued until in 1918 he married the ballerina Olga Khokhlova, but this was shortlived as, while looking for inspiration, his wondering eye spotted Marie-Therese Walter in 1927. He and Khokhlova separated but remained legally married until her death in 1955, because he wanted to avoid losing any of his work in a costly divorce settlement. Walter herself was soon dumped in favour of photographer and painter Dora Maar, who survived until 1944 when he started seeing art student Francoise Gilot (not that any of these relationships were completely exclusive on his side; he *was* Picasso after all).

Miraculously, despite all the bed-hopping high jinks, his output in the studio remained even more prolific, inspired by his muses. Regardless of his fame and talent, this is not the type of man your mother would wish you to be involved with.

In 1953 Gilot, with whom he'd had two children – Claude and Paloma – did the unthinkable and left him (fed up with his infidelities and abusive behaviour). It was karma. The great Picasso was humiliated and dumbstruck. Not to worry – he soon found comfort in the arms of other women and captured them on canvas. Jacqueline Roque and Picasso were married in 1961, not as a great love gesture on his part – more a final stab of revenge at Gilot whom he'd always 'hinted' that he would marry.

Picasso died on 8 April 1973 leaving many a *Weeping Woman* in addition to his most popular work.

'Art is not the application of a canon of beauty but what the instinct and the brain can conceive beyond any canon. When we love a woman we don't start measuring her limbs,' he said – and he certainly tested this theory.

'Only put off until tomorrow what you are willing to die having left undone.'

'I don't say everything, but I paint everything.'

The Musée National Picasso in Paris, the Museo Picasso, Malaga, and Museu Picasso, Barcelona are three museums permanently dedicated to showcasing his work. Be sure to visit at least one. Or hire the 1996 film about him, *Surviving Picasso*, starring Anthony Hopkins as the artist, which tells the story through the eyes of Francoise Gilot. Alternatively wear defiant red lipstick today, *à la* Paloma, his daughter.

As October comes to a close, summertime ends too, and the clocks go back (remember *Fall back, Spring forward* to get the right direction).

28th October

Designed by French sculptor Frederic Auguste Bartholdi and engineered by
Gustave Eiffel, the Statue of Liberty was officially dedicated to New York
on this day in 1886. Though a decade in the making, it was a gift from
France to America to celebrate the centenary of American Independence,
and represented liberty and democracy.

Who the model was remains uncertain – some think it is the widow of
Isaac Singer (the Singer sewing machine industrialist), Isabella Eugenie Boyer,
others think it is the architect's mother, Charlotte Bartholdi, while others
guess it was his lover, Jeanne-Emilie Baheux de Puysieux. Whoever it was,
she is now lost but forever stands for liberty.

Lady Liberty is 151 feet tall and resides on a 150-foot pedestal. She
arrived in June 1885 at New York harbour in 350 pieces – quite some excess
baggage. She is dressed as a Roman deity, a goddess, in a *palla* – a female
version of the toga and cloak – and would need 4,000 square yards of fabric
to change her look. Her greeny complexion took twenty years to weather,
starting off black, to copper, to signature hue.

Aim to climb her stairs, sail around her or at least celebrate *your* independence and what she symbolizes – 'Liberty Enlightening the World' – with
her torch illuminating the struggle for freedom. What have you done for the
cause lately? Today's the day to go to *www.amnesty.org* for human rights, *www.inter-
nationalpen.org.uk* where writers defend freedom of speech, and *www.global-cool.com*
where carbon emissions and keeping the world turning is the point of focus.
Think about what liberty means and try to make a difference.

29th October

In 1891 Fanny Brice was born. She was the burlesque dancer who made it
to the legendary Ziegfeld Follies – the ultimate dance troupe and stage act
of the time. Her Follies signature song was 'My Man'. This was not only a
huge hit in her lifetime but was also immortalized in the story of her life,
on stage and on film, with Barbra Streisand starring as Brice in *Funny Face*
(and winning an Academy Award for the performance in 1968).

Brice finished her career as the voice of radio character Baby Snooks –
not how *Funny Face* ends at all.

31st October

In 1795 English poet John Keats was born while in 1902 the first telegraph cable
across the base of the Pacific Ocean was completed – two great excuses to communicate but, bearing in mind the date, you may want to keep the door firmly shut.

How to Halloween

Halloween originated in the fifth century, when summer officially ended for
the Irish Celts. It was believed that on this night all the spirits of those who
had died in the preceding year came back to find a living soul to possess for
the year. The living weren't keen to share their souls and certainly didn't fancy
being possessed, so the practice of dressing up as ghouls and ghosts and fright-
ening the spirits away with pumpkins and spooky houses began. The Romans
adopted this custom and even added a few games, such as apple bobbing –
after the Roman goddess of fruits and trees, Pomona, who was celebrated in
October. By the ninth century 'trick or treating' had been added, but why be
clichéd? Tonight could be the perfect excuse for a night of revelry with a mask.

Foot Note

The platform shoe

If you are feeling a bit below eye level, or are worried about getting
your feet wet, this is the shoe for you. The platform has been the unsung
hero of the diminutive diva and the perfect way to add inches since

ancient times. In ancient Greece this was the style important figures wore in order to tower over their followers. Leaping forward, it was then adopted by the lower-moralled, but high-born courtesans of Venice and was similar in style to that worn by the Japanese geisha – which helped them stand out from the crowd and catch a client's eye. From geishas' getas to the (husband-helpful) chopines, an early form of the platform-soled shoe, Venetian husbands liked to encourage this shoe to be made so thick that their wives would look good but not be able to stray with such cumbersome attire. They caused many grumbles in marriages where wives halved in size once vows were exchanged and the shoes came off, and they were later banned after being blamed for many miscarriages.

It wasn't until the thirties that the thick soles stepped firmly into the front line of fashion in partnership with the court shoe, evolving through the forties. By the fifties the platform was the perfect date to take to the Prom or be worn with your New Look, *circa* 1947, though what could be more this than the raised rainbow sandal from 1938 Ferragamo? It gave height to the hair-raising seventies and let you dance away in the disco era without any discomfort to your twinkle toes. It only phased out in the eighties when shoulder pads and spikes became the weapon of the working girl. But the portable pedestal went back onto the dance floor with the rise of the brand Buffalo as worn by the Spice Girls in the early nineties.

The platform now looks set to stay safely in vogue for as long as people need to add length to their legginess. Just be wary of adding too many inches as it will cause even a supermodel to topple, as Naomi Campbell famously did when her sky-high (8-inch) Vivienne Westwood creations caused her to fall to earth with a bump on the runway in 1994. Luckly she had a well-padded bustle to cushion the fall and had the sense to smile.

November

'Having money is rather like being a blonde. It's more
fun but it's not vital.'
Mary Quant

Wish You Were Here

Diane von Furstenberg from New York

I love NY because of its energy! It is built on granite and I think that is why everyone in NY has so much of it. NY is a great place to live because it has so much to offer and yet it is not that big . . . you can find everything, see everything, meet anybody. Everyone comes here to realize a dream . . . merchants, artists, writers . . . I love the spontaneity and the fact that everything is possible here.

When I first visited NY in 1969, I fell in love with the city and knew that I wanted to move there, which I did as a young bride. Seven years ago, I moved to the West Village and it was a revelation . . . I hardly move from there, but I am discovering new things about New York all the time, and I continue to fall in love all over again. There are so many neighborhoods, so many lives . . . you can get lost.

My favourite New York moment is when I drive back from Connecticut on Monday morning. I get on the West Side Highway and drive down along the Hudson River – the fact that Manhattan is an island and that water is everywhere makes it very special, peaceful and freeing. Along the Hudson River is also my best place to walk . . . it is both quiet and fun. You can see the Statue of Liberty and breathe the air of the sea.

For me, NY is work so I do pretty much just that, but a perfect day in NY is walking everywhere, going to the museums and ending up at the theatre, while having great meals in between.

My favourite restaurant is Pastis, but I also love the Waverly Inn, owned by my close friend Graydon Carter. It is on the corner of Bank Street in the West Village. It is a charming, intimate space and the food is excellent! If you want a great deli, push east and go to Katz's Deli.

Shopping in NY is an experience. I love Scoop for T-shirts and sweaters, but I mostly shop at my shop on 14th Street. For the best vintage, there is Resurrection.

Part of visiting New York is staying in some of the best hotels . . . My favorites are the elegant Carlisle Hotel, the Gramercy Park Hotel, and the hip and trendy Mercer.

Once a week, I visit Tracie Martyn for her electric facials. She is my favourite by far . . . If you have time, she is worth visiting.

If you have only 24 hours in NY, hit the streets . . . walk from uptown to downtown and see the museums.

Love, Diane

1st November

After all the ghosts and gremlins of Halloween comes a holy day to celebrate every saint – All Saints' and All Souls' Day. Regardless of whether or not you wake up with Dracula's fang marks in your neck or with a pumpkin by your side, the black cat and broomstick will be exhausted after an evening dancing with the devil – so compensate by spending the day doing good deeds. No need to go crazy – total overhauls are saved for new year's resolutions – but little things like opening a door for someone, offering someone needy/cute your seat on the bus, taking out the trash without being asked, should bring the sparkle back to your halo.

2nd November

Today in 1960, Penguin was finally given permission to publish D.H. Lawrence's novel *Lady Chatterley's Lover*, thirty years after the author's death. Originally it was deemed indecent, with its four-letter words and sex scenes, and Lawrence's publishers had to wage a court battle before Chatterley's affair with her gardener could be released. It went on sale on 10 November and was sold in brown paper bags. Its first print-run of 200,000 copies sold out on the first day of publication. As is so often the case, the forbidden fruit was all the more enticing – did we learn nothing from Adam and Eve?

Also on this day Marie Antoinette was born in 1775. Along with a reputation for glamour and fashion, this queen of France will for ever be remembered as woefully extravagant. One of the many scandals attached to her, before her beheading, was the 1785 Affair of the Diamond Necklace.

To say Louis XIV's monarchy was unpopular with the masses is putting it mildly. A plan was cooked up to discredit the throne and making Marie Antoinette look bad was an added bonus. The cunning Comtesse de la Motte secretly went to the eminent, and out of favour, Cardinal de Rohan, Bishop of Strasbourg, and proposed a plan that would reinstate him at court. The bishop was all ears. The comtesse suggested he present a gift of a rare and beautiful diamond necklace – as luck would have it, she had just the one in mind. A few forged notes from the queen and a nocturnal interview through the shrubbery later (with a lady of the night rather than her majesty) and his holiness was convinced that the necklace was a capital plan. He entered into a contract with the jewellers, rationalizing that the cost of diamonds was a small price to pay to find favour again with the king. However, when the bishop missed the very first payment the jewellers went directly to the (baffled) queen, who knew nothing of the diamonds, and very soon the plot was foiled. Rather than concealing the entire sorry episode and brushing it away, no harm done, Louis XIV made the mistake of thinking he could use it to their PR advantage. He arrested and tortured the witless bishop before exiling him, regardless of his innocence, while his subjects continued to believe the story circulated by the comtesse of the queen's greed and cunning in getting a man of God to shower her with diamonds. What about innocent until proven guilty? The comtesse was imprisoned, flogged and branded – but she had her own contacts and managed to escape to England, where she published her scandalous memoirs against the queen. As for the queen – even when she was in the right she was in the wrong.

Diamonds are said to be the 'teardrops of the gods' and are believed to hold special magical powers. They have long been treasures of kings, queens and all who can wear them – as well as been used to cast spells of love.

Records from 1074 tell of a Hungarian queen's crown set with uncut diamonds, and by the thirteenth century they were all the rage in England and France. In 1477 Archduke Maximilian of Austria gave a diamond ring to his bride-to-be, Mary of Burgundy, and the tradition of the engagement ring was born. The placing of the ring on the third finger of the left hand dates back to the Egyptians who believed that *Vena Amors* – the vein of love – ran directly from the heart to the tip of the third finger. And so it became the indestructible symbol of love.

In the sixteenth century 'scribbling rings' were used by lovers to etch (permanent) sweet nothings and declarations of their love on the window-panes. Evidence of diamond damage can be found in the *très cher, mais très chic* restaurant La Pérouse in Paris.

In 1766 Mr Lefèvre, one of King Louis XV's bar-keepers, purchased an old mansion on the quayside of the Seine and named it La Pérouse after the famous navigator. By 1850, La Pérouse was *the* place for the literary, political and gallant gentry of Paris to meet, and its regular patrons included Alexandre Dumas, George Sand, Alfred de Musset, Victor Hugo, Émile Zola and Gustave Flaubert. The mirrors in the former living rooms are still covered in scratches. Courtesans of centuries past took the diamonds their lovers had offered them and dragged them over the mirrors to check they were real.

It is now favoured by celebrities, who can be hidden in the private cabine rooms. Go to its website for reservations, but be sure to go with a king's ransom: *www.restaurantlaperouse.com*

How to pick a diamond

Now we can't all know as much as Elizabeth Taylor about diamonds, but when a jeweller wafts a velvet cushion under your nose and confides that this is a blue white diamond what do you say? Is this good, bad or bonkers? It's actually a very misused phrase and is used to throw you off guard. It refers to the way in which fluorescent and natural light and UV wavelengths react to it. Basically if the stone looks milky or oily that will bring the price down. Exit with cash rather than stone; you don't want to have to travel with an entire lighting gig to be able to show off your gem to its best advantage.

The key to diamond shopping is: Cut, Clarity, Colour and Carat.

You want all four Cs ticked before you sign on the dotted line. Look out for any scratches, marks or blemishes and read the diamond certificate to check you have picked a winner.

'Diamonds are a girl's best friend.' Marilyn Monroe knew a diamond ring was often more enduring than the man. Shame.

The four Cs

Cut can be brilliant, emerald, princess, cushion, oval, baguette, heart, brico-lette, marquis . . . Marcel Tolkowsky developed the 'brilliant' cut in 1919 and since then cutting techniques have developed, allowing diamonds to become ever more sparkly as more and more light can be bounced off the facets.

Round   The simplest and most popular – and due to its shape the most sparkly and enduring classic shape.

Princess   A modern classic with clean, square lines and sparkle. Developed in the 1970s it combines emerald cut and triangular facets.

Marquise   Regal and elongated with tapered points at both ends, it will make the finger look longer.

Emerald   One of the most classic diamond shapes with clean lines from step-cutting or parallel-line facets. It is always cut in block corners and often with a rectangular outline.

Radiant   A combination of the classic emerald cut with the sparkle of the round brilliant with rectangular-shaped outline.

Cushion   An unusual diamond shape and a good alternative to the oval or princess cut. Because it is a softened pillow shape it is relatively rare, based on an antique cushion-cut.

Pear   A beautiful and feminine shape with rounded end that tapers on one side – perfect for pendants or drop earrings.

Oval   The most similar to the round brilliant cut, it combines the round's sparkle with a flattering and elongated outline. Perfect if you want a unique shape but all the fire and brilliance of the round.

Heart   Of course the most romantic, and similar to the pear shape apart from the cleft in the round end. Skilled cutting and setting is required to keep a true heart diamond sparkling.

Trillion   A dramatic and bold cut that was developed in the 1970s which varies the radiant cut with step-cutting and brilliant faceting, and comes in a triangular shape.

'Square-cut or pear-shaped these rocks don't lose their shape.' Song by Jule Styne

Clarity refers to the diamond's pureness, which is due to the depth of the earth it has been dug from. Remember only 20 per cent of those mined are good enough to become a bit of bling. You don't want too many cracks, imperfections or flaws on your diamond, and if this mirrors the relationship, upgrade on both.

Colour can enhance or diminish the diamond's value. It's all about the lighting, darling. Always ask to see the object of your affection in natural light. Pink and blue trues (think of the Hope Diamond) are good and add value, while off-yellow and murky hues bring it down. Even if you're going for the clear and classic, diamonds are a bit like Dulux paint: there is no such thing as 'just white'. See what suits you – and the budget – best.

Don't forget vintage heirlooms can be real treasures (sentimental and sensational) so don't rule this option out – look in the box before tossing it over your hopeful fiancé's shoulder. See page 433 for vintage sourcing.

Carat refers to the weight (one carat is one-fifth of a gram). The more carats the more bling, but go for something you can lift. The Koh-i-Nor 'Mountain of Light' remains one of the most famous diamonds in the world, weighing in at 191 carats. When it was presented to Queen Victoria she cut it into a more 'manageable' 108.93 carats and wore it as a brooch.

For more sparkling information look on *www.diamondhelper.com*

Where to get your diamonds

Do you really need to ask this? Yes, there is Harry Winston, Bvlgari and Asprey but when diamond digging you *have* to go to Tiffany's.

A brief history of Tiffany's

Founded in 1837 by Charles Lewis Tiffany and John B. Young (and originally called Tiffany and Young), by 1853 Charles Tiffany was the sole owner. He was dubbed the 'King of Diamonds' and, true to his title, in 1887, he bought the French crown jewels.

But it was Mr Walter Hoving (2 December 1897–27 November 1989), the Swedish-born American businessman, who really transformed Tiffany's into a beacon of everything chic during his reign as head of Tiffany's and Co., 1955–1980. Hoving commissioned the designers Jean Schlumberger, Angela Cummings, Elsa Peretti and Paloma Picasso as well as Gene Moore to dress the windows. He told them: 'Design what you think is beautiful and don't worry about selling it. That's our job.' What a boss.

Mr Hoving's uncompromising vision took the company from $7 million in 1955, to $100 million in 1980. He had rules that had to be followed:

No diamonds for men
No silver plate
No charge accounts for rude customers
No Sellotape

Things had to be done properly, and the packaging had to be the signature eggshell blue and tied with a white satin ribbon.

As well as demanding perfection in-store, Mr Hoving was fastidious about good manners. In addition to his bestselling book called *Your Career in Business*, he penned *Tiffany's Table Manners for Teenagers*, inspired by his grandson's atrocious table manners.

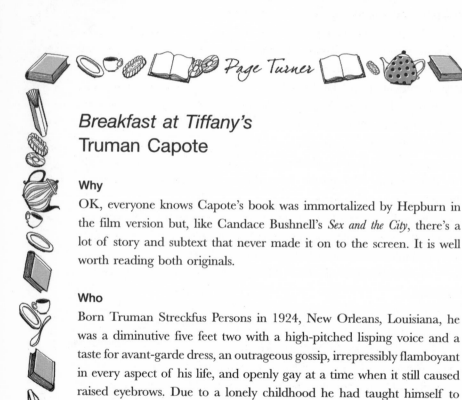

Page Turner

Breakfast at Tiffany's
Truman Capote

Why

OK, everyone knows Capote's book was immortalized by Hepburn in the film version but, like Candace Bushnell's *Sex and the City*, there's a lot of story and subtext that never made it on to the screen. It is well worth reading both originals.

Who

Born Truman Streckfus Persons in 1924, New Orleans, Louisiana, he was a diminutive five feet two with a high-pitched lisping voice and a taste for avant-garde dress, an outrageous gossip, irrepressibly flamboyant in every aspect of his life, and openly gay at a time when it still caused raised eyebrows. Due to a lonely childhood he had taught himself to read and write before he even got to school, and aged ten he won a writing competition with his first story *Old Mr Busybody*.

In 1933 he moved to New York to live with his mother and her second husband, Joseph Capote, whose surname he decided to adopt as his own. In 1945 *Mademoiselle* magazine published his novella *Miriam* which won him the O. Henry Award and a substantial advance for his next novel, the semi-autobiographical *Other Voices, Other Rooms*. The character of Isabel was based on his friend the novelist Harper Lee (who returned the compliment and used Capote as her inspiration for Dill Harris in her bestselling novel). The Harold Halma photograph Capote had taken for the jacket said it all – and heralded a big personality exploding onto the scene. Capote had arrived. He loved to hang out with the stars – all the name-dropping and schmoozing. Life was just *fabulous*.

In 1958 he published the novella *Breakfast at Tiffany's* as the lead story in his latest work, a collection of short stories. But it was *Tiffany's* that changed everything and was brought to the screen in 1961. Though Capote lamented and lambasted the producers, announcing he was appalled by the casting (he wanted Monroe for the part) and the ways in which the screenplay changed his original novel, he was soon appeased by the results and his increased fame. He was now an international star.

Capote's next project bizarrely took him from diamonds to death row. *In Cold Blood* followed the (true) trial that was gripping America of the men accused of murdering the Clutter family. The writing of this book, as well as one of the main convicts, became an obsession for Capote. It was the subject of the 2005 Oscar-winning film *Capote*, though you shouldn't miss the star-studded 2007 film *Infamous* which focuses on more aspects of his fabulous life. Maybe watch one today and one on his birthday.

Capote is also remembered as a legendary party-goer – and party thrower. He was the host with the most. His Black and White Masked Ball for the *Washington Post*'s Katharine Graham, on 28 November 1966, has gone down in history as *the* party everyone wishes they had been to.

Sadly as Capote got older he became more and more dependent on alcohol, had a series of dreadful boyfriends and was said to have become a bitchy caricature of his former self. He had a brief comeback in the eighties, writing features for Andy Warhol's *Interview* magazine, but died in 1984, aged fifty-nine, at the home of TV host Johnny Carson's ex-wife, from liver disease, complicated by multiple intoxication.

The plot

So you think you know the story of Holly Golightly? You don't.

For a start the original was blonde, with an upturned nose; but don't worry, that chic sense of style was always there.

In the novel Capote's Miss Golightly has a much tougher reality to cope with than the one her on-screen incarnation encounters. If you want to find out about what shapes her as a character, more space is given to her past in the book, as well as to some of the shady characters and sadnesses she would much rather forget in a sea of champagne bubbles. As much as the effervescent enigma dazzles on the party scene, she knows she hangs out with all the 'phoneys'; did this girl reflect Capote's own world? Golightly entertains millionaires and gangsters; all very exciting and exhilarating, but she never really knows who anyone is. She also never remembers her own key, much to the annoyance of her neighbours, and to the secret delight of the shy nameless writer who lives in the same block as her. The boy is instantly star-struck by Golightly – mesmerized by her madness, smitten by her eccentricities – and she too decides to befriend him, or at least adopt him when she's not entertaining, providing she can christen him Fred, after her brother.

'Fred' is hopelessly in love with her, but Miss Golightly is far too busy running away from reality and surrounding herself with beautiful people and objects that she doesn't seem to notice. In fact the only time our heroine feels totally at peace is when she is at the Fifth Avenue jeweller's, Tiffany's, or the library.

Read the book, compare Capote's to Hepburn's Golightly and see who you identify with most.

Hosting

How can you hope to compete with Holly Golightly or Truman Capote? When it comes to hosting this soirée make high heels and little black dresses obligatory. Cater with canapés, or convene at the hottest new restaurant – one chic enough for a true Miss Golightly to consider attending.

Alternatives on America

To Kill a Mocking Bird by Harper Lee
Little Women by Louisa M. Alcott
East of Eden by John Steinbeck
The Age of Innocence by Edith Wharton
Catch-22 by Joseph Heller
Catcher in the Rye by J.D. Salinger

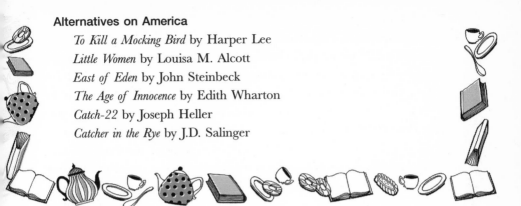

3rd November

In Ancient Rome today was April Fool's Day, while in more modern times it has become National Sandwich Day, appropriately celebrated on the birthday of John Montagu, the fourth Earl of Sandwich.

He is the man credited with creating the first sandwich. Legend goes the earl was up all night engaged in a particularly crucial game of cards, and while gambling he got the munchies, but he refused to leave the table and risk losing his lucky streak. There's nothing like hunger to make a man lose his concentration, so fearing the worst he told his servants to run down to the kitchen and bring him some meat placed between two slices of bread so that he could eat with one hand and continue to play with the other. His wish was granted, and it was very tasty and did the trick. His fellow gamblers looked enviously on and by the end of the night sandwiches were had by all.

A similar story, told on the menu to diners at Claridges hotel, London, is of the Duchess of Bedfordshire's ladylike attack of the nibbles. This time there was no gambling involved but the genteel ladies solved the potential hunger pangs by refining the sandwich and instigating one of the most well-loved of English traditions – High Tea. Delicate sandwiches, a pot of tea, perhaps some scones, oh, why not some cream with the jam? That should carry you through to dinner.

Book a table to experience it there for yourself: *www.claridges.co.uk*. As Spencer Tracy said, 'I don't want to go to heaven, I want to go to Claridges.' Couldn't agree more. Alternatively you can book one of their master classes from tea-tasting to wine-sniffing.

4th November

English archaeologist Howard Carter discovered the entrance to King Tutankamen's Tomb in Luxor, Egypt, on this day in 1922.

In 1905 Carter had resigned from his position at the Egyptian Antiquities Service over a dispute, and started to lead his own searches. Two years later the independent archaeologist and adventurer was introduced to Lord Carnarvon, a keen amateur, who agreed to pump money into Carter's expeditions in exchange for reflected glory, and maybe a few days on the dig if he or his daughter were in town.

The arrangement had gone on for about fifteen years and his patron was, understandably, starting to get a little frustrated with the lack of return and lack of glory he'd been hoping for. But then, just in the nick of time, Carter quite literally struck gold in the Valley of the Kings. The find was better than either of them could have hoped for and the tomb of Tutankamen turned out to be one of the most well-preserved tombs of all the Egyptian kings.

After the initial euphoria, it took a few more weeks to carefully prise their way into the inner chamber. Everything was beautifully intact and the only slip occurred when Carter unwrapped the mummy of the ancient king and his majesty's ancient skull fell to the floor and cracked. Some feared this would fulfil an eerie Ancient Egyptian prophecy that said if a king was left undisturbed he would remain immortal – but if not he would haunt the person that woke him for eternity. Despite the threat, Carter lived, richly and famously, until he was sixty-four, a good twelve years after the discovery. He even borrowed a phrase found inscribed on King Tutankhamen's wishing cup for his own epitaph:

May your spirit live,
May you spend millions of years
You who love Thebes,
Sitting with Your face to the North Wind,
Your eyes beholding happiness.

How to find your own treasure

You don't need to go back as far as Ancient Egypt to find treasures. Anything a few years old is now classed as 'vintage', and though this is rather indiscriminate you must agree it sounds so much better than 'second-hand'.

How can you put a price on finding something unique, something covetable, something wow, something to turn all your friends green with envy? You simply can't. Finding a collector's item is a great way to show off your great eye, know-how, and creative flair – a stylish hat-trick if ever there was one. Above all, the thing with vintage is to aim for something that you wear rather than wears you. As soon as an outfit makes you feel anxious, start again, move on; it doesn't matter about the label, it is not the look for you. You have to be able to breathe, walk, talk, laugh and eat without risk of exploding out of the corset, or impaling yourself on one of its hooks and causing permanent damage.

Rummage in the thrift stores on city breaks, take regular trips to Portobello and other markets as you won't get results every time. The brilliant thing about wearing vintage is that you don't have to be a budding fashion designer, art student, 'muse' or dab hand with the sewing machine and glue gun to get a unique look. Vintage is an instant and, if you are clever, a cost-effective way of guaranteeing you won't see someone else in the same LBD, jacket or skirt (jeans and T-shirts really don't matter). Why risk it looking better on them? Shudder. Why risk it indeed?

Vintage = different = individual = no comparison. Not next season or that forgotten season but *your* season is what you are aiming for.

Starting the search

Some days are fruitful, some days are frustrating, but unlike Howard Carter's fifteen years of sand-shifting angst, we are only talking *off-days* here, not years in the style wilderness. Some days you will leave with a teapot and a Ming vase when you were after a T-shirt and mink coat (fake fur, obviously). Others you'll find a satisfied smile and a new look impatient to hit the town.

Be serious: leave no stone unturned but remember, just because it's old doesn't mean it's valuable – you wouldn't want a used tea bag. Search markets, charity shops and vintage sales at the town halls. Try a few different sales – local, in town and out of town. Sample which ones work for you, your tastes and your budget, and always remember to bring enough cash or a cheque book as this lot don't tend to take plastic. This is another era after all. Do you want twenties and deco or sixties Courreges? Biba, Ossie Clarke, YSL and Dior are always 'hot' labels. Look after any modern labels that you think will stand the test of time – McQueen, Galliano, Alaïa, Westwood are obvious examples.

That said, don't be a label junkie: a flapper dress without the label can be equally show-stopping. You can feign it is an original Poiret (and keep the change) then go on to trash it without regrets. The price of your find will depend on beauty, condition, label and (most of all) the mood, and madness, of the seller. You then have to consider if you want to wear it or savour it and whether it is what you came out in search of today. Before you write a cheque for the next two months' worth of rent, work out if the parasol is in good enough condition, if you really do need another wedding dress and why you want that shoe with no buckle and broken heel. What do you want to invest in and what will make you happy *now*?

For further advice pick up Funmi Odulate's *Shopping for Vintage: The Definitive Guide to Vintage Fashion* with a full directory of all the websites, where to go and who to buy, and what you should keep a guarded secret.

How to source vintage and valuables

by Lulu Guinness, accessories designer

I have always loved vintage, mainly because I like to look different and to feel different to everyone else. There is a vintage shop that I love in New York called Legacy, which is wonderfully eclectic. It's owned by two girls, Rita Brookoff and Joanna Baum, and is down on 109 Thompson St: *www.legacy-nyc.com.*

I have always collected vintage for a number of guises, and why I love this store is threefold – it has its vintage pieces, it mixes in new (local and global) designers that are on the cusp of their careers taking off as well as being sympathetic to the feel of the shop, and there they also do these brilliant reprints of old crêpe de Chines. They are the most flattering dresses I know – I must have about nine of them now, navy, polka dot, floral, abstract . . . every possible combination. I wear them so often that people sometimes ask me if I made them; how I *wish* they were my design! The thing I love about Legacy is that everything has a very feminine essence; even the modern pieces retain that vintage charm with frayed hems, hooks and eyes and such like. I think you *can* find great value vintage if you look, particularly if you look when out of town – Legacy has a few pricier pieces like good Jackie O-style coats and movie-shaped silhouettes, but you can always find something – well, I can. Above all you'll find something that is unique which, after all, is what is so special about vintage.

The reason I like vintage all started from the great driving force to be different – and that has filtered into everything in my life from the egg timer to my saucepans to my clothes. *Everything* has to be a one-off, and I like things to be a mix of different eras. But I'm not a snob about vintage – I am too poor for that! I believe if you buy something you shouldn't be precious with it – you should wear it and enjoy it, that's what it's there for. It doesn't then matter if it's not a mint condition Schiaparelli; it has lived a little and can continue to do so with you.

I don't collect jewellery or clothes *per se*, that would be too 'predictable' for me; any clothes or trinkets I find I wear, I buy on impulse rather than on a quest. But I do collect powder compacts – simply because no one else was when I started. And again I don't think it matters if it's a copy of a Miriam Haskell or whoever – it still looks the same and it's the look and the antiquated charm I am going for.

I never really have time to shop when I'm in London as I'm either with my family or I'm working. When I get to New York I can explore – wander the fifth floor of Bergdorf Goodman and see all the young designers, go to big vintage fairs at The Pier and browse unnoticed at the market stalls and get a few trinkets as well as ideas. I like to float around unrecognized – once you become a regular, the bad can outweigh the good as they think they know what you are looking for as well as your budget. Try and rummage quietly through the shimmer and surprises and see what you can find, adapt to what you see – 'precious' all depends on the buyer, not the price tag.

I like the whimsical as well as the functional – I used to design bags around fitting in a packet of cigarettes; now it's a mobile phone! Without sounding too fey, the idea for my flower handbag simply came about when I was trying to work out a way to always carry a flower about with me – indeed the first bag I made was a Girl Friday-type briefcase as I was working with a film company, and I made different compartments, all totally functional, black on the outside and a frivolous red or purple lining inside. As for my compacts? I used to have my treasures lined up on my dressing table; now I have a table with a special glass lid over a sunken ledge for my finds to rest on – it's nice to have them out on display, but you also have to be practical in a house with children and a dog!

How to care for your pearls

Pearls, a favourite of everyone from Coco Chanel to Lulu Guinness, are often found in charity shops and vintage fairs. Just perfect to style a bourgeois twist into your second-hand, sorry, *vintage* finds.

Pearls are delicate and sensitive to their surroundings – how very *you*. Be careful to only put them on as the finishing touch once all the perfume, lotions and potions have been applied, as chemicals will affect their shine and lustre. Try and buff the little dears with a silk cloth and put them away in their box, often velvet, to keep them safe. Never leave them on a radiator or, worse, on the television, as this will send them into shock and they will be discoloured and brown by the next morning. Despite professing to hate your perfumes, pearls are in fact happiest when worn, with your body oils as a little moisture. So fussy. They also like to be stored flat – a good idea as you don't want the string stretching and snapping. True pros say you should restring your treasures once a year on pure silk thread. A perfect antiquated alternative to all the bling.

5th November

Remember, remember, the fifth of November. Gunpowder, treason and plot. I see no reason why gunpowder treason should ever be forgot . . .

Today in 1605 the gunpowder plot was foiled.

When James I came to the English throne (in 1603) the Catholics wanted to get rid of him; he was Scottish and had converted to Protestantism. While plotting they came upon the slightly extreme idea of blowing up the state opening of parliament which would be attended by James I, his queen and his eldest son, as well as all the government that had refused to grant any extra tolerance to the Catholic demands. The hope was that while the country was in chaos following the death of the king and key MPs, they could step into the breach. It has to be said the idea was not *totally* thought through.

The plot was lead by Robert Catesby. His four co-conspirators were

Thomas Winter, Thomas Percy, John Wright and the name we all know – Guy Fawkes. The plan was hatched in the spring of 1605 when they managed to conceal twenty barrels of gunpowder beneath parliament. They then set about covering their tracks until the state opening later that year – patience is a virtue. In preparation for the coup Catesby cautiously enlisted a few 'key Catholics' in the scheme, one of which was Francis Tresham, who warned his brother-in-law, Lord Monteagle, that he'd be better off skipping parliament that day. Once he heard this Monteagle raised the alarm. Fawkes was the man we all blame because he was caught red-handed and, quite literally, over a barrel. A little bit of torture later and they had all the names, details and the plan was foiled. Guy and his team were executed.

Burning effigies of the conspirators and collecting 'a penny for the Guy' (though perhaps a little too late for charity to help him) became popular on this day, and today fireworks fill the sky without any of the carnage and chaos that was originally planned. If you don't want to stage a firework display in your garden, why not try a sparkler in your pudding?

7th November

Marie Curie was born in 1867. With her husband, Pierre Curie, she researched and pioneered radioactivity. She was not only the first woman to ever win a Nobel Prize, she won it twice.

9th November

In 1989 the Berlin Wall came down. Cross your own hurdle or boundary today or, somewhat randomly, listen to David Hasselhoff. Let me explain. While the wall symbolized the division between East and West and was a twenty-eight-mile barrier dividing Germany's capital city at the height of the Cold War, the Hoff, the American actor best known for his roles in *Knight Rider* and *Baywatch*, released his single 'Looking for Freedom' in Germany, just as the wall came down. Mr Hasselhoff's hit song became an anthem and he even performed it on the remains of the Berlin Wall on New Year's Eve 1989.

10th November

English artist William Hogarth was born in 1860. He is best known for his moral and satirical engravings such as *The Beggars' Opera*, 1728, and *A Rake's Progress*, 1732.

Go and find his work at the Tate Britain today or, at the very least, look him up online: As J.M.W. Turner said, 'Hogarth has no school, nor has he ever been imitated with tolerable success.'

12th November

Another artist, the French sculptor Auguste Rodin, was born in 1840. This is the artist who created *Le Penseur* ('The Thinker') in 1880, and *Le Baiser* ('The Kiss') in 1886.

Rodin began sculpting when he couldn't get into Paris's famed École des Beaux Arts, but when his sister died Rodin was so traumatized he nearly gave up art to enter the Church. He then met seamstress Rose Beuret en route to this decision and she became his life companion and encouraged him to sculpt full-time. Like a true 'creative', Rodin had a turbulent private life, including an affair with sculptor Camille Claudel – sister of popular French poet and diplomat Paul Claudel – but, as with Picasso it all helped his work, as she was said to inspire his famous *Kiss*.

16th November

In 1959 *The Sound of Music* opened on Broadway. The film version was not released until March 1965.

Make a list of your favourite things ('Raindrops on roses and whiskers on kittens . . . *Tiffany's treasures and no credit limit* . . .) today.

How to deal with moths

Curie didn't solve this problem and Maria wanted the children to wear curtains rather than risk couture. So if you don't want to end up looking like an extra in a Hogarth scene, it is time to know how to take on the moth and protect your heirlooms.

Moths are like mice and other unmentionables – they travel in packs. If you open your wardrobe and find a hole has been inflicted on one of your most prized possessions, it's time to go to war before too many of your labels unravel.

Moths are unfortunately fashion victims – they enjoy a nibble of a Vuitton as much as a Dior and the purer the cashmere, cotton or chenille the more they like to sink their mothy teeth in. This is not fair, as let's face it they didn't pay for it and you wouldn't dream of nibbling a stranger's sweater – but life isn't fair.

In the initial stages of panic you can send everything over to the dry-cleaners, summon Rent-a-kill and shroud everything in plastic, but you have to be cleverer than that. Mothballs, moth sprays and sachets of lavender are all very well but you have to clean, vacuum and remove any eggs to prevent an army swelling its numbers. If you find a jumper with a nibble, empty the drawer or surrounding area, clean away any dust and see if they have attacked anything else nearby. When it gets to the white gunk stage you have to accept your sweater has gone to the fashion shop in the sky – if it's still at the bite mark stage a few stitches, a hot wash and full steam-iron should blast any remnants of the beast away. It's an urban myth that moths eat only natural fibres – they like the same labels as you. Moths are not attracted by light but they are by areas of infestation, so don't let things build up.

Store out-of-season clothes properly – dry-clean or wash them in hot water before storing. Brush out any pockets, along the seams and under the collars and seal them in airtight containers.

If you have floorboards, be prepared for an attack – and consider fumigating your property every six months. Or if this is serious warfare you can, like Linda Evangelista, invest in cedar-wood wardrobes (this has a similar effect on the moths to kryptonite on Superman).

Thank goodness these horrors haven't got a taste for Manolos.

18th November

The American artist and photographer Man Ray, who had made Paris his home, died in 1976, aged eighty-six. As he explained, 'Dada cannot live in New York,' and indeed the bohemian had to live in Paris. Here he led the social and artistic scene of the era along with Duchamp, Max Ernst and the artists' model and leading muse of the day, his lover Kiki de Montparnasse (Alice Prin). Kiki was Man Ray's companion for most of the 1920s, and the subject of some of his most famous photographic images and experimental films. However, in 1929 he found a new muse and began a love affair with the surrealist photographer Lee Miller. Strike a pose in his honour today.

19th November

Calvin Klein was born in 1942. Don't let anything come between you and your Calvins today as you douse yourself in the perfumes Obsession or Eternity to celebrate the man who launched Brooke Shields, Kate Moss, Christy Turlington, Natalia Vodianova and many a career through his global campaigns.

20th November

Emilio Pucci was born in 1914 in Naples, Italy.

You may already know his name – and his bright psychedelic prints – but you might be surprised about how he got into fashion. Don't ignore destiny.

Born Marquis di Barsento, he was a wealthy aristocrat and diplomat with a Ph.D. in Social Sciences, the *ideal* bachelor (straight) – and yes, that is what he was enjoying being. He was an Italian stallion. As well as the girls, he had a penchant for skiing and competed in the 1934 Winter Olympics. Being a style-conscious Romeo he insisted that *he* design the outfits, and indeed so stylish was the look that an après-ski shot of a girlfriend wearing his jacket ended up in *Harper's Bazaar*. He was then besieged with requests – not for dates, but by women wanting that jacket. He had only lent her his as she was getting chilly. What a gentleman. Emilio Pucci then became the first person in his family to work for over a thousand years. How modern. Soon his brightly coloured swirls and sportswear had taken off, and an empire was created. When he opened a store in Capri in 1949 his capri pants took the world by storm.

Mr Pucci died in 1992 and his son took over the business, but died in a car accident in 2000. Later that year his daughter sold the company to LVMH, and Julio Espada was given the design reins. Christian Lacroix became the design director in 2002 and most recently British designer Matthew Williamson took on the boho brand and debuted his designs on the Milan runway for Pucci in February 2006. Leave the house in big prints and bold colours to celebrate innovation today.

22nd November

In 1963 the thirty-fifth President of the United States, John F. Kennedy, was assassinated. Watch Kevin Costner in the 1991 Oliver Stone film *JFK*, or read on.

Jacqueline Kennedy Onassis

Though she didn't seek fame, for a time Jacqueline Kennedy was the most influential and photographed woman in the world. Her life story reads like a Shakespearian tragedy, but she carried herself with such dignity and poise throughout that she commanded respect. She was a powerful player in American politics, a journalist turned iconic First Lady, but above all else she was a devoted mother. She was born into a privileged family and married a dashing president. Did she have it all? Well, her wealth couldn't guarantee her happiness, or protect her from what was to come. If your love life is getting you down, your family are driving you up the wall, stop worrying about how to juggle everything, take a deep breath, and hold your head high. Think determination and dedication: think Jacqueline Kennedy.

Her life and times

Jacqueline Lee Bouvier was born on 28 July 1929 in Southampton, New York. Born to John 'Black Jack' Vernou Bouvier III and Janet N. Lee, she was half Irish and raised a Catholic, the eldest of their two daughters. Her father was a stockbroker who had a reputation as a notorious womanizer and gambler, which led to a bitter divorce in 1942. Later that year her mother remarried the wealthy Hugh D. Auchincloss Jr. But despite the anguish her father caused, Jackie always doted on her daddy and her later romantic choices reflected her love of a rogue. Learn from this tale.

In 1947 Jacqueline (as she preferred to be called) started her college education at Vassar, New York, and was named 'Debutante of the Year'. She studied at the Sorbonne in Paris before returning to graduate from George Washington University in Washington DC with a degree in French

literature. In 1951 she was a finalist in the *Vogue* 'Prix de Paris' writing contest. Her first job as 'The Inquiring Camera Girl' at the *Washington Times Herald* led her to interview, amongst others, the dashing young Massachusetts senator, John F. Kennedy. The Kennedy charm was legendary – but this time he'd met his match, and pretty soon her previous engagement was called off. While she was in England covering the coronation of Elizabeth II, JFK proposed over the phone. They married on 12 September 1953, in Newport, Rhode Island and it was the society wedding of the year. The only cloud on her dream day was that her father failed to sober up in time, leaving her stepfather to walk her up the aisle.

She was soon to have a new father figure in her life. By marrying JFK she had become part of the formidable Kennedy clan. John Fitzgerald Kennedy, known as 'Jack' to his family, was the second of Rose and Joseph Kennedy Senior's nine children. This generation of Kennedys would become one of America's most famous political families. Her new father-in-law quickly spotted Jackie as a great PR asset for JFK's political aspirations, and she became their secret weapon – brilliantly capturing the hearts and minds of the American public.

The demands of such a high-profile marriage and all the political campaigning meant that Jackie's own ambitions to become a novelist had to be put on hold. In 1960 democrat JFK (narrowly) beat Richard Nixon in the Presidential Election, and became the thirty-fifth President of the United States of America.

Between tramping the campaign trail and becoming First Lady, Jackie gave birth to their first daughter, Arabella, who was tragically stillborn. But on 27 November 1957 their daughter Caroline was born, and their son John Jr arrived on 25 November 1960, neatly between JFK's election and inauguration ceremony. Jackie set about turning the White House into a home for her young family, charming the nation, claiming that she was 'wife and mother first, then First Lady'. With her great eye for style she spearheaded the renovation of the White House, which gave American heritage a new sense of purpose and elegance and it also became one of her proudest lasting legacies.

Being in the spotlight, it was only natural she would worry about what to wear. Fashion designer Oleg Cassini (who at one time was engaged to Grace Kelly) was appointed to look after her wardrobe. While she was aware of her style-setting status, she was wary of seeming too preoccupied by superficial matters. Though the best designs were coming from Europe, Jackie was determined to embody the American Dream and wear home-grown talent . . . as long as it was unique. 'I want all mine to be originals,' she told Cassini; most specifically there were to be 'no fat little women hopping around in the same dress'.

To the world, Jackie and JFK seemed like the perfect family, and thanks to her, they (almost) were. On 14 February 1962 Mrs Kennedy took CBS, and America, on a tour of the White House to show the work she had done. When asked what her role was, she replied with typical modesty, 'I take care of the President.' (Quite a task.) She also famously remarked that 'if you bungle raising your child I don't think whatever else you do well matters very much'. Maintaining appearances required a certain determination. They hid JFK's crippling back and health problems from the world and their children, as well as the real whammy that, like Jackie's father, he was an absolute flirt and philanderer. While the world marvelled at their united front, she turned a blind eye to his numerous affairs, including those with Marilyn Monroe, Kim Novak, Jayne Mansfield, Angie Dickinson and a succession of secretaries.

When Kennedy went on state visits, it was often Jackie who was the star attraction – she spoke French, Spanish and Italian fluently. She made the biggest impression in France: not only had she studied in Paris but she was very proud of her French ancestry. Her husband quipped, 'I am the man who accompanied Jacqueline Kennedy to Paris, and I have enjoyed it.'

By 1963, the strain of perpetuating the myth was evident. When her son Patrick Bouvier Kennedy was born, and died, in August she hid from the public eye. Post-natal depression and grief overwhelmed her, but there was also hope as it brought her closer to her husband than she'd been in years. In November she agreed to join him as the campaign trail hit Texas.

22 November 1963 was a day that played in slow motion. Air Force One landed at Love Field, Dallas and Jackie came off the plane wearing

a pink tweed Chanel suit, with matching pillbox hat. She sat next to her husband in the open motorcade. 'Take your glasses off, Jackie,' JFK told her as they waved at voters and drove past the Depository Building. They were the last words he ever said to her. Moments later Lee Harvey Oswald fired two shots and JFK was dead. Everything was captured on Abraham Zapruder's home video. JFK died, his head blown off, in Jackie's arms in the back of the car. Chaos ensued.

Jackie managed his death with style and dignity, protecting his reputation and ensuring his legacy. Lyndon Johnson was sworn in on the same plane that carried her husband's coffin, and Jackie stood beside him, defiantly wearing her blood-spattered Chanel suit. While others discussed conspiracy theories, Jackie took control and led the nation in mourning. She wanted his funeral to emulate that of the assassinated President Abraham Lincoln. Over 250,000 people queued to pay their respects while the coffin was lying in state, and 300,000 lined the streets for the funeral. Jackie broke with protocol and insisted on walking behind the coffin, in front of all the international heads of states, and lit his eternal flame. 'Jacqueline Kennedy has given the American people . . . one thing they have always lacked . . . majesty,' wrote the *Evening Standard*. The image of their son John Jr, on his third birthday, saluting his father's coffin is unforgettable. In an interview with *Life* magazine she spoke of her husband's 1,000-day administration: 'He is a legend when he would have preferred to be a man. Don't let it be forgot that for one brief shining moment there was Camelot.' The legend was born.

After his death, as much as the young widow wanted to disappear the nation wouldn't let her; they wanted to know every detail of her life. She relied more and more on her brother-in-law, Bobby, and they began an affair. He was close to becoming president but then, with victory in sight, on 5 June 1968 he too was assassinated. Out of his huge family it was only Jackie who had the strength to turn off his life support machine, but without him Jackie was terrified. 'They're killing Kennedys,' she is said to have remarked, and she needed to get the prime targets – her children – out of the spotlight. (Tragically the Kennedy Curse was to hit again, when on 16 July 1999 her son's plane crashed, killing him, his wife and his sister-in-law.)

On 20 October 1968 she married billionaire Aristotle Onassis, a Greek shipping tycoon twenty-three years her senior. They seemed an unlikely couple, yet he broke off his engagement to opera diva Maria Callas to be with her, and had the means to offer her the protection and security that she craved. She, in return, was his prized catch. But soon things were strained, and they were in the process of divorcing when, in 1975, he died. Due to a prenuptial agreement she received only $27,000,000 of his estate, admittedly not bad by anyone else's standards, but only a fraction of his fortune.

It was now time for another reinvention – behind her signature bug-eyed shades she had evolved from First Wife to trophy wife and now it was time for Career Jackie to walk again. With her children at college she returned to her passion for books and became an editor, first at Viking and then at Doubleday.

Despite her desire for anonymity, ironically, just like Marilyn, she was immortalized in one of Warhol's screen prints, and has remained a source of fascination and style inspiration. Read *The Secret Letters of Marilyn Monroe and Jacqueline Kennedy* by Wendy Leigh for a fictional yet fascinating insight into how the two women might have corresponded.

Jacqueline Kennedy died on 19 May 1994 of lymphoma cancer, with her partner Maurice Tempelsman at her side. At her funeral her son said that three of her greatest attributes were 'love of words, the bonds of home and family, and her spirit of adventure'. She was laid to rest alongside her assassinated husband at Arlington State Cemetery.

Jackie-isms

'I want to live my life, not record it.'

'A newspaper reported that I spent $30,000 a year buying Paris clothes and that women hate me for it. I couldn't spend that much unless I wore sable underwear.'

'I don't understand it. Jack will spend any amount of money to buy votes but he balks at investing a thousand dollars in a beautiful painting.'

'The first time you marry for love, the second for money, and the third for companionship.'

'I don't think there are any men who are faithful to their wives.'

How to write a letter

Mrs Kennedy was a great letter writer, as any lady with lovely manners should be. But do you know how?

If it is a formal letter, the etiquette of 'how to start' and 'how to finish' is a complex hive of dos and don'ts. For the *absolute* authority on this you should look at Debrett's *Etiquette and Modern Manners* which will answer every question and query, but you only need to really nit-pick when writing to someone as high up as the Queen. For most other occasions clear presentation and good layout will help you get away with any innocent slips; just try to find the right tone to suit your reader.

Correct letter-openers include:

'Dear Sir' or 'Dear Madam' is correct if you know the sex but are not sure of the name of the person you are writing to.

'Dear Sir/Madam' for when you have absolutely no idea whom you need this to get to, but you still have to be polite.

'Dear' followed by Mr or Mrs, and their surname, is the correct 'I know who you are' opening, but increasingly first names are acceptable, although a *lot* less formal.

'Dearest', 'Darling' and so on depend on your devotion and flirtatiousness, and of course, there's 'to whom it may concern'.

The contents

Even if it's a personal note you still need to write on a nice, unscrumpled, clean piece of unlined paper. No tea stains or ink splodges – you are not in prep school. Tear splashes can be charming and add to the emotion, but are *only* permissible if the writing is still legible. In a personal note content is not prescribed, it can simply flow in a chatty way. But be sure that for every question you ask them, you tell them a piece of your news. Don't overwhelm the reader with a thousand questions and no news of what you are up to – presumably you are not setting a quiz. Similarly, don't just talk about yourself and forget why you have gone to the effort of writing to them. Surely you are hoping to hear a bit of news in return? Ask them a few questions. No one likes a me-me-me letter. Sign off with love and kisses.

When things are slightly more formal, such as invitations to weddings or events that require an RSVP, a small card (with stamped return-address envelope) is often enclosed. These usually require nothing more than a tick or a cross, Yes/No. But you *must* reply promptly as hosts do need to know numbers to cater accordingly. Use your logic: if an invite is fancy enough to warrant an RSVP it is usually worth going to, and how kind that you were invited.

The handwritten RSVP

If there is no simple 'tick yes or no' option, or indeed no printed card, you must reply in the proper way. There are rules. As with emails or conversations, you should echo the style or wording of the invitation. (Jane Austen was also a fanatical letter writer – see page 14.)

For example:

'Miss Elizabeth Bennet thanks Miss Caroline Bingley for her kind invitation to visit her at home on January 4 at three o'clock in the afternoon, and has the pleasure of accepting.'

Make sure you state your name, their name, where, when, and that you can come. Alternatively, when replying in the negative, you could write:

'Miss Elizabeth Bennet very much regrets that she is unable to accept the kind invitation [as she has a prior engagement/will be out of town].'

N.B. The bracketed information is extra; decide if you really need any other details. Waffle and chitchat should be cut here – just say what has to be said in a chic little card. No further explanation is needed; you don't have to justify yourself.

And to close

For a really good finale let's go back to Beethoven: he ended his infamous *Immortal Beloved* letter thus:

> What tearful longings for you – you – you – my life – my all – farewell.
> Oh continue to love me – never misjudge the most faithful heart of your beloved.
> Ever thine
> Ever mine
> Ever ours

Crumbs. Might be a bit much for a letter to the tax inspector. Why not try the following instead:

'Yours sincerely' is the correct businesslike sign-off for those whom you know, but whom you can't be *too* casual with (say, the bank manager). Be professional yet respectful. This is also the coldest sign-off for those colleagues and so on you loathe but have to correspond with.

'Yours faithfully' (note only the first word has a capital letter, a common mistake) is for formal business letters – the ones that start 'Dear Sir or Madam'. It is for those people you haven't met but to whom you wish to convey a slightly warmer tone than 'sincerely'.

'Yours truly' is slightly out of date but good for old school teachers or distant aunties.

'Yours' is the neutral ending – neither too formal nor too affectionate – just right. Leave them to interpret the level of affection.

'Kind regards' is the more friendly, up-to-date version of the 'Yours truly' option, and can be adapted to 'Kindest Regards', which is a mere whisker away from 'Love from', but slightly more grown-up.

One lovely lady letter writer who would have adhered to all these rules was born on 22 November 1819. We know 'her' as George Eliot (her real name was Mary Ann Evans), though she explained she chose this name because 'George was Mr Lewes's Christian name [her partner] and Eliot was a good mouth-filling, easily pronounced word'.

Eliot was her adopted pseudonym for works 'far too good to be written by a woman' (a popular opinion of the day, most certainly not today) – including *Adam Bede*, 1859; *Mill on the Floss*, 1860; *Silas Marner*, 1861; *Middlemarch*, 1871–72 and *Daniel Deronda*, 1876.

'Our vanities differ as our noses do . . .' she writes in *Middlemarch*. Which of her books have you got your nose in today? You can always curl up with the audio version and drift away from modern-day and man-made problems and go back to rural England.

23rd November

Stay in the wilds of the countryside as Thomas Hardy's classic *Far from the Madding Crowd* was published in 1875. Set in the nineteenth century, this is the love story of Bathsheba Everdine and Gabriel Oak, and how opposites attract.

It opens with one of literature's most beautiful descriptions of a face and the power of a smile.

> When Farmer Oak smiled, the corners of his mouth spread till they were within an unimportant distance of his ears, his eyes were reduced to chinks, and diverging wrinkles appeared round them, extending upon his countenance like the rays in a rudimentary sketch of the rising sun.

How to celebrate Thanksgiving

If you are an American yourself, are married to, dating or living with one, or even have an American friend, it's a good day to celebrate, or at least content yourself with knowing *why* they are on vacation today.

The first Thanksgiving feast took place back in 1621, when the English colonists and the Wampanoag Indians joined together to celebrate all they had grown. In 1863 President Lincoln declared it a public holiday, giving spirits a lift during the civil war that was raging at the time.

Thanksgiving is celebrated on the fourth Thursday of November in America and the second Monday of October in Canada. The nearest celebration we have in England is in the first few weeks of the autumn school term when, with an abundance of crêpe paper and tinned foods, Harvest Festival is celebrated.

The turkey

The Thanksgiving meal itself is essentially very similar to English Christmas fare – so this could be your dummy run if you like. You basically need a turkey, a family, a brewing quarrel and a large table. For a breakdown (rather than cause a breakdown) visit: *www.e-gourmet-recipes.com/how-to-cook-a-thanksgiving-turkey-gourmet-turkey-dinner* which promises to make you feel like the *'best goddamn cook or gourmet cook that there ever was'*. Just reading the instructions, not undercooking your fowl and keeping the peace will be enough. For advice on uninvited guests, cooking with a hangover, gift giving or enjoying thanksgiving on your own (what a relief that would be), try Amy Sedaris's delightfully unconventional look at entertaining, *I Like You: Hospitality Under the Influence*.

Top billing should go to the turkey – today is sometimes referred to as Turkey Day. The bird should be accompanied by mashed potatoes, vegetables, sweet potatoes, cranberry sauce and gravy. It was actually first brought to Britain in 1526 by a Yorkshireman, William Strickland, who acquired six birds from American Indian traders on his travels, and sold them for a tuppence each in Bristol.

You won't need to catch your bird, just cook it, unless all this turns you into a staunch vegetarian. But do not despair – there are loads of sites to help you with the challenge of the big meal, such as *www.turkeyhelp.com* and *www.britishturkey.co.uk*.

The most crucial thing with turkey is making sure that you neither overcook nor undercook it – it has to be just right. When roasting your turkey the British Turkey's website suggests that you cook it upside down so that the juices from the back and legs run down to the breast and keep it moist. But be warned, if you do this the cooking time will be reduced, so keep an eye on it thirty minutes before you calculated for it to be done.

Cooking tips

Order in at least four to six weeks in advance – fresh birds are available as well as ready-basted, free range and frozen.

Know how many are coming to dinner and buy a bird big enough. Follow this turkey chart:

Size of Bird (kg)	Portions
1.5 – 1.75	3 – 4
3 – 3.5	7 – 9
4 – 4.5	10 – 12
4.5 – 5	12 – 15
5.5 – 6.5	16 – 18
6.75 – 7.75	20 – 24

- If frozen, allow enough time for it to thaw. If the bird is under 4 kg you should allow roughly 20 minutes per kg and then add 70 minutes. If the bird is over 4 kg allow 20 minutes per kg and then add 90 minutes.

- Weigh the turkey after stuffing to calculate the cooking time and remember that oven temperatures vary. Fan ovens are faster than gas. If the bird is 2–4 kgs, allow 3–3.5 hours. If the bird is 4–6 kgs, allow 3.5 to 4.5 hours.

- On big holiday days remember the power may be reduced slightly due to a serge on the grid (as everyone will be cooking at the same time).

- Constantly opening and shutting the oven door will reduce the heat.

- Allow the turkey to stand for 15–20 minutes before carving.

The pumpkin pie

You are not home and dry and free from the kitchen yet and unfortunately there will be no using the pumpkin you hollowed out for Halloween. That ghoulish deterrent will be well and truly rancid by now, with no chance of a starring role in your Thanksgiving feast.

You can of course buy canned pumpkin (as well as the entire pie or an alternative) but purists argue that home-made fresh pumpkin pie is the essential accessory of the Thanksgiving feast. You can download a good recipe from: *www.everydaycook.com/recipebox/pies/pumpkinpie*.

Family time

Above all it's not about the food: Thanksgiving is about family.

Great families that you could imagine celebrating Thanksgiving with, or be thankful that you're not with, include:

The Simpsons
The Partridge Family
The Brady Bunch
The Kennedys
The Osbournes

Who would you choose? Or would you head to Wisteria Lane and knock on the door of one of the *Desperate Housewives*?

America's unofficial First Family are the Simpsons. Created by Matt Groening, their twentieth anniversary was marked with the first movie-length version of the cartoon in 2007. They were first seen in America on 19 April 1987, as part of the *Tracey Ullman Show* (she cannily took shares in the cartoon). By December 1989 it earned its own solo slot in the US, and in the UK remained the 'best reason to get satellite' until it finally came on terrestrial BBC, airing on Saturday, 23 November 1996, five years after 'Do The Bartman' went to number one in January 1991. It is now the longest running animated series on television, even beating *The Flintstones*.

Special guests on the show have included:

Larry King
Danny DeVito
Ringo Starr
Aerosmith
Paul and Linda McCartney
Donald Sutherland
Kirk Douglas
Jay Leno
U2
Bob Hope
Elizabeth Taylor
Bette Midler
Meryl Streep (as Bart's girlfriend Jessica Lovejoy)

Michelle Pfeiffer's Mindy Simmons caused Homer a lot of stress and nearly seduced him away from Marge altogether in the *Last Temptation of Homer* – but even Michelle Pfeiffer couldn't compete with his blue-rinse missus and break up the Simpson family. There is a god.

26th November

'I think this is the beginning of a beautiful friendship.' *Casablanca* premiered at the Hollywood Theatre, New York in 1942.

Set in World War II, the film was based on the Murray Burnett and Joan Alison play *Everyone Comes to Rick's* which was sold to Hollywood for $20,000, the most an un-produced play had ever cost at the time. The history-making gamble paid off and the film went on to win three Academy Awards, was voted second greatest movie of all time, and crowned Bogart as America's number one screen legend. See page 358 for more Bogart moments.

Watch the original today – or Steven Soderbergh's homage to *Casablanca*, the 2007 film *The Good German*, which uses the same technology and sepia shades as the original (there was an outcry when a Technicolor version of

Casablanca was shown – no, no) with Cate Blanchet, George Clooney and Tobey Maguire as the leads.

Today, 26th November, was also the day when, in 1943, a new toy, the Slinky, first appeared. Like Pucci, another example of how some of the best career moves happen accidentally.

It was created when naval engineer Richard James was trying to develop a battleship monitor – as you do. He was mid-experiment with some tension springs when one fell to the floor and began to 'walk' by itself. A eureka moment occurred and, as the springs kept moving, the idea for the toy was hatched.

James introduced the Slinky at Gimbel's Department Store in Philadelphia, Pennsylvania in 1945. He persuaded all his friends to turn up to bolster the crowd, but he needn't have worried – within ninety minutes four hundred had been sold, and over quarter of a billion have now been sold worldwide.

Ideas can come from anywhere and anything – you just have to be ready to run with them.

29th November

C.S. Lewis was born in 1898. Irish author and scholar Clive Staples Lewis taught at Magdalen College Oxford, where he was friends with J.R.R. Tolkein before becoming the first Professor of Medieval and Renaissance Literature at Magdalene College, Cambridge. Lewis is remembered most for his *Chronicles of Narnia* – the seven novels about children who went through wardrobes and pictures to escape war-torn England and encountered an enchanted other world.

His life was turned into the 1993 weepy film *Shadowlands* starring Anthony Hopkins. Watch this today, dip into Narnia or see what you can find hidden in the back of your wardrobe.

 *Foot Note*

The trainer

There are all sorts of styles, and all sorts of names – the running shoe, the gym shoe, the sneaker, the sports shoe and the trusty plimsoll. In addition to this there are all sorts of brands that promise to deliver (the best control and support, rather than first place and instant fitness; curses). There's Adidas, Reebok, Puma and, just as Hoover monopolized the vacuum-cleaning world, Nike dominate those who want to get fit and physical (and also bought Converse in 2003, so that means you're part of the Nike empire when hanging out in baseball boots, like the kids at Rydell High). No trip to New York is complete without a bend round the corner of Tiffany's iconic Fifth Avenue store into Niketown, whether you are competing in the New York marathon or not. Believe it or not, there was life before Nike; the company was only founded in 1964.

The first soft plimsoll was invented back in 1893 for boaters so that they didn't scuff the carefully waxed deck with their leather dress shoes. The term 'sneaker' was coined in 1916 by the US rubber company Keds to describe just how quiet an entrance the soles could make – they allowed you to 'sneak' up on someone. In Britain the name is far more functional and purpose-led – it became known as a trainer because, frankly, it was a trainer. It didn't sound like fun because getting fit wasn't meant to be fun in those days.

Back to Nike (as this is most likely to be in your wardrobe): this name is derived from the Greek goddess of victory – perfect for your competitive streak; you've got to be in it to win it. The legendary 'swoosh' or trademark tick first appeared in 1971 and was designed by graphic design student Carolyn Davison when she was at Portland University. She was paid a puny $35 for it. Yup, you read right. She did later receive Nike stock and a gold 'swoosh' ring for creating one of the most recognized logos of the modern day. John McEnroe, Michael Jordan, Maria

Sharapova and Anna Kournikova are amongst the iconic names in the celebrity Nike endorsement folder. Adidas are their main rivals and count Beckham and Jonny Wilkinson among their 'faces'. Adidas have also collaborated with designers such as Stella McCartney and Yohji Yamamoto, and had Run DMC and pretty much every pop and hip hop artist adopting the white tops, high tops and three-striped brand as their uniform. It just depends which team you want to be on. As Nike told the world in 1988, 'Just Do It'. If you're going to get physical, just do it in style.

December

'God bless us every one!'
A Christmas Carol by Charles Dickens

John Galliano from near and far

Wish you were here – oh, how I wish you were! As much as I love to travel – and to see all the corners of the world from Argentina to Asia, the southern hemisphere to the far reaches of the North – sometimes there really is no place like home! There is so much to see, so much to learn. Travel is so inspiring: the geishas in Japan, standing in Red Square in the snow, the elephant in Rajasthan with his pink-painted toenails, the bull fights and flamenco dancers in the houses of Seville. Be sure to see the world and experience every adventure and corner of the globe – but never neglect what you have when you come home, because this is where the heart is.

Collect all you have seen, all you have learnt and create your own kingdom, your own Utopia where your imagination can reign supreme. As the nights draw in, let memories of touring the Forbidden City, of losing your luggage in long haul and it adding to the adventure, of sunsets in Hawaii with sand inbetween your toes, and of the bright lights and nightlife of the Big Apple warm and spice up your evening. Let the raw hides and tales from the Gauchos hang in your kitchen, the silks of India and the East give colour, as well as a different culture, to your bedroom and the jacket you found in the car-boot sale in Prague, or that teapot from the beach bric-a-brac market sit in pride of place. Mix your favourite childhood curiosities – games, gramophones and photo frames – with elements from your adventuring, such as antiques found in seafront markets in St Tropez or Alfie's in London, textiles from Virginia, tea from Fortnum's, and shells from the Maldives and a weekend break in Brittany. Let them collide to create a collage of your life.

Travel through books, films, friends and memories. Open your mind to new places, new sites, new lands and you will find magic.

Get your passport stamped at least twice a year and take adventures

near and far and then you really will be my 'girl for all seasons', as Sinatra sang – the best is [always] yet to come – so find it!

Love, *John*

1st December

Today is United Nations World AIDS Day. Wear a red ribbon and visit: *www.worldaidsday.org*.

Today also marks the start of Advent and the opening of the first window of your advent calendar. The word comes from the Latin word 'coming', and marks the approaching feast of Christmas, parties and time off – yay. Begin the countdown.

2nd December

'*La Divina*', opera singer Maria Callas, was born in 1923, and fashion designer Gianni Versace was born today in 1946. Two fabulously high-octane icons to end the year in style with and encourage you to indulge in all excesses.

After all, you will need all your creative juices flowing this month as this is the time of year when your social calendar should/will be bulging. In addition to your present-shopping there are parties to be seen at, as well as to organize. Work on your stage presence (we're not talking panto dame here); mesmerize your audience with what you wear, what you say and what you do. Do the diva – 'tis the season.

Gianni Versace was famed for his neo-classical ornate prints, the gold medusa-head logo, and for combining the glamour of Italian Renaissance luxury and excess with a tribe of A-list devotees. It was Versace who created 'the supermodel' by agreeing to pay the girls astronomical fees, which led to remarks such as: 'We don't do *Vogue* – we *are Vogue*.' And of course there is Linda Evangelista's legendary comment that has been wildly misquoted. What she actually said – 'We have this expression, Christy [Turlington] and I: We don't wake up for less than $10,000 a day,' – is often changed to, 'I don't get out of bed for less than $10,000.' But look at her in front of the camera – an actress with no script, the clothes her sole prop and only one pose to sell the dream for the season. Versace, like others, clearly thought she was worth it, to misquote L'Oréal. Evangelista told American *Vogue* in 2001, 'I feel like these words are going to be engraved on my tombstone. It was brought up every time I did an interview . . . Do I regret it? I used to regret. Not any more. I don't regret anything any more . . .' Thanks to the supermodels and beautiful people the Versace empire grew and grew.

Tragically on 16 July 1997 Gianni Versace was murdered outside his Miami home. Despite the loss of its founder the label continues with his sister and muse, Donatella Versace, as the head of design, and brother Santo Versace the CEO, keeping his sexy spirit and the family business alive.

Maria Callas would have liked Versace – glamorous, talented, famous, and the ultimate label for the red-carpet diva. 'Versace' says success as well as sexiness, and he would have loved her too.

Maria Anna Sophie Cecilia Kalogeropoulos was born in New York. Her Greek parents had emigrated and squished the family name to Callas so people could pronounce it. Her great musical career did not take flight until 1937, when, aged fourteen, she returned to Athens with her mother, following her parents' separation. In 1942 she made her stage debut in the leading role of *Tosca*. She shone and got rave reviews: '[Callas is] one of those God-given talents that one can only marvel at,' wrote critic Alexandra Lalaouni.

With this success she left Greece and returned to America but soon was touring Italy, opera's homeland, where she met and married wealthy industrialist Giovanni Battista Meneghini who was also her manager. She remained devoted to him until she met her soulmate Aristotle Onassis.

Between 1953 and 1954, touring mixed with vigorous dieting meant that she lost around eighty pounds and transformed into the glamourpuss people remember. Some argue this affected her voice but wherever she sang she was always a sensation, and now she looked as good as she sounded, and sexy suited the diva. Callas didn't have three voices; 'she has three hundred,' a conductor commented and, as well as her range and versatility, she was a great actress who could bring the characters to life. All this was fabulous, but it has to be said that offstage she was an A-grade bitch – and enjoyed a well-covered rivalry with Italian soprano Renata Tebaldi. Callas was quoted as saying that to compare them was like comparing 'champagne to cognac', to which a bystander added, 'No, Coca-Cola,' and for years Callas was considered even ruder than she'd intended (though she rarely corrected the slip). But her greatest ever rival was not found on the stage but in her private life when the great love of her life, Onassis, dumped the diva for Jackie Kennedy. 'First I lost my voice, then I lost my figure and then I lost Onassis,' she said bitterly.

Not only did the diva lose her man, but she also lost her fight, and after his death became a recluse. She died in 1977, yet her recordings remain on the bestseller lists. As Leonard Bernstein said, 'She was pure electricity,' while Franco Zeffirelli sighed, 'Maria is always a miracle.'

5th December

This is the day to download K626, the *Requiem*, because on this date in 1792 Mozart died. Eerily this was to be Mozart's last composition and had to be completed after his death by Joseph Eybler, before it was finally finished by another of his pupils, Franz Xaver Süssmayr. Contrary to legend, and the film *Amadeus*, the commission was not anonymous, a scary premonition or written by his rival composer Salieri. Mozart's final requiem was paid for by Count Walsegg to commemorate his wife's death. Walsegg had intended to pass it off as his own work, with Mozart merely employed as the 'ghost writer', but due to the untimely death of the composer the score was not delivered to Walsegg until December 1793 and was finally performed in a memorial for the count's wife on 14 December 1793. However, it will always be thought of as the composer's own requiem.

Also on this day, Walt Disney was born in 1901. He must be the (unofficial) patron saint of cartoons and modern-day folklore. After working for the Red Cross during the First World War Disney returned to America and headed straight to Hollywood with twenty dollars in his pocket. His cartoon *Alice Comedies* was a huge success, and Disney became a recognized name. In 1932 he produced the first colour cartoon, *Flowers and Trees*, and in 1937 released *The Old Mill*, which was the first short to use multi-plane camera action, i.e. a cartoon using film angles. It was as clever as conventional film-making, except that the stars in this were two-dimensional and didn't have diva tantrums – unless scripted to do so.

'I only hope we don't lose sight of one thing – it all began with a mouse,' Disney said of his greatest creation. Mickey Mouse was 'born' on 19 November 1928, making his on-screen debut in *Steamboat Willie*. Along with his own original characters, Disney was a great fan of the fairy tale and, on 21 December 1937, Disney released the first full-length animated feature film *Snow White and the Seven Dwarfs*. The cartoon cost a staggering $1,499,000 – a big amount today; an obscene one at the height of the Depression – yet it goes down as one of the greatest triumphs of motion picture history (phew). Walt Disney Studios went on to complete other animated films including: *Pinocchio, Fantasia, Cinderella, Dumbo, Sleeping Beauty* and *Bambi*. But don't think about settling down to watch any of these on DVD without a box of tissues.

Muse of the Month

Cinderella

Just like the beautiful girl next door, the fairy-tale princess, the ultimate heroine, we've all grown up 'knowing' Cinderella. As well as being a regular at pantomime time, she has been the basis for Gioacchino Rossini's opera *La Cenerentola*, Johann Strauss II's ballet *Aschenbrödel* and *Cinderella* by Sergei Prokofiev. Along with Shakespeare's most popular works, or Bram Stoker's *Dracula*, *Cinderella* is one of the most frequently adapted of all fairy stories.

Cinderella is the heroine that no one tires of hearing about, and no one tires of seeing – the message is clear: good shoes equal love and happiness.

In 1899 Georges Méliès made the first film version to hit the big screen. Every telling has its own take, shoe fixation, and happily ever after. In 1957 the great musical duo Rodgers and Hammerstein gave the story their spin in a version for television; the first recording starred Julie Andrews, the second Lesley Ann Warren and the third appeared in 1997 with Brandy in the title role, Whitney Houston as the wicked stepmother, and Whoopi Goldberg as the fairy godmother. Another musical version worth watching, particularly if you're planning to relandscape your garden with roses and swings, is the 1976 *The Slipper and the Rose*, starring demure Gemma Craven and dashing Richard Chamberlain in the leads. In 1998 *Ever After* hit the big screen, starring Drew Barrymore in Ferragamo shoes and butterfly wings and still we hadn't had enough. In 2004's *A Cinderella Story*, Hilary Duff played the lead, the same year as Disney's *Ella Enchanted* gave the role to Anne Hathaway.

As the year comes to an end it's time to work out your own 'Happy Ending'. Don't let bad situations (jobs, romances, quarrels, etc.) simmer and messily follow you into a new year. Though we might not all have

a[n obvious] fairy godmother, there *are* guardian angels out there, with or without wands and wings. Cinderella's goodness, kindness and grace will never be out of fashion so take her as your lead and cut down on your cursing, and quit smoking, chewing gum and other unprincess-like habits. Don't roll your eyes. Cinderella should also inspire your romantic side as well as encourage you to polish your manners and housekeeping skills. Indeed, think 'Cinderella' and you will have your outfit sorted for the Christmas party in record time, make a killer entrance and, who knows, you might even find the whole handsome prince thing works out too.

Who says there's no such thing as magic?

Her life and times

There are an estimated 3,000 versions of this tale, with at least one in every culture, so the precise origin of this classic has been lost in the telling. The first known version is thought to trace back to Ancient Egypt and Ancient China. Later, around AD 850, it was published in *The Miscellaneous Record of You Yang* – 酉阳杂俎 – by Tuan Ch'eng-Shih, where the heroine is known as Yeh Shen and the benefits and beauty of tiny feet are highlighted. Across the globe she has many different names, including the Burnt Face Girl, according to the Native American Mik'maq legend. In England she was originally known as Tattercoats.

Today, however, the most widely recognized version is the story told by French writer Charles Perrault in 1697 (see page 186). Perrault was the first to christen our heroine Cinderella as he reworked the 1634 tale *La Gatta Cenerentola* by Giambattista Basile. In 1812 the Brothers Grimm gave it their edit, called her 'Aschenputtel', and gave a gruesome demise to the stepsisters. But Perrault's far kinder and more wholesome version is the one that survives as the definitive romantic account, and was the basis for Walt Disney's animated feature film. Disney's *Cinderella* was released on 15 February 1950. The quest to find the girl to voice the title role was something of a Cinderella story of its own. Ilene Woods beat 309 girls for the part, although they hadn't been told what they were auditioning for. As Cinderella sang, 'A dream is a wish your heart

makes when you're fast asleep,' and with her as your heroine, a 'happily ever after' is practically guaranteed.

But back to Cinderella . . .

Once upon a time, as all proper fairy stories begin, our heroine was born with all the best attributes and a loving family. If she weren't so nice you too would have hated her. But she didn't always have it easy, no, not at all. Her mother died when she was very little and sadly she would go and put flowers on her grave every day. Her heartbroken father couldn't bear to see his daughter growing up without a mother so he remarried, way too soon – as they say, marry in haste, repent at leisure; but at least Cinderella had a mother figure once more.

All accounts agree that this second wife was a horror and, thanks to her, the stereotype of the wicked stepmother has stuck. In addition to her new stepmother, our heroine had to contend with two stepsisters who turned out to be as rotten as their mother. The three were spoilt and cruel and so jealous of the girl's beauty that when her father died (or, in other versions, was simply overpowered) they forced her to become a servant –and nicknamed her 'Cinderella' as she slept by the fireplace in the kitchen and was always covered in cinders. They forced her to do all the chores: the cooking, the cleaning, the washing – you name it, she did it, and without complaint.

All versions wax lyrical about her kindness and beauty and the impossible situation she was bullied into – something no modern-day heroine would stand for. But fear not: this is no Greek tragedy; this is one story with justice and a happy ending.

The king and queen of the land decided to host a ball to find their dashing bachelor son and heir a bride, and all the eligible ladies in the land were invited. There was much excitement: who doesn't want to end up with a handsome prince? Plus this one turned out to be a real catch and was kind as well as handsome, so all the maidens went into meltdown getting their look together. Cinderella was even busier than usual as she had to sew and mend gowns for her stepmother and the two wretched sisters, who needed more than a pretty frock to catch his eye. (In some versions of the tale there are three balls to attend, but finding a gown for one occasion is surely stress enough.) As the invite was for 'every maiden in the land', Cinderella tried to reason with her stepmother that technically this included her too, but she had nothing to wear except rags, and no time to make anything, so she was left at home as they went off to the social event of the year.

At this point accounts vary as to how Cinderella's transformation took place. In some versions the clothes appear on a tree beside her mother's grave, but, thanks to Perrault and Disney, the more popular opinion is that her fairy godmother turned up (the puff of smoke an optional extra), a pumpkin became a coach, mice transformed into white horses, and Cinderella's rags became the most glorious gown that no one else had and was simply not available in stores. Wow! So she went to the ball looking so radiant and sensational that no one recognized her.

Now to the feet. The legendary glass slippers she wore, which technically it would have been impossible to dance the night away in, are now in fact thought to have been a poetic typo. The fantasy footwear angle in Perrault's original French said she wore a fur slipper (*pantoufle de vair*) – a colloquial word for fur with the same pronunciation as *verre*, meaning *glass* – and here it is thought the slip was made and the glass slipper (*pantoufle de verre*) appeared. But let's face it, when has looking good honestly ever involved comfort?

Cinderella spent the whole evening dancing with the prince. It was love at first sight. But there was a catch (isn't there always?) She had to leave at midnight, before the magic ran out. On the stroke of midnight, as the clock started to chime, she made a run for the door. Here is another tip you can take from Cinderella – leaving early makes you seem far more mysterious and enchanting and will make a much bigger impact: always leave them wanting more. The love-struck prince chased after her but Cinderella had a head start and vanished. All that was left of his dream date was one of her glass heels on the staircase. (As you will know it is nearly impossible to run in heels, let alone ones made of glass. Ditching them was one option, but if they had been Manolos better to have pulled them off and made a dash carrying them.)

The prince was heartbroken, and rather than going back to the party and trying his luck with another lovely he vowed to find this girl and marry her. He decreed that *anyone* who fitted the shoe would be his bride. This might have been a bit rash. Soon girls were queuing up from all over the kingdom to squeeze their feet into the dainty shoe. (In some versions they chop off toes to try and claim his hand. The emphasis on the smallness of her feet probably came from the original Chinese version – where small feet were considered a symbol of beauty. Also in this version Cinderella's fairy godmother was a fish – which isn't half as romantic.) Shall we carry on?

Her prince was about to give up as there seemed to be no maidens left, when Cinderella, in her 'servant girl' look, appeared and pulled the other slipper out from under her apron. Although she was dressed in rags, when she put on the slipper he saw at once that she was his princess. Her inner beauty and princess-like poise were no longer concealed (well, that's what happens when you fall in love). He of course swept her off her feet, put her on his horse, took her back to his palace and married her. He promised they would live 'happily ever after', and on this occasion they really did. In the classic version she is such a good soul she doesn't even seek revenge on her horrible stepmother and siblings, but in others they are forced to become servants, or are pecked to death by birds. Each to their own.

How to panto

This will fill you either with delight or dread, but December marks the start of the pantomime season. Cary Grant, despite moving to America and becoming an international movie star, never missed an opportunity to return home to see one and relive a moment of his childhood. Find out where there is one playing near you by going to *www.bigpantoguide.co.uk*

The history of panto dates back to Ancient Greece and gained huge popularity in the reign of the Roman Emperor Augustus. The word comes from a single masked dancer called Pantomimus. As the performance evolved through the ages it took elements of Commedia dell'Arte from Italy, which also went on to influence vaudeville and music hall in America, and reached England in the sixteenth century. The great clown Joseph Grimaldi, who leapt onto the stage in 1800, loved the genre and can be credited with many of the plots, characters and staging that are used today. *Oh yes he is . . .*

Once you get over the kitsch factor – and the probability that you will end up showered in sweets if you're lucky, water if you are not – panto is a perfect way to get you in the mood for the season's festivities.

There are three key conventions you need to consider before you go to, or think about writing your own, panto: that the principal boy is played by a woman, that the men dress up in drag, and that the audience is expected to be part of the show; hissing, booing and shouts of 'he's behind you' are compulsory. Once you have these elements in place, throw in a couple of singalongs and you know you'll reach 'happily ever after'. Staging your own version could offer a unique twist to the gap between Christmas lunch and Christmas supper or be the perfect punchline for that moment after the clock has chimed in a new year and you don't know what to do with yourselves. Is there someone – an uncle, a male friend in touch with their feminine side – who is desperate to don a pair of tights? Make a classic tale your own by including lots of topical and insider jokes that could only be understood by your personally selected audience. You probably have most of the props you'll need lying round the house – a broom for Cinders, some smarties to act as beans in *Jack and the Beanstalk,* and a pair of thigh-high-what-were-you-thinking boots for *Puss in Boots.*

How to throw a fancy-dress party

You shouldn't need too many excuses to party at this time of year. If you're hosting a party you could ask guests to 'bring a bauble' (as well as a bottle). Place a Christmas tree at the entrance and each guest can hang their present on it – you'll end up with a tree full of your friends. The best thing about it being your party is that *you* get to pick the theme, one that you know you have a great look lined up for. Clearly mark on the invite that effort is required (or words to this effect). Be kind, give some notice and try to hit upon an idea that everyone will want to make an effort dressing up for. Don't make it too obscure; if it's too hard to find a costume for your party it could be just too much hassle to attend. Yikes! Don't want that.

Themes could include:

Pride of the nation – Time to swing the kilt? Britannia? Liberty? If you're feeling brave, don a bikini and lots of lipgloss and go as an entrant to Miss World.

Landmark achievement – Do you fancy stepping out with Big Ben? As Eros? Tube stations are a popular theme – backcomb your hair and go as High Barnet.

Literature – Recreate the characters of Oscar Wilde, Austen, Brontë, the *Beano*, Jilly Cooper, Dickens or Roald Dahl.

Era – You could simply name a decade, or make it more specific – Woodstock, a seventies roller disco, eighties Wall Street. Are your friends more likely to go all out for hotpants or shoulder pads?

Trailer trash – Set a budget on the invite and ask people to come in whatever they've managed to cobble together from the local charity shop.

Soap dish – J.R. Ewing or Dot Cotton? Let's just hope they don't stay in character all night.

Seasonal – Dress as a decoration, deck yourself in holly and ivy (could be prickly), be the Ghost of Christmas Past or simply gift-wrap yourself.

When searching for themes, think of venues, the catering and hosting as well as the costume. *www.costumesalon.com* suggests starting points such as:

Arabian Nights – Remove all furniture and throw rugs over the floors, drape white fabric (DIY dust sheets) over the walls and surfaces to create a tent-like vibe for your belly dancers. Serve pitta bread, hummus and Turkish Delight. Dress: Cleopatra, Lawrence of Arabia (horse optional).

Speakeasy – Think smoky jazz clubs and Ronnie Scott's, Jodie Foster singing 'My name is Tallulah' in *Bugsy Malone*, card games (snap to poker), cigarette girls and Cuban cigars. Hire a jazz pianist. Dress: Zoot suits and flapper dresses, think *Some Like It Hot* and Al Capone.

For something glamorous, refer to Truman Capote's Black and White Ball (page 429) or photographer Nick Knight's Masked Ball (see page 392).

A fancy-dress party is the perfect excuse to try on a new personality, so *nil points* for those doctors or nurses who come in their everyday uniforms. Take a night off from yourself, stop being a shrinking violet and step out as someone you always wanted to be. Whether taking your inspiration from fairy tales or film, drag or drama, there is another you in there just waiting to burst on stage – just make sure you know your entrances and exits.

All the world's a stage,
And all the men and women merely players.
They have their exits and their entrances,
And one man in his time plays many parts,
His acts being seven ages.

As You Like It, Shakespeare

The good fairy must always enter stage right and the evil villain from the left. Originally with the Commedia dell'Arte, the right-hand side of the stage symbolized heaven and the left hell. Try and ensure you only have heavenly entrances and entrants at your soirée; it will prove very difficult dividing up the dance floor otherwise.

Decide on your costume in light of the theme, the venue, your budget, your dressmaking skills and the time you have to create/find the look. Fancy dress takes longer than you think: you need time for the idea, time to source, time to create or hire. Time to regret issuing/accepting the invitation? Be realistic, time is not in great supply in December. If your dressmaking skills are zero you can hire (Angels, Shaftesbury Avenue, London is a famed treasure chest), or work with what you've got – if you've got a sheet, you've got a toga. With a tea towel you can be a shepherd. Look in charity shops, eBay or vintage sales. Find an old prom or wedding dress that you can dye or sew sequins onto. Do you still have your school uniform, anything Hepburn-nesque, or is it time to show what you've learnt at your burlesque classes? Is there any muse or anything amusing you resemble? For a quick fairy fix, tinsel is a great wrist and waist trim and can easily twist into a crown. Miniskirts and mini looks done right can have an added something, done wrong and you look ridiculous; tread the line with care. Wings, wands and masks are usually in abundant supply at toy stores. For a more upmarket look try Butler and Wilson or Slim Barrett. Sadly, the Crown Jewels are only lent to royalty. If modelling a complicated outfit, be sure to book a taxi – mermaid tails, flippers and wetsuits can make getting on and off a bus very tricky.

When weighing up your fancy-dress options, decide if you're going alone (like the original Cinderella) or, if going with someone, can your looks coordinate? Two heads are better than one. Sadly there's only one head in a pantomime horse outfit. Aim to be the front of the horse. Do not attempt a costume that a glamorous ex of your man's has immortalized or that is likely to be ten a penny at the party. You want to stand out for the right reason. Besides it's really dull spending the whole evening going up to every Captain Hook in your Tinkerbell costume trying to find your Peter Pan.

Great pairs:

The Ugly Sisters
Antony and Cleopatra
Romeo and Juliet
Laurel and Hardy
Hansel and Gretel
Bonnie and Clyde
Napoleon and Josephine
Posh 'n' Becks
Kate and Pete
Batman and Robin
Punch and Judy
Salt 'n' Vinegar

Going in a group is a good option for several reasons – but mainly for safety in numbers, particularly if you're all planning on coming home on the night bus dressed as pixies, fairies and goblins. You can also split the responsibility of finding different parts of the look and not only help each other to assemble the ensembles, but give each other the courage to leave the house. If doing 'groups' you should have all members present – do not form the Stones without Mick Jagger – similarly, the Supremes would be in trouble without Diana Ross. If in doubt, St Trinian's school uniform, doctors and nurses, or sports stars are easy-peasy; you don't need to specify which sportsperson you are exactly – unless you want to spend the night swearing in sweat bands, in which case John McEnroe will do you nicely. American footballer is perfect if you don't want anyone getting too close, and remember, if you're a cheer-leader you get to have pompoms.

Groups can include:

Abba
The Spice Girls
Three Little Pigs
The Jackson Five
The Seven Dwarfs

6th December

The real St Nick was born in AD 343. The original Father Christmas dedicated his life to serving God and is the saint of goodness and giving. His acts of kindness range from pilgrimages to paying dowries. You don't need to go so far, but today is the perfect date to remind yourself to send your Christmas cards, especially international ones. Make sure your seasons greetings get there in time.

Any requests to Father Christmas better be sent sooner rather than later to:

Father Christmas
Santa's Grotto
Reindeer Land
SAN TA1

Enclose a stamped addressed envelope and you'll get a reply.

8th December

Singer, songwriter and peace activist John Lennon, a founding member of the Beatles, was murdered in 1980. He was forty years old, living in New York with his wife, artist Yoko Ono, when he was shot by madman Mark Chapman, who was carrying a copy of *Catcher in the Rye* and some Beatles cassettes.

Download one of his great anthems, 'Give Peace a Chance', 'Make Love Not War' or 'Imagine'.

How to make punch

With the holiday season and all the end-of-year festivities dominating this month, it's worth having something with a bit of a kick up your sleeve. You'll need something exotic to toast all those old acquaintances and glamorously greet the new. Punch, or mulled wine, is the traditional English tipple to bring a flush to your cheeks at this time of year, but egg nog or your own invention can also take centre-stage in a cauldron or punch bowl at any gathering you might be hosting. This could be the time to patent a recipe for Mistletoe Martinis (note: not a good idea to use real mistletoe as this is poisonous rather than aphrodisiacal), Reindeer Rum Punch, Santa's Shakers and so on.

Mulled wine ('mulled' meaning heated or spiced) dates back to the medieval ages, and was originally called *Ypocras* or *Hipocris* after the physician Hippocrates, before becoming a favourite in Victorian England. It was considered to be healthier than water as the wine was heated, so it was cleaner. Don't use your best vintage bottle of red – the taste will change so the gesture will be a wasted one. And don't let it boil. Mix your wine with fresh nutmeg and cinnamon, and chuck in a pre-mixed 'mulled wine' sachet.

The best way to pull your punches is with your punch.

Ingredients:

A bottle of dark rum

Two bottles of red wine (note, these portions are for a party of more than one, hic)

$1/2$ cup of orange juice

$1/2$ cup of lemon juice

2 cups of sugar

Optional: three cups of tea (just black English Breakfast, no milk)

To make:

Mix the wine, juice and tea in a simmering saucepan, heat it through – avoid bringing it to the boil – and stir in the sugar and the rum. Add brandy for extra kick.

You can slice oranges and lemons and add cinnamon sticks for decoration. Serve warm and, most importantly, with a ladle.

10th December

Edward VIII shocked the world when he announced his abdication in 1936. He had been king for less than a year. He did it for love. In his speech he

explained: 'I have found it impossible to carry the heavy burden of responsibility and discharge my duties as King as I would wish to do without the
help and support of the woman I love.'

The woman in question was American divorcee Mrs Wallis Simpson and
their affair proved to be a constitutional no-go – but Edward's mind was made
up. So he left England and the throne and they set up home together in Paris.

How to get the Simpson look

To get a man to abdicate from the throne is a tall order – to get her look
is not. The romance between the twice-married Mrs Simpson and the dashing
Duke of Windsor was one of the biggest scandals the British monarchy has
had to weather. She was said to have commented, 'I am nothing to look at,
so the only thing I can do is dress better than anyone else.' If you feel as if
you have the whole world turning against you, rather than run and hide,
take Wallis's advice and shine so they can see their green envy reflected in
all your glory.

When Wallis Simpson died on 24 April 1986, her jewellery collection alone
sold for over $50 million (£31 million). Many of the pieces were designed by
her devoted husband. A plume-shaped diamond brooch, designed in 1935 by
the then Prince of Wales, was bought by the actress, and friend of the couple,
Elizabeth Taylor. 'It's the first important jewel I have ever bought myself,' she
said. In fashion terms Simpson was frequently on the Best Dressed lists. She
favoured Chanel and Schiaparelli and was photographed by Beaton in Hart-
nell, and although she was never recognized as being part of the monarchy,
more a blight on it, she was a muse for an era, and continues to influence
fashion today. It is Mrs Simpson who is often credited with saying 'no woman
can be too rich or too thin' – both of which are very hard to be in December.

Read about Wallis and her extraordinary life in:

The Darkness of Wallis Simpson by Rose Tremain
Wallis Simpson's Diary, ed. Helen Batting

The Duchess of Windsor: The Uncommon Life of Wallis Simpson by Greg
King

12th December

Author Gustave Flaubert was born in 1821. His novel *Madame Bovary* caused
a scandal when it was first published as it vividly described the affairs and
indiscretions of the heroine, Emma Bovary. Curl up with the book, the 1933
Jean Renoir film or someone tall, dark, handsome, and utterly devoted.

Another great lover born today was Frank Sinatra (12 December 1915–14
May 1998). See his official website *www.franksinatra.com* for the full list of
films, music and his biography.

Sinatra was not just a singer, he was an Oscar-winning actor and leader
of the legendary Rat Pack. Sinatra was an entertainer in the truest sense.
His career spanned seven decades and his record sales topped 250 million
worldwide, all from doing it His Way.

He started with big bands before RKO pictures signed him in 1944 and
his film career began. His schedule of singing, touring, acting, love affairs
and family life was hectic to say the least and, on 26 April 1950, his vocal
chords haemorrhaged on stage. Ouch. His singing career looked like it might
be over – but don't worry, Ol' Blue Eyes was very distracted by something
else: Ava Gardner. Their affair bust up his marriage to his childhood sweetheart, but to prove it was more than just a fling, the A-list icons married on
7 November 1951, only ten days after his divorce had come through. 'I love
her, and God damn me for it,' he said. But while Gardner's career took off,
Sinatra's fell into decline. Not only had he damaged his vocal chords but he
kept getting cast in dud films. Then, just as it appeared it couldn't get any
worse, he was dropped by his record label and his film studio in 1952.

But it wasn't over – not by a long shot.

Sinatra made a spectacular comeback in *From Here to Eternity* in 1953, a
role which earned him the Academy Award for Best Supporting Actor. Sadly,
though, his success had a price and he split with his siren Gardner as work

went crazy and his star was firmly on the up again. In 1955 he starred with Marlon Brando in *Guys and Dolls* and, in 1956, with his childhood hero Bing Crosby in *High Society*.

'If he could stay away from the broads and devote his time to being an actor, he'd be one of the best in the business,' Bogart commented – but how could he when there were so many on offer?

The original *Oceans 11* gang partied with starlets and presidents. Rumour has it that Sinatra introduced JFK to several of his liaisons, including Marilyn Monroe. To quote Frank: 'Fairy tales can come true, it can happen to you, if you're young at heart.'

In 1967 he was one of the biggest names in the world – so it was high time he took his third trip up the aisle. This time it was with Mia Farrow, who was thirty years his junior. This marriage only lasted two years after Sinatra gave her an ultimatum – him or her career. She chose her role in Roman Polanski's *Rosemary's Baby*. He served her divorce papers on set.

Sinatra had links with the mob as well as the White House. He turned down the role of Dirty Harry in 1971, yet inspired the character of Johnny Fontane in *The Godfather* (in 1972), and, in true mafia style, allegedly called Farrow and offered to get both of Woody Allen's legs broken when he left her for their (Allen and Farrow's) adopted daughter. Farrow declined.

His fourth and final marriage was to Barbara Marx in 1976, and lasted till his death in 1998. He had one of the most successful runs ever in Las Vegas and 'My Way' was the longest charting single in the UK ever.

His epitaph reads: 'The best is yet to come.'

How to deck the halls with boughs of holly

Frank's epitaph is the perfect motto to use when starting to spruce up your home for the holiday season. Less is not more at this time of year.

Start at the door, with a wreath, or up the ante with an outdoor illumination display that will ensure your house can be viewed from space. Electric lights were invented in 1895 and still no one has found a way to stop them all fusing.

Twist fresh holly and ivy around mantelpieces or picture frames or through the banisters. Go green – evergreen – and place laurel leaves on table tops. Have even more candles lit (safely, and not too near your cards – remember you'll hopefully get as many as you sent the year before).

Above all ensure that you get that tree up. The tree is a fairly essential part of the holiday season tradition. Prince Albert started the craze in Victorian England and each year around 36 million trees are produced to cope with demand. Don't try and put a tree up all by yourself unless it is a mini version that comes up no higher than your elbow. Anything larger needs two people to manoeuvre it and share tinsel distribution.

If choosing a false tree, opt for the biggest one you can find. The bigger it is, the more lifelike the branches can be. You can go for a variety of colours (black, white, full rainbow) but unless you own a restaurant or live at the Tate Modern, best go for evergreen.

If you can't bear to fake it, you can opt for potted – and let it grow a little each year inbetween; simply wedge it securely in a bucket. For real trees you need to liberally spray the needles with water and, if potted, water the roots regularly (water not waterlog). Don't stand the poor thing next to a radiator or, if this is the only place with Christmas-tree feng shui, turn this particular radiator off. Just until the Epiphany. You try sitting pretty on a radiator – you'll be fighting a losing battle as it is with the needles, so don't aggravate your hoover any more than necessary.

How to present your presents

'"Christmas won't be Christmas without any presents," grumbled Jo, lying on the rug . . .' And so begins *Little Women* by Louisa May Alcott.

While it's getting late to start ordering online, the shops will be getting really frantic. Try not to leave your shopping to the stage when you have to fight your way through the hysteria. Remember *it is better to give than it is to receive*, so try to make it pleasurable and allow time for thoughtful perusing rather than panicked purchasing.

First editions of childhood books and treasures from a flea market – things they don't need but might want – can be found all over and show that time and effort rather than just money have been thrown at the problem. Presentation is key: be sure your gifts, whether an heirloom or home-made jam, are beautifully wrapped.

How to wrap
by Michael Howells, set designer

There are two types of wrapper and 50 Cent is not the one you'll be needing at this precise moment. Don't neglect the wrapping – you want your gift to make an entrance. Can you get creative with the photocopier at work when no one is looking and print and design your own wrapping-paper designs? Or scan lots of photos and print up a year's worth of memories to wrap your tokens in. If you are feeling you want to be more environmentally friendly, try and find a paper-free alternative, or use recycled paper from last year, or wallpaper, fabric remnants, glossy magazines or newspapers. Make a collage and tie it with string. Use shoeboxes and ribbons. For bikes and bulky objects you could find a cupboard or a shed and drape an old curtain or sheet over the surprise. Can you keep it simple on the outside and exploding with sequins, feathers and all sorts of delights as Pandora's box opens? Always double- if not triple-wrap layers to increase the suspense. Try it in different colours and textures and even add sweets – why not create the ultimate pass the parcel? The more layers, the more you will conceal the shape and contents and excuse any haphazard sellotaping techniques. Wrapping is as much a part of the present as the gift itself, especially if finished with a gift tag and lots of love.

17th December

Charles Dickens's *A Christmas Carol* was first published in 1843. The novel is so associated with Christmas that when Dickens died in 1870, a girl was heard to ask, 'Mr Dickens dead? Then will Father Christmas die too?'

A Christmas Carol was written when Dickens was in a tight spot, similar, though less drastic, to Bob Cratchit's. There wasn't a Tiny Tim but Dickens's wife was pregnant with their fifth child and the royalties on *Martin Chuzzlewit* were proving slow in coming.

The book opens with the death of Marley. His business partner Scrooge is a man described as 'a tight-fisted hand at the grindstone' sort of man who was so 'cold within he froze his own features'. With the help of the ghosts of Christmas past, present and future, Marley shows him the error of his ways. There have been over seventy film and television adaptations, including Michael Caine in *The Muppet Christmas Carol* and Bill Murray in *Scrooged*.

Inspired by the reformed Scrooge, make a donation to the charity of your choice, prove the spirit of the season is alive and well, and do a good deed. Make someone's day.

Also on this date, in 1892, the Russian Imperial Ballet performed Tchaikovsky's *The Nutcracker* ballet for the first time, this beginning another holiday tradition.

A trip to the theatre is as essential as the bowl of uncrackable nuts that adorn every coffee table in December. The ballet/theatre trip is an excellent idea for:

a) an original Christmas present or treat. Note – it's hard to wrap and keep a secret.

b) an office outing for those who want to stay on the wagon.

c) a great way to get in the mood and get inspired for your costume party.

21st December

Celebrate the release of Disney's *Snow White* on this day in 1937, and make fairy cakes.

How to customize your cakes

This is the season to forget the diet in favour of everything fanciful. Once you've made or bought your cakes let your creativity take flight and decorate them with as many silver balls, sparkling hundreds and thousands and as much coloured icing and additives as possible. You could customize each cupcake by icing on a different letter, and lay them out to form a message, or use a cake stand to build your cakes into a Christmas-tree formation, lather them in green butter icing and, for that 'dusted with snow' effect, sprinkle them in icing sugar. Alternatively there are several fantastic cupcake delivery companies; try *www.frufru.co.uk* and let someone else lick the spoon.

How to avoid the kitchen but still be creative

The pomander originated in France – *pomme d'ambre*, 'apple of the amber' – and was a little ball of scents and spices, ideal to waft away all the unpleasant everyday odours of court in the Middle Ages. As much as an odour eater it became a stylish accessory for the gentry, worn either on neck chains or attached to girdles.

Traditionally when they were made the pomanders would have their sweethearts' initials drawn in cloves on the surface. Originally pomanders were made of lemons, which could only be found in the Holy Land, and cloves, which were equally rare – so when a maid received one of these it was clear how serious her knight's intentions were. Much, much later Aliza-unde de Bregeuf of Canton Towers, Boston, Massachusetts was looking for a way to jazz up the holiday games and decided to update the popularity of the pomander. She orchestrated a game where the person would give a lemon-clove pomander to their sweetheart, who would then bite one of the cloves from the pomander (instant breath freshener) and give them a kiss. The game proved hugely popular and spread across the States; just don't swallow the clove.

To make a pomander properly you need to allow four to six weeks as they have to dry. But the effort will be worth it – they are easy to make and are cheap gifts, as well as a great way of adding a festive flavour to your home. All you need is a fresh citrus fruit (orange, lemon or lime – preferably one with an oily skin), a ribbon, a box of cloves, a thimble and some imagination.

First loop your ribbon (as this is what the pomander will hang from), and pin this to the fruit with a safety pin. Use a big bow to conceal the join. Now for the fun part: take the cloves and push these into the fruit so that the buds are on the surface, first marking rows or swirls or initials in pen or pencil. Use a thimble to protect your fingers as there is a lot of clove pushing to be done; the more cloves you use the stronger the scent will be. Lay the fruit on a sheet of greaseproof paper and shake powdered cinnamon over it. Then wrap it up and place it in a warm, dry cupboard (the airing cupboard is ideal) and forget about it. After six weeks or so you can unwrap it. You will no longer have an orange, lemon or lime – you will have a hard, dry little ball that will have emerged from its chrysalis as your very own pomander.

22nd December

Italian composer Giacomo Puccini was born in 1858. For the story behind his most famous opera, *La Bohème*, see 1 February, page 48. His most beloved work, however, was *Madame Butterfly* which he finished writing on 27 December 1903, just two months before its scheduled debut at La Scala, Milan on 17 February 1904. The debut was a fiasco; everything went wrong and his opera was savaged by the critics. Determined, Puccini still maintained it was his favourite work, and with a bit of editing, on 28 May that year at the Teatro Grande in Brescia he proved his detractors wrong and his Butterfly was pronounced a triumph.

Use Puccini to get your singing voice warmed up for carolling. Do you know all the words to 'Silent Night' or 'Away in a Manger'? And can you remember the descant part to 'O Come All Ye Faithful'? This is the flashy frilly bit that swoops and screeches over the soprano part and adds another layer to the harmony. If you can't remember the words, go to *www.carols.org.uk*

23rd December

The Night Before Christmas was first published in 1823. Written by Clement Clarke Moore, it was originally a tale to help his children sleep, but a family friend loved it so much they sent it to the *New York Sentinel*, who published it.

It was an instant hit, but Moore didn't acknowledge he was the author until 1844, by which stage it was already a classic.

> 'Twas the night before Christmas,
> When all through the house
> Not a creature was stirring,
> Not even a mouse;
> The stockings were hung by
> The chimney with care,
> In hopes that St Nicholas soon would be there . . .

In addition to his description of the preparations, Moore wrote of a man with a 'broad face and a little round belly, that shook, when he laughed, like a bowlful of jelly'. And with that, and a Coca-Cola advertisement, the first image of Father Christmas appeared.

Rather than following a kiss under the mistletoe (and don't pretend you didn't know it was there) with a blush and a quick exit, why not dazzle your admirer with this story?

According to a Scandinavian myth, when the goddess Frigga's son, Bladur, was killed with a spear fashioned from mistletoe, his death brought winter and sadness. It took a lot of magic to bring him back to life but once she had, Frigga decreed that mistletoe would never again be able to cause death and harm, and those passing under it should celebrate her son's resurrection by kissing.

Who are you to argue with a goddess?

24th December – Christmas Eve

Now it really is the night before Christmas – and it might as well be the longest day of the year as there's the last-minute shopping, wrapping, cooking, well-wishing, and annual family gathering to get through before you can hang up your stocking. You'll probably be wanting a drink as well.

If there is anyone in your house under the age of ten you won't get much sleep tonight. You can try the Clement Clarke Moore routine – a nip of sherry (for you), some of your potent home-made punch or a trip to midnight mass.

One last job before you go to bed, regardless of your age, is the hanging of the stocking. Stockings have been hung since 1870 – and it's important to go for the knitted or the felted variety as nylons may snag and lose all they contain.

The tradition came about when Father Christmas accidentally dropped some gold coins down the chimney. Luckily they fell into the stockings that were drying in front of the fire rather than down the ash grate.

There is much myth and magic about tonight – an old wives' tale says that if you bake bread on this night it will never go mouldy. It is also said that on this day all the animals can speak – but it is also bad luck to test either theory, particularly the bread one.

Page Turner

The Little Princess
Frances Hodgson Burnett

Why

Indulge in the tale of a 'princess' to inspire your good grace and imagination during this giving season.

Who

Frances Hodgson Burnett (24 November 1849–29 October 1924) was born in Manchester, England and was four years old when her father died. Her mother was left to bring up five children alone, as well as manage the family wholesale business. In 1864 the family moved to Knoxville, Tennessee after one of Frances' uncles offered to look after them, but sadly this help failed to materialize so the children grew up with next to nothing. Frances escaped their bleak reality by writing stories and poems with happier endings.

But a happy ending was not yet hers – when she was eighteen her mother died and she was left to care for her four younger siblings. Frances used her imagination – literally – to survive and started to submit stories to magazines, earning the money for postage and paper by picking and selling wild grapes. She began to be published in *Godey's Lady's Book* as well as other magazines and managed to write five or six stories a month, at ten dollars apiece, to support her family.

In 1873 she married Dr Swan Burnett, a childhood sweetheart, and in 1874 gave birth to her first child, Lionel, followed by a daughter, Vivian, while they were travelling in Paris. She took her husband's name in addition to keeping her own when they married, and became the Hodgson Burnett we all know. Her first novel, *That Lass o' Lowrie's* earnt rave reviews, but due to the copyright laws in place in those days she didn't receive any royalties from sales of her book in the UK.

In 1877 they settled in Washington DC and she mixed in affluent literary circles, threw lavish parties and took a keen interest in fashion, a far cry from her childhood. When *Haworth* was published in 1879 she made sure she was standing on British soil, Canada, to ensure she was eligible for her royalties, but there was still no law protecting authors from their work being translated to the stage by eager playwrights without the author's permission.

It was not until her first children's novel, *Little Lord Fauntleroy*, in 1886, inspired by her own son Lionel (and which made velvet suits all the rage) that she managed to address this. Hodgson Burnett sued a playwright for using her novel as the basis of his play without her permission. She won. It became a landmark case, ensuring that copyright would remain with the author. She was now famous on both sides of the Atlantic, but her victory was a short-lived triumph as her son Lionel died in 1890 of consumption. While in England she wrote *Sara Crewe*, which she revised and published in 1905 as *A Little Princess*, and this was followed by her other most famous children's novel, *The Secret Garden*, in 1909.

The plot

Seven-year-old Sara has come to England to get educated at boarding school. With her mother long dead she has been brought up in India by a loving and wealthy father, but now it is time for him to enrol her at Miss Minchin's Seminary for Young Ladies. Captain Crewe makes the steely headmistress promise she will take extra special care of his 'Little Princess' as it breaks his heart to leave her.

Impressed by her charge's great wealth, Minchin indulges her prized pupil and allows her to be lavished with ponies, private rooms and special

treats. Despite all the preferential treatment, and bulging bank balance, Sara is not bratty or flashy; far from it, as she has been raised to have a kind heart and is a good judge of character. She befriends Becky the maid, as well as pupils Ermengarde and Lavinia. All seems carefree for the Little Princess until her eleventh birthday when word comes that her father has died and her fortune is lost.

The headmistress turns on Sara, furious at the money she has spent on the child, and sets her to work as a servant, stripping her of all her privileges and making her sleep in the attic. But the little princess manages to survive by using her imagination, just as the author survived her childhood.

Unbeknownst to her, Crewe's fortune is not lost and her father's friend is desperately looking for her. At the house next door to Miss Minchin's school, an old gentleman and his Indian manservant watch the little girl in rags doing her chores in the winter and decide to help her. They leave clothes, food and make a cosy fire in her attic room as if by magic. Sara's luck is on the up, but will she get the happy ending she deserves, the one that Hodgson Burnett so wanted in her own childhood? You may have seen the film with Shirley Temple, but this shouldn't replace curling up with the original book version.

Hosting

Do you have Becky's budget or that of the Little Princess? Whichever is fine if you have a lot of imagination, and as this is the last book club meeting of the year, why not throw a party to celebrate? Have party games and party foods from the Victorian era. You could make a cracker quiz with different questions about all the books you have read this year. You could theme a secret Santa around the stories, or, more simply, around anything that a princess would love. Use your last book club session to celebrate all that you have read and make a pact to continue next year.

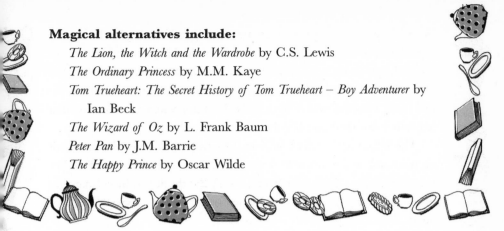

Magical alternatives include:

> *The Lion, the Witch and the Wardrobe* by C.S. Lewis
> *The Ordinary Princess* by M.M. Kaye
> *Tom Trueheart: The Secret History of Tom Trueheart – Boy Adventurer* by
>   Ian Beck
> *The Wizard of Oz* by L. Frank Baum
> *Peter Pan* by J.M. Barrie
> *The Happy Prince* by Oscar Wilde

25th December – Christmas Day

Depending on what time you arise you could work up an appetite – or get hypothermia – by going to watch the annual Serpentine Swimming Club race at 9 a.m. in Hyde Park. It is a race for the Peter Pan Cup, originally presented by club member author J.M. Barrie, and is only open to members, so the most you can do is watch. But why not start Christmas reading *Peter Pan*, because who *does* want to grow up? Or watch Johnny Depp as J.M. Barrie in the film *Finding Neverland* while persuading the turkey to defrost. If hell-bent on outdoor swimming, you can get icicles on your toes and join the swimmers at Brighton beach for a different Christmas Day swim – some even do it in fancy dress (perhaps to conceal their madness).

How to be trivial

Rather than talking about the turkey, marvelling at how your presents have been wrapped or how, yet again, your auntie guessed you wanted lime-green hand-knitted socks, change the subject. Trivia is key at family get-togethers.

- Did you know that the abbreviation Xmas is Greek? It comes from the Greek letter X which stands for *Chi* – the first letters of Christ's name in Greek.
- The first Christmas celebration was not actually recorded in Rome until AD 360 and it didn't become part of the Christian Church calendar until AD 400.
- In 1647 Oliver Cromwell banned Christmas. The puritan leader got parliament to pass a law arresting anyone in England who celebrated on this day, which sounds just like Narnia, where it was always winter and never Christmas. Thankfully Christmas was restored by 1660 after thirteen years with no presents. (This is not, however, where the association of bad luck with this number comes from. Friday the thirteenth is thought to be the day the crucifixion took place and ever since, doom and gloom has been predicted for this date.)
- 'Jingle Bells' was originally written for Thanksgiving in 1857.
- The Queen's speech – a three o'clock date for the nation – has been televised to time with the Christmas pudding since 1957. In 2006 Her Majesty made her first podcast – so you can now download her Christmas message wherever you are in the world.
- Though everyone dreams of a 'White Christmas' – let's not get started on climate change – in England there are not that many 'just like the ones we used to know'. In fact in the last century there were only seven white Christmases, and most of these only just qualified. The best places to go for a white Christmas include the Alps, Vermont, St Petersburg and pretty much anywhere in Austria. On the other hand, the most popular places to get a tan with your turkey are Australia, the Virgin Isles, Jamaica, the Bahamas – all of Columbus's favourites.

26th December – Boxing Day

In some countries gifts are given on Christmas Eve, in others on Christmas Day – and for those with wills of steel, it's today. Long, long ago Boxing

Day was the day for gift giving as the actual birthday of Christ was far too holy a day for frivolity.

Boxing Day got its name because it was the day all the servants who worked over Christmas would be given the day off to go and see their families – with a box from the master of the house. This tradition hails from medieval times when alms boxes were placed at the back of every church to collect money for the poor.

Today – unless they really spoilt you over Christmas – is the day your true love can start all that giving, if you are quoting the famous song below. Today is the day that the three kings set off, following the star, to Bethlehem to see Jesus, and the twelve days of Christmas began.

The twelve days of Christmas are the last six days of the old year (26, 27, 28, 29, 30, 31 December) and the first six days of the New Year (1, 2, 3, 4, 5, 6 January). And the song you *think* you know actually has a lot more meaning than you realize. It was sung at a time when Catholics had to conceal their faith and celebrations and used analogies instead. If you add all the gifts up, there are 364 in total – one for every day of the year bar Christmas (and ignoring a leap year, clever clogs).

The lyrics:

My true love represents God.

The partridge in a pear tree is Jesus Christ.

Two turtledoves are the Old and New Testaments.

Three French hens stand for faith, hope and love.

Four calling birds are the four gospels of Matthew, Mark, Luke and John.

Five golden rings recall the first five books of the Old Testament.

Six geese a-laying stand for the six days of creation.

Seven swans a-swimming represent the seven gifts of the Holy Spirit: prophecy, serving, teaching, exhortation, contribution, leadership and mercy.

Eight maids a-milking are the eight beatitudes.

Nine ladies dancing symbolize the nine fruits of the Holy Spirit: love, joy, peace, patience, kindness, goodness, faithfulness, gentleness and self-control.

Ten lords a-leaping are the Ten Commandments.

Eleven pipers piping represent the eleven faithful disciples.

Twelve drummers drumming symbolize the twelve points of belief
in the Apostle's Creed.

(For this and more information on customs go to *www.woodlands-junior.kent.sch.uk/customs* – a site far too good to be for just one school.)

How to get what you really want

Self-control isn't what you're going for here. Rework the words of the classic tune along with what is currently in the magazines – well, you've got to move with the times here – and get your true love to shop the twelve days of Christmas: Twelve issues of *Vogue*, eleven Top Shop dresses, ten diptyque candles, nine books from Borders, eight bags from Harrods, seven tops from Stella, six Dior sunglasses, five Blahník heels, four Chanel lipsticks, three Cartier watches, two Tiffany diamonds and one Hermès Kelly bag . . . just a thought.

If diamonds and duplexes are more to your taste than partridges and pear trees, you might prefer to purr 'Santa Baby' in a receptive ear: 'Santa honey, one little thing I really need, the deed to a platinum mine'.

Just one thing before you dash to pull out the platinum-blonde wig – it was never sung by Marilyn Monroe. Madonna – yes, Kylie – yes, Pussycat Dolls – yes, Eartha Kitt – yes. The breathy version you are thinking of is by a flaming redhead model turned actress, Cynthia Basinet, and could be perfect to lip-sync for a holiday edition of your burlesque routine.

27th December

German actress Marlene Dietrich was born in 1901. Her signature song – with strong accent – was 'Falling in Love Again' and she did this several times; her conquests included JFK, Sinatra, Yul Brynner and James Stewart.

30th December

Rudyard Kipling, the British poet and author, was born in Bombay, India, in 1865.

His best known works are the children's books *The Jungle Book* and the *Just So Stories*, a collection which explains *How the Camel Got His Hump* and *How the Leopard Got His Spots*. His own childhood was miserable – he was sent away from his parents, abused by foster parents and considered a failure at school. His own children both died tragically young – his 'best beloved' daughter Josephine, for whom he wrote the *Just So Stories*, died of influenza and later his son died serving in the war.

Kipling always turned down the honours offered to him, including a knighthood, Poet Laureate and the Order of Merit, but in 1907 he did accept the Nobel Prize for Literature.

Kipling wrote the much quoted poem 'If' first published in 1909.

If you can keep your head when all about you
Are losing theirs and blaming it on you,
If you can trust yourself when all men doubt you . . .

In other words no doubt, no lies, no stress about how you look – live for dreams and focus on your triumphs rather than dwelling on disasters. Hmmm. A great verse to inspire you in the build-up to a new year. Start planning what your new year's resolutions will be.

31st December – New Year's Eve

This is the date to wrap up all you've achieved, to tidy up loose ends and go out and celebrate the end of the year. Party your way into a new diary.

In Scotland, New Year's Eve and Day celebrations are known as Daft Days, Night of the Candle or, most often, Hogmanay. This is because, in addition to the copious amounts of alcohol that's consumed, a three-cornered biscuit called Hogmanay is eaten, along with haggis, shortbread, scones, oatmeal cakes and black buns to line your stomach.

In the Highlands the tradition continues with carrying burning juniper branches throughout the house – to cleanse it of germs. The modern consequence will be to totally stress your smoke alarm out, but this could be considered effective multi-tasking as you can test it works while you flap those burning branches about. You will get rid of the demons as well as wake up the neighbours.

Tidying the house shouldn't be a 'tradition' solely in Scotland, it should be adopted by everyone. What better way to greet the new year than with a clutter-free, clean home? (Unless you are holding a house party, in which case this is a total waste of time. Leave it until the morning after.) Even if you are entertaining, do a light dusting before you lay out the drinks, as it will make a world of difference. Wait for the real dust to settle before you tackle the serious cleaning or call in the professionals.

This is the last chance to learn all the words to 'Auld Lang Syne' by Robert Burns, to the melody thought to be composed by William Shield. You need a degree to understand them, but the basic thrust is in the first line about old friends and not forgetting them. Call or text them. The phrase *Auld Lang Syne* itself literally means *old long since* – so long ago – but the translation doesn't fit with the tune.

> Should auld acquaintance be forgot
> And never brought to mind?
> Should auld acquaintance be forgot
> And auld lang syne?
> For auld lang syne, my dear,
> For auld lang syne,
> We'll tak' a cup o' kindness yet,
> For auld lang syne.

And there's a hand, my trusty fere
And gie's a hand o' thine!
And we'll tak' a right gude-willie waught
For auld lang syne.

There's no denying it – New Year's Eve does require slightly more planning than an average night out, especially as most pubs and restaurants are reservation only. In some countries it's believed that what you do on this night offers a glimpse of how the year will unfold. This is partly true – so give things a helping hand and arrange something you will enjoy, with people you love.

Is this the date to throw your fancy-dress party? Maybe get your guests to come as the headline of the year, or indeed in the best bargain found in the sales so far.

A tradition from Yorkshire says it's lucky to close one year saying 'black rabbit, black rabbit, black rabbit' and then, once the clock strikes midnight, to say, 'white rabbit, white rabbit, white rabbit'. 'Auld Lange Syne' and a kiss seem a more sociable option than tongue-twisters or riddles.

The first fireworks to mark the dawn of a new year explode in Sydney, Australia. They then ripple up through the continents from Asia into Europe. A New Year's Eve addict can cross timelines and celebrate twice. But whatever you do on this occasion you *have* to stay beyond midnight, Cinderella. No losing a shoe, and if you do, no running away – see the new year in with a smile and start the next year an all new, all improved Girl for all Seasons.

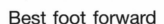

Foot Note

Best foot forward

- It is said that the Romans and Ancient Egyptians drew the faces of their enemies on the soles of their shoes so that they could, quite literally, walk on them. Not very grown-up, but pass the pen, let's learn from the ancients.

- Cobblers didn't label shoes 'left' or 'right' until 1822, which brings a whole new meaning to having a dance partner with two left feet.

- Madame Bovary's lover gave her pink satin shoes with a swan-down trim, similar in style to the shoe which is shown flying off in Jean-Honoré Fragonard's famous oil painting *The Swing*. You need at least one pair of pink shoes in your wardrobe.

- The shoemaker Olga Berluti recommends polishing shoes with Venetian linen dipped in Dom Pérignon before exposing them to the quarter-light of the moon for best results. 'Alcohol makes shoes shine, but it must be a chilled, dry and grand champagne,' said Berluti. Forget spit and polish and go for bubble and squeak. And as for the moon? Berluti continues, 'The moon gives transparency to the leather. The sun burns; the moon burnishes.' Well, now you know to polish after dark.

- Paul Simon sang it, and you can have it – 'diamonds on the soles of your shoes', that is. For the 2000 Dior haute couture show Galliano was famously inspired by the *clochards* (down-and-outs) that he passed during his daily jog along the banks of the Seine. He made the ordinary extraordinary by printing news, not on paper, but on chiffons and silks, and finishing bias-cut gowns with trinkets and tying them with string. And the shoes had diamonds on the soles. These might not have been intended to be practical, but diamonds are the most durable material available, so are a sound investment.

- Diana Vreeland, the legendary editor of American *Vogue*, who, amongst other achievements, set Manolo Blahník on the pathway to eternal (footwear) fame, was fastidious about keeping hers polished, especially the soles – proof that you really should have a driver on call. Manolos aren't known as 'limousine shoes' for nothing.
- But ultimately, as Bette Midler said, 'Give a girl the right shoes and she can conquer the world.' And so she should.

Acknowledgements

There are so many people to thank that it is impossible to know where to start – there are those who helped, those who distracted, and those who contributed. Then there's you – the person reading this right now – and all the people who made *How to Walk in High Heels* such a success – thank you.

For those who made this happen – Grainne Fox my unswerving protector and agent, Jocasta now Hamilton my electrifying editor, the beautiful illustrations by Natalie Ferstendik, the proof readers and the faux-pas checkers, phew, Antigone and Alice for laying out the tome, Ruth, Emma, Jamie and everyone else at Hodder & Stoughton who made this book happen – thank you.

Writing a book like this is like opening Pandora's Box: with an unending mountain of possibilities, names and dates to research and include, this is only the tip of the iceberg. Never judge a girl – or a book – simply by its cover.

I must of course give my love and thanks to my family and friends, as well as to those who helped me, those I met along the way and those who I hope stay with me for always. Thanks for all the incredible contributions, and especially for the foreword by Manolo Blahník that I shall spend the rest of my life living up to. Love to my mum and dad and brothers, Mrs B, Stephen Jones, Sarah, Romilly, Michael the World's Tallest Man, Gisele, Bill, Alex, Alexis, Jelka, Amy, Natalie, Evelyne, Sam, Steven and always and forever my dearest most beloved John.

Index